JOJO'S
BIZARRE ADVENTURE

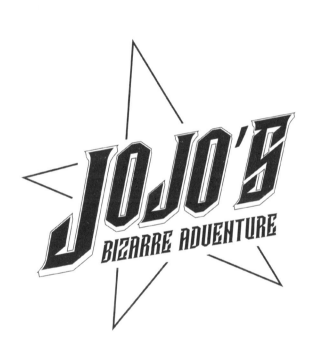

JoJo's Bizarre Adventure: Manga's Refined Oddball
by Frederico Anzalone
published by Third Éditions
10 rue des Arts, 31000 TOULOUSE, FRANCE
contact@thirdeditions.com
www.thirdeditions.com

Follow us:
: @Third_Editions
: Facebook.com/ThirdEditions
: Third Editions US

Publishing Directors: Nicolas Courcier and Mehdi El Kanafi
Editorial Assistants: Ken Bruno, Ludovic Castro and Damien Mecheri
Author: Frederico Anzalone
Foreword translation: Satoko Fujimoto
Foreword adaptation: Anthony Prezman
Proofreading: Zoé Sofer (copy preparation) and Charles Vitse (proofs)
Layout: Julie Gantois
Classic cover: Solène Pichereau and Steffi Girinon
First Print cover: Boell Oyino
Pictograms: Steffi Girinon
Intern: Elsa Pecqueur
Translated from French by Michael Ross, ITC Traductions

This informative work is Third Éditions' tribute to the manga series *JoJo's Bizarre Adventure* and to its mangaka, Hirohiko Araki. The author presents an overview of the story of the *JoJo's Bizarre Adventure* manga in this one-of-a-kind volume that lays out the inspirations, the context, and the content of these titles through original analysis and discussion.

JoJo's Bizarre Adventure is a trademark of Shūeisha Inc. and Lucky Land Communications. The manga was originally published by Shūeisha Inc. in Japan. All rights reserved. Cover art is inspired by the works of Hirohiko Araki.

English edition, copyright 2021, Third Éditions.
All rights reserved.
ISBN 978-2-37784-300-8
Legal submission: November 2021
Printed in the European Union by Grafo.

FREDERICO ANZALONE

JOJO'S BIZARRE ADVENTURE

MANGA'S
REFINED
ODDBALL

03.rd ThirD
éditions

To a loyal fan, stand tall and stand strong.

Johnathon Nicolas Roman

❧ ❋ ☙

Table of Contents

JOJO'S BIZARRE ADVENTURE

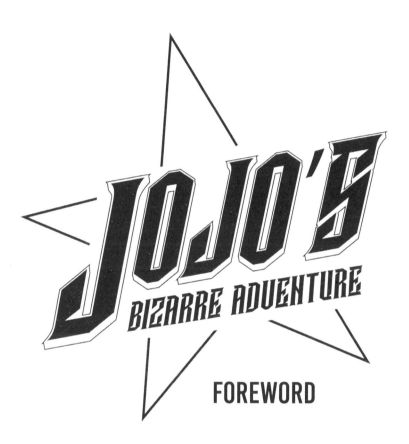

FOREWORD

IRST, as a Japanese person, I would like to give my sincere thanks to Mr. Frederico Anzalone for taking on the challenge of writing this book.

JoJo's Bizarre Adventure by Master Hirohiko Araki is an incredible series that has enabled manga–lord of the counterculture–to rise to the level of intellectual culture. But I'll let the work speak for itself. Instead, I'd like to shine a spotlight on the series' author, Hirohiko Araki, who I've been fortunate enough to meet in the flesh while working on the audacious, live-action film adaptation of the saga.

OUR FIRST MEETING

Master Araki, who up to that point had always refused to see his manga adapted into a film, wanted me to direct the project. We had an initial meeting to discuss the script. In the room, his editor and the film's producer were waiting with nervous looks on their faces. Master Araki arrived right on time with a big smile on his face and said in a good-natured tone:

"A pleasure to meet you, I'm Hirohiko Araki."

His voice was soft and he spoke with kindness. He didn't try to dominate the meeting. On the contrary, I could sense his modesty.

"*JoJo* is a celebration of humanity's greatness."

His message was both simple and profound.

DURING FILMING

Accompanied by his lovely and radiant wife, Master Araki arrived sporting his constant smile. He tried to encourage the young, intimidated actors and carefully watched each of them do their work. Then, he left to return to his work: drawing the *JoJo* series, still in progress.

"All films belong to their directors. Feel free to tear apart the original universe."

His words gave me chills.

EDITING AND GRAPHICS CREATION

Two or three times, I asked him to view the film during editing to get his unvarnished opinions.

He gave me valuable advice from his personal point of view. I also asked him to supervise the design, particularly the colors and movements, of the Stands, which are full-fledged characters in the film. Apart from the realism and flow that are specific to feature-length films with actors, he paid particular attention to the way in which these things appeared, as well as to the different shades of colors. His comments were both spot-on and extraordinary.

"It's really interesting to direct a film."

His candid smile deeply touched me.

AT THE PREVIEW SHOWING

Finally, the end credits finished rolling and the lights came back on. Nervous, I wondered what the audience's reactions would be. It's always a terrifying moment for an anxious director like myself. And at that same moment, Master Araki gave me a beaming smile.

"It's a terrific film, it was very interesting."

We clinked our wine glasses. I'm sure that he must not have liked certain details, but he didn't say a word about that. He had unconditional kindness and expressed great respect for the work of the team of actors.

"To us! Here's to hoping we can all make another film together!"

His wonderful, sincere words marked the successful conclusion to our collaboration. This unflappable author also knew how to celebrate others. He personally embodied the *JoJo* universe.

Now, it's your turn to experience the wonderful world of Hirohiko Araki!

Takashi Miike
三池崇史

ABOUT TAKASHI MIIKE:

A cult filmmaker, born near Osaka, Japan, in 1960, Miike is known for both his bold artistic choices and the length of his films. Experienced at adapting manga into live-action films (notably, he brought *Ichi the Killer* and *Blade of the Immortal* to the silver screen), Takashi Miike directed the 2017 film *JoJo's Bizarre Adventure: Diamond is Unbreakable – Chapter 1.*

PRELIMINARY REMARKS

All of the names, concepts, and excerpts of dialogue from *JoJo's Bizarre Adventure* used in the English translation of this book are, when possible, those of the latest English version of the manga, published by VIZ Media. Where an existing English translation is not available, the translation is based on the French version of the manga, published by Delcourt-Tonkam. For the English names of characters and Stands that depart radically from the original Japanese names, the "real" names, the ones used by most fans, will be provided.

Additionally, the numbering of parts, volumes, and chapters follows that of the original Japanese version. For each, the equivalent in the English version (up through Part 4 as of the writing of this book) is provided in a footnote.

Finally, because the *JoJo* saga is intimately tied to music, the beginning of each chapter offers suggestions of songs to listen to while reading.

All of the songs are collected in the following Spotify playlist: open.spotify.com/playlist/4vBRQMEv3f3GNsxX9V4ayp. Of course, you're more than welcome to listen to them on physical disks if you have them.

JOJO'S BIZARRE ADVENTURE

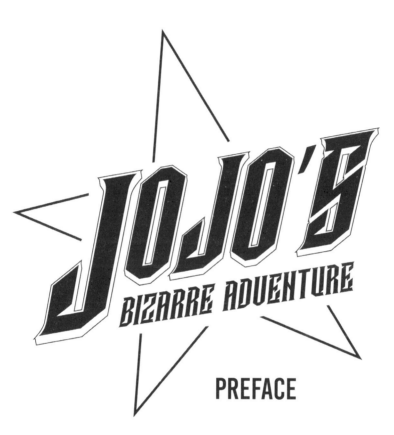

PREFACE

STAR CHARTS

To listen to while reading:

Tangerine Dream – *Love on a Real Train*

Thursday, October 25, 2018, 7:52 p.m. Brussels, underground. Artificial lighting, machinery, in the belly of a giant serpent. I was sitting on the brown, worn leather of a seat in a streetcar rapidly passing through the tunnels beneath the city center under reconstruction. I try to remember now, was the car noisy or quiet? Deserted or packed with people? I don't remember. But all that doesn't matter. The only thing that matters is this phrase that came to me that night, at 7:52 p.m, as all of my thoughts focused on the book that I was planning out: "Between what and what is *JoJo* the missing link?" It's an odd question, right? It came to me just like that, as if my mind had drawn an *Oblique Strategies* card–a deck of cards, created by Brian Eno and Peter Schmidt in 1975, intended to stimulate creativity by having the user read and interpret enigmatic phrases. It was in that moment, beneath the streets of Brussels, that the book you hold in your hands was truly born. The serpent's egg.

Of course, I had already established the foundation of the book. I had a general outline for it, but that phrase gave words to a personal obsession that had been bothering me for some time: it's a question of influences and how they're visually represented. Diagrams, trees, maps. A work of art, unlike a human being, can have 20, 30, 40 parents, who sometimes even have connections between them. When you connect the dots, big, strange constellations appear. That's how I created a star chart of the Araki star system, which thereafter always stuck in my mind. Or perhaps I should say the star charts, plural, because there are many answers to the question of the missing link, all different ways of modeling cause and effect. What I think my mind was trying to tell me is that *JoJo's Bizarre Adventure* holds such an important place in Japanese pop culture and I needed to observe these links on a larger scale; I needed to zoom out to try to understand what groups of stars the Araki system had connected to. So, I let that question continue burning in me as I wrote this book, hoping that in the end I would be able to provide an answer.

I couldn't possibly put a definitive date on the text you're reading. I believe that I started this preface in Tokyo's Kōenji district in May 2018. At that time, I would comb through specialized Japanese bookstores in search of books and documents. I wandered, my heart pounding, through the second exposition celebrating *Weekly Shōnen Jump*'s fiftieth anniversary. I observed the city and took notes. I talked with locals about manga in neighborhood cafés that had become my regular spots. For what it's worth, I was able to verify a fact that I had never actually doubted: in Japan, everyone knows *JoJo*. At least by name. So, this preface evolved over time, until it reached its final form in July 2019 in Brussels, after a year of work and (at times extreme) isolation. I needed to focus on the heart of the book. It was a year of reflections, interviews, revisions, and cross-referencing of information. A year of obsessive inquiries, seeking out the slightest clues in art books, the archives of *Vogue*, the captions of videos of Italian fashion shows, manga and films from each of the relevant time periods, the streets of Sendai in *Google Street View*, and many other documents, often obscure and often in Japanese. As for that, I would like to thank my bilingual friends for their invaluable help, since my Japanese skills are fairly rudimentary. Sometimes, my discoveries changed the content of this book. I let it come to life. I wanted it to evolve organically, even if that meant adding a curve in the road and letting unexpected plants grow wild on the shoulders; but I never lost sight of the horizon. As I write these lines, I realize that I adopted a method similar to that of *JoJo*'s author who, you will soon understand, has a habit of building a very precise, solid foundation before improvising upon it.

I would love to be able to tell you that I was born the same year as *JoJo's Bizarre Adventure*, in 1987. Really, I would have loved that. However, in reality, while the first chapter of the saga was indeed published in the issue of *Shōnen Jump* dated January 1, 1987, the issue in question actually went on sale in December 1986. How's that for luck? It was at the end of the 20th century, a decade later, that my fascination with *JoJo* took hold, thanks to a famous adaptation of the series into a fighting game. At the time, I was blown away by the originality of *JoJo*'s universe. I was a voracious reader of manga (as I am to this day) obsessed with series like *YuYu Hakusho*, which, as I would later understand, had actually been heavily influenced by the works of Araki, an author who nonetheless remained unknown to French-speaking audiences. It wasn't until the third part of *JoJo* was published in French (like many readers, the first two parts had put me off) in the early 2000s that I finally came to understand what the series is really about and the true magnitude of the phenomenon. It was in 2005, I think, while reading the fourth part, which was the one that spoke to me the most, that I developed a visceral desire to write about *JoJo's Bizarre Adventure*. And that's something that I've done sporadically. Some years later, I had a second jolt of realization.

Sitting in a university auditorium, immersed in studies of Renaissance and baroque statues, I realized just how much *JoJo* had an energy similar to those creations. In 2019, some months after that, I went to see my history of modern period art professor to show him Araki's work and the things he had borrowed from art history. Everything came full circle. So, that's where I'm coming from. That's how I developed an urge to write about this saga that, in my opinion, for reasons that will become apparent as you read this book, is one of the most remarkable of all Japanese comics. It's a saga that, for the past two decades, has intrigued me, astonished me, electrified me, and nourished me. It has also at times disappointed me. It breaks my heart, but I will sometimes severely critique Araki's manga, just as I will sing its praises. I don't want to simply idolize his work; I think it's important that I keep things in perspective. And I will try to keep the right perspective, balancing rigor with fondness.

Thus begins this book. It aims to offer a portrait of an artist, a textual analysis of a series, the history of its creation, and, as I've already suggested, a critical review. I wanted the book to be a hybrid, to be meditative; I wanted it to not go exactly as one would imagine. I wanted it to be like *JoJo's Bizarre Adventure*. While it's impossible to put a label on it, the book's structure can be summarized as two simple components: a horizontal, chronological history, then, in the last part, a vertical leap for a bird's-eye view. This book is not an encyclopedia or an academic work; rather, it is a personal essay. A meticulously researched one, yes, and put together with as much rigor as possible, but it is infused with my own opinions and analyses. I will touch on various aspects of Japanese history and society in order to draw parallels with Araki's work and the general evolution of manga. In that regard, I would like to stipulate that the view—by nature a Western one—of Japan that I offer in this book has been informed by my travels and experiences all across the archipelago, by lengthy discussions with my friends (including Japanese people, expats, and former residents of the country), and by reading valuable documents, such as works written by historian Jean-Marie Bouissou.

Friday, July 12, 2019, 9:24 p.m. Brussels, aboveground. It's almost dark outside. Near me sit my voice recorder, annotated extracts of my manuscript, and miscellaneous documents: a copy of the magazine *Ultra Jump*, an informational book by Hirohiko Araki, piles of manga, a Japanese mook called *JOJOmenon*. Among other things. You will soon become familiar with all of these objects. On my side, I will soon put them all away. It's the beginning for you and the end for me. I'm preparing to close out this text and begin a final one: the book's conclusion. So, "between what and what is *JoJo* the missing link?" I haven't quite yet decided. We'll come back to it later, a few hundred pages from now. Until then, enjoy the journey.

ABOUT THE AUTHOR: FREDERICO ANZALONE

Born in Brussels in 1987 to Italian parents, Frederico is a graphic artist, a speaker, a podcaster, and a journalist. And now an author. He wears five hats, one on top of the other; isn't that ridiculous? Elsewhere, perhaps yes, but not in *JoJo*! Frederico Anzalone's writings, specializing in manga and Japanese culture, can be found every three months in the French magazine *ATOM*. He has also written for *BoDoï*, *Les Cahiers de la BD*, and *Chronic'art*.

JOJO'S BIZARRE ADVENTURE

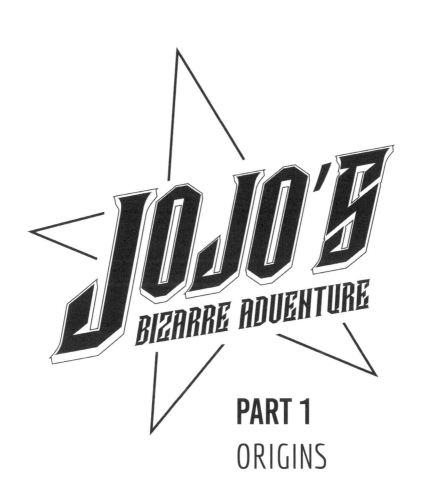

PART 1

ORIGINS

CHAPTER ZERO: ARAKI BEFORE JOJO (1960-1986)

Legacy. If I had to summarize Hirohiko Araki's work and career in one word, that would be it. Whether we're talking about bloodlines or artistic legacies, the concept of things being passed down will always be associated with Araki. And his pen. As such, over time, *JoJo's Bizarre Adventure* has become one big repeating cycle of filiation, with its central pillar remaining, to this day, the Joestar family tree. The saga itself is the hybrid offspring of numerous spiritual progenitors: certain Japanese manga classics, of course, but also Italian sculpture and American films, among others. When it comes down to it, there may be no manga with DNA more mixed than *JoJo*'s. The first base pairs of this genome came together in the 1960s and '70s in Sendai, Japan, where Araki, whose real first name is Toshiyuki, was born (June 7, 1960) and raised.

Starting in his childhood, Araki inherited from his parents two very specific interests that are partially responsible for the unusual character of his manga. That said, there was nothing out of the ordinary about Mr. and Mrs. Araki: he was an office worker, she was a homemaker. The classic situation for Japanese families at that time. However, there was one peculiar detail about them: when they would read stories to their little angel, they always chose Western tales. Never Japanese. What could have remained just a fun fact would go on to take on crucial importance because those "exotic" stories left a strong mark on young Araki's imagination, which was shaped by books like Mark Twain's *The Adventures of Tom Sawyer* and Jules Verne's *Twenty Thousand Leagues Under the Sea*. As an adult, Araki has even assessed that these stories were directly responsible for his interest in foreign countries, including his musical and culinary tastes (he says that he's not in love with Japanese cuisine[1]), which clearly lean toward the West. In connection to this preference for the exotic, let's take a closer look at a crucial event. A spark was born in a dark movie theater when Araki went with his father to see the Sergio Leone film *The Good, the Bad and the Ugly* (1966, released December 30, 1967 in Japan[2]), a masterpiece of Italian Western films, also known as "Spaghetti Westerns." Araki, a schoolboy at the time, became fascinated with Clint Eastwood, who played the part of "Blondie," a.k.a. the Man with No Name, a character with a piercing gaze and a cigar frequently between his lips. Anyone who's seen the film will remember Eastwood's taciturn performance, each line delivered with a punch–the most famous probably has to be, "You see, in this world there's two kinds of people, my friend: Those with loaded guns and those who dig. You dig," as he forces Tuco, "the Ugly," to dig for treasure. For Araki, it was a revelation. Eastwood's character would remain for him *the* perfect image of a hero, the paragon of an independent, adept, and unflappable man, charismatic and powerful, who effortlessly projects a commanding presence just by standing there. Two decades after that initial thunderbolt, the *mangaka* would actually base the attitudes and disposition of his most famous character, Jotaro Kujo, on those of Eastwood's iconic roles! This filiation actually makes perfect sense when you learn that the character Blondie was a Wild West transposition of the Japanese figure of the wandering samurai.[3] But we'll come back to that later.

The second predilection Araki inherited from his father is somewhat more obvious: his love of art. At home, young Araki had to put up with the dirty tricks of his twin younger sisters, who were apparently little tyrants, to the point that he fought with them daily. The situation even got quite desperate: Araki got to the point where, to avoid conflict, he didn't want to come home after school... The story doesn't say if, as in Stanley Kubrick's *The Shining*, the twin girls would wait for him in the entry hall, hand in hand, with creepy smiles on their faces! In any case, to get away from them, Araki developed a habit of isolating himself in his bedroom with his father's collection of art books to keep him company. He immersed himself in them as an escape; many of those images imprinted themselves on his young mind.

---

1. Araki provided these details in a joint interview with Kazuma Kaneko (artist for the *Shin Megami Tensei* video games), given in 2001 for the magazine *Thrill*. The detailed list of interviews used in writing this book can be found in the final pages, in the "Bibliography" section.
2. Source: *Internet Movie Database* (IMDb).
3. *The Good, the Bad and the Ugly* is part of the *Dollars Trilogy*, entirely directed by Sergio Leone and whose first installment, *A Fistful of Dollars* (1964), was a remake of the Akira Kurosawa samurai film *Yojimbo* (1961). Clint Eastwood played the role of Toshiro Mifune's character and he went on to play the same silent, mysterious hero in the trilogy's other two installments.

Without realizing it, the future *mangaka* began developing the contours of his artistic knowledge, which would later splash across the pages of *JoJo's Bizarre Adventure*, where you'll find jumbled together the influences of Paul Gauguin (with his uninhibited chromatic contrasts), of Michelangelo's body images, and of American pop art's immoderate use of Ben Day dots.

In his time spent in isolation, Araki also read manga. A lot. What did he read? What were the comic books that he read over and over, that would deeply influence his work? We'll reveal the answers soon. But before that, let's look at some key points from the past. Keys that you will find useful throughout the rest of this book. After all, how can we speak of legacy without knowing where it stems from? Given that the saga of *JoJo's Bizarre Adventure* is rooted in a very specific vein of manga, of which it embraces the conventions as much as it twists them, we have to study the history and nature of that vein, called *nekketsu shōnen*, but also the status of the manga universe and its center, Japan, when Araki became old enough to read. It is a story of defeat, revenge, upheaval, and catharsis. To really understand it, let's first look at the cradle of modern manga. In the year 15 B.A. (before Araki).

Manga Before Araki, Act 1: From nuclear trauma to story manga

Gyokuon-hōsō, the "Jewel Voice Broadcast." That is the name given to the famous speech[4] broadcast on August 15, 1945, in which Japanese Emperor Hirohito announced to his subjects (most of whom were hearing the solemn voice of their sovereign for the first time) the country's surrender, shortly after the bombings of Hiroshima and Nagasaki. It marked the final moments of the war in the Pacific Theater, and thus of all of World War II. Everything had to be rebuilt. In Japanese, they speak of *zero nen*, "the year zero." It was in this context, starting from a blank slate, that modern manga was born. In a Japan that was wounded, hungry, and impoverished. They were suffering from post-traumatic stress on the scale of an entire nation, in a territory occupied by their recent enemy: the Americans. In that difficult and uncertain situation, the Japanese needed to dream, to laugh, to escape from their daily lives for a few brief moments, and manga turned out to be an ideal response to those needs. That is, for those who could afford the luxury of amusement. And then, paper became scarce. For these reasons, post-war manga developed largely through *akahon*, "red (cover) books," booklets made of low-quality paper that were thus cheap to produce, but also through a network of lending bookstores that offered books specially designed for such circulation called

4. You can listen to a digitized copy of the speech on *Wikipedia*, at the following address: https://en.wikipedia.org/wiki/File:Imperial_Rescript_on_the_Termination_of_the_War.ogg.

kashi-hon ("rental books"). Both *akahon* and *kashi-hon* were widely available in the Osaka region.

Before long, the young author Osamu Tezuka (born November 3, 1928, in Toyonaka, Osaka prefecture) became the leader of this renaissance and his first long-form story, *New Treasure Island* (*Shin Takarajima*, edited by Shichima Sakai), published in 1947 as an *akahon*, became an instant classic of what would come to be known as "story manga," a new form of comics with stories more developed than those that came before. Up to that point, Japanese comics mainly offered stories in short episodes independent from one another, heavily inspired by the theater: we see this in the panels of Suihō Tagawa's *Norakuro* (1931-1941 in its first version, never published in English) with their zoomed-out views of characters on their feet, reminiscent of actors on a stage. Tezuka added elements of cinematography to the mix, such as close-ups and framing changes, for more dynamic storytelling. His version of the medium also came with a slew of Western inspirations that gave it an exotic flair: there was, of course, Robert Louis Stevenson's *Treasure Island* (1883), but also *Tarzan* (a character created by Edgar Rice Burroughs in 1912) and *Robinson Crusoe* (Daniel Defoe, 1719). In terms of graphic style, there were very clear American influences, first and foremost the childlike, curvy lines of productions by Walt Disney and the Fleischer brothers (*Betty Boop*, *Popeye*, etc.). With *New Treasure Island*, Tezuka laid the first stone of modern manga and, by doing so, established himself as the spiritual leader of practically all story manga authors to come. As such, we can say that from the very beginning, manga as we know it has been created from a strong blending of cultures.[5]

While at the time Japanese comics were intended for children, Tezuka raised the medium's ambitions: in addition to enhancing its form, he also enhanced its content. His series *Lost World* (1948), for example, loosely inspired by the Arthur Conan Doyle book of the same name, went beyond mere entertainment to offer an underlying warning about dictatorial regimes, the reoccurrence of wars, and the amoral usage of scientific progress. Essentially, issues anchored in his era of "the aftermath." Tezuka was an incredibly prolific manga writer. With one success after another, he rose to dizzying popularity and in the 1950s, his influence became so great that he dominated all manga production. His *Astro Boy* series (*Tetsuwan Atomu*, 1952-1968), starring a little robot running on—not coincidentally—nuclear energy, went on to become an ultra-famous icon, and even an emblem of the Japanese nation. If you had to remember a score of names from the history of manga, you'd have to include Hirohiko Araki. But if you had to remember just one, it would have to be Osamu Tezuka.

---

5. This was even the case earlier, since early manga was largely inspired by European caricature art, first imported to Japan by English cartoonist Charles Wirgman (who moved to Japan in 1861 and created the satirical magazine *Japan Punch*, published from 1862 to 1887).

Manga Before Araki, Act 2: Explosions and mutations

Although Tezuka, today nicknamed *manga no kamisama* ("the god of manga"), continued to reinvent himself and deliver numerous masterpieces throughout his life, he was no longer considered avant-garde by the time Araki was old enough to read. It was the mid-1960s and the most popular authors, at least the ones who influenced *JoJo*'s creator, included Sanpei Shirato (*The Legend of Kamui*, 1964-1971) and Mitsuteru Yokoyama (*Babel II*, 1971-1973, never published in English). It's worth noting that these many newcomers were often inspired, or even discovered, by Tezuka himself: Yokoyama, for example, who was a major inspiration for Araki, produced pages in keeping with Tezuka's style.

At the time, the country had been recovered for some time already–the period of occupation ended in 1952. Japan was reborn. The Japanese began leaving the countryside to move to expanding megacities where they could find progress, verticality, and more money. The country entered what's now known as the "Japanese economic miracle," a period of dizzying growth that led it to become the world's second largest economy in the late 1960s. Thanks to that growth, Japanese wallets got fatter–well, not for *all* Japanese, but we'll come back to that–and people could afford to save or travel outside the country, for example, but also to indulge in many and varied pleasures. As such, the culture of entertainment exploded. The hordes of spectators that filled baseball (*yakyū*, as they say in Japan) stadiums to watch a sport that had become very popular since the American occupation[6] is a perfect example. Similarly, there was spectacular growth in the tie-in product and cartoon industries, which changed manga readers' relationship with their favorite heroes, who left the pages of their books (to go anywhere and everywhere). Of course, baseball was not the only bit of American culture to take hold in Japan: for example, American films started becoming available on Japanese screens shortly after release in their home country.[7] That gave Araki plenty of opportunities to slake his thirst for Western films.

Meanwhile, the capital of manga moved from Osaka to Tokyo and a new model of publication made its debut in 1959 with the advent of two future popular magazines dedicated to *shōnen manga* (manga for boys): *Weekly Shōnen Magazine* from Kōdansha and *Weekly Shōnen Sunday* from Shōgakukan. A totally new concept at the time, their weekly rhythm–instead of monthly, which was the norm up to that point–allowed authors to expand their stories and provide readers with a steady stream of entertainment: each week, the next

6. Note, however, that the sport had already existed in Japan since the late 19th century.
7. Since we know that Araki is fond of Clint Eastwood, note, for example, that *Dirty Harry*, directed by Don Siegel, came out on December 21, 1971, in the United States and less than two months later in Japan, on February 11, 1972 (source: IMDb).

installment in the stories would be published, creating events that brought fans together. This format became—and has remained—a very popular one. Even though it takes a toll on the authors... At the same time, a more dramatic form of comics emerged, one closer to (the dark side of) reality and with even more techniques borrowed from cinematography than before, drawn from current Japanese productions and from American noir films. This form became known as *gekiga* and it first appeared in *Kage* (1959-1962), a crime-drama magazine for lending bookstores featuring working-class authors (unlike Tezuka who came from a wealthier family). Then, *gekiga* gained prestige with *Garo* (1964-2002), an ambitious monthly magazine that was actually first targeted at children. By publishing a story like *The Legend of Kamui*, about a young ninja, but also, above all, about class conflict and peasant revolts, *Garo*, with its leftist bent, aimed to educate the youth about societal issues they would face in life. However, the magazine quickly transformed into a high-quality, adult, avant-garde publication. It went on to play a decisive role in distributing the works of distinguished authors—whether in the *gekiga* genre or not—and attracted intellectuals, chief among them politically aware students.

The 1960s in Japan was a turbulent time. The "children of the bomb" grew up and many young people took firm stances against American imperialism and social injustices. For example, they railed against how to give rise to the "economic miracle," which benefited the most fortunate, the working-class people worked themselves to death without reaping a just reward. Things came to a head in the spring of 1968, when a violent student revolt broke out in Japan, particularly in protest against the American war in Vietnam. For these young people of the activist left, fighting for their beliefs and reading manga was a natural pairing: the *gekiga* author Yoshihiro Tatsumi, for example, wrote about contemporary issues, depicting in a naturalist style the despair and difficult daily lives of the common people he saw around him, the people left behind by the economic boom. And he did so without sheltering readers from the destitution and crude bodily fluids that stained reality—blood drawn in anger, hidden tears, and sad ejaculate.

At the time, the dramatic drawings and rawness of *gekiga* also influenced *shōnen*, with a wave of very socially conscious works, such as *Hikaru Kaze* ("the winds of wrath," never published in English, 1970, *Weekly Shōnen Magazine*) by Tatsuhiko Yamagami or *Harenchi Gakuen* by Go Nagai ("shameless school," never published in English, 1968-1972, *Weekly Shōnen Jump*), which were clearly inspired by the student uprisings. Eiji Ōtsuka, a manga theorist born in 1958, two years before Araki, remembers that time of daring editorial choices and audiences breaking down barriers: "There were lots of socially and politically engaged manga and their authors tackled very personal themes. I remember reading such titles when I was in the year six of elementary school, for example. You have to understand that these manga were more for university students and such, but since it was called a '*shōnen manga*,' children ten years old or so would read it too. It was part of counterculture."[8] Counterculture distributed on a mass scale: in 1966, *Weekly Shōnen Magazine* crossed the symbolic threshold of a million copies printed per issue. What's more, *shōnen* was not simply "influenced" by *gekiga*: *shōnen* magazines actually picked up and published *gekiga* authors. A large proportion of *Rien ne fera venir le jour* ("nothing will make the sun rise"), a French anthology dedicated to Tatsumi's works from the 1970s, was in fact originally published in *Weekly Shōnen Magazine*. In 2013, looking back, the author commented in the anthology's foreword on this interesting editorial choice: "This selection includes some extremely shocking stories. You'll even find a scene in which a child commits murder. [...] In hindsight, I'm surprised that high-circulation magazines published these stories 40 years ago."[9] So, that's the kind of comics that young Araki, a faithful reader of *Shōnen Magazine*, would have encountered at the time.

The truth is, in that period of authors seeking formality and sophistication, all of manga was evolving and the borders between publishing categories were porous. Authors with an adult approach like Tatsumi and Shirato published in magazines labeled both *gekiga* and *shōnen*, but also *seinen manga* (manga mainly for young men). This new category called *seinen*, which borrowed and, in a way, mainstreamed the adult approach started by *gekiga*, exploded in popularity with the magazines *Manga Action* (1967) from Futabasha and *Big Comic* (1968) from Shōgakukan. As a side note, since Araki has mainly written manga for men, in this book we won't get into *shōjo manga* (manga for girls), but this category, too, underwent a modernization at that time thanks to the "Year 24 Group",[10] whose most notable figures were Riyoko Ikeda (*The Rose of Versailles*, also known as *Lady Oscar*, 1972-1973) and Moto Hagio (*The Heart of Thomas*, 1974-1975). Again in this case, there was a certain fluidity: in the 1960s, it was not unusual for authors labeled as *shōnen* to also publish in girls' magazines, like the king of horror Kazuo Umezu[11] or Fujio Akatsuka, a key *mangaka* in the comedy genre. This was also the case for Tetsuya Chiba, whose

---

8. "Eiji Ōtsuka et le manga engagé" ("Eiji Ōtsuka and socially engaged manga"), remarks by Eiji Ōtsuka collected by Frederico Anzalone for *BoDoï* October 8, 2015. http://www.bodoi.info/eiji-otsuka-et-le-manga-engage.
9. Remarks from 2013 reported by Jean-Louis Gauthey in the foreword to *Rien ne fera venir le jour* (Cornélius, 2018).
10. This was a name given retrospectively by critics to a group of women *mangaka* who revolutionized *shōjo* in the 1970s. "Year 24" refers to the 24th year of the Shōwa era (1949): these authors were (just about) all born in that year.
11. This was notably the case for the entire collection *Hebi Onna* ("the snake woman," never published in English), the content of which was pre-published in 1965 and 1966 in *Shōjo Friend*. More generally, it's worth noting that in Japan, horror manga has always been closely associated with female audiences.

name will come up often throughout this book: although he became famous for his virile, rough-and-tumble *shōnen*, Chiba actually got his start in *shōjo*.[12]

In general, the period from the 1960s to the early 1970s was a golden age for avant-garde Japanese artists, a great cultural melting pot, with manga as one of the key ingredients. Artists mixed and mingled.[13] That includes in *Garo*, which began to incorporate media other than comics, such as literary texts and photography portfolios. A great example of this artistic cocktail: in 1967, the Japanese New Wave filmmaker[14] Nagisa Ōshima directed *Tales of the Ninja* (*Ninja bugeicho*), a feature-length film entirely composed of fixed and traveling shots of panels by Sanpei Shirato! Meanwhile, Shūji Terayama, an icon of underground theater, showed his interest in manga in an even more remarkable fashion. In March 1970, following the death of a key character in the hit boxing manga *Ashita no Joe*[15] (published in *Shōnen Magazine* from 1968 to 1973), Terayama called for a funeral to be held in Tokyo in honor of the fallen fighter. Tetsuya Chiba, who was the manga's artist, thought it was a joke. And yet... "The streets were filled with people. All of these readers had come out, even though it was a weekday. People had left their work—businessmen, students. They were all dressed in black. They sported black armbands, black ribbons, many brought flowers and incense,"[16] Chiba recounts. Over 700 readers in mourning joined the author in Kōdansha's offices to attend a ceremony led by a Buddhist priest... held on a replica boxing ring! This one quirky event alone shows the state of manga culture during Araki's childhood. Manga captivated people; it stimulated them; it brought them together. It was a real cultural boom.

---

12. Tetsuya Chiba's first series, *Mama no Violin* ("mama's violin," never published in English) is a manga for girls that was published in 1958 in the magazine *Shōjo Club*. In an interview published in the magazine *ATOM* No. 10, Chiba explains that the reason why there were so many male authors in early *shōjo manga* is because there was a lack of women *mangaka*. "In *shōnen* magazines, spots were hard to come by and were largely already taken up by more experienced authors. It's funny to note that my contemporaries were in the same boat [as me]: Shōtarō Ishinomori, Fujio Akatsuka, Kazuo Umezu, Leiji Matsumoto… They all got their start in *shōjo*", he explains.
13. There's still a very strong following of 1960s art and avant-garde thinkers in certain bars of Tokyo's Golden Gai neighborhood, where you'll find numerous celebrations of filmmakers and photographers from that era. There's even an establishment (Lonely Bar) dedicated to *Ashita no Joe*!
14. Called the "Japanese New Wave," in reference to the French New Wave, this movement was made up of a fringe group of Japanese filmmakers who, starting in the 1950s, broke with classic film styles, both in terms of form and content.
15. Literally, "tomorrow's Joe."
16. Original English text in Paul Gravett, *Manga: Sixty Years of Japanese Comics*, Harper Design, 2004.

Manga Before Araki, Act 3: Boiling blood

Nekketsu. That's the name given to a particular form of *shōnen* manga, a category that exploded in popularity in the late 1960s. The term, which literally translates as "hot blood," refers to extreme zeal, throwing yourself fervently into a task. In practice, *nekketsu* manga deal with sports, combat, and adventure, and they glorify the quest for victory. They also highlight heroism, courage, and the hard work needed to achieve that victory. So, why did this genre take off like wildfire? Perhaps it can be seen as a response to the "need to learn to win again" for a nation whose fighting spirit had been severely injured in 1945. Before the American occupation, stories for boys (on sword fighting or martial arts) shaped and exalted the patriotism of young Japanese men. For example, in the 1930s, they would read training novels called *nekketsu shōsetsu* that praised the virtues of physical discipline, bravery, and military and sports victories. However, starting in 1945, the culture became subject to American censorship, which prohibited stories about samurai and combat sports out of a fear that they would dangerously awaken the Japanese fighting spirit and *bushido* values, "the way of the warrior." This explains, for example, why Akira Kurosawa, the samurai film master, did not make any works in this genre until after the occupation. Starting in 1950, the censorship was lifted and all kinds of sports manga started to appear: the *nekketsu* spirit was back.

However, the great *nekketsu* works of the '60s, the classics still remembered today, were often filled with that extra dramatic spirit brought by the influence of *gekiga*. Two of the most popular manga of that era (incidentally, published in *Shōnen Magazine*), had no shortage of theatrical flourishes and their stories were founded on tragedy, with strong accents of social marginalization. On the one hand, there was the baseball manga *Kyojin no Hoshi* ("Star of the Giants," in reference to the team called the Tokyo Giants; 1966-1971, never published in English), written by Ikki Kajiwara and illustrated by Noboru Kawasaki, a former assistant to one of the founding fathers of *gekiga*, Takao Saitō (known for *Golgo 13*). On the other hand, there was the boxing manga previously mentioned, *Ashita no Joe*, written by a certain Asao Takamori... which was actually a pen name for the very same Ikki Kajiwara! At the time, Kajiwara was a pillar of the *nekketsu* spirit: his work was everywhere and was easily recognizable. For example, he was also the writer for the highly popular *Tiger Mask* series (1968-1971, never published in English), a wrestling *shōnen* that, of course, had the obligatory doses of blood, sweat, and tears. In addition, he wrote *Ai to Makoto*[17] ("love and truth," 1973-1976, never published in English), a manga that mixed romance and fighting between bad boys. The dramatic

17. Ai and Makoto are the first names of the two main characters, but the title has the double meaning of "Love and Truth."

dimension of this manga strongly influenced Araki. As a fun fact, the manga has had several adaptations for TV and film, including a feature-length musical (!) directed by Takashi Miike (*For Love's Sake*, 2012).

In *Kyojin no Hoshi* as in *Ashita no Joe*, we observe the spectacular rise of the heroes (Hyūma Hoshi and Joe Yabuki), who must overcome obstacles, such as their absent, dead, or disapproving parents. Two boys who grow up in poor and dirty neighborhoods of Tokyo, in the shadows of endless rows of tall buildings. The two stories also include different versions of coaches with broken dreams who transfer their hopes for revenge to their young prodigies. Without necessarily asking for their opinion... Indeed, Hyūma's father is a former player for the Tokyo Giants who had to abandon his promising career after being injured in World War II. The heavy-handed father, who drinks sake like it's his job, forces his puppet of a son to follow a nearly-impossible training regimen so that he can restore the family's honor—and perhaps, allegorically, the country's honor. Hyūma, a rebellious and reluctant child, ends up developing a true love for baseball and starts his race to the top. Between devotion to the sport and macho rivalries, the *nekketsu* spirit fits perfectly with baseball, which, in many ways, is quintessentially Japanese: just look at how the face-offs between batters and pitchers resemble sword duels, with the two sides observing each other, slowly, before the situation comes to a head in an instant. The hero of the boxing manga *Ashita no Joe*, meanwhile, is a 15-year-old orphan who has never spent much time in school. And who has nothing to lose. He puts up his fists and displays his cockiness in the slums of northeast Tokyo, trying to get a few yen, a place to rest his head for the night, or any number of little favors. He's surrounded by yakuzas, day laborers, and street urchins. Then, one day, an old, washed-up boxer spots his potential during a fight. Long before Sylvester Stallone's popular character in *Rocky* (1976), Joe was the archetypal outsider, the underdog, from an underprivileged background: rebellious and unusually combative, he even went on to become a total icon of working-class rebellion. In March 1970, the terrorist organization Sekigun-ha ("Red Army Faction"), which was an outgrowth of far-left student movements, hijacked an airplane and flew to North Korea. The group proclaimed in a statement announcing their actions, "*Wareware wa Ashita no Joe de aru*" ("We are *Ashita no Joe*" or "We are the Joe(s) of tomorrow")...

So, that's the background behind today's *nekketsu*, which remains *the* ambassador genre for manga worldwide: when mass-market consumers think of "manga" or "manga style," they first and foremost think of archetypal *shōnen nekketsu* images that have had global success, like *Dragon Ball* (1984-1995) or *Naruto* (1999-2014). Indeed, without those 1960s works and without Ikki Kajiwara, there would be no *Dragon Ball* or *Naruto*, no *Saint Seiya* (1986-1990) or *One Piece* (1997-present). Also no *JoJo's Bizarre Adventure*, of course.

However, the way in which *nekketsu* energy is used has changed. Since those classics from 50 years ago, the genre has been mainly oriented—and this is not a value judgment, just an observation—towards more superficial, more carefree entertainment and has increasingly moved away from those dramatic, socially conscious works that mirrored the big issues of their time. Why? The answer to that question could fill a whole book on its own, but here are a few ideas.

Starting in the 1970s, manga became increasingly segmented in very targeted magazines according to the age, gender, and social group of readers. That meant you'd no longer find dark and tragic stories from someone like Tatsumi in *shōnen* magazines: that more adult current started moving to "big people" magazines (a clear example is the semi-autobiographical manga *Barefoot Gen* by Keiji Nakazawa, a very painful story, which was dropped by *Shōnen Jump* in 1974) and the serialized *shōnen* moved more towards pure entertainment, the excitement of romantic comedy, and the enchantment of imaginary worlds, to the point that much of mainstream manga production reached a certain degree of superficiality in the 1980s. The manga of the entertainment virtuoso Akira Toriyama, both exciting and lighthearted, perfectly embody this movement toward pure enjoyment. We can probably say that Toriyama's *Dragon Ball* popularized and imposed a standard for *nekketsu* heroes, via the character Son Goku, that lasts to this day: the archetype of the carefree, radiant, idealistic, cheerful guy, which we find, for example, in *One Piece*, the world's best-selling manga series ever. The big *shōnen* hits—whether *nekketsu* or not—would no longer often feature heroes who, like those in *Barefoot Gen*, *Hikaru Kaze*, and *Otoko ippiki gaki daishō* ("the ideal gang leader," by Hiroshi Motomiya, 1968-1973, never published in English; a manga that features a young gangster who ends up clashing with the adult world and confronting the complexity of the political system), rebel against the dysfunctional parts of society.[18] Son Goku does not embody vengeance and incitement of the downtrodden, but rather a more carefree and individualistic race to the top. Like a symbol, essentially, of Japan having moved to the side of the oppressors. We should also note that, starting in 1967, a government agency dedicated to protecting the youth began adding "suspect" manga to a blacklist. Authors like Tetsuya Chiba who were responsible for *shōnen* considered inappropriate for children faced pressure from

---

18. Of course, this aspect has not entirely disappeared. *Shūjin Riku* ("prisoner Riku," 2011-2018, never published in English) by Shinobu Seguchi, for example, features an enraged hero in a context of abject poverty and, as such, fits into the legacy of the older works mentioned. There's also *Kunimitsu no Matsuri* ("the election of Kunimitsu", 2001-2005, never published in English) by Masashi Asaki and Tadashi Agi, which stars a rebellious hoodlum who decides to enter politics.

this agency,[19] which can help explain the changes in that segment of manga. We can view the transition to "*nekketsu* à la Toriyama" as a reflection of the shifts that began in the 1970s, considered an era of political disillusionment in Japan. The 1968 uprisings did not change Japanese society and they even deteriorated into deadly shootings and, as we've already seen, far-left terrorism. Winter 1972 marked a turning point: 30 or so members of Rengō Sekigun ("United Red Army") gathered in the mountains near Nagano to prepare for an armed revolution... and ended up killing each other on orders from their leader. It was a national trauma. For Michaël Prazan, author of the book *Les Fanatiques: Histoire de l'armée rouge japonaise* (2002, French only, "Fanatics: The History of the Japanese Red Army"), this event discredited the entire Japanese left; however, more generally, it also "discredited politics and political engagement in the long term."[20] It was the twilight of a great era of protests, a slide toward a more sanitized age in politics: in Japan, they use the term *shirake sedai*, "the apathetic generation," to refer to youth of the 1970s–which thus included *shōnen* readers and new-age manga authors. For some Japanese intellectuals like Eiji Ōtsuka, the period after 1972 marked the transition from an era where collectivist values (i.e., ideologies) took precedence over the individual to an era where, conversely, personal enjoyment was the dominant force, via the consumption of fashion items and cultural products tied to fiction stories.[21] This phenomenon reached its zenith in the 1980s. It was an era in which money flowed freely in Japan, and since the middle class no longer wanted for anything, new desires were created for them: it was an age of consumerist capitalism, where entertainment was king. An age that saw an explosion in *otaku* culture, the culture of obsessive fans (and consumers).[22] Starting in the 1990s, the Tokyo neighborhood of Akihabara became the focal point for *otaku*, being a bastion

19. At his studio, Chiba received a visit from agents investigating *Ashita no Joe* and complaints were filed with the publisher. However, although the series ultimately finished in 1973 with an open ending, Chiba stated in an interview given to *Kaboom* ("Tetsuya Chiba : L'étendard de la révolte" ["Tetsuya Chiba: the standard-bearer for rebellion"], No. 11, August 2015) that he did not give in to pressure and indeed drew what he wanted to all the way to the end.
20. In Christophe Paget, "Japon 1968 : la révolte étudiante la plus longue et la plus violente du monde" ("Japan 1968: The world's longest and most violent student uprising"), *Radio France internationale*, April 11, 2018. (www.rfi.fr/asie-pacifique/20180411-japon-1968-revolte-etudiante-plus-longue-violente-monde).
21. To learn more, read the article "L'héritage impossible du 'mai 1968' japonais : comment le manga dessine-t-il les mouvements sociaux de la fin des années 1960 au Japon ?" ("The impossible heritage of Japan's 'May '68': How does manga depict the social movements of the late 1960s in Japan?") by Julien Bouvard, in the journal *Cahiers d'histoire*, available online at the following address: journals.openedition.org/chrhc/7927.
22. On this subject, the blog *Baburu Jidai* (baburujidai.tumblr.com), named for the Japanese economic bubble (*baburu* from the English *bubble*), is a fascinating collection of symbols of consumerist-*otaku* culture from the 1980s and '90s: ads for electronics, magazine covers, boxes for models, videos from the period, and more. While we're on the subject, it's important to note that the term *otaku* is quite vague because there are as many categories of *otaku* as there are passions in the world: *anime otaku* for Japanese animation, *tetsudō otaku* for trains, etc.

for manga, anime, video games, and electronics more generally, since the neighborhood has previously specialized in selling electronic goods. Thus, it seems logical that, in this context of growing wealth in Japan, social justice was no longer a major concern for the heroes of the 1980s.

In any case, to this day, *nekketsu* still packs a punch and still promotes the values of hard work and going above and beyond. It has even amplified them! Although we can say that the genre has lost its original main function (to galvanize the Japanese people during their post-war reconstruction), *nekketsu* manga offer a universal message: quite simply, they convey the fortifying and enchanting idea that, no matter who you are, "where there's a will, there's a way." When it comes down to it, it's as simple as that. That's why the genre attracts such a broad audience, both young and old. It's not unusual for people, as they grow up and become adults, to keep reading the adventures of their childhood heroes. Did you know that when the soccer manga *Captain Tsubasa* (1981-1988) began publication, Japan didn't even have a professional soccer league yet? The author, Yōichi Takahashi, was so moved by watching the 1978 World Cup that he attempted to popularize the sport with his now-famous manga. And there's no doubt: the spectacular and vibrant adventures of Tsubasa supported soccer's rise to prominence in Japan: today, there are countless world-class professional players—and not just Japanese!—who recognize *Captain Tsubasa* for the series' influence on their career choice.

That's the incredible power of *nekketsu*. And it's also why Araki, too, was fond of the genre as a child. Even though he grew up to be an author of baroque, iconoclastic *shōnen*, young Araki was a fan of an absolute paragon of '60s *nekketsu*: one of his first obsessions, early in elementary school, was the baseball manga *Kyojin no Hoshi*. He became a huge fan of the work of writer Ikki Kajiwara. The star manga on the country's most popular sport, brimming with the energy of a hero for poor neighborhoods. Since Araki's adolescence was spent in a prosperous, conservative Japan, years in which the country had returned to law and order, far from the violence of the 1970s, and since *JoJo's Bizarre Adventure* was born in the heart of the 1980s, a period when it was all entertainment, all the time, in this book, we have to ask ourselves: in *JoJo*, what remains of the messages of social justice found in the manga of Araki's childhood, those works still marked by the difficulty of life in the post-war period, mixed with the tumult of the late 1960s. Also, of course, how have other aspects of manga from the '60s and '70s been infused into the work of the *mangaka*, who, having been a voracious reader as a child, had interest in numerous genres?[23]

23. Araki also read the *shōjo* magazine *Bessatsu Margaret*, for example. He says in the second volume of the spin-off *Thus Spoke Kishibe Rohan* (published in July 2018 in Japan) that it may have been the first magazine that he had ever read. He has also said that "a girl in [his] family had issues of it in the bathroom." This comment followed the episode *D.N.A.* of *Thus Spoke Kishibe Rohan*, published in the September 2017 issue of *Bessatsu Margaret*, for which he made the cover.

The pen is mightier than the sword

June 1973: *Ashita no Joe* hung up its gloves. Two months later, Tetsuya Chiba started running *Ore wa Teppei* ("I am Teppei," 1973-1980, never published in English) in *Shōnen Magazine*. It was the story of an untamed boy living outdoors in the mountains whose life changes when he has to go to school for the first time—a metaphor for the "return to law and order" for the new generation of Japanese? Radiant and energetic, Teppei shows unusual talent for sports, particularly *kendo*, a martial art that becomes central to the story. The magic of *nekketsu* struck again: under the influence of *Ore wa Teppei*, Araki put on a *kendogi*[24] and signed up for the *kendo* club at his school. Although he was a shy boy, Toshiyuki nevertheless felt a real need for recognition: in the *kendo* club, whether the young fencer won or lost a duel, no one noticed him... which inevitably frustrated him. At the time, Araki had already been drawing for several years. He started around the age of six by imitating works like the ninja manga *Watari* (1965-1966, never published in English) by Sanpei Shirato and *Harris no Kaze* ("Harris' wind," 1965-1967, never published in English) by Tetsuya Chiba, in which the author featured his first bad-boy hero. Toshiyuki even began creating his own manga, with stories "about musclemen who fight villains," as Araki stated in 1993 in the artbook *JoJo6251*! It was his source of enjoyment, but he never thought he'd be able to do it for a living one day. It was also his secret. That is, until he decided to share his work with his classmates. And when he did so... surprise: Toshiyuki suddenly became the center of attention. Everyone was interested in the budding artist. In a way, his friends at school were both his first readers and his first editors. It's fun to imagine them standing over his shoulder, pushing him to turn his stories in one direction or another! His confidence boosted, Araki put down the *shinai*[25] and brandished a pen. He had found his calling in life.

In the past, just like today, the best way to break into the manga world in Japan was to win one of the competitions held by *shōnen* magazines. As a way of discovering talent, they encouraged young people to send in their work—with a standard length of 31 pages, generally, for story manga.[26] The winner would come away with a prize, their first publication, and the possibility of a future career. Starting in his first year of high school, each summer, Araki would send the fruits of his labor off to Tokyo, the heart of the manga industry. But to no avail. At best, he would see his name listed among the finalists... but he suffered one disappointment after another. He would never receive any feedback, advice, or suggestions for improvement. Teenage Araki was on his own. In hindsight, Araki says that his work lacked originality.It copied the style of his favorite

---

24. Traditional outfit of kendo practitioners, or *kendoka*.
25. Bamboo sword used for training by *kendoka*.
26. And 15 for gag manga, another major genre.

manga:[27] *Babel II* (1971-1973, never published in English, published in *Weekly Shōnen Champion*) by Mitsuteru Yokoyama, who, to remind you, was one of the most illustrious heirs of Tezuka's style. The thing is that, of all the authors that Araki admired, Yokoyama was the one that had most deeply moved him, the one whose books he'd read over and over. Unfortunately for him, at that time, manga editors were known for their severity and their scorn for novices who lapsed into simple imitation of established *mangaka*. Newcomers had to digest and respect the work of their elders, yes, but not simply walk in their footsteps. Given that fact, it's surely not by chance that two future giants of the manga world, on the verge of making it big, incorporated strong outside influences into their manga: Katsuhiro Otomo (*Akira*, 1982-1990) took inspiration from Franco-Belgian comics, first and foremost Mœbius, and borrowed gray themes from the engravings of Gustave Doré; Akira Toriyama (*Dr. Slump*, 1980-1984; *Dragon Ball*, 1984-1995), meanwhile, drew from American comics and films from Hong Kong. The same ended up being true for Hirohiko Araki, who perfected his drawing style by taking inspiration from the art of a certain European country... but it's still too early for us to get into that.

Time went by and Araki grew older. At 16 years old, when he saw that authors his age (like the duo Yudetamago, known for *Kinnikuman*, a.k.a. *Ultimate Muscle*) were debuting in *shōnen* magazines, he redoubled his efforts and, under the influence of the trauma from his many rejections, became obsessed with the idea of producing original work that would win over the editors of a magazine. Basically, a manga that would make them want to keep reading past the first page. That is crucially important. After all, with the number of submissions they receive, editors often judge a manga after only just—partially!—taking out the first page from the envelope containing all of a beginner's hard work. So, Araki observed the most popular authors of the day. He studied art in depth and how to catch someone's eye, how to pique their interest, through both form and content. By doing this, he developed the basics of an approach he would continue to use throughout his life: total coherence in the ingredients that go into his work. Granted, *JoJo's Bizarre Adventure* has no shortage of craziness and uses plenty of improvisation, but it's also the work of an architect who knows exactly where every piece goes. Thus, young Araki continued teaching himself to be a *mangaka*; but, how could he make himself stand out? What secret weapon could he deploy? He ended up getting his answer from his love for Spaghetti Westerns. At that time, few manga were set in the Wild West.

---

27. Hirohiko Araki, *Manga in Theory and Practice: The Craft of Creating Manga*, p. 20. This book is an English translation, published in June 2017, of *Araki Hirohiko no Manga Jutsu*, released in Japan in April 2015. In it, the author reveals his trade secrets, as well as abundant information about his career.

There was *Kōya no Shōnen Isamu* ("Isam the desert boy," 1971-1974, never published in English, illustrated by the very same Noboru Kawasaki who drew *Kyojin no Hoshi*), a story about a half-Japanese, half-Native American boy in search of (a classic plot device for *shōnen* stories) his missing father. The anime version of the story (on which Hayao Miyazaki worked as an animator!) was partially broadcast on French TV under the name *Willy Boy*. However, besides that classic, there weren't many other manga like that. Araki recognized that there was territory there where he could stake his claim, especially since, being a fan of Clint Eastwood, he was already familiar with the subject matter. This was his chance! Indeed, the story that launched his career was set in America's western frontier. It was a brief story that was nevertheless filled with ideas, published in the first issue dated 1981 of a magazine that was on track to become legendary: *Weekly Shōnen Jump*.

Jumping into *Shōnen Jump*

What would the history of *shōnen manga* look like if *Shōnen Jump*, launched in 1968, had never existed? Well... I have no idea, I am but a humble human being. However, what we can say for sure is that this magazine by the publisher Shūeisha, although it was created a decade after *Shōnen Magazine* and *Shōnen Sunday*, has had a profound effect on the *shōnen* genre. In its early days, the only distinguishing feature of *Shōnen Jump* was its outsider positioning. Initially, the idea was to create a 100% manga magazine—its competitors also offered articles on cultural news and other related content—and to target an audience from seven to 14 years old, i.e., a younger audience than *Shōnen Magazine*, which, as we've already seen, trended toward an adult style and themes at that time and even hosted the depressing tales of Yoshihiro Tatsumi. That doesn't mean that *Shōnen Jump* only offered sanitized content: as early as 1968, the magazine included the famous series *Otoko Ippiki Gaki Daishō* with its rebellious hero, as well as the scandalous *Harenchi Gakuen*, a manga that was both humorous and perverse, likely too risqué and subversive for young readers, and that like *Ashita no Joe* was among the titles that drew the fury of parent associations. That's not to mention, not long thereafter, *Toilet Hakase* ("Dr. Toilet," 1970-1977, never published in English) by Kazuyoshi Torii, a series that took its scatological humor quite far, and *Barefoot Gen* with its taboo subject matter, starting in 1973. Incidentally, early in the magazine's history, it included translations of American comics (the very first volume included a *Flash Gordon* story). Then, as *shōnen* gradually evolved, *Jump* shifted its editorial focus and the version of the magazine in the 1980s, the era when Araki got his start, was already far from the original 1968 version. In the intervening years, *Shōnen Jump* had become the most popular magazine in its category.

To this day, *Jump* remains the heart and soul of mainstream manga and the *nekketsu* style in particular. We can even say that it's THE manga magazine: the most sold, the most influential, the most coveted, the one that has made *shōnen* such a global success, with worldwide hits like *Dragon Ball* and *One Piece*. At the height of its popularity (from the mid-1980s to the mid-1990s), when the company printed up to 6.53 million copies a week, *Jump* launched numerous best-sellers that set the standard for their respective genres. If you ask a *mangaka* born in the 1970s or later what their sources of inspiration are, just to mention the most obvious, there is a strong probability they'll mention Akira Toriyama as a major, or at least minor, influence.[28] Moreover, Hirohiko Araki said in 2015 that, from a visual standpoint, he thinks "every manga popular today belongs to this continuing movement best represented by Toriyama":[29] a masterful balance between realism and stylization or, to put it another way, between academic expertise and personal touch. As if to signal this paradigm shift, Osamu Tezuka prophetically declared in 1982: "Perhaps comics must now follow the path forged by Akira Toriyama because it's a path that surely leads to success. I can't outdo Akira Toriyama."[30]

Unsurprisingly, in 2018, *Dragon Ball* was the opener for the spectacular exhibition in Tokyo dedicated to the magazine's golden age–"Weekly Shōnen Jump Exhibition Vol. 2: The 1990s - A historic 6.53 million copies in circulation"–on the 52nd floor of the luxury skyscraper Roppongi Hills Mori Tower. Before entering the exhibit, the staff would ask visitors to wait in a vestibule wallpapered with magazine covers where they could hear, from the next room, the cries of the hero Son Goku, expressing his anger with the emblematic tyrant Frieza. The hype would build... Next, visitors would enter a few people at a time into the first part of the exhibition, a fantastic intro: a vast, dark room with an impressive projection of an animated (and thus with sound as well) version of the manga's panels with a 3D effect. And not just any old panels, of course: those of Son Goku's "Super Saiyan" transformation, with his golden hair, a climax at the height of the series' popularity in 1991 on the pages of *Weekly Shōnen Jump*. At that same time, Japanese fans could read in *Jump* the famous Egyptian chapter of *JoJo's Bizarre Adventure*.

And yet, Araki could have ended up never appearing in that magazine. Indeed, the aspiring *mangaka* liked *Jump*, of which he bought the very first issue when it came out, but his real favorite was *Shōnen Magazine*. That's the magazine that published the famous series *Ai to Makoto*, *Ashita no Joe*, and *Kyojin no Hoshi* by writer Ikki Kajiwara. Araki's goal was simple: to work with

28. I have personally heard this several times from *mangaka* that I've met, including from both those who produce *shōnen* and those who don't.
29. Hirohiko Araki, *Manga in Theory and Practice*, p. 122.
30. Source: catalogue of the exhibition *Osamu Tezuka – Manga no Kamisama*, p. 134.

this leading author. As such, *Shōnen Magazine* was the first publication that Araki targeted when trying to break into the profession. However, when he realized in the late 1970s that Kajiwara no longer appeared in the magazine's table of contents, young Araki decided to try his luck elsewhere.[31] Especially since, at the time, *Shōnen Magazine* was increasingly drifting toward romantic comedy, a genre that was trendy, but not at all to Araki's taste.

The story of Araki's first visit to the *Jump* offices is one that will make you smile. Once again, it confirms that Shūeisha's magazine was never his first choice. In the late 1970s, Araki had started higher education,[32] but he still kept sending in his work to publishers from his home in Sendai. Tired of never receiving any positive responses, Araki pulled an all-nighter studying his drawings, drew up all the determination he could muster, and headed to Tokyo to get some answers in person. Initially, he intended to visit the offices of *Shōnen Sunday*, from the publisher Shōgakukan. Was that because, at the time, the magazine hosted Ikki Kajiwara's work?[33] Possibly. In any case, after a four-hour train ride (the high-speed train line known as the Shinkansen, which now connects Sendai to Tokyo, did not exist yet), Araki stood in front of Shōgakukan's building. What happened next can be explained by the difference in perception a young man can have when standing on the sidewalk in front of two towering figures of imposing stature: the buildings of Shōgakukan and Shūeisha, located right next to each other. It just so happened that the second was smaller than the first. Intimidated, Araki changed plans at the last second and entered the smaller of the two buildings. Tucked under his arm were the unfinished pages of what would become *Busō Poker* ("poker under arms"), his very first published story.

Russian roulette

Unsurprisingly, Araki was not received like a prince. While a junior editor at *Jump* agreed to take a look at his work, the editor pointed to a lack of attention to details in the panels before he even began to read! As he turned

31. Araki provided these details in a joint interview with Kazuma Kaneko (artist for the *Shin Megami Tensei* video games), given in 2001 for the magazine *Thrill*.
32. Araki has a degree from the school of applied arts Sendai Design Senmon Gakkō. *Senmon gakkō*, which means "specialized schools" in Japanese, offer short professional training courses, similar to a community college education in the United States. However, we don't know what course of study young Araki chose.
33. Although we don't know the exact date of Araki's expedition, it's possible that at that time *Shōnen Sunday* was running *Pro Wrestling Superstar Retsuden* (a manga about the lives of famous wrestlers from that time, never published in English), written by Kajiwara. This manga began in 1980, in the 23rd issue of the weekly magazine. What's more, Kajiwara had already previously collaborated with *Shōnen Sunday*: he was responsible for writing the manga *Tenkaichi Ōmonoden* (started in 1975), illustrated by Yasuichi Ōshima.

each page, he added more criticisms to the pile. However, unbeknownst to him, in that moment, Araki reached a decisive turning point in his career. That editor, Ryōsuke Kabashima,[34] went on to become Araki's personal editor, an exceptional creative partner who helped *JoJo's Bizarre Adventure* become a reality in all of its eccentricity. Kabashima's influence would be just as big as him—standing at six feet, one inch-tall (1.85 meters). In any case, Araki left that meeting armed with encouragement, valuable advice, and a new goal: to rework his story to be able to present it as a 31-page manga to the Tezuka Award, which Shūeisha has been giving out twice a year since 1971.[35] The award is intended to encourage new story-manga authors. It has launched the careers of numerous manga stars, such as Tsukasa Hōjō (*City Hunter*), who took second place in the 18th edition in 1979, and Masakazu Katsura (*Video Girl Ai*), who took second place in the 21st edition in 1981 and who also placed in 1980. With *Busō Poker*, Toshiyuki Araki also won second place, in the 20th edition of the Tezuka Award in the second half of 1980.[36] Along with that came 100,000 yen. Interestingly, the first place is often left vacant: the judges only give it if they feel that a work really deserves it. Even worse: during the 96th edition, in the second half of 2018, they didn't even name a second place! Moreover, the panel in 1980 was not kind to Araki: even though he won the award, his work was described as "entertaining, but poorly drawn."[37] He had some work to do, that's for sure. But he had done it, the young author received a bit of recognition, which came with his first official publication: in its issue dated January 5, 1981, *Shōnen Jump* presented *Busō Poker* to its readers.[38]

Similar to Sergio Leone's Western films, like *The Good, the Bad and the Ugly* (in which "the good" is no better than any of the others), *Busō Poker* features

---

34. He is the grandson of the pioneering *mangaka* Katsuichi Kabashima (1888-1965), who was the co-author of *Shōchan no Bōken* ("adventures of Shōchan," created in 1923, never published in English), a manga with a number of similarities to the Belgian comics *Tintin* and *Spirou* (which it preceded). Ryōsuke Kabashima joined the editorial staff of *Shōnen Jump* in 1979 and, notably, he worked on *Sakigake!! Otokojuku* ("Charge!! Men's School," 1985-1991). In 1995, he launched the *seinen* magazine *Manga Allman*. Last I heard, he retired after directing the editorial department of Shūeisha's branch dedicated to contemporary literary essays (Shūeisha Shinsho).
35. This was not Araki's first time participating in this contest. For the 14th edition (second half of 1977), he submitted a story called *The Bottle*, another Western, of which you can see a sample on this Japanese blog: http://atmarkjojo.org/archives/15678.html. Interestingly, at the time, his pen name was Arakino Toshi (荒木之利), or Toshi Arakino in the Western order of names. However, we don't know if that was his very first time participating in that competition.
36. A *YouTube* video shows when Araki met Tezuka (www.youtube.com/watch?v=ImktRhu3T-GQ). The master, who the award is named for, congratulates the newcomer for his success and advises him to move to Tokyo. Not many *mangaka* come from the Tōhoku region (northeast Japan), he remarks. Araki replies that there's Shōtarō Ishinomori. Tezuka concedes that point and invites him to take up the helm of Ishinomori.
37. Hirohiko Araki, *Manga in Theory and Practice*, p. 138.
38. It was number 631, which, incidentally, also contained the 49th chapter of *Dr. Slump* and the 201st of *Ring ni Kakero* (1977-1981, never published in English), a famous boxing manga by Masami Kurumada, influenced by *Ashita no Joe*. A few years later, Kurumada went on to create *Knights of the Zodiac*.

morally ambiguous characters. The story begins in a lawless town in the middle of the desert in the United States. With his dark hair, thick eyebrows, and sardonic attitude, Don Peckinpah (likely a reference to the director of Western films Sam Peckinpah) is a scumbag, an outlaw with a $10,000 price on his head. Dead or alive. Because of this, lots of people want to take him out and the story starts with one of these attempts. In a barber shop, a pistolero is lying face down on the floor: he bit the dust after trying to take down Peckinpah while he was getting a haircut. It was a nice try, but the outlaw is an awfully good shot. A few pages later, Peckinpah enters a saloon and joins a poker game that caught his attention. A dangerous game of poker. This is because at the table sits a blonde man named Mike Harper, another sharp shooter and outlaw with the same $10,000 reward on his head. Don't let your guard down, gentlemen, opportunistic shooters could come from anywhere. Thus begins a tense card game that culminates in a final bet: for their guns. The loser must give in to the winner and thus expose himself to extreme danger... On the 31ˢᵗ and final page, the story ends with a sudden twist: both men perish when a Molotov cocktail is thrown by an old drunk who's been lingering around since the beginning. It turns out to be none other than the narrator in disguise, the person who introduced the story just after the title page–similar to how Alfred Hitchcock would start off episodes of the series *Alfred Hitchcock Presents*, for example. A man who appeared to be external to the story of the two gunslingers turns out to be the equalizing force.

Unlike the rules of poker, Araki doesn't leave much up to chance. It's fair to say that the young author did not yet have his own visual identity–he even later said that he had the drawing skills of a child![39] However, he made up for his lack of experience by delivering pages with careful layouts, with the panels playing off one another intelligently (this includes the way he created a nice visual coherence when Peckinpah handles the cards), for a story that may have been bogged down by some very pedantic repetitions, but that still proved to be gripping and well structured. Other than the abrupt ending, that is; but that's understandable when you learn that *Busō Poker* was originally a story around 100 pages long and that it had to be cut down to meet the standard requirement of 31 pages.

In that first one-shot, Araki's affinity for suspense (he carefully ensures on each page that the last panel, in one way or another, makes you want to keep reading on the next page), gambling, and unusual confrontations were already present and foreshadowed future card and dice games in seasons 3 and 4 of *JoJo*. A *mangaka* was blossoming.

---

39. Hirohiko Araki, *Manga in Theory and Practice*, p. 138.

The day after

While Araki had just taken one small, timid step into the manga industry, he then had to dive in head first. And stay there. Immediately after *Busō Poker*, his editor was categorical: there was no way his one-shot would be turned into a series (developing a complete series based on a pilot story is a common practice for manga magazines). And yet, every young author's goal is to get their own series to establish their presence within the magazine, issue after issue. Of course, that's also what the editors expect when they invest in their young protégés. And I'm not simply using the word young as a turn of phrase: as we've seen, a number of *Jump*'s leading authors began their series while they were still teenagers; compared to the norm at that time, Araki, at 20 years old, was already practically an old geezer. There was no time to waste!

So, why couldn't they turn *Busō Poker* into a series? Because as a pure thriller, it relied entirely on a story and a concept, while its two dueling gunmen were really just tools for building suspense. The problem is that what actually builds the loyalty of *shōnen* readers is the characters. They are the glamorous stars who appear on the cover, the ones who readers identify with and become passionate about. What's more, the magazines poll their readers to create rankings of the most popular figures. The fact is that Araki was exploring creative avenues that were not well adapted to the needs of a periodical like *Jump*. Indeed, in his book *Manga in Theory and Practice*, Araki recounts that he had a project that he abandoned and never published, *Suna arashi* ("sandstorm"), that he created about a year before going pro and whose pages were lost. In that manga from his youth, Araki told the story of a boy who sets out to save his sister from a strange storm in a desert. Additionally, we should note that the theme of a boy in the desert, which echoes the first chapter of the famous manga *Babel II* (in which the sandstorm in question was created to protect the ruins of the Tower of Babel!), is one that Araki is particularly fond of and it went on to be one of the inspirations for Jotaro in *JoJo's Bizarre Adventure*. So, *Suna arashi* put its emphasis on neither the characters, nor even the story, but instead on the atmosphere. For Araki, the failure of this story was attributed to the fact that a natural phenomenon like a sandstorm cannot be the only antagonizing force in an action *shōnen*. It's just not enough. At least, not with his skill level at the time: "Had I been a better artist at the time, my work might have found acceptance," he says modestly. "I think that's the defining characteristic of mood-based manga: if you're not an incredibly skilled artist on the level of Akira Toriyama or Katsuhiro Otomo, the manga won't come together."[40]

---

40. *Ibid.*, p. 154.

So, when he was getting started, Araki felt out of step. With the expectations of editors, on the one hand, but also with the expectations of his potential audience... "I was well aware that what I liked and what became smash hits were two different things,"[41] says Araki, who, when *Star Wars* (1977 to 1983 for the original trilogy) became a blockbuster franchise, preferred instead the intimist, uncompromising horror of Brian de Palma's *Carrie* (1976). How could he reconcile what his gut was telling him with what was most likely to sell? Did he need to ignore his own wants and just create a series that would pay the bills, then dedicate his free time to "real" passion projects? He thought about it. In any case, the years that followed *Busō Poker* were years of trial and error.

In the world of young *mangaka*, there's two kinds of people: those with a series and those who dig. Araki was digging. A lot and for a long while. Immediately after his first publication, he had no other choice but to keep studying on his own, imitating the style of his favorite authors and relying on guides like the book *Hitchcock/Truffaut* (1966), which contained an interview between filmmakers Alfred Hitchcock and François Truffaut, and which can be seen as a sort of filmmaking manual, whose advice also applies to manga creation. What Araki really wanted was to learn the secrets of drawing by becoming the assistant to an established *mangaka*, which is a classic path followed by authors just getting their start, but that option was not feasible since he was still living in Sendai, far from Tokyo, where all the action was (and he never ended up playing that role, either at that time or later). For that same reason, Araki had to send photocopies of his drafts through the mail to the capital. While his packages made their way across Japan, he felt like he was off wandering in the desert. He produced pile after pile of *name* (*nēmu*, the Japanese term for rough drafts, storyboard-like pages that can be more or less developed, depending on the author), but he suffered one failure after another: around 500 pages were turned down... Nonetheless, that period gave us two short stories which, although they were not turned into series, were indeed completed, published in magazines, and later included in some editions of the collection *Gorgeous Irene* (1987, never published in English). Their titles: *Outlaw Man* and *Virginia ni Yoroshiku* ("say hello to Virginia"). Each one was 31 pages long, following the standard format.

Outlaw Man (published in a special edition of *Jump* dated January 10, 1982) kept the Wild West setting, but this time focused more on the action, instead of reprising the unique style of *Busō Poker*. The story follows a cat-and-mouse game between an outlaw and agents of the Pinkerton National Detective Agency, the famous American company founded in 1850—a sort of cross between police, which didn't really exist at that time, and mercenaries. In

41. *Ibid.*, p. 76.

Outlaw Man, you get the feeling that Araki wanted to shine the spotlight on one particular character, a gunslinger with thick eyebrows, a sort of doppelganger for Peckinpah from *Busō Poker*. Alas, there was nothing especially memorable about him. In his drawings, still lacking maturity, Araki still hadn't broken away from his influences: his panels, in spite of offering a good sense of his nascent dynamism, looked like straight copies of Shirato or Yokoyama. Two authors whose style was outdated by that time.

A more unusual story, *Virginia ni Yoroshiku* (also published in a special edition of *Jump*, dated August 1, 1982) is a time capsule that offers some interesting insights into its era. And into its author. This manga kissed the Wild West goodbye: the story takes place in outer space, inside a cargo ship that's home to two men (a Japanese and an American), an AI computer (Bonnie), and a robot (Clyde). In the manga world, *shōnen* has never been a major forum for science fiction, which performs much better in the more cerebral *seinen* and *shōjo* categories. At that time, there had been the great epics of Leiji Matsumoto (*Galaxy Express 999*, 1977-present) and of Osamu Tezuka, as well as the space opera *Cobra* (1978-1984, *Shōnen Jump*) by Buichi Terasawa, but nothing notable other than a handful of classics, stories about giant robots or other *tokusatsu* (Japanese costumed heroes). On top of this, *Virginia ni Yoroshiku* had none of the grandeur of those other works: the story went in the opposite direction of *Star Wars*, instead taking place in a more muted setting that sets the stage for a total thriller (again?). Quite far from the standards of *shōnen*. *Virginia ni Yoroshiku* is a race against the clock: the crew must deal with a masked psychopath who explains in a video transmission that he has placed two bombs aboard the vessel; he then challenges the crew to disarm them in time. There's a flavor of *2001: A Space Odyssey* (1968, Stanley Kubrick) in the stressful, confined space where, right up to the end, we get the impression that the antagonist might be the ship's artificial intelligence, just like the computer system HAL 9000 in Kubrick's film —in fact, in *Virginia ni Yoroshiku*, Bonnie bears the serial number 8000! However, the truth is much more cynical. The person responsible is one of the two men aboard the spaceship: Captain Matt Jackson, a disillusioned former military man who appears to have become a misanthrope and whose main hobby is to do target practice on the different parts of a portrait of a woman, like a perverse game of darts. The one-shot ends like a horror story: knife in hand, Jackson is hunting down his colleague and we fully expect there to be a bloodbath. The end. Araki says nothing else about the motivations of the killer, who on the final page is only shown from behind. In this way, he becomes dehumanized, an incarnation of pure evil, just like the antagonists of slasher films.[42] An explanation for this is that horror films and stories about psycho killers had exploded in popularity around

---

42. A type of horror film that features a game of cat and mouse between a killer (often masked) and their prey. The series *Halloween*, *Friday the 13th*, and *Scream* are emblematic examples.

that time, and it's easy to imagine the impact that movies like *Halloween* (1978, John Carpenter) and *The Shining* (1980, Stanley Kubrick) would have had on Araki, a big fan of horror who published in 2011 a book on his favorite horror films, *Araki Hirohiko no Kimyō na Horror Eiga-ron* ("Hirohiko Araki's bizarre analysis of horror films," Shūeisha Shinsho, never published in English), of which an entire chapter is dedicated to iconic killers, with sketches to boot.[43] As for *Virginia ni Yoroshiku...* it was a valiant effort, but it remained nothing more than a one-shot, probably because it was hard to imagine turning its story into a full series.

The Sherlock Holmes from the dark side

"B.T." is a trickster. He's an arrogant 12-year-old boy with diabolical intelligence who manipulates his adversaries with mischief, magic tricks, and other moves reminiscent of ninja tactics from the pages of *Kamui Den*. His real name? There's no point in asking: no one knows. B.T., that brat with a shock of blonde hair, is the hero of the very first series by Araki, who began signing his work Hirohiko[44] instead of Toshiyuki.

He did it! Araki finally managed to create that cross between a charismatic figure and a protagonist of a suspense story. To get there, he drew inspiration from the detective novels of Arthur Conan Doyle, whose work he's very fond of, from which he replicated the dynamic between Sherlock Holmes and his assistant and admirer John Watson, the narrator of most of the stories. An influence that the *mangaka* openly claims. Moreover, it was partially because of the Holmes connection that the manga was actually published in *Jump*. Indeed, after an initial short story starring the character was published in *Fresh Jump* in 1982, the project *Mashōnen B.T.*, of which the kanji "*ma*" (魔) can mean both magic or the devil (as such, the title can mean "B.T. the magic boy" or "B.T. the diabolical boy"), didn't convince the editorial board of *Shōnen Jump*. They didn't see why they should feature a fiendish boy in a magazine whose motto is "friendship, effort, victory"—a trio of keywords chosen when the magazine was first created based on the results of a survey to find out what its readers were interested in. So, putting forward the name "Sherlock Holmes" helped

43. He also published a second essay dedicated to films, in 2013, that was no longer limited to just horror, notably examining the concept of "suspense": *Araki Hirohiko no chō hen'ai! Eiga no okite* ("Hirohiko Araki's super-favorites! Rules of movies," Shūeisha Shinsho, never published in English).
44. The Japanese website *Livedoor News* (news.livedoor.com/article/detail/13498403) reported on a rumor that might explain this pen name. The kanji *hi* (飛) is the first character of *hikōki*, "airplane" in Japanese, and the *ro* (呂) is supposedly a reference to *Roshia*, "Russia" in Japanese. The rumor goes that Araki's mother felt her first contractions while she was on a plane headed to Russia!

reassure the magazine's editorial board. In addition, Araki could count on support from Ryōsuke Kabashima, who had become his official editor and who, severe though he may have been, was nevertheless an influential ally. Even so, that was not the only sticking point (the English letters "B.T." were considered too unorthodox and vague to be the name of a character, leaving the editors skeptical) and it took close to two years of insistence for *Mashōnen B.T.* to finally be published in September 1983...

You can read the pilot one-shot (a detective story) in the collection *Gorgeous Irene* and the actual series (more focused on action and misadventures) in a single volume entitled *Mashōnen B.T.* (1984, never published in English) and subtitled *Cool Shock B.T.* Although it's clumsy and halting, the series is worth a read for its nonconformist aspects. Selfish, vengeful, and morally ambiguous, blonde-headed B.T. represents the exact opposite of everything a *shōnen* hero is supposed to be; moreover, his appearance and personality laid the foundations for the future *JoJo* antagonist, Dio Brando. His cold and calculating demeanor doesn't have much in common with the fervent spirit of *nekketsu*, the magazine's main genre. That said, while B.T. represents a sort of evil-against-evil situation, his opponents are worse than he is: they are often sadistic, more violent, and more detestable, even while some of them demonstrate an interesting sort of ambiguity. It's the kind of situation where there's a boy who appears perfect in every way, but his attitude changes and he crosses over a moral line when he's at risk of being charged with manslaughter, which would put his future in jeopardy. For a *shōnen*, Araki strayed quite far into the territory of human malevolence and brutality, even for the '80s, a time when gratuitous violence was commonplace in *Jump*. In fact, *Mashōnen B.T.* began just after the launch of *Fist of the North Star* (*Hokuto no Ken*, 1983-1988), a series that was about as gory as it gets, but the violence of Araki's manga was more moral than graphic. Take this for example: B.T. and his Watson-like foil Kōichi (which, by the way, is also the first name of the hero from *Babel II*) grapple with different adversaries in each chapter. In one of the stories, they're faced with a duo of depraved killers in Nazi uniforms who are galvanized by the sense of authority they get from their getups. The two killers trap B.T. and Kōichi in a forest, in a territory they call a "detention camp" (!), and then proceed to torture the two boys and try to take their lives. It's a story line more like something out of a horror movie like *The Last House on the Left* (1972, Wes Craven), rather than the kind of thing you'd expect from a manga for boys... Araki also amused himself by making references like the long eyelashes of the protagonist in *A Clockwork Orange* (1971, Stanley Kubrick), which B.T. sports at the start of a chapter, or the name "de Palma" (a likely reference to the director of *Carrie*, Brian de Palma) written across Kōichi's sweatshirt. The series leaves no doubt about the author's proclivities, which are laid out for all to see.

Araki was trying to find himself. His drawing style, with more childlike lines than in his previous work, still lacked assuredness. He lacked a clear direction that could firmly establish his identity–the characters didn't always seem to belong to the same series, for example. In any case, Araki experimented: he inserted decorative geometric forms into his drawings, like the distinctive black and white arrows that point to B.T. at key moments in the story. At the time, it was a modern visual vernacular, reminiscent of New Wave album covers[45] and the flashy motifs favored by the Memphis Group, an influential design movement from the 1980s. Again in terms of experimentation, the author liked to spice up his duels: B.T. fights his enemies with magic tricks–explained in tutorial sequences–something Araki is clearly fond of, or he makes risky bets, foreshadowing *JoJo's Bizarre Adventure* and its story arc "D'Arby the Gambler"[46] in particular.

Mashōnen B.T. was a flop. In *Jump*, readers are encouraged to judge the quality of the stories published by sending in votes; those votes can then influence what's published in the future. In the case of *Mashōnen B.T.*, due to a lack of interest from the audience, the series ended after six chapters with a final story that, ironically, received many positive votes. In that last chapter, B.T. evolved: he no longer acted purely in his own interest; instead, for the first time, he tried first and foremost to defend his partner in crime, Kōichi, from a major adversary, a horrible, crafty boy who was B.T.'s first real rival intellectually. With that shift, the final chapter managed to find the path toward the holy trinity of "friendship, effort, victory" and proved the importance of playing to reader's expectations... Apparently, in 1983, audiences just weren't ready yet for an antihero in *Jump*. Two decades later, ironically, that ended up being the main attraction of the famous series *Death Note* (2003-2006), which, to be fair, also stood out for its meticulous drawings and carefully crafted plot.

In spite of its short run and its sad fate, *Mashōnen B.T.* nevertheless left a legacy that prevented it from slipping into total oblivion. In 1996, the manga *Yu-Gi-Oh!* (1996-2004, Kazuki Takahashi) first appeared in *Shōnen Jump*, featuring Dark Yugi (the dark spirit that dwells within the series' hero), a wicked being who fights his enemies through dangerous games and who behaves similarly to B.T. Given that Takahashi is open about his admiration for the work of Hirohiko Araki (additionally, Yugi dresses in a style reminiscent of Jotaro from *JoJo's Bizarre Adventure*), it's likely that B.T. was indeed an influence.More recently, the deluxe edition of *JoJo*, called *JoJonium*, launched

45. For example, it makes you think of the work of fashion illustrator Patrick Nagel—who specialized in using solid blocks of color and minimalist geometric shapes in his compositions—produced for the band Duran Duran. The album cover for *Rio* (1982) and the cover of *Mashōnen B.T.* are both imbued with similar energy, made up of uninhibited contrasts and bold diagonal lines.
46. *JoJo*, volume 23; *Stardust Crusaders*, *JoJonium* edition, volume 7.

in December 2013 in Japan, included on its covers motifs of black and white arrows, just like those from *Mashōnen B.T.* Motifs that also appeared in the opening credits for the anime series *JoJo's Bizarre Adventure: Phantom Blood* (2012-2013), which adapted the manga's first part. Moreover, as I write this book, the August edition of the monthly *Ultra Jump*, where *JoJo's Bizarre Adventure* currently appears, has an illustration of Araki surrounded by the same type of arrows. Nothing is lost; everything transforms into something else.

The muscle and the brains (behind the muscle)

1982: Katsuhiro Otomo launched *Akira*, which would become a classic. A manga categorized as *seinen* that, to simplify things, is a story of teenage rebellion in "Neo-Tokyo" (set in 2019), built after a nuclear holocaust, taking place on a backdrop of military experiments to develop metapsychic abilities in humans. Experiments that go terribly wrong. In this case, "science without conscience" doesn't create robots or cyborgs (humans with augmented abilities, particularly thanks to mechanical prostheses) as seen in Osamu Tezuka's *Astro Boy* or Shōtarō Ishinomori's *Cyborg 009*. In *Akira*, the human body and mind are directly altered and transformed into weapons. And in spectacular fashion at that: anyone familiar with the series will remember Tetsuo, whose right arm degenerates into a grotesque mass of organic matter mixed with bits of metal and wires.

It was a new era. One of new fashions and new kings of manga. While Otomo was deeply impacted by a trio of classic manga authors—Tezuka, Yokoyama, and Ishinomori—to whom he aimed to pay homage in various works,[47] his way of approaching the art of manga moved away from their influence. So much so that *Akira*'s author went on to have his own deep impact on Japanese comics: through his visual style, of course, which was totally new in manga, and his innovative processes,[48] but also through the precision and quality of scene-setting in his panels, which raised the standards for the medium and, more

---

47. In an interview given to *Forbes* in 2017, he said, for example, that *Akira* has a general concept similar to that of Yokoyama's *Tetsujin 28-go* (1956-1966, never published in English), the manga that started the trend of giant robots (of which Otomo would copy the drawings when he was a schoolboy, just like he'd do with Tezuka's *Astro Boy*). In both cases, we see secret weapons designed during a war whose discovery during peacetime sets off the action of the story. That in addition to other similarities and homages.
48. In his short story *Fireball*, for example, published in 1979, he drew a panel that has become famous, one showing a man who puts a bullet in another man's head. In a single image, without any speed lines or effects for emphasis, he drew both the shooter's arm experiencing the recoil from the shot, the movement of the case ejected into the air, and the bullet piercing the skull of the unfortunate victim. At the time, in a manga, it would have been more orthodox to cut the action up into several panels with a frantic pace.

than ever before, heightened the cinematic dimensions. When *Domu: A Child's Dream* (1980-1981), a one-shot that was purposefully cadenced and laid out like a film, was published, no other manga author had gotten closer to being so movie-like. Just reading that foundational manga, you can understand very quickly the artist's sense of showmanship and attention to detail, which reach their culmination in *Akira*, with its incredible sequences of destruction, the most famous of which is the spectacular apocalyptic scene in volume 3, in which a black sphere in the heart of Neo-Tokyo unleashes a destructive force on the surrounding buildings. Otomo's drawings influenced countless numbers of artists, including Tetsuo Hara, whose *Fist of the North Star*, which mixes martial arts with a post-apocalyptic world (borrowed from 1981's *Mad Max 2*), added excitement and gore to the pages of *Shōnen Jump* in the '80s.[49]

Once again, as legacies so often work, Hara in turn started his own trend: he established a new way of drawing the human body in manga, based on accentuated muscles and realistic shadowing. In other words, a drawing style influenced by Otomo, but also by Tetsuya Chiba (who devoted plenty of attention to the ruggedness of the male body in *Ashita no Joe*) and by artists of American comics like Neal Adams and Frank Frazetta, two virtuosos of realistic drawing. The path taken by Hara was part of a phenomenon that was common throughout the 1980s: body worship. At that time, increasingly muscular action movie heroes took over the big screen (the physique of Kenshiro, the protagonist of *Fist of the North Star*, was inspired by Mel Gibson and Sylvester Stallone, among others) and that imagery, which reached its apex with movies like *Rambo: First Blood Part II* and *Commando* (both from 1985), was reflected abundantly in manga for men and boys.[50] Tetsuo Hara's style of drawing, an ode to exaggerated masculinity, was the supreme example and was very quickly copied left, right, and center, including in *Jump* itself, for example with *Sakigake!! Otokojuku* by Akira Miyashita, a particularly macho series.

Now, let's get back to the future author of *JoJo*. Where was he to go next after *Mashōnen B.T.*? It was October 1984 and Araki, tired of traveling back and forth between Sendai and *Jump*'s offices, had moved to Tokyo and started work on a second series called *Baoh Raihōsha* (*Baoh: The Visitor*), the word

49. We can consider its main character, Kenshiro—a severe man in mourning with a scarred body—to be one of the last great tragic *shōnen* heroes, before *Dragon Ball*'s Goku definitively took the archetype of the carefree, strapping young man to its pinnacle. After Kenshiro, the same approach of a character with very "ostentatious" virility flourished above all in the *seinen* segment, with, for example, the works of artist Ryōichi Ikegami, like *Sanctuary* (1990-1995; written by Buronson, the author of... *Fist of the North Star*).
50. At that time, in *Dragon Ball*, Goku had to actually storm the "Muscle Tower" (in several chapters published in early 1986), a headquarters of the Red Ribbon Army. Lying in wait for him there was a colossal enemy with an uncanny resemblance to Arnold Schwarzenegger in *Terminator* (1984).

Baoh being derived from "biotechnology," a term that the author was hearing frequently at the time. Like *Akira*, *Baoh: The Visitor* dealt with experiments on human beings and, as in *Fist of the North Star*, it included an obvious glorification of the male body. The *mangaka* developed a new, more virile and rugged style. He moved away from the childlike, round forms of *Mashōnen B.T.*, which were more based on the old school of Yokoyama and Tezuka. Of course, it was still far from the style of all-out strange and beautiful muscle appearing in *JoJo*, with lines much closer to those of Tetsuo Hara. But, from the very first appearance of the hero Ikuro in *Baoh: The Visitor*, his physique is on display for the reader. He is shown in a getup that wouldn't be hard to imagine on a slave in Ancient Rome: a small loincloth, leather straps, and not much else.

The 17-year-old Ikuro is a test subject. After a car accident, his dying body was picked up by a secret military project led by Dr. Kasuminome[51]—whose face bears a resemblance to Colonel Shikishima from *Akira*! Dr. Kasuminome created a biological weapon: the "baoh," a parasitic worm capable of transforming its host into a mutant with heightened abilities and supernatural powers when faced with a dangerous situation. However, the infection also condemns the host to death, since the worm grows in size and eventually escapes violently from the host's body. *Baoh: The Visitor* begins with a getaway. That of Ikuro and Sumire, a girl with psychic powers who is also a test subject. The two are held in captivity in a train occupied by the organization Doress which, in the story, has been responsible since World War II for all sorts of human experiments—ones that the Americans, who pull the strings from the shadows, have decided to pursue. Ikuro escapes from the train (in his skimpy outfit) with Sumire. On the run, they're chased by assassins hired by Doress to bring them back, dead or alive.

Although it was a blend of action, horror, and science fiction, *Baoh: The Visitor* did not have a profound effect on the history of any of these genres, but it did allow Araki, in his first real continuous story, to develop his explosive chemistry and start his future trend toward farcical horror. In the second volume, the hero, in a slimy remake of the Trojan horse, hides inside the body of an enormous and repulsive, genetically modified spider, before bursting out of its belly to take his enemies by surprise! The author also enriched and modernized his formula by incorporating aspects of contemporary action movies: in *Baoh: The Visitor*, there's a robotic skeleton that looks like T-800 from *The Terminator* (1984, James Cameron), for example, while a scene of a character crying in the rain is reminiscent of one of the final moments in *Blade Runner* (1982, Ridley Scott). In a way, Ikuro's transformation was also a precursor to the "Stands" from *JoJo's Bizarre Adventure*, alter egos with extraordinary abilities that take control of individuals with supernatural

51. Literally, "mist eye."

powers. However, in *Baoh: The Visitor*, Ikuro turns into a dehumanized avatar with special abilities (bio-blades attached to his forearms, rapid healing, etc.), a fixed expression on his face, incapable of speaking–which might explain why the manga has some slightly tedious soliloquys. Ikuro's alter ego passes through different stages of evolution over the course of the story and its general appearance bears a resemblance to Star Platinum, the most famous of *JoJo*'s Stands. A wild mane of hair, a jewel on the forehead, a scarf around the neck, their posture... The similarities are striking.

That said, while Ikuro's powers evolve, he nevertheless remains quite bland; his transformation doesn't make him any more remarkable. That's the opposite of a character like Akira Fudo, the hero of *Devilman* (1972-1973, Gō Nagai, *Shōnen Magazine*), a young man who's really, truly consumed by his mutation into a demonic creature. *Devilman* is probably one of the last great *shōnen* tragedies, with a story that's terrifyingly dark, both brutal and sexually charged, and we can see some traces of this action-horror series in *Baoh: The Visitor*. We see it in the exaggerated violence and in Ikuro's transformation into a beastly being. However, his mutation, which is supposed to pose a great danger to the hero, remains mostly aesthetic. Araki put an emphasis on Ikuro's exploits and on his special attacks: he presents Ikuro as a nearly-invincible superhero, more admirable than repulsive, whose methods are certainly brutal, but who is nonetheless guided by principles of justice; *Devilman*, on the other hand, abused notions of morality and ended in the most tragic way possible. These two different approaches ultimately represent changing times.

All in all, *Baoh: The Visitor* lasted for nine chapters (compiled into two volumes published in 1985) that, this time, did not come to a premature end and instead offered a real conclusion, a bittersweet "happy ending." In the second volume, Ikuro ventures into the secret Doress laboratory, beneath a seaside cliff: he aims to rescue little Sumire, who has been captured and is being subjected to unbearable torture. Of course, she's being used to lure the host of the precious Baoh. Ikuro, after fighting his last adversary, a brawny man who bears a striking resemblance to the hero from *Violence Jack*[52] (1973-1974, *Shōnen Magazine*; never published in English) by Gō Nagai (him again!), sacrifices himself to save Sumire and finds his final resting place at the bottom of the ocean. In the epilogue, a few years later, Sumire stares out at the sea and feels that Ikuro is not dead. That he'll come back to her when she turns 17. We can tell that Sumire harbors feelings for Ikuro, being willing to wait until she comes of age so that she can be with her star-crossed lover who shares the same condition as her.

---

52. A precursor to *Fist of the North Star* and even *Mad Max*, set in a post-apocalyptic world where violence and desolation reign supreme. It's also an alternative sequel to *Devilman*.

At the time, Hirohiko Araki was still far from being as famous as *Jump*'s illustrious flagship creators, but *Baoh: The Visitor*—with its good balance between current manga trends, the spirit of "friendship-effort-victory,"and a few unusual artistic choices, like the tendency to place his hero in affected or overly dramatic poses (we'll come back to this in a bit)—did not go unnoticed. It was featured on the cover of *Jump* (No. 45 of 1984, just six issues before the first chapter of the future blockbuster *Dragon Ball*), an honor that *Mashōnen B.T.* never received. Sometime later, it even got a nice, 48-minute-long anime adaptation, produced by the renowned studio Pierrot, which came out in 1989 in Japan and 1995 in France. Incidentally, in that adaptation, the hero did not wear his loincloth at the beginning of the story, further accentuating the glori-fication of the male body. So, *Baoh: The Visitor* was a modest success and thus ensured financial security for young Araki and earned him a bit of a reputation as a young *mangaka* with an unusual style.

While the official story goes that the money he made from this series allowed him to travel outside of Japan for the first time and, in so doing, find inspiration for his future "*JoJo* style" in sculptures he saw in Italy, it's evident that Araki already had an interest in modern Italian statuary—and its Greco-Roman ancestors—while writing *Baoh: The Visitor*. I'll explain in just a moment. But first, let's talk about the splendors of antiquity. We'll start in Rome, a city that's a living museum, where we'll find THE key of all keys.

The mad contortionist

That's not the nickname of a circus sideshow, but rather one that we could give to Araki, from the time of *Baoh: The Visitor* to today. I say that because if there's one element that defines the characters drawn by the author, it's the famous "*JoJo dachi*" (*JoJo* poses), that affected body language that contorts the human body, pushing up against the limits of credibility. Araki's obsession with swinging hips and flexed or twisted members took root in Rome when the author fell in love with a masterpiece by Gian Lorenzo Bernini; after that, there was no going back. Bernini is probably the most famous baroque Italian sculptor and you can view a number of his works in Rome, whether outdoors, in churches, or in museums.[53]

Rome is a captivating place. You have to see it with your own eyes. Did you know that it was Rome that helped the famous Japanese architect Tadao Ando establish his signature style, when he went on a sight-seeing trip in the

---

53. I won't get too much into it, but Bernini was not just a sculptor; he was also an architect and painter.

1960s?[54] The Roman Pantheon (a monument built in the first century BCE), whose dome has a large circular hole at the top, letting in a gentle light, inspired Ando's famous artistic style balancing solid and open spaces. As for Hirohiko Araki, what he discovered in Rome was not the first of Hegel's five major arts, but rather the second: sculpture. I think we can say that the artist behind *JoJo's Bizarre Adventure* was truly born in the Galleria Borghese. This gallery is home to, among other things, a major collection of paintings and statues from the 16th and 17th centuries. It's where you'll find Bernini's *Apollo and Daphne* (1622-1625), one of the most beautiful baroque marble statues and one that changed Araki's life forever.

Baroque: a term used for things that are grotesque, extravagant, or flamboyant. The term arose in the 16th century in the field of jewelry to describe an irregularly shaped stone. The term was later used to describe an artistic movement that took shape around 1600 in Rome as an offshoot from Renaissance art. Receiving financial backing from the ultra-wealthy Catholic Church, baroque works of art aimed to glorify the faith and idealize the power of God. Baroque is an over-the-top, dramatic style of art. As such, it diverged from the order, balance, and rectilinear compositions of classicism, a movement that existed alongside baroque art (at least for a time) and which aimed to return to the rigor and reason of the Renaissance. Baroque art distinguished itself in its preference for movement, curvy lines, and pathos. In sculpture, subjects were not shown in stable, stationary positions, freezing them for all eternity in an ideal state, as was the case during the Renaissance; instead, they were captured in action at very precise moments, putting the subjects in positions that were as dramatic as possible. To do this, baroque artists relied heavily on muscular tension, body contortions, and grimaces. The goal was to dazzle viewers and stir their emotions.

Apollo and Daphne is a perfect example of baroque sculpture and, more generally, of the Italian "Seicento" (meaning "six hundred" for the 1600s) period. This sculpture depicts two figures at the end of a chase, astounded by an extraordinary event. An acme. The exact moment in which the nymph Daphne, fleeing from Apollo, begins her metamorphosis into a laurel. The statue shows remarkable virtuosity (among other prodigious details, Daphne's toenails are seen turning into plant matter and fusing with the ground). In the room housing the statue, it inspires in the viewer an irresistible urge: to walk around the work and photograph it from every angle. This is typical of baroque statuary. Many such works have a spiraling composition, such as *The*

---

54. It's important to note that before 1964, the Japanese were not really able to travel outside the country without special permission. As a consequence, the Japanese naturally developed warped notions about foreign cultures and countries. Once the restriction was lifted, Ando went out to see the world with his own eyes. He talked about this experience in an interview shown on one of the main screens in the exhibition "Tadao Ando: The Challenge" (Centre Pompidou, 2018).

Rape of Proserpina (1621-1622), another marble statue by Bernini found at the Galleria Borghese. It's worth noting that these two works depict myths from Greco-Roman antiquity, the culture of which was rediscovered and gained renewed interest from the Renaissance onward. Naturally, statuary from that period was no exception: artists were inspired by unearthed masterpieces, like the spectacular *Laocoön and His Sons*, the lyrical spirit of which can be seen as close to that of Bernini. It's a Greek marble sculpture discovered in 1506 near the Roman Colosseum, attributed to the Hellenistic period (from 323 to 30 BCE), an era of innovation equivalent in Ancient Greek art to what the baroque movement represented in Italian art in the early modern period. Basically, there's an eternal cycle: many major artistic movements have had their own "baroque evolution," one of transcendence of and distancing from classical roots. The baroque itself evolved into the rococo, an artistic movement that arose in the 17th century. We'll get into that more later, but what's important to note is that *JoJo's Bizarre Adventure* is such an extensive work of art that we can apply this same chronological pattern to it to distinguish a classical foundation, a baroque emancipation, a rococo excess, and other evolutions... We'll get back to this in a few chapters, I promise!

For Araki, this tendency to draw inspiration from the poses of both ancient and modern sculptures really took off in *JoJo*, of course, but it was already present in *Baoh: The Visitor*. In the very first chapter, we see Ikuro half-naked like many of the statues from those periods; at the same time, when Ikuro runs, his body appears in exaggerated positions reminiscent, for example, of the defining elements of Bernini's *David* (1623-1624; another marble statue housed at the Galleria Borghese), with his leaning torso and flexed legs. Moreover, the very last panel, covering a full page, of the first chapter shows Ikuro making a circular movement that looks like an exaggerated version of the *Discobolus* of Myron, a famous Greek sculpture from the 5th century BCE that depicts an athlete preparing to throw a discus. It's fair to say that the borrowed imagery was still gratuitous at that point, inserted here and there for no other reason than the fact that Araki liked how they looked; he still needed to digest them. In any case, the artist had found the touch of originality that would come to define his style. At the time, it was unusual in manga to come across characters with their hips tilted or bodies twisted like those Western statues. You certainly wouldn't see that in the work of Tetsuo Hara, whose big, strong men in *Fist of the North Star* maintained a stiff posture inspired by martial arts. Hara's characters are like tree trunks; they're monoliths whose hips hardly move and whose stiff arms and legs don't snake around. Immediately after his trip to Rome, Araki began pursuing an aesthetic that was different from that of Tetsuo Hara: he aimed to reproduce the intensity, beauty, and sensuality of *Apollo and Daphne* in his manga.[55] That said, in *JoJo*, that sophistication is blended with the macho, martial-arts-inspired exactness of *Fist of the North Star*. That's because legacies are also about genetic hybridization.

Still, there remains a riddle to be solved. On the covers of *Baoh: The Visitor*, why were the hero's arms and hands displayed in the way that they were? Why the eccentric angles, the play on parallel and perpendicular lines? The answer is Antonio Lopez. This Puerto Rican artist (1943-1987) was a giant in the world of fashion illustration and without a doubt the artist in that field who, in the 1970s (mainly), demonstrated with the greatest vivacity that fashion drawings had not been made obsolete by photography. Moreover, Lopez showed incredible versatility, being capable of making drastic stylistic changes. Looking at the covers of *Baoh: The Visitor*, you can see that they're obviously inspired by Lopez's work for the Italian brand Missoni[56] in the 1980s. Particularly, a 1984 illustration in which the subject shows off a red glove whose design is similar to that of the gloves worn by Ikuro on the cover of the second volume. But why did Lopez choose to draw subjects in such positions in his Missoni campaigns? The simple answer is that Lopez, as an artist, was like a sponge, soaking up everything that caught his eye and infusing it into his work. He took an interest in emerging urban cultures and included in his illustrations popular dance moves. Of greatest interest to us, the mechanical movements we see on the covers look similar to popping, a funk dance movement related to breakdancing. The basic principle of popping is the rhythmic contraction and relaxing of the muscles. In the way that influences work, this dance style indirectly made its way into Araki's drawings. It should be noted that this tendency for mechanical gestures was already discreetly present in *Mashōnen B.T.* In the very last panel of the last chapter, the hero's arms are held in a "Lopez style." Undeniably, Lopez's work had a spectacular influence on Araki. While the *mangaka* considers Italian sculpture to be the spark that ignited the fire of his style, it would be a mistake to reduce the "*JoJo* poses" to that. Instead, you have to understand that they are a composite in which fashion is an important ingredient, drawn from both illustrations and photos of models. In fact, we can say that a lot of the *JoJo* spirit comes from the work of Antonio Lopez, but also from another fashion illustrator, Tony Viramontes, who we will come back to later.

55. That said, Araki was not inspired solely by baroque art. We will delve more into sculpture's impact on *JoJo* in chapter nine.
56. The brand is known for its multicolored knit garments, of which we see the influence in *JoJo* starting with *Battle Tendency*.

JoJo's Bizarre Mother

Araki's last manga before *JoJo*, *Gorgeous Irene*, created a sort of mold for the series... and was also an anomaly in the author's career. *Gorgeous Irene* is made up of just two chapters, independent from one another and only loosely connected. They were published in the *Shōnen Jump Autumn Special* in 1985 (for which Araki made the cover) and in the very first issue of *Super Jump*,[57] dated December 20, 1986. Logically, the pair of episodes was later published in a compilation named *Gorgeous Irene*.

The anomaly has to do with the fact that in this brief series, Araki veered toward (a fantasy of) femininity, whereas up to that point, he had focused solely on masculinity. The "gorgeous"[58] Irene Rapona was his very first heroine, at a time when few female characters were given leading roles in the *shōnen* segment—there was Arale from *Dr. Slump* and the trio of thieves from Tsukasa Hōjō's *Cat's Eye*, published between 1981 and 1985 in *Shōnen Jump*, but not many others. So, Irene was Araki's first, but also his last heroine for a long time: it wasn't until the turn of the 21st century that *JoJo*, in its sixth part, gave the lead role to Jolyne Cujoh.

Gorgeous Irene stars a quirky female assassin. Irene is a 16-year-old girl living a secluded life in a mansion with her butler for company. However, when she puts on makeup, she's able to transform into a grown woman—her body becomes more shapely, her demeanor changes, and... she moans with pleasure! Irene becomes a femme fatale, in the literal sense. Her dance-like movements and strange perfumes are capable of hypnotizing her adversaries. She then controls their movements and can even make them commit suicide! Irene has some similarities with *Cutie Honey* (1974, *Shōnen Champion*) by Gō Nagai (yet again!), which was actually one of the first *shōnen* series to feature a female lead. *Cutie Honey* is a cheeky and gory play on the "magical girl" genre, a type of story focusing on a girl with magic powers that are often unleashed when she undergoes a transformation into a costumed heroine. The *shōjo Mahōtsukai Sally* ("Sally the witch," 1966-1967, never published in English) by Mitsuteru Yokoyama, is an iconic example, as are the manga *Sailor Moon* (1992-1997, Naoko Takeuchi) and *Cardcaptor Sakura* (1996-2000, Clamp). While these works are mainly intended for female audiences, Nagai's Honey aimed to win over and excite readers of the opposite sex. The heroine's costume is constantly being torn apart in the heat of the action—but no matter to her, she just keeps on fighting her outrageous enemies, including a gang

---

57. *Super Jump* (1986-2011) started as a supplement to *Weekly Shōnen Jump* before becoming its own fully-fledged, *seinen*-oriented publication.
58. The original Japanese text uses the English word "gorgeous," transcribed into the Japanese katakana syllabary; the same is done for other words spoken by the heroine ("Dancing!," she exclaims before doing some choreography).

leader with long hair and a voluptuous chest who "wants nothing to do with men!"[59] So, somewhere between voyeurism and women's empowerment. We can see *Gorgeous Irene* as a successor to Nagai's manga: the same eroticism with slight S&M tendencies, the same kind of bad guys (Irene faces a giant woman who wields a king-size chainsaw!), the same unfettered violence, and the same lampooning of men. The series is an '80s remix, even more inspired by the fashion illustrations of Antonio Lopez (by that point, the "mechanical" poses were out of place, but there are also sophisticated outfits and hair-styles that defy the laws of physics, in the spirit of some of Lopez's works). It also appears to be infused with glam rock and British new-wave culture (the over-the-top looks of the characters look like they're straight out of some of the most flamboyant music videos of that era), with a contemporary graphic style that, in the second chapter, is very similar to Tetsuo Hara's work in the way that bodies are drawn. Also in that chapter, we start to see the clear influence of Tony Viramontes' vibrant and sensual work on Hirohiko Araki, particularly in the design of a black-gloved female assassin, posed with a hand on her face, obviously inspired by the illustrator's work for the British edition of *Vogue* in December 1983. In that issue, Viramontes drew the model Leslie Winer, his muse, with her androgynous face and punk vibes, in a sassy and affected pose.[60] As for the overlapping-disk earrings worn by Araki's titular character, those came directly from an illustration by Antonio Lopez dated 1983, in which a subject is wearing several hats, one on top of another.[61]

Unlike the influences of Hara and Viramontes, you don't have to wait until the second chapter to see the spirit of the '80s shine through in *Gorgeous Irene*: it makes its presence known from the very first panel of the first episode. Looking at that first page, you can practically hear a synthesizer and a beatbox. It's laid out like a cosmetics ad, showing off make-up products associated with certain parts of the female body. The panel leaves no doubt: we are totally immersed in the flashy consumerist and lighthearted pop aesthetic of 1980s Japan! It was a decade that saw an explosion in worship of Japanese pop-culture "idols," young, multi-talented starlets who worked as singers, models, and actresses, the most emblematic example from the '80s being Seiko Matsuda. Araki's manga was perfectly in keeping with the times.

59. *Cutie Honey* (translated from the French edition published by Isan Manga), p. 159.
60. The session during which Winer posed for Viramontes is recounted and documented in photos on the website *Fashion Sphinx* (fashionsphinx.com/?p=986), maintained by Eugenia Melian, who was Viramontes' agent. There you can see the resulting illustrations, similar to Araki's drawings on p. 81 of the compilation *Gorgeous Irene*.
61. This illustration can be seen on the cover of the book *Antonio's People*, published by Thames & Hudson in 2004.

All of the seeds of the future *JoJo* spirit were already present in the modest-yet-refreshing *Gorgeous Irene*. In the series, Araki went all-in with the farcically gory universe filled with eccentric characters with equally eccentric powers (the chainsaw-wielding woman also uses chewing gum as a weapon), body worship, pop-culture extravagance, and a highly affected attitude. The second chapter, part of which is set in a destroyed version of New York's Harlem neighborhood[62] (the scenes of devastation further reinforce the spiritual similarities with *Fist of the North Star*), even offers the physical basis for Jonathan Joestar from *JoJo's Bizarre Adventure* via the character Michael: the two men are practically twins. Similarly, the chapter offers a primitive version of the future character Stroheim from the second part of *JoJo*, with his trapezoid-shaped hairstyle, which without a doubt was inspired by an illustration done by Antonio Lopez for Missoni that appeared in a magazine ad published in 1985.[63] In that ad, an androgynous subject sports that very same hairstyle and is wearing a monocle that, once again, inspired Stroheim's look. These outrageous hairdos, which we also find in other images from that same Missoni campaign, can be explained by the fact that Lopez and his close collaborator Juan Ramos had a keen interest in science fiction and integrated futuristic fantasy influences into their work.

However, what *JoJo* did not keep from *Gorgeous Irene* was the focus on women. Moreover, in *Gorgeous Irene*, Araki let loose and wasn't shy about showing some nipples in the first chapter, something he would never again do until... 2011, in *JoJolion*,[64] the eighth part of the saga. It's important to note that, unlike today, in the 1980s, female nudity was allowed in *Shōnen Jump*: during that same era, you would occasionally see nudity in early installments of *Dragon Ball* and *City Hunter* (1985-1991), for example. This was also the case for *Stop!! Hibari-kun!* (1981-1983) by Hisashi Eguchi, an author known for his pretty girls who Araki, sometime before *JoJo*, claimed as an inspiration for his own female characters... until his editor reprimanded him for sticking too close to the original![65] In any case, *Gorgeous Irene* does not bear any obvious traces of this influence and that's not the reason why Irene's adventures came so

62. In the 1980s, New York had a reputation for being ravaged by crime. After that, in the '90s, crime fell precipitously under the leadership of Mayor Rudy Giuliani (who took office in 1994).
63. You can see it on the cover of the Japanese book *Antonio Lopez Monogatari* ("the story of Antonio Lopez"), published in 1987.
64. There are a few scenes with female nudity in the sixth and seventh parts of *JoJo*—*Stone Ocean* and *Steel Ball Run*—but "strategic" parts of the body remain covered. Strategically.
65. Araki provided this information in a joint interview with Tetsuo Hara, conducted in September 2017 for an event in Japan to celebrate the 50th anniversary of *Jump*, called "Legend Talk Show." A report of the event can be found on the Japanese website *Mantan Web* (mantan-web.jp/article/20170910dog00m200002000c.html). The drawings that Araki talks about, those that were too close to Eguchi's drawings, were most likely unpublished sketches. Why is it that, conversely, Araki was allowed to develop a style undeniably similar to *Fist of the North Star*? That remains a mystery...

quickly to an end. So, what was the reason then? In 2012, Araki talked about the decision: "Today, there are lots of stories in which strong women fight, but at the time, it was unheard of in a *shōnen* magazine.[66] Intuitively, I sensed that it wouldn't fly and I avoided extending the series. I told myself that readers wouldn't like it and it couldn't last. [...] At the time, after the release of the film *Aliens* with the strong Ripley, played by Sigourney Weaver, I wanted to give it a try myself. But as a man, I had a hard time drawing a woman who takes hits. It was too cruel."[67] So, that's why Araki returned to totally male-dominated storytelling. That said, I think it's fair to say that *Gorgeous Irene*, even more than *Baoh: The Visitor*, laid the groundwork for the carefree, pop spirit of *JoJo* and, as such, that the model for this very male-focused saga was... a woman.

66. For example, there were examples of fighting heroines in *shōnen* in the 1970s, like *Sukeban Arashi* (never published in English) by Masami Kurumada, with its female thugs, published in 1974 in *Shōnen Jump*, or the series *Cutie Honey*, discussed in this chapter. However, the norm was, of course, to feature male characters.
67. *JOJOmenon*, 2012 (never published in English).

JOJO'S BIZARRE ADVENTURE

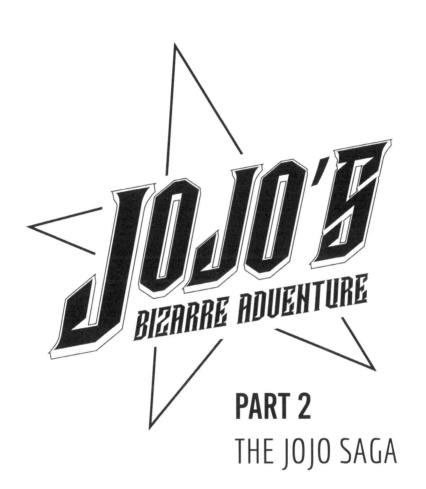

PART 2

THE JOJO SAGA

WARNING

You are about to enter the world of *JoJo's Bizarre Adventure*.
In this saga, a number of the characters use "Stands," which are like
guardian spirits with powers that are specific to each user.

In the next part of this book, strange events may occur.

Because just like Araki's characters, each chapter will now have its own Stand.

Beware, all ye who enter here.

CHAPTER I: STRANGE AND BEAUTIFUL (1986-1987: JOJO'S BIZARRE ADVENTURE, PART 1)

Stand: New Order
Do you really think there's only one way of counting things?

To listen to while reading:

Goblin – *Profondo Rosso*
Led Zeppelin – *Immigrant Song*
The Rolling Stones – *Gimme Shelter*
Van der Graaf Generator – *Necromancer*
Jack the Ripper – *From My Veins to the Sea*

"I found my style in Italy." These are the words of Hirohiko Araki in his book *Manga in Theory and Practice: The Craft of Creating Manga.* It's even the title of an entire section in which the author lays out his famous "Aha!" moment as an artist that came to him during his first trip to Rome. In fact, we get a very strong Italian flavor from the outset of *JoJo*. Indeed, from its very first panel! In it, a dark hand (that at first glance appears to be gloved due to the lighting) points a rustic dagger at a terrified young woman. Lying on her back, her privates barely covered, she's about to be sacrificed. The scene appears to be presented through the eyes of the killer. Have you heard of the *giallo* movie genre? If so, you can probably see where I'm going with this. If not: *giallo*[1] refers to a category of exploitation films that started in the 1960s in Italy with Mario Bava's *The Girl Who Knew Too Much* (1963). Directors like Dario Argento and Lucio Fulci went on to take the category to new heights. Being early slasher films, these over-the-top movies were a cross between crime, horror, and erotica. In particular, they built their dramatic tension around the identity of the killer, of whom—and this became a sort of cliché for the genre—

---

1. *Giallo* means "yellow" in Italian. This name comes from the color of the covers of crime novels published by the company Mondadori.

the audience often only saw the hand doing the deed (with a knife, razor, or other sharp object) for a good portion of the film. If the hand was wearing a black leather glove, even better. And if the point of view is subjective, i.e., through the eyes of the murderer, that's absolutely iconic. Particularly, we see all of these characteristics in Argento's *Deep Red* (*Profondo Rosso*, 1975), a masterpiece of the genre. As such, it puts a smile on your face when you realize that the very first page of *JoJo* is a sort of stereotypical image from the *giallo* genre—even though you have to feel bad for the poor victim! I smile because of the fact that this scandalous, unflattering, nasty side of Italian culture is not what the author had in mind in that quote from his book on theory. When he talks about Italy, Araki only mentions the splendors of the country's statuary. So, we don't know if the *giallo* reference is purposeful or not in the first chapter of his manga, but we do know of the author's lover for horror thrillers and it's worth noting that he named one of his characters "Dario." No matter. Whether it's conscious or not, *JoJo's Bizarre Adventure* always maintains close ties to multiple facets of Italy, as that first page so brilliantly shows. Moreover, that's just one of the many influences that appear immediately in the series, called *JoJo no kimyō na bōken*[2] in the Japanese version, the first chapter of which was published in the issue of *Shōnen Jump* dated January 1, 1987.[3]

Baroque 'n' Roll

"*Dogyaaaan!*" screeches the Japanese onomatopoeia in the first panel. "It's a saturated sound, like distortion coming from an electric guitar. A rock 'n' roll way of saying 'ta-da!,' explains Satoko Fujimoto, the current French translator of the manga.[4] From the beginning, Araki makes a habit of punctuating his pages with sound effects from rock music and horror films. For example, he took inspiration from the diaphanous sounds of the mellotron, a keyboard instrument typical of horror movie soundtracks—it was used abundantly by the Italian musical group Goblin, which created the soundtracks for some of Argento's most famous films—and that was also heavily used in progressive rock, a musical genre that Araki loves.

2. The international title, *JoJo's Bizarre Adventure*, is a faithful translation.
3. Issues of *Jump* always come out several weeks before the date marked on their cover. This issue was actually released in early December 1986.
4. Remarks collected by us on January 25, 2019. Satoko Fujimoto has translated *JoJo's Bizarre Adventure* in collaboration with adaptor Anthony Prezman since volume 8 of *Steel Ball Run*, published in April 2014. They're the ones who translated the new French edition of *Phantom Blood*, *Battle Tendency*, and *Diamond is Unbreakable*, as well as the latter volumes of *Stardust Crusaders*.

In fact, *JoJo*'s panels—and this has been even more true as the series has progressed—are really cadenced like musical compositions. According to the action taking place, they are accented with riffs, abstract noises, and percussion. We can call it a "*JoJo* rhythm": the pulses in katana characters like "*Do Do Do Do...*" or "*Go Go Go Go...*"—which are not exclusive to Araki, but which he uses frequently and in a very particular way, with emphasis and razzle-dazzle—keep time for the growing tension, for example, or tap out a beat, of varying speed and strength, to underscore the impact of an incredible moment. A score that will give you shivers. Sometimes from anxiety, sometimes from turmoil and clashes.

With a first panel like that, what follows can't be good, right? Blood spurts out. We witness a tribal ritual, a sacrifice in which a giant Aztec man—the one with the dagger—is spattered with the fresh blood of a young woman. He's wearing a stone mask that suddenly, feeding off the red liquid, shoots out bony needles that lodge themselves in the man's skull. The man, triumphant, standing tall, then proclaims that by completing this ritual, he has just obtained eternal life. And yet, the tribe vanished from history, leaving nothing but ruins. That is the curse of the stone mask, the narrator tells us.

Starting from the prologue, the manga brings movie images to mind. In addition to the trend of masked killers in '80s slashers, the stone mask in *JoJo* also calls to mind, in the way it brutally latches on, the "facehugger" from *Alien* (1979, Ridley Scott), a spider-like creature that hooks itself onto the head of an unfortunate host to implant an embryo in their body. By association, it might also make you think of another mask with frightening characteristics, one that's well-known for fans of fantasy movies and that also involves ritual killing: the mask from *Black Sunday* (1960, Mario Bava), the beginning sequence of which features, in a gothic black-and-white atmosphere, the execution of a woman condemned for witchcraft in the 17th century. As punishment, a muscular executioner places on her face a mask with spikes, which are then, of course, driven into her skull. Although in this case, the function of the mask is reversed between the executioner and the victim, the emphasis Bava places on the mask, which the camera lingers on with a direct shot, barely visible against a black background, is not unlike the way in which Araki presents his stone mask at the end of *JoJo*'s prologue. Thus, even before *JoJo*'s story actually begins, right off the bat, it foreshadows what makes the series special: visions of horror, rock 'n' roll beats, and an exotic flair.

The main story takes place in an equally exotic locale, at least compared to the norm for *Jump*. Araki takes us to the countryside of Victorian England in 1880. The narrator tells us that "our story centers around this stone mask excavated in Mexico and the adventures of two boys whose fates take a rather bizarre turn!" These boys are named Jonathan Joestar,[5] the son of an English lord, and Dio Brando, from a working-class family: two teenage boys who would normally never cross paths. However, they end up living under the same roof when Dio loses his father: Lord George Joestar, out of gratitude to Dio's father for supposedly saving his life in the past, takes in Dio and raises him as a second son, never suspecting that young Brando, under his facade of being the perfect son, is hiding a sly, violent predator with no moral limits, looking to steal the family's fortune. Even if that means killing His Lordship. Up to this point, Jonathan, nicknamed JoJo, has had a happy life; however, it soon turns to torment. When no one is looking, Dio bullies him. Dio unleashes on JoJo all of his hatred for the upper class.

When *JoJo's Bizarre Adventure* was first published, presenting a non-Japanese hero was practically taboo in *Jump*. Outside of a few stories set in imaginary universes, of course, almost all of the magazine's titles took place in Japan, or at least featured Japanese heroes. In *Knights of the Zodiac*, for example, the heroes visit Greece and other places, but the main character is still a young Japanese man. Of course, there were already other manga starring non-Japanese heroes, but they were mainly found in *shōjo*. Female authors were crazy about a certain type of Western beauty and weren't shy about infusing it into their manga. On that note, I have a telling anecdote that can help explain the overrepresentation of foreign boys in *shōjo*. The actor Björn Andrésen visited Japan in 1971. The androgynous youth, who played the teenage character Tadzio in the Luchino Visconti film *Death in Venice* (1971), quickly became a sensation. The boy appeared in ads on local television, recorded songs, and the girl's manga magazine *Margaret* described him as "the most beautiful boy in the world": he became a sort of archetype for Western beauty in the Japanese imagination. The archetype of the slender prince with elegant, golden hair, the influence of which we find in girls' manga of the 1970s (and later), a time when many major *shōjo* titles were set in the West, like the classics *The Heart of Thomas* by Moto Hagio (1974-1975), set in Germany, *Kaze to Ki no Uta* ("the poem of wind and trees," 1976-1984, Keiko Takemiya, never published in English; set in France), and of course *The Rose of Versailles*, also known as *Lady Oscar* (1972-1973, Riyoko Ikeda). While in the 1970s this archetype of the androgynous European boy with venomous charm was closely associated with *shōjo*, it also made its way a bit into *shōnen* via *Ring ni Kakero* by Masami Kurumada (1977-1981), a boxing manga known for its parade of handsome young men, including, for example, the Frenchman Napoléon Valois, a character

---

5. Named after "Jonathan's," the family restaurant where Araki and his editor would have their editorial meetings at the time. The full name Jonathan Joestar comes from the fact that Araki wanted to come up with something strong and easy to remember, with alliteration between the first and last names, like "Steven Spielberg."

with a very *Rose of Versailles* air about him. In 1987, in *JoJo*, we can potentially consider Dio, a young European with foppish attitudes and poisonous beauty, to be another in this lineage of beautiful, blonde *shōjo* boys, and thus of Tadzio.

As for Araki, his desire to set *JoJo* in Great Britain came, quite simply, from a trip to Europe. As we already know, the money that Araki made from *Baoh: The Visitor* allowed him to travel for the first time outside of Japan, and it was after spending some time in England that he got the idea to set his manga in that country, especially since he liked the atmosphere of the Sherlock Holmes stories, which were also set in the Victorian era. Given the chosen setting, he figured it would only be normal to feature a British hero, right? Even if that meant going against the status quo at *Jump*. And that was just the first of his transgressions, the first bizarre feature in a series that has accumulated numerous eccentricities.

Negative penalty

From the very beginning, *JoJo's Bizarre Adventure* follows paths that are so non-conformist that you have to ask yourself how the heck the series got the green light from the editorial team, and then was able to keep going. Especially given that the editor in chief of *Jump*, Hiroki Gotō, was not a big fan.[6] It's likely that Ryōsuke Kabashima, who had previously gone to bat for *Mashōnen B.T.*, was instrumental in making it happen. He was the audacious editor that Araki needed: "Without him, I wouldn't be drawing manga like I do today," the *mangaka* recounted in 2009. "He always encouraged my choices to do something that no one else at *Jump* was doing. He would tell me that publishing a non-conformist story in a popular magazine would be interesting. It was thanks to his words that I was able to have creative freedom."[7] Be that as it may, audacity alone is not enough: the first few chapters left readers unconvinced. The problem was that the hero, who filled the stereotype of the prim and proper boy scout, was constantly being clobbered by his nemesis, Dio, who humiliated him in a boxing match (in which, of course, the deceitful adversary cheated), who planted a kiss on the girl Jonathan liked, Erina, and who even murdered his dog Danny! Jonathan was broken, both psychologically and physically. Of course, Araki was trying to set up Dio's gradual intrusion, to pose him as the invader, and then follow that with Jonathan's comeback. However, a manga in *Jump* is supposed to convey positive values and a hero

---

6. Hiroki Gotō, *Jump – L'âge d'or du manga*, Kurokawa, 2019, p. 250. Gotō explains that when he more recently re-read the first four parts of the saga, he finally got hooked and even now says that it's a "brilliant manga."
7. *Ibid.* p. 254.

can't afford to stay stuck in a mire for so long without any light at the end of the tunnel. As Araki tells it: "In a weekly manga magazine, each manga only gets nineteen pages an issue. That meant that Jonathan remained on that negative side for two or three weeks. That can be tough on a weekly manga, and sure enough, the readers didn't take to it, and I could feel their growing dislike of the constantly beat-upon protagonist. When an installment ends with a feeling of defeat, the readers' emotions will stay down on that negative side with the protagonist, and that will be reflected in the reader surveys."[8] The infamous satisfaction surveys, which can decide whether a series lives on or is laid to rest...

It's important to note that originally, Araki wanted to focus on Dio, not Jonathan. The insolent blonde boy was a direct and purposeful extension of the hero from *Mashōnen B.T.*, a "version 2.0" whose programming was pushed to the extreme, giving him more adult traits—Araki has admitted that Dio's appearance was influenced by Roy Batty, the antagonist from *Blade Runner*. We can clearly see that the author tried to make Dio as charismatic and impressive as possible (from the moment he makes his sensational appearance at the Joestar's home), even with his first name, which comes from the heavy-metal artist of the same name, but which also means "God" in Italian! The *mangaka* became attached to his character, perhaps almost too much so: "Dio is even more spiteful and jealous than B.T., and when I created him, that may have had an influence on my own mindset. [...] For example, in my daily life, I would think dark thoughts and, like Dio, I looked at people as if they were insects,"[9] explains the author.

Interestingly, the beginning of *JoJo* is like an inverted version of the *nekketsu*-style manga from Araki's childhood, like *Kyojin no Hoshi* and *Ashita no Joe*. Jonathan, the protagonist, is an affluent, carefree young man while Dio, the antagonist, plays the part of the angry kid from the slums who's devoted to pulling himself up by his bootstraps by channeling his rage. Young Brando is a sort of evil twin to those old dirt-poor rebels and, without a doubt, his personality is more intriguing that of Jonathan, who is just a simplistic person-ification of justice. In fact, Dio's hatred of the upper class and his thirst for power did not come out of nowhere. Throughout his childhood, he endured poverty and violence, particularly from his alcoholic, abusive father who would beat his mother, so much so that she ultimately died from the injuries. It's quite clear that Dio no longer has any positive feelings toward humanity. There remains nothing but bitterness, animosity, and resentment. And to get his revenge for his lot in life, Dio won't shrink from any excess; he won't hesitate to violate the rules of morality or quite simply crush any human being—any

8. Hirohiko Araki, *Manga in Theory and Practice*, p. 92.
9. Hirohiko Araki, *JoJoveller*, Shūeisha, 2014.

pathetic insect—who crosses his path. When it comes down to it, when we observe the care that Araki put into Dio's character, we can tell that he is marked by the difficulty that the author had in creating a *shōnen* centered on a hero who transcends notions of good and evil. Ultimately, the spirit of B.T. lives on in Dio Brando.

While the early chapters of *JoJo* presented a simplistic concept, a clash between two avatars representing good and evil (one seems to possess only virtue, the other only vice!), there were many ways to read into that conflict between the well-off Jonathan and the destitute Dio, at a time when Japan was still living out its "economic miracle." That trend didn't come to an end until the 1990s when the bubble burst, bringing an end to the famous *bubble jidai*. In some ways, *JoJo* is a product of its time, whether or not those aspects were consciously captured by Araki, a man who spent his teenage and young-adult years in a prosperous and calm Japan, compared to the tumult of the '60s. Perhaps we can consider Dio to be a symbol of revolt by those left behind by the economic boom, people who were burning to take what they had always been left out of. As for Jonathan at the start of the manga, he can be viewed as a reflection of a certain category of young Japanese in the 1980s who were well-off, apolitical, and sitting pretty in the pacifying comfort established by their parents. After all, in spite of his innate virtues, the heir to the Joestar fortune, who, on the whole, is quite naive and passive, doesn't he also live a life of luxury that he takes for granted? Doesn't he owe it all to the hard work of his father? That said, young Jonathan evolves. After the first five chapters, *JoJo's Bizarre Adventure* leaps forward in time to show Jonathan and Dio, seven years later, now young adults finishing their university studies. At the same time, each is well on his way to success in his chosen pursuits. With nothing in common.

The vampire masquerade

To recap, the fates of these two boys are tied together by a mysterious stone mask discovered in Mexico. That mask, in fact, is now hanging in the Joestars' home. It's a souvenir that Jonathan's late mother bought while traveling. And it will soon resurface in the story.

For seven years, Dio has feigned friendship with JoJo, waiting for his chance to steal the Joestar family fortune. He's now finally old enough to legally collect an inheritance. And it just so happens that Lord Joestar is sick... Of course, none of this is a surprise to Dio: he's been gradually poisoning his adopted father by replacing his medicine with a fake. However, Jonathan figures out the scheme and manages to prove, in front of witnesses, Dio's guilt. Dio is now backed into a corner. In the heat of the action, Dio uses the stone mask on himself. He has discovered its effects; he knows that the artifact trans-forms humans into vampires, thus giving them eternal youth and superhuman strength. And with that, in volume two, the real battle between Jonathan Joestar and Dio Brando begins. "I quit being human, JoJo!," exclaims Dio in a now-famous line. And there's no lack of famous lines from *JoJo's Bizarre Adventure*, often in Japanese using peculiar phrasing or other eccentricities, such as the prominent usage of words from European languages or of Latin characters. While it's not always possible to transpose these oddities into a translated version, you'll nonetheless find surprising lines like "HELL 2 U!," left as-is from the original text. Interestingly, there are actually two books in Japanese on the most unusual choices of language in Araki's saga: *JoJo no kimyō na meigen shū* ("collection of JoJo's bizarre quotations," 2012), also known as *JoJo's Bizarre Words*. "I'm often told that the dialogue in my manga is distinctive, but I'm only writing lines based on the way I actually think and talk in my daily life," Araki explains. "When it comes to expressing a manga's world and characters, a *mangaka* shouldn't rule out straying from what's in the dictionary. By using more vernacular speech, you can make your characters more distinctive."[10] Moreover, there's no shortage of onomatopoeias in the series. When Dio kisses Erina, for example, the Japanese sound effect is a very surprising "*Zukyuuuun!*" Satoko Fujimoto comments on this: "It's like the onomatopoeia you'd use for a gunshot! Or an arrow piercing a heart, for example. And then, again, there's a side to it that's like distortion from an electric guitar. But it's not a sound effect you'd typically associate with a kiss."[11] As such, this sound shouldn't be interpreted as that of the kiss, but rather a sound effect for a dramatic event, something terrible that's happening. Paired with the image, this onomatopoeia produces a particularly unorthodox effect. That's totally typical of Araki: he uses quirky sounds that don't match the norm for manga, and sometimes ones that are even more strange than the one in the kiss scene. According to the French translator, these bizarre sound effects are often impossible to transpose into French: that's because to do so, there aren't any references that all francophone readers would share (a single onomatopoeia can be translated in different ways); as such, it's very difficult to convey to those readers that an onomatopoeia doesn't correspond to its typical usage, whereas the Japanese are familiar with a whole series of codes for sound effects, to the point that some of those sounds are actually used as slang. Still, Satoko Fujimoto thinks that, in spite of that, the written form itself of the onomatopoeias—left as-is in the French version and accompanied by a caption provided by the adaptor Anthony Prezman—conveys specific emotions. And that's true. When Dio forcibly kisses Erina, the Japanese onomatopoeia

10. Hirohiko Araki, *Manga in Theory and Practice*, pp. 109 and 110.
11. Remarks collected by us on May 15, 2019.

has sharp lines and produces a violent effect that contrasts with the theoretical tenderness of a kiss.

While one of the influences that Araki claims for the first part of *JoJo's Bizarre Adventure* is the novel *East of Eden* (by American writer John Steinbeck, published in 1952 and adapted to the big screen a few years later by Elia Kazan), with its theme of intergenerational heritage, we can also consider volumes three to five to be a sort of mix between the *Dracula* literary saga (1897, Bram Stoker) and martial arts films, which were popular in the 1980s, particularly thanks to Hong Kongese actor Jackie Chan. In those volumes, Jonathan goes to confront Dio, who's more of a megalomaniac than ever, living in a theatrical, luxurious ambiance, with ornamented columns and a coffered ceiling, in a sumptuous castle overlooking the seaside village of Windknight's Lot. On the hilltop, surrounded by henchmen he's turned into bloodthirsty vampires (including Jack the Ripper, the famous serial killer of London's Whitechapel district!), he drinks the blood of girls and basks in his new position as a self-proclaimed emperor. Dio is now the ultimate lifeform, ruling over the top of the food chain. And he has many powers: capable of reanimating dead bodies, he's preparing to send an army of zombies out across all of England.

The general direction of *JoJo*'s story is clear. Everything leads up to the great final battle between the hero and his rival. After the seven-year leap forward, Jonathan and Dio both look like bodybuilders, as if to signal the coming duel of champions. You have to remember that this was created in the middle of the boom in bodybuilding movie heroes and Jonathan, while he sometimes makes you think of Kenshiro from *Fist of the North Star*, also has an air of Sylvester Stallone. And that actually makes perfect sense given that the actor was one of the references used by Tetsuo Hara to draw Kenshiro—at the time, that type of movie inspired both *mangaka*, each in his own way. Araki, influenced by this era of worshiping physical prowess, aimed to portray in his manga a clash of titans, between the greatest justice-seeker and the ultimate bad guy: "People always love to compare who's stronger or who's cooler. You've got Godzilla versus Mechagodzilla, Schwarzenegger versus Stallone... I wanted there to be [in *JoJo*] that sort of contest or struggle between Dio and Jonathan."[12] In the end, everything leading up to that great battle is just the tale of how one becomes the avatar of good and the other of evil. The emergence of that antagonism gives direction to Jonathan's life: in the beginning, he's submissive, but he ultimately rises up, as a hero, to face the enemy of humankind. For Araki, that story resonates with his own experience: "There were limitations on how I could write the character because he was a 'symbol of justice,' so he may be a little on the boring side. I solidified his character as I went. [...] Just as

12. Words of the author in *JoJonium*, *Phantom Blood*, volume 3.

Jonathan was unsure as to how to live his life, I was unsure as to where to take the character. Maybe I grew as an author a little with Jonathan as he trudged on through his hardships."[13] That said, the core of the protagonist remains the same from beginning to end: a personification of the idea of justice, a living tribute to human virtues. As he matures, Jonathan simply becomes more determined and better armed.

In volume three, we meet the man who will do that arming. The man who will introduce *JoJo's Bizarre Adventure* to the world of martial arts. Will Anthonio Zeppeli, the eccentric master of "the Hamon," wants to destroy the stone mask and offers to teach Jonathan a fighting technique from the East that will allow him to hold his own against Dio. This new direction in the story, offering many training sequences and loaded with *nekketsu*-style values of stretching one's limits, brings *JoJo* closer to the traditions of *Jump*. And when it comes to training plot lines, the figure of the mentor is an essential archetype. With his dandy mustache,[14] his checkered hat, and his odd habits—he fights with a glass of wine in his hand without spilling the precious liquid—the Italian, Zeppeli, is also the saga's great eccentric. What's more, his name, which pays homage to the rock band Led Zeppelin, reflects a unique point that remains parts of *JoJo* to this day: many of the characters created by Araki, who is crazy about music (background music is important in his studio, where he draws while listening to songs that fit the atmosphere he's trying to create), have names inspired by musical artists. Western artists, of course.

The Hamon, "the way of the immortals." The light side of the stone mask. It's a method that aims to master the energy coursing through a person, based on the idea that a precise breathing technique induces ripples of energy through the body. Araki illustrates this invisible phenomenon by placing Zeppeli in a river: on the surface of the water, circular waves spread out around him. For the author, who has a strong interest in magic tricks and other illusions, this new plot line allowed him to explain in a (more or less) scientific way the extraordinary phenomena found throughout his manga. His story also reveals that the stone mask and the Hamon both have connections to blood: when the age-old mask's spikes plunge themselves into a victim's brain, they awaken a hidden potential in the person, who must then feed on blood (of others); the Hamon, on the other hand, works through the circulation of blood thanks to its oxygen richness. Moreover, the reason why vampires created by the mask are vulnerable to both daylight and Zeppeli's technique is that the waves of

13. Words of the author in *JoJonium*, *Phantom Blood*, volume 1.
14. An attribute inspired by the artist Salvador Dali and by Iyami, a character from the famous comedic *shōnen Osomatsu-kun* ("Mr. Osomatsu") by Fujio Akatsuka, originally published between 1962 and 1969 in *Weekly Shōnen Sunday* (the series has since had runs in other magazines). Iyami is also known for his eccentric poses, making him a sort of forerunner for the "*JoJo* poses," even if they were intended to be comical with Akatsuka's character.

energy produced by the Hamon have the same form as those emitted by the sun. Supposedly, the best strategy to defeat Dio is to fire a powerful charge of Hamon at him. But that's purely theoretical. Jonathan first has to train under his Italian sensei, in training sequences reminiscent of martial arts films, on the one hand, but also, of course, fighting manga.

With the Hamon, Araki came up with a way to make the invisible visible. To make the forces of life tangible, without them taking the form of giant pulses of energy like in *Dragon Ball*. Araki's techniques are more strange, more unexpected. For example, Zeppeli uses the "Hamon Cutter" technique: when he spits a liquid–in this case, wine–with extreme pressure, he's able to transform it into super-sharp disks. Then there's the "Sendo Wave Kick," which shoots a wave of concentrated energy, and the "Sunlight Yellow Overdrive," which creates a whirlwind of energy–the characters cry out the names of the moves in foreign languages, following the trend started by Masami Kurumada's *Ring ni Kakero*, with its attacks like "Winning the Rainbow" and "Galactica Phantom." By synchronizing the energy present on the surface of the water with the energy in his body, Zeppeli is even able to walk on water. It's quite a sight to behold. And it's a good thing that it's pleasant to look at because the secrets of the Hamon cover numerous pages. Before getting to Dio, Jonathan and Zeppeli have to use all of their techniques to vanquish formidable enemies, such as Blueford, the zombie knight, with his eccentric "Danse Macabre Hair," a move in which he moves his long black hair like a third arm. As always, with a view to explaining extraordinary events, Araki justifies the movement of the undead warrior's hair by comparing it to the way in which a plant called touch-me-not is able to "expand and retract its leaves at an incredible speed by manipulating turgor pressure, which is produced by the movement of water through the cells."[15] But hold on a second... did you say a knight? Yes: the final volumes of the first part of *JoJo* have some interesting medieval European accents, particularly since it's the only time in the entire saga that we find that kind of atmosphere. The fourth volume, in particular, features a fight against another undead knight, Tarukus (whose appearance and head-on attacks are reminiscent of Taurus Aldebaran from *Knights of the Zodiac*), in the "Lair of the Two-Headed Dragon" at the castle of Windknight's Lot. There, Jonathan and his adversary engage in a constrained battle, each one being connected to the ceiling by an unbreakable chain. Iron, stone, and chivalrous (dis)honor: that's the formula for this fight to the death, which ends in tragedy.

---

15. *Phantom Blood*, volume 4.

Macho, macho man

It's during fight scenes that you can see all of the eccentricity that had become part of Araki's way of drawing the human body. At first glance, you can see the first part of *JoJo* as a baroque version of *Fist of the North Star*. From a distance, the similarities are obvious. For example, in *JoJo*, you see ways of shading the skin—with bold hatch marks—and of drawing light, on black clothing in particular, that are reminiscent of Hara's drawings. Not to mention, of course, the same penchant for square-jawed, leather-clad giants. However, whereas Tetsuo Hara drew stable fighters, firmly planted on the ground in logical, functional martial-arts positions (even if their techniques were works of fantasy), Araki put his characters in strange positions. He would put them off balance or have them leaning for no logical reason. He would set them in absurd defensive martial-arts positions that seemed to serve no other purpose other than their visual appeal and the artist's desire to reproduce body positions from the worlds of fashion and modern Italian sculpture. In volume three (*JoJonium, Phantom Blood 2*, p. 273), for example, Dio's body bends in the shape of an S for no good reason as he blocks an aerial attack from Zeppeli. You can see it as a way of echoing the rounded features and tension of marble sculptures like *Bacchanal: A Faun Teased by Children* (1616-1617), attributed to Bernini and his father, Pietro. However, whereas the children in this Seicento statue use their weight to push back the faun's head, producing tension and an off-balance effect, Dio leans voluntarily. While having total control of the situation, he puts that tension on his own body. Moreover, Dio's right arm and left hand adopt those famous 90° angles "*à la* Antonio Lopez," giving the antagonist's body an interesting combination of angles and curves. An amalgam of contrasts that we often find in Araki's drawings of his characters. These bizarre body positions show that *JoJo* is not, and never will be, a "true" martial arts manga: in Araki's series, the fundamentals of combat—how a person effectively positions themself in situations of defense and attack—have no real importance. We see this more and more as the saga progresses: the only things that count are special abilities, intelligence, and the context of the fight. Bodies are there for show; they elegantly occupy space and give substance to a certain view of human beauty.

The other major difference of visual philosophy between *JoJo* and *Fist of the North Star* is Araki's strong tendency to inflate and deform the body. And in spectacular fashion at that. For example, a person's thigh may be shown three times larger than usual for a single panel showcasing a kick. Or a character's limbs may be drawn extraordinarily long, using surprising expressionist effects. In addition, we can tell that Araki, who illustrates with detailed muscles and heavy shading, is not the greatest master of anatomical drawing—for example, in his panels, there are many shadows that seem to have been placed at random. Do these deformations of the body hide some clumsiness or, conversely, do they make it more visible? Probably a little of both, depending on the case. In the end, it doesn't really matter: his illustrations are exciting and that's what really matters. Furthermore, those visual oddities have the advantage of giving *JoJo* a unique aura that distinguishes it from all other manga. The greatest point of divergence between Araki and Tetsuo Hara is this: Hara is much more skillful at anatomical drawing than Araki—once again, all you have to do is look at the positioning of shadows—and his body illustrations remain relatively faithful to reality. That's excluding passages that play around with scale, of course: in some panels of *Fist of the North Star*, the bad guys are two or three times the size of the hero. We also see this manipulation of scale in the work of Araki, who even associates it with a special move: Jonathan's "Zoom Punch." It's an attack in which his fist seems to grow to four times its normal size, dwarfing the enemy in front of him.

There is one aspect where the two *mangaka* truly overlap: extreme violence. In the first part of *JoJo*, we see numerous heads ripped off and bodies cut to pieces. With an abundance of detail. Who can forget Araki's version of Jack the Ripper hiding inside the body of a galloping horse? It's a bizarre horror scene that echoes the part of *Baoh: The Visitor* in which the hero bursts forth from the belly of a giant, eight-legged beast. It's a theatrical kind of horror that Araki covers his pages with, being a big fan of horror who, in the 1980s, went as far as to import films from the genre not released in Japan. Unsurprisingly (given Dio's zombies), his favorite category of horror at the time was stories of the living dead.

Ashita no JoJo

Coming back to the concept once again: legacy. What do we keep from the people who came before us, and what do we do with it? When we reach the fourth volume of *JoJo* (*Phantom Blood 3* of *JoJonium*), no doubt remains: legacy is the story's central theme. In this volume, Zeppeli dies after intervening in the battle between Jonathan and Tarukus. With his last ounce of strength, the mentor infuses what remains of his power into the hero's body. His death will not be in vain. Zeppeli sacrifices himself to save and empower young Joestar, who then becomes humanity's only home of defeating Dio. It's a sad but necessary passing of the torch.

On the inside flap of the first Japanese volume of *JoJo*, Hirohiko Araki presents his work as an ode to humanity. A sort of statement of purpose on what the series will be. However, the author explains in *Manga in Theory and Practice* that he wrote that brief text without giving it too much thought. Above all, he wanted to state that his characters would forge their own paths, that

549

they wouldn't need machines to fight their battles, and they wouldn't need divine intervention to save them. That's how he wanted to pay tribute to the brilliance of humankind. Also in his work on theory, Araki connects this idea of an ode to humanity with the notion of legacy and, in so doing, gives us a personal and essential key to understanding the series: "In hindsight, I can see what led me to that theme [of the greatness of humanity]. When *JoJo* was just starting to be serialized, my grandfather passed away, and it made me think about how people die, but that some part of us is left behind to be passed on to the following generations. *East of Eden*, a work I deeply admired, also dealt with the theme of connections across generations, and at the time, everyone was talking about *Roots*, the American drama series [from 1977]. On the surface, the series appeared to be about slavery and racial discrimination, but as I watched it, I thought it was at heart a story about a family. When I started *JoJo*, I wanted to write about a battle between good and evil, but these influences led me to make my series about passing the torch."[16] That says it all. To this day, the theme of "passing the torch" is still the central concept of *JoJo's Bizarre Adventure.*

Jonathan Joestar and Dio Brando. The inheritor of human virtues versus the man who has rejected humanity. Dio, who was born to a terrible father, ends up himself–following the idea that evil begets evil?–becoming so nefarious that humanity's dark side is no longer enough to define him. At the end of the fourth volume, the two enemies face off in a fateful scene that, once again, is reminiscent of *Fist of the North Star*. It makes you think of another duel between polar opposites: the fight between Kenshiro and Shin, who is another famous megalomaniac of the manga universe. Dio and Shin are both tyrants posing as emperors, both have blonde hair and wicked smiles, and they both ultimately meet the same fate: falling from a balcony of their palaces. Dio, however, doesn't take much baggage with him on his flight. After Jonathan's Hamon penetrates deep into Dio's body, the vampire is reduced to nothing more than a head without a body.

A happy ending? Well... yes, for the time being. Dio is vanquished, the mask is destroyed, and Jonathan marries his beloved Erina. However, the author saves one last surprise for us. We find ourselves on a ship carrying the two lovebirds to the United States on their honeymoon. However, Wang Chan, Dio's most faithful servant, has infiltrated the ship and is carrying the head of his master who, deprived of a body, aims to steal Jonathan's. The ultimate battle has arrived. On the ship, there's total chaos. And when the vampire attacks our hero, the sworn enemies end up mortally wounding one another.

On February 7, 1889, while at sea near the Canary Islands, Jonathan Joestar passes on. He rests on the deck of the ship, sitting, in an illustration bathed in

---

16. Hirohiko Araki, *Manga in Theory and Practice*, p. 171.

light whose lines melt away into a plain white background—a color associated with death in Japan. The composition and ethereal nature of the image are very reminiscent of the famous final page of *Ashita no Joe*, one of the best known images in the history of manga, in which the boxer sits in a corner of the ring, slumped over, his head bent forward, and a smile on his lips. He's resting in peace.[17] Surprisingly, Jonathan gives his last breath while cradling Dio's head in his arms, with a calm bordering on friendship. Brotherhood even. As if Jonathan and Dio, two sides of the same coin, had united and resolved their fate in death.

In 1987, in *Jump*, killing the hero of a manga was an iconoclastic act. It was very unusual. Moreover, the death of Araki's hero preceded the "death" of Goku in *Dragon Ball* by one year, an event that took place at the very end of 1988. It's not out of the question that Jonathan's fate opened the way for Toriyama—but in any case, Goku's death was less impactful because in *Dragon Ball*, the dead continue to live on in their own dimension and it's possible to bring them back to life by making a wish to the dragon Shenron. By having his protagonist pass on, Araki initiated the legend of the Joestar family, which continues under the spiritual guidance of this ancestor who died a hero to protect his wife and their unborn son. "I sensed that in order for the Joestar family's noble lineage to be passed down, Jonathan needed to die. I know that readers might have been disappointed by his death, but Jonathan's blood and spirit passed on to the second protagonist, Joseph,"[18] explains Araki.

Finishing in fall 1987, this first story arc, consisting of five volumes and later renamed *Phantom Blood*, constitutes what we can call the early period of *JoJo's Bizarre Adventure*. A bit naive in its themes and, admittedly, not always captivating, this first part doesn't share much with what *JoJo* would become some years later, even though it planted the seeds for many subsequent developments. For this reason, very few readers cite it as their favorite part. However, in spite of it all, *Phantom Blood* has an old-fashioned charm that fits with its setting in Victorian England, and its many unique characteristics— some unique for its time, others in absolute terms—are noteworthy.

Phantom Blood sets the tone right from the beginning: *JoJo* is a living organism that's constantly shaking things up and transforming. It's fed by the curiosity of its creator, a man who, while a manga enthusiast, is perpetually looking beyond that universe—to film, fashion, music, sculpture, and more. The organism breathes; its lungs absorb the air of its time—the effervescent 1980s—and transform that air into Araki-style "Hamon." In a recent interview, the *mangaka* talked about this process of absorption back when he was trying

---

17. He appears to be dead in the ring, but Tetsuya Chiba has denied that. "Joe is drained, but still alive," he stated in the magazine *Kaboom No. 11*.
18. Hirohiko Araki, *Manga in Theory and Practice*, p. 102.

to find his own style and he took the opportunity to express his gratitude for his forebears, the manga artists who opened up so many opportunities and gave him so much inspiration: "The idea for *JoJo* was born of the desire to depict something different, something that doesn't resemble the works of Osamu Tezuka, Fujiko Fujio, Tetsuya Chiba, or Katsuhiro Otomo—all great masters that I used to read. It simply wouldn't have been possible without such predecessors. [...] Looking back, so many manga artists of the 1970s and 1980s were geniuses. It was also an era in which new forms of music and fashion emerged incessantly. Maybe making a debut and beginning to work on *JoJo* around that time was good for me."[19] These are honest words filled with humility. When it comes down to it, perhaps Jonathan Joestar inherited his deep sincerity from his creator. Unless the reverse is true? Who knows. But one thing is for certain: the heart of the living organism that is *JoJo* beats in sync with that of Hirohiko Araki, an artist devoted to his work and who has undertaken the mission, somewhat by chance, to celebrate the beauty of humanity.

19. Masanobu Matsumoto, "Draw Close to the Unexpected — The Chemical Reactions of Manga Artist Hirohiko Araki," *The New York Times Style Magazine: Japan*, 2018. https://www.tjapan.jp/entertainment/17230475.

CHAPITRE II: INDIANA JOJO
(1987-1989: JOJO'S BIZARRE ADVENTURE, PART 2)

Stand: Babel Fish

How many languages do you speak?
You'll have to know more than one if you want to play archaeologist and reveal
the deepest, darkest secrets.

To listen to while reading:

Guns N' Roses – *Welcome to the Jungle*
Wham! – *Club Tropicana*
AC/DC – *TNT*
The Cars – *Just What I Needed*
Creedence Clearwater Revival – *Suzie Q*

Did Jonathan really die? Many readers surely asked themselves this question when they saw Joseph Joestar appear in late 1987, in chapter 45 of *JoJo's Bizarre Adventure*. You can't blame them, given that JoJo, the second of his name, is the spitting image of his grandfather Jonathan. Why did Araki make them look so much alike? Because after killing off his original hero, he didn't want to disorient his readers too much. He didn't want them to feel like they were starting a whole new series. But don't be deceived: the only thing Joseph shares with his grandfather is his appearance. An inveterate fighter and prince of troublemakers, he doesn't align with the supreme righteousness of Jonathan and instead embodies, like good old B.T., the art of the shortcut: instead of perseverance and heroism, Joseph prefers escapes and cunning. "My least favorite word is 'work'! My second least favorite is 'try'!" he declares.[20] Araki once again thumbing his nose at *Jump*'s values. In reality, of course, Joseph harbors an extreme sense of justice that's just waiting for the right moment to burst out. After all, he's a Joestar. And that's what *Battle Tendency* goes on

20. *Battle Tendency*, volume 3.

to prove (once again, this international title was given after the fact). This second story arc, in seven volumes (in the original Japanese version; four in the *JoJonium* version), takes place a half-century after the events of *Phantom Blood*.

Welcome to the Jungle [21]

As always, it's the Nazis fault. They awakened the beast. In 1938, the German army discovered a strange place deep in the jungle of Mexico: ruins of a techno-logically advanced civilization (bearing a strong resemblance to the inside of the derelict ship in *Alien*), at the center of which stands a sort of living statue. It has the body of a large man, with his eyes closed, that seems to have fused with a pillar. The half-man, half-edifice is alive, but sleeping: he gives off heat and pulses, yet remains immobile. He's surrounded by a constellation of stone masks, the artifact that was at the heart of the drama in *Phantom Blood*... Why are the Nazis interested in this mystery? Because their *Führer* is on a quest for immortality, believing it would allow him to rule the world. The soldiers then remove the Pillar Man from his chamber to study him in a laboratory. Big mistake! For many of them, that place of experimentation will be the last thing they see before dying.

Everything is bigger than before in *Battle Tendency*. It's a zoom out, both in terms of the time scale and what's at stake. Araki goes back several millennia to recount the origins of the stone mask and adds a new level to the food chain, above the vampires. The Pillar Men. They are the last remnants of a species that was present on the earth in prehistoric times and which we could describe as augmented human beings. And it turns out that one of these ancients created the stone mask for the purpose of accelerating evolution. As we know, the mask awakens latent abilities in living things. When a human wears it, the mask transforms them into a vampire. However, when one of these prehistoric beings used the mask, they became a sort of demigod: this lifeform referred to as the Pillar Men. And those Pillar Men fed on vampires. That means that Dio, if he were still around in 1938, would likely have ended up as a meal for one of them! Lucky for him he got away.

Joseph starts his odyssey in New York. Dio's influence has not entirely faded away and one of his old admirers intercepts Jonathan's heir. His name is Straizo and, obsessed with the idea of eternal youth, he has become a vampire himself. For this same reason, he has a keen interest in the miracle of the Pillar Man. After a high-flying battle, Straizo, repentant but close to death,

---

21. *Bienvenue, ici Babel Fish. Je pirate temporairement cet espace mais, soyez-en assuré, je viens en paix. Le but de mon intervention est simple : je suis ici pour vous donner l'opportunité de – tenter de – découvrir quelques secrets cachés à propos de la conception de l'ouvrage que vous êtes en train de lire. Voulez-vous relever le défi ? Alors tenez-vous prêt, je réapparaîtrai bientôt.*

explains to the hero that Speedwagon, an old friend of Jonathan (a former hoodlum from the slums of London who, since *Phantom Blood*, has made a fortune in the oil business), had died near the aforementioned archaeological site. Joseph needs to go search for Speedwagon's body to give him a proper burial. First of all because "Granny Erina" is attached to her old friend and, secondly, because Joseph wants to get to the bottom of this "Pillar Man" matter. Destination: Mexico. Meanwhile, blood spatters the Nazi laboratory. In a passage reminiscent of one from *Baoh: The Visitor* in which the parasite is observed, the Pillar Man (who the German officer Rudol von Stroheim has named Santana, known in some translations as Santviento) awakens and demonstrates his terrifying abilities. One after another, the soldiers of the Third Reich are exterminated by this being from a "master race"–ironic, no? Meanwhile, Joseph arrives on site. To hold his own against Santviento, he must use all of his cleverness and mastery of Hamon, and he must exploit the Pillar Men's weakness: they're afraid of the sun, just like the vampires. Coming within an inch of losing his life, Joseph comes out of the battle victorious.

A recurring pattern then plays out. Once again, a dying person informs JoJo of his next destination. Stroheim, mortally wounded, tells Joseph about how the German army discovered other Pillar Men in Europe, and the fact that those creatures are about to awaken. Santviento and his kind have a very particular biological clock: because of their extreme energy consumption, they are forced to sleep for 2,000 years so that they can recuperate. And that period is about to expire. Stroheim adds that the Germans are also studying these creatures to find a way to tame them because when the Pillar Men awake, all of humanity risks being subjugated by its natural predator. Great. If that's how it is, then let the games begin. One last detail: Speedwagon has actually survived... and it's a good thing, too: the ultra-rich gentleman will be a very useful ally for Joseph. Together, they take a private plane to Rome, where the petrified creatures lie dormant.

Club Bizarre[22]

A few paragraphs ago, I described *JoJo* as a living organism. This is particularly true in this second part. Open your eyes and listen with your heart: you will feel the energy of life. A flow, a murmur, pulses. An energy that runs through the floorboards and seems to act like a DJ: there's a sort of groove that makes the "dance floor" come alive, invisible strings that put

---

22. *Babel Fish*, volume 2. *Los Stands estaban previstos desde el principio del proyecto, pero no se mantuvieron todas las ideas. Por ejemplo, al principio existía el "Stand de la honestidad", que obligaba al autor de estas líneas a expresarse en la primera persona del singular; esta idea fue finalmente recuperada en el prefacio y en la conclusión del libro.*

people in sophisticated positions, stretching choreography to its limits. In this world, people adopt theatrical positions; they twist and sway. And I'll remind you, they do so for no good reason: in combat, fighters have nothing to gain from prancing around like that. And the onomatopoeia, constantly keeping the tempo, add a soundtrack to this manga which, more than ever, feels like a giant music video. Or like a festival that flamboyantly celebrates the beauty of the human body.

The reason why the characters in this second part of the series project so much panache is that Araki, even more than before, drew inspiration from the world of fashion. And it was women's fashion, in particular, that influenced him, especially through the sophisticated poses of models in magazines. When you read *Battle Tendency*, you feel like you're watching a performance of voguing, a style of urban dance that first developed in the late 1960s in New York's African-American and Latino LGBT community, a group suffering from poverty and marginalization. This style of dance, intended to be liberating, borrows imagery from the luxury fashion world and rhythmically reproduces the poses seen in fashion magazines (that's the heart of it, but it also includes inspirations from funk and kung fu). Hence the name "voguing," as in the magazine *Vogue*. In 1990, the music video for Madonna's *Vogue* brought this style of dance into the mainstream, and in recent years, voguing has received renewed interest and, notably, has appeared in the Gaspar Noé film *Climax* (2018) and in the American TV series *Pose* (2018-present). An example of a passage in *Battle Tendency* reminiscent of voguing is the famous joint pose, in volume seven (*JoJonium Battle Tendency*, volume two, p. 76), in which Joseph and Caesar seem to set their bodies in dynamic dance moves, as if driven by the same energy: it's one of the pages that's most typical of the ambiance of this story arc. This drawing also bears the influence of illustrator Tony Viramontes: the way in which Caesar positions his body and his hand, for example, with his fingers splayed in front of his face, looks like a generic dance move, but actually, it comes directly from a 1983 work by Viramontes, in which he drew, in his own style, the transgender model Teri Toye.

In *Battle Tendency*, the spirit of Viramontes is so clearly present that it's worth taking a closer look at this artist for a moment. From a Spanish-Mexican family, Frank Antony Viramontes was born in Los Angeles in 1956. He rose to fame as a fashion illustrator (and photographer) in the early 1980s. He distinguished himself with his jittery drawings, purposely conceived with urgency, which were largely inspired by the turbulent body language of works by Egon Schiele and by the sparing lines of drawings by Jean Cocteau—the sketches with free-flowing strokes that really began to blossom between two chapters of the collected volumes of *JoJo* bear a very strong resemblance to this approach. For Dean Rhys Morgan, author of the monograph *Bold, Beautiful and Damned: The World of 1980s Fashion Illustrator Tony Viramontes*, the artist "crystalized an image of femininity that was to become emblematic of the 1980s. [...] There was a certain insolence about the Viramontes women. They adopted an air that was confident, aloof, nonchalant. They were not pretty faces. They were strong, with a full mouth, a prominent nose, and graphic brow."[23] Viramontes used the same approach in drawing men. "He liked to recreate typically macho men into softer, more feminine images, stretching the bounds of masculine identity."[24] In Viramontes' work, both women and men have the same flamboyance, the same haughty and resplendent air about them. Antonio Lopez, his mentor, also played around with gender: his famous campaigns for Missoni always blurred the lines between masculine and feminine, as we can see from Lopez's famous androgynous figure with a trapezoidal haircut, which inspired Stroheim's hair. Moreover, works by Lopez and Viramontes are very (homo)sexually charged, both latently and conspicuously. And that makes sense when you learn that both had as an influence, for example, the artist Tom of Finland, who is very well known for his erotic works centered on gay leather culture–the relation is clear in some of Lopez's virile, well-built figures. In the works of Lopez and Viramontes, the princes of '80s fashion illustration, the body is accentuated just as much as the garment covering it: the body is celebrated, glorified, shown in elegant and innovative positions.

As I said before, when talking about *Gorgeous Irene*, the hyper-masculinity in *JoJo*, in a way, comes from a woman. This is particularly true in *Battle Tendency*, an effervescent universe in which the male characters adopt many poses inspired by Viramontes' strong women or by Lopez's often-feminized men–at the very least, Lopez liked to give them attitudes and highlight their beauty in ways more commonly associated with women. The influence of these two artists, and of women's fashion in general, has a lot to do with the (involun-tarily?) crypto-erotic aura given off by *JoJo*'s characters starting in the second part. That fetishizing gaze on the male body that's inextricably linked to *Battle Tendency*. Of course, that omnipresent glorification of (a certain conception of) masculine beauty, which mainly consists of celebrating the body's vigor and muscle tone, also comes out of the famous muscle culture of the 1980s. Indeed, Joseph, like Jonathan before him, has an air of Sylvester Stallone about him, while Rudol von Stroheim looks remarkably like Dolph Lundgren, the actor who played the iconic character Ivan Drago in 1985's *Rocky IV*.

The bodies become more extravagant in *Battle Tendency*, and thus the outfits, too. Once again, Araki drew inspiration from the world around him at that time. All he had to do was turn his head and let his eyes wander: the flamboyant

23. A *YouTube* video with the author presenting the monograph: https://www.youtube.com/watch?v=eYFDY3fxrnE.
24. *Ibid.*

1980s had no shortage of iconic looks, whether conveyed by a new kind of model (like the tall, androgynous Grace Jones, one of Antonio Lopez's muses) or by very visual movements in music, like the New Wave. Caesar Zeppeli, with his headband and mussed-up blonde hair, bears a resemblance to Nick Rhodes, the keyboardist from Duran Duran.[25] A headband whose two-tone triangular pattern undoubtedly comes from... well, once again, the patterns that are ubiquitous in Antonio Lopez's work for Missoni! Just like for the drawings of bodies, the clothes of Araki's characters contribute to the eroticism of the masculine forms: from small, form-fitting tops that leave little to the imagination, to tank tops that show off biceps, Araki's pages are constantly celebrating muscle and skin. As for the Pillar Men, they're practically naked, as if to give them a legendary, or even divine, dimension. Indeed, to design their appearance, Araki took inspiration from Roman sculptures and statues of Japanese Niō, divine guardians of Buddhist temples, to give them a mythical aura while maintaining a feeling of familiarity. These intimidating giants have the biggest and most athletic bodies of the second story arc. Their muscles shine, their hips sway, and their hair waves—like the mane of rocker-like hair hiding under Kars' turban, giving the knight with the "Danse Macabre Hair" from *Phantom Blood* a run for his money. They are the pillars of this wild discotheque we call *Battle Tendency*.

Around the World [26]

For the first time, Araki drew the country that had given him so much inspiration: Italy. We find ourselves in Rome, where Joseph meets Caesar Zeppeli, the proud successor and grandson of the Hamon master from *Phantom Blood*. For several generations, the Zeppeli family has fought against the stone mask and Caesar is no exception. As such, he's a valuable ally for our hero. However, between Joseph and him, it all starts with... a battle of the pastas. Spaghetti versus macaroni. Stuffed with Hamon. The thing is that Joseph—undoubtedly jealous!—can't stand the arrogance of "that Italian playboy," who's flirting with a girl in a restaurant in the heart of the city. Joseph decides to tease him with an attack of spaghetti, hoping to shut his trap. Unbeknownst to him, Caesar is a Hamon master! In a matter of seconds, a rivalry is born. In volume three of *Battle Tendency*, *JoJonium* edition, of which Caesar appears on

---

25. Tony Viramontes also illustrated the cover of the album *So Red the Rose* (1985) from the group Arcadia, a spin-off from Duran Duran. A symbol of the crossover between the world of fashion and New Wave music.
26. *Babel Fish*, volume 3. *Eine der anfänglichen Ideen war es, den Leser das Buch umdrehen zu lassen um Abschnittes des Textes lesen zu können, die auf de Kopf gedruckt wurden – der Stand hätte sich "Das Rad des Schicksals" oder "Der Goldene Schnitt" genannt.*

the cover, Araki recounts the genesis of this character: "For Part 1, I wasn't able to draw the friendship aspect of a rival pairing. Jonathan and Dio didn't really have that sort of relationship. That's why I had Caesar, who inherited the Zeppeli bloodline, appear along with a Joestar. *Weekly Shōnen Jump* is a *shōnen* magazine after all, so I wanted to include something that portrayed friendship in a positive light." A good old bromance between two rivals: always a winning recipe.

It's beneath the Roman Colosseum, no less, that the last three Pillar Men lie in slumber. Once again, the Nazis are on the case, but they're no match for the titans. Once revived, the impressive Kars, Esidisi, and their subordinate Wamuu[27] have no need to worry about the Germans, who they massacre within a few seconds. Newly awakened, the three giants set themselves the task of finding the "Red Stone of Aja," a mysterious gem that, once set in the stone mask, would give it new powers. By using the augmented mask, the Pillar Men would undergo a final stage of evolution, turning them into ultimate lifeforms who would no longer have reason to fear the sun's rays. When they arrive at the Colosseum, JoJo and Caesar get the beating of their lives. They weren't counting on the fact that their adversaries had already fought against Hamon users, long ago, and can thus counter their attacks without difficulty. Joseph is on the ground and near death when he gets an idea. "If only I had a month! Then I could get strong enough to defeat you," he shouts at Wamuu. The Pillar Man, a proud fighter who loves a challenge, can't resist the temptation of the hero's proposition. But Wamuu's not stupid: the warrior inserts a ring infused with poison inside of Joseph's body, next to his heart; the ring is set to dissolve in 33 days. Joseph has just one option: confront the Pillar Man again before then... and beat him so that he can drink the antidote hidden in Wamuu's lip ring (incidentally, doesn't that seem to have a bit of homoerotic symbolism to it?). As if that wasn't enough, Esidisi also places a poisoned ring around Joseph's throat, so our hero will have to defeat him too.

Training: an obligatory stage in every martial arts story. The last three Pillar Men aren't kidding around and if Joseph is going to have any hope of challenging them, he'll have to learn to perfectly master Hamon. For that purpose, Caesar takes JoJo to meet his master in Venice. On an island shrouded in mystery, off the coast of the City of Canals, the two thieves submit themselves to the trials of the beautiful Lisa Lisa, who, beneath her fashionista exterior, with her dark

---

27. These three names are inspired by the bands The Cars, AC/DC, and Wham!. In the original Japanese, their names are written in katakana characters (resulting in カーズ/Kāzu, エシディシ/ Eshidishi, and ワムウ/Wamū), thus referencing the musical artists without actually reproducing the exact written form of their names. The latest French version, unlike the English version, chose to totally embrace these references. However, here, we'll stick with the names as published in the English version. Note that Esidisi, on p. 55 of volume three, swallows a stick of dynamite: a reference to the song *TNT* by AC/DC, with its famous chorus "*Cause I'm TNT, I'm dynamite*"?

glasses and stilettos, is also a skillful fighter. She immediately has an imposing presence: to this point in the series, she is probably one of Araki's most charismatic characters. The actor tells about how she was created: "When this part was originally serialized, the girls that showed up in *shōnen* manga were all cute types–essentially the stereotype of 'a man's ideal girl.' Readers weren't looking for a realistic portrayal of women, but instead, the type of girl that giggles during a conversation with heart marks appearing next to her. [...] That's why I think a warrior-type character like Lisa Lisa felt fresh. Mr. Zeppeli in Part 1 was a very gentle character, and to contrast with that, I made her what you would call a 'sadistic' character today."[28] Indeed, Lisa Lisa does not coddle her protégés and subjects them to ordeals that nearly kill them! She's not teaching Joseph how to use Hamon to save his life, she says pitilessly, but rather to train a warrior to fight those who threaten the human race. Offering plenty of excitement, this training phase is the most successful passage in *Battle Tendency*; after it, the story arc enters a (too) long series of confrontations all over the place–near Venice, in the Swiss Alps, and on the island of Vulcano. A battle tendency, you might call it.

Closer to God[29]

Who is Kars, the leader of the Pillar Men? To find out, we have to go back in time 10,000 years. At that time, there was a tribe of humanoid creatures who the prehistoric humans feared as if they were gods. Or demons. Weak against the sun's rays, these beings were forced to move underground and would only come out at night. However, they were capable of absorbing energy from flora and fauna, thus increasing their lifespans. While they were peaceful and free from conflict for a time, their lives took a sinister turn when a genius emerged in their ranks. Kars. He wanted to rise to a higher level and achieve immortality. In a way, the appearance on earth of this maverick was like a rebel yell from nature against its own status quo: a rejection of the rule that says that every living thing must perish one day. To achieve his goals, Kars created the stone mask, capable of conferring eternal life by unleashing the brain's hidden abilities. However, the process couldn't have been more selfish: the person who uses the mask becomes a creature requiring vast amounts of energy, forced to kill and feed on insane numbers of living beings. Because of the mask, Kars' tribe came to see him as a danger and they all threw themselves

28. Remarks from the author in *JoJonium*, *Battle Tendency*, volume 2.
29. *Babel Fish*, volume 4. *Onder meer was er de idee om songteksten toe te voegen (van de liedjes die aangeraden worden om naar te luisteren in het begin van het hoofdstuk) tussen twee paragrafen in het tweede hoofdstuk, in de zin van een muzikaal onderbreking.*

on him. "Fools! Do you not wish to conquer the sun?! Do you not wish to rule over all?" he cried. And he ultimately massacred the entire tribe. Kars then began a long journey, accompanied by his only friend, Esidisi, and two infants who survived: Wamuu and Santviento. Throughout human history, the four beings would emerge from time to time before returning to their required two millennia of slumber.

Battle Tendency is actually a work on (the cruelty of) the hierarchy of living beings. After all, can't the battle waged by Joseph and his companions against the Pillar Men be seen as humanity's refusal to lose its spot at the top of the food chain? Should we see it as *JoJo's Bizarre Adventure* always praising the beauty of humankind, including in this case, or rather as the series highlighting the selfishness of humans in relation to all other living creatures, humanity's supposedly dominant position over all flora and fauna? It's only natural that humans would refuse to be reduced to simply being food for others; they don't want to die. However, to what extent are they right to proclaim their supremacy when creatures superior to them in every way appear? This view of the series may seem cold and prosaic, but we can actually consider this "battle tendency" to be a series of struggles between two species—the humans and the Pillar Men—filled with egotism and trying to claim the position as the dominant beings on the planet. Kars, too, of course, demonstrates egotism: in volume 12 (*JoJonium Battle Tendency*, volume four), his companions are killed and he becomes the last survivor of his species, but this actually suits him because, in his mind, there could only be one supreme ruler. And Kars takes that position. Thanks to the Red Stone of Aja, the Pillar Man becomes the ultimate lifeform. A perfect creature that never ages, never dies, has the abilities of all living things put together, and has a body to rival that of the most beautiful statues of ancient Greece. The equal of a god.

To take on Kars, Joseph can count on support from the Speedwagon Foundation's fighting technology team. But they're not the only ones. This is going to sound really bad, but just try to appreciate the irony: to defeat this total embodiment of supremacy, Joseph receives help... from a squadron of Nazi soldiers! Rudol von Stroheim, the German officer from the beginning of *Battle Tendency* —the one who Joseph called "Nazi scum!" and who responded by calling Joseph a "damned Englishman!"—survived as a cyborg[30] thanks to German military technologies. And he has no intention of letting Kars subjugate humans. Of course, in 1938, World War II had not yet been declared, but we can still marvel at this alliance between Joseph and an officer of the Waffen-SS! Or laugh at it. Because, ultimately, it reminds us just how much *Battle Tendency*, with its very pulp fiction-like tone, is lighter and wilder than *Phantom Blood*. Moreover,

---

30. He now has a monocle that's even more reminiscent of the figure with trapezoidal hair drawn by Antonio Lopez for Missoni.

this second part references more than once the *Indiana Jones* saga (in volume eight [*JoJonium Battle Tendency*, volume two], we even see a reference to the mine cart scene from *Indiana Jones and the Temple of Doom*), which is also quite "pulpy" and also features heroes crossing paths with Nazis trying to steal mythical powers. However, there's a clear divergence between how the two series approach German soldiers. Indy would never ally himself with one of Hitler's men. We can probably chalk this contrast up to the difference between the countries of origin of the American films and the Japanese manga, given that in Japan, depicting Nazism is not as taboo as it is in the Western world–for example, some members of famous Japanese rock bands, like the guitarist Die from Dir En Grey, have dressed as Nazi officers, which would be unimaginable in my corner of the world. In any case, we should note that *JoJo* never once defends Nazi ideology: Joseph does not in any way support Stroheim's ideas, in spite of their alliance. Instead, we should see their partnership as JoJo taking all the help he can get to face Kars. Fighting fire with fire, basically.

Explosions in the Sky[31]

If *Phantom Blood* was a baroque version of *Fist of the North Star*, then *Battle Tendency* would be the baroque version of *Phantom Blood*. The wild teenage years of *JoJo*'s early period. In part two of his series, Araki took out all the stops. He drew characters who were even more glam and didn't hesitate, from time to time, to deform and amplify parts of the body, even more spectacularly than before–an approach that reached its apex in the second part and already began softening in the third part. *Battle Tendency* also marked a shift to a lighter tone, in spite of its story raising the stakes. While comic relief was not absent from *Phantom Blood*, it moved to center stage in part two thanks to the shenanigans of Joseph, who often messes around, who's clumsy at times, and who uses all sorts of trickery and deception. JoJo, the second of his name, amuses himself by infuriating the Pillar Men, who, you have to admit, don't have much of a sense of humor. We also see more confrontations with very specific contexts, much like the duel between Jonathan and Tarukus in the first part. In *Battle Tendency*, there's even a fight to the death on Roman chariots and, in volume 12 (*JoJonium Battle Tendency*, volume four), Joseph has to fight while maintaining his balance on top of an ancient sanctuary, all while having

31. *Babel Fish*, volume 5. *L'idea di usare the footnotes has évolué.* このスタンド *era at the beginning appelé "アンダーワールド" et il n'agissait pas to use le lingue straniere but to "verbergen" anécdotas à propos de la conception du 本 y some thoughts del autor dans le "下の世界" delle note a piè di Seite. それから het idee is geworden d'écrire frasi in varie lingue che de lezer would have rendu compte, une fois translated, dat ze zou absurd of umoristico zijn geweest. Endlich is het idee again geëvolueerd et voici comment moi,* バビルフィッシュ, *werd geboren. Gracias por su atención y have une good Tag.* 敬具, B.F.

to hold on for dear life to a rope attached to Lisa Lisa's feet after she fell into Kars' cunning trap. These are the beginnings of a future basic ingredient of *JoJo*: in the coming parts, Araki will constantly spice up his battles by adding special rules or challenges. The second part's new variations of Hamon are also more original and foreshadow the future of the series: we can see Lisa Lisa's "silk dance" or Caesar's Hamon bubbles as prototypes for the kinds of abilities offered by the Stands, who will make their debut in the next part—incidentally, don't you think Caesar Zeppeli's power is a precursor to Soft & Wet's bubbles in *JoJolion*?

In many ways, this second part is a zany remix of *Phantom Blood*. That's not to mention the physical resemblance between Jonathan and Joseph. You've got to admit, the story repeats itself. As if the weight of legacy is also the weight of determinism. Joseph, like his grandfather, is again humanity's last hope against a direct threat, and Caesar, like Will Anthonio Zeppeli, plays the role of the ally destined to meet a tragic end. Before dying, Caesar, like his grandfather before him, passes his last remaining Hamon to JoJo who, as a sign of friendship, then puts on his former rival's headband. The second part also offers another Hamon training sequence, of course, under the aegis of a new, quirky master. In the first part, the master is a sort of surrogate father; in part two, Lisa Lisa plays the role of a maternal figure—and we later learn that she is actually Joseph's long-lost mother! Then, as one might expect, it all ends with a clash of titans between the Joestar scion and the new ultimate lifeform. Indeed, titans, because it's a final battle of mythical proportions: Joseph, aboard a military plane (from the Nazis, I might add!) crashes at the top of a volcano and, in one final trick, finds a way to trigger an eruption of lava that propels Kars into space. Unable to re-enter Earth's atmosphere, Kars is condemned to drift among the stars for all eternity. The ultimate being, the one who cannot die, then undergoes one final biological evolution: he transforms into a lifeform that's half-mineral, half-animal, a sort of rock with humanoid features that, perhaps to avoid descending into madness, has even ceased all thought. As for Joseph... Caught in the flames during his heroic act, he dies on February 28, 1939, on the island of Vulcano, in the Mediterranean Sea. Or at least, that's what Araki wanted us to think, until we learn in an amusing epilogue that, in fact, the series' second hero did not suffer the same fate as Jonathan. In that final chapter, Joseph stumbles across his own funeral—his new wife, Suzie Q, forgot to let his friends and family know that he was still alive!—and *Battle Tendency* ends on that lighthearted note.

Have you seen the second *Indiana Jones* movie, *The Temple of Doom*? It's an odd sequel, a detour with a different tone that has no influence on the third installment, which is itself considered the real continuation of the first installment. In *JoJo's Bizarre Adventure*, the second part holds this same sort of isolated position. We hear nothing more about Kars, nor about the stone mask, and the only real link between *Battle Tendency* and its sequel is Joseph Joestar... as an old man who bears little resemblance to the JoJo he once was. Should we see the second story arc as nothing more than an intermezzo, a story that could be told while waiting–as Araki planned–for Dio to return? Maybe. That said, by having his hero face a god-like being, Araki showed his ambition to totally thrill readers. Perhaps the series needed that detour, which could then be forgotten, in order to feature such an extreme threat. Because in the *JoJo* saga, humanity will never again face a danger on the magnitude of Kars. The one who defied, with all of his being, the great family tree of all living things.

CHAPTER III: FIRE IN CAIRO
(1989-1992: JOJO'S BIZARRE ADVENTURE, PART 3)

Stand: Emperor Time
He who controls the flow of time is invincible? Don't be so sure.

To listen to while reading:

The Cure – *Fire in Cairo*
Devo – *Some Things Never Change*
George Thorogood and the Destroyers – *Bad to the Bone*
Dio – *Holy Diver*
The Beatles – *Get Back*

Shōnen Jump in the 1980s was not a warm and nurturing place. At least, not for its authors. The working conditions were Spartan and the editors were harsh. Many *mangaka* have recounted what it was like behind the scenes: Hisashi Eguchi, for example, who joined the *Jump* team in the late 1970s, in an interview, talked about how the atmosphere there changed in the '80s. "Over the years, the working conditions got more difficult; I felt the difference when I started *Stop!! Hibari-kun!* in 1981. [...] At the time, the magazine's circulation was increasing exponentially and the publication's goals were no longer the same as when I started there. The magazine's future heavyweights like Akira Toriyama, Yudetamago, and Tetsuo Hara established a standard of very strong universes and authors had to be able to hold their own in the reader polls."[32] Because of this, the editors turned up the heat. And the authors were the ones who paid the price: "I had a reputation for working very slowly and to alleviate that problem, my *tantō*[33] installed me in a tiny room wedged between two offices, where I was supposed to work and where I could sleep. A little. I

32. Interview published in the magazine *ATOM* No. 8, 2018.
33. The Japanese term for editor.

remained for two years in that unhealthy storeroom, where there was just an old, smelly blanket to keep me warm in the winter. [...] I wasn't until I'd turned in all of my pages that I could finally leave... to stay in a hotel or hostel near the Shūeisha offices!" That's what it was like backstage at *Jump*, the dark side of the energetic, joyful characters splashed across the pages of the magazine.

Did *Jump*'s stars enjoy more enviable conditions? No. In a 2017 interview, Hirohiko Araki and Tetsuo Hara reminisced about their early careers in the 1980s. Hara recounted that he, too, suffered from the pressure. In the interview, he drew a parallel—with a bit of humor—between Nobuhiko Horie, who was his editor for *Fist of the North Star*, and Raoh, the manga's hulking, menacing antagonist.[34] When work wasn't progressing as fast as he would like, the *tantō*, normally kindly, would become two-faced, to the point of giving off the same aura as Raoh! "Editors control the *mangaka*, you know. They're very smart,"[35] Tetsuo Hara said. As for Araki, he revealed in that same interview that he also, at times, was confined to a meeting room so that he could work. Sometimes, he was accompanied by other artists, like the duo Yudetamago. Araki also recounts that one day, while he was bringing in a manuscript to Shūeisha's diminutive office building, next door to the big Shōgakukan tower, he witnessed a shameful scene: a *mangaka* in tears, standing in front of his editor, while the editor threw the poor man's pages, judged to be "unworthy," into the shredder... Araki says that he got scared, wondering what sort of humiliation might be in store for him.

Let's be clear: I don't intend to present a uniformly dark impression of the relationship between authors and editors. Many *mangaka* have publicly praised the qualities of their *tantō* and that includes, of course, Hirohiko Araki, who, at the end of volume 28 of *JoJo* (the last of part three, *JoJonium Stardust Crusaders*, volume 10), slid in a touching homage to Ryōsuke Kabashima, the man who supervised the saga up to part three before passing the torch: "It goes without saying, but I'd like to express to him my deep gratitude. Each of his words has given me the strength to see things through. Without him, the *JoJo's Bizarre Adventure* series would not have seen the light of day." Instead, my point is to show the extent to which editors can influence the *mangaka*, on the one hand, but also influence the works of manga themselves. Some of these women and men behind the scenes have had so much influence over manga that they can be considered veritable unofficial co-authors. In *JoJo*, it would be

34. Nobuhiko Horie was also an editor for Hisashi Eguchi and Tsukasa Hōjō. In 1993, he became the magazine's fifth editor in chief: under his management, *Jump* achieved its all-time record for circulation, with 6.53 million copies printed. In 1996, Kazuhiko Torishima—the *tantō* for Akira Toriyama during *Dr. Slump* and the first part of *Dragon Ball*—took over from him.
35. Joint interview during a special event called "Legend Talk Show," a report of which can be found on the Japanese website *Mantan Web*. https://mantan-web.jp/article/20170910dog-00m200002000c.html.

impossible to determine with precision what points are more attributable to the decisions of the author or of the editor—you would have to be a fly on the wall and listen in during every editorial meeting. As such, when talking about the progression of the series, everything must be attributed to the nebulous pair of "the *mangaka* and his editor at the time." Except, of course, if you have insider information on the source of an idea.[36] As for that, we learn from the joint interview between Araki and Hara that Kabashima was responsible for the change in direction taken by *JoJo* in its third part, in the late '80s: Kabashima "strongly pushed" the *mangaka* to visit Egypt in preparation for what was supposed to be *JoJo*'s last story arc. Kabashima had decided that Dio the vampire, who was to make his big comeback, as expected, would now be based in Egypt because the *tantō* loves the country and is very familiar with it—according to Hiroki Gotō, the editor in chief of *Jump* at the time, Kabashima "had studied archaeology and Western history, from antiquity to the present," and "was a scholar, the likes of which are rarely seen among manga editors."[37] It's interesting to note that Araki, contrary to what you'd expect from his love of foreign cultures, has stated numerous times that he doesn't like to travel. As such, he was strongly opposed to the recommendation from his editor... but apparently you can't say no to your boss because Kabashima got his way anyhow. So, together, the two men prepared to explore the land of pyramids.[38]

There in Egypt, the *mangaka* had a strange experience. Falling victim to a kind of paranoia, he felt like he was surrounded by suspicious gazes and shady looking people everywhere he went. In spite of the friendliness of the locals, Araki trusted no one and imagined that there was a bad guy waiting to attack him around every corner. Ironically, this Kafkaesque atmosphere inspired one of the most important concepts of *JoJo*'s third part, and even of the rest of the saga! In part three, seemingly ordinary people, who actually have hidden evil powers, slyly blend in to the crowd; some of those evildoers then try to fool the heroes in order to lead them into an ambush. In the end, Araki's bad experience was to the benefit of... well, of himself, actually.

36. In this book, if I attribute an idea to Araki, it's because, according to my sources, the idea was his. However, it's always a good idea to stay on the safe side and, above all, not underestimate the importance of editors. Additionally, you have to realize that Araki, like most *mangaka*, creates his panels with help from a team of assistants. So, when talking about the series' visuals, you actually need to view them as the work of "the author and his assistants." Kei Sanbe, for example, now known for his manga *Erased* (2012-2016), assisted Araki from the second to the fifth part of *JoJo*, particularly handling illustrations of vehicles.
37. Hiroki Gotō, *Jump – L'âge d'or du manga*, Kurokawa, 2019, p. 254. Based on this statement, we can imagine that Kabashima must have had a hand in the presence of ancient civilizations and archaeological dig scenes in *Phantom Blood* and *Battle Tendency*.
38. A photo from that time could be seen on the defunct Japanese website *Nobury*, which offered a report of the "Legend Talk Show." In that photo, Ryōsuke Kabashima looked strangely like Lord George Joestar, Jonathan's father in *Phantom Blood*!

Without pausing after the end of Joseph's adventures, *JoJo* began a new adventure in *Shōnen Jump* dated April 3, 1989. Welcome to the third part: *Stardust Crusaders* (a name given after-the-fact to this story arc). The part that would propel the series to new heights.

Jailhouse Rock

The bizarre adventure has a tendency to skip a generation in the Joestar family. This time, Araki featured Joseph's grandson, Jotaro Kujo. Aged 17 years old, standing six feet and five inches tall (1.95 m), and built like a tank. Strong-headed, with unruly hair and a manly scowl. His father, a renowned Japanese jazz musician, is always off touring—we never see him. Jotaro's mother, an American with English roots, coddles him way too much: her name is Holly Kujo, née Joestar, and she is the daughter of Joseph and Suzie Q. For the first time, *JoJo*'s story is not set in the past, nor—for the moment—in a foreign country, but instead in contemporary Japan. It all starts in Tokyo in 1987. Behind bars. Jotaro is in police custody after getting into a brawl and he refuses to leave his cell. He feels like he's possessed by an evil spirit that he struggles to control and, since he doesn't know what the spirit might be capable of making him do, he prefers to voluntarily remain locked up, rather than committing some irredeemable act.

Meanwhile, Joseph Joestar arrives in Japan. He's changed a lot: he now looks like a man who's seen some things in his day, a cross between Indiana Jones and his father in *The Last Crusade* (1989, Steven Spielberg), a fedora perched on his head and a white beard adorning his face. The elder JoJo knows the truth about this evil spirit. Accompanied by his Egyptian friend Mohammed Avdol, Joseph pays a visit to Jotaro and explains to him that what he's taken to be a malevolent spirit is actually a "Stand" a manifestation of his own fighting spirit, and that each of these supernatural beings has special abilities that are specific to its user. They're called "Stands" because they stand next to their user.

The reunion is an eventful one. Joseph tells the statuesque Avdol to forcibly remove Jotaro from his cell, in what becomes the very first duel between Stands in the history of *JoJo's Bizarre Adventure*. This battle remains a true classic because it simply pits two basic powers against each other: super-strength and super-speed (for Jotaro) versus control of flames (for Avdol, whose Stand, a brawny figure with the head of a falcon, gets its appearance from Horus in Enki Bilal's *Nikopol Trilogy*). However, the change is notable because, like the Roman chariot race before it in *Battle Tendency*, for example, in *Stardust Crusaders*, battles will no longer simply be about combat. This jailhouse brawl does not feature just two unique parameters—the abilities of fighter A versus those of fighter B—but rather three, since in this case there's a specific goal, which is to get Jotaro to leave his cell. An additional rule to the game. *JoJo's Bizarre Adventure*, to this day, has kept this formula: it's never a matter of just having two adversaries face off and seeing what happens, no matter how complex their powers may be; instead, they're faced with a particular situation or a very specific configuration of the battlefield. Even in a flat desert setting, where it seems that there's nothing to complicate the clash, there's always a third parameter (or set of parameters). All in all, logically, it fits into the legacy of *Busō Poker* with its tense card game... or good old *Babel II*, in which the battles regularly featured cunning, strategy, and special abilities–indeed, in volume two, Kōichi must trick self-guided tanks that are trying to attack his fortress that's protected by a sandstorm.

The idea of Stands comes from the concept of Hamon in the first two parts of *JoJo*, resulting from the *mangaka*'s desire to make the invisible visible–note that the *Fist of the North Star*-style epaulettes on Jotaro's Stand have a spiral motif, seemingly a vestigial nod to Hamon. To be more precise, the Stands are the result of Hamon being laid to rest. The reason was that Araki's editor eventually got tired of the idea, which pushed the author to refresh it: "I concluded that he had likely grown tired of the effect because it was only one kind of thing. I concluded that a broader assortment of powers wouldn't have that same pitfall, and that's how Stands were born."[39] However, Araki had an idea more ambitious than just an array of special abilities. The next level up from making superpowers visible: turning them into full-fledged characters, inspired by the hero's guardian spirit in the horror manga *Ushiro no Hyakutarō* ("Hyokutaro behind," 1973-1976, never published in English) by Jirō Tsunoda. Araki believed in this idea. He knew that he was onto something. However, the *mangaka* had a hard time convincing others of his concept: when he declared, during a meeting, that he wanted to have guardian spirits come out of the bodies of fighters, no one got his idea! Maybe what convinced his superiors was the fact that he explained that he could use the concept to create tons of characters with diverse appearances and abilities–because let's not forget that in *Jump*, the characters are king. When he introduced Stands into his story, at the beginning of *Stardust Crusaders*, Araki set about making his concept as intelligible as possible. He clearly showed the beings coming out of the characters bodies and sometimes made them translucent–which he soon stopped doing, probably figuring that the readers had already gotten the gist. Araki also explained the rules governing his concept: only Stand users can see the Stands, only a Stand can injure another Stand, and the hard suffered by a Stand is passed on to the body of the user, etc. Rules that would go on to be twisted at times... but I digress.

39. Hirohiko Araki, *Manga in Theory and Practice*, p. 143.

In the first volume of part three, Joseph reveals to his grandson that "he" has returned. Dio, the megalomaniacal vampire, the nemesis of their ancestor Jonathan. Even though he was reduced to nothing more than a bodiless head at the end of *JoJo*'s first part, Dio survived for a century at the bottom of the ocean, asleep in his coffin. Sailors then dragged it up by accident. Dio was able to survive all that time because, before he sank to the seafloor, he ended up succeeding in taking over Jonathan Joestar's powerful body, to which he attached his own head. As proof of this evil deed, the new Dio has a star-shaped mark (a reference to the "star" of "Joestar") on his upper back, like all Joestars do.[40] From Egypt, where the vampire wisely hides out, Jonathan's body sends out spiritual signals to the bodies of his descendants, triggering the emergence of their Stands. Also affected, Holly Kujo is not as lucky as the men: unfortunately for her, in *JoJo*, women fighters are still anomalies. The power that emerges within her becomes an illness that might kill her. Even though she's the granddaughter of the illustrious martial artist Lisa Lisa, "This kind, peaceful woman doesn't have the power to resist Dio's curse! She doesn't have the strength to control her Stand!"[41] explains Avdol. This makes Joseph's blood boil. The same is true for Jotaro, who's usually loath to show his emotions. How can they save Holly and break the curse? The answer's quite simple. All they have to do is go to Egypt to find Dio and eliminate him once and for all. When it comes down to it, this situation is similar to the race against time to save Athena in the manga *Knights of the Zodiac*, when she is pierced through the heart by an arrow that only the Grand Pope can remove. Same time period, same magazine, same chivalrous spirit. Our heroes are on the case, with adventure in store for them.

Rebel Rebel, Make My Day

Jotaro Kujo, the iconic hero. He's easily recognized by his hulking stature, his customized school uniform, and, of course, his hat that defies the laws of nature—it fuses with the young man's messy hair, to the point that it seems to be an extension of his body![42] Let's not forget his famous line in Japanese, "*Yare yare da ze*," which can be translated as "good grief" (in the VIZ *JoJonium* edition). It's a phrase that signifies exasperation, with a macho, slang tone, the ending "*ze*"

---

40. Note that this is an invention of the third part that was never mentioned earlier. The TV adaptation, which started in 2012, rectified this inconsistency and placed the mark on the bodies of the Joestars starting in *Phantom Blood*.
41. *JoJonium Stardust Crusaders*, volume 1; original Japanese, volume 13.
42. Araki takes a few chapters to really establish Jotaro's appearance and behavior. For example, in the beginning, there's a definite distinction between his hair and his hat. Sometime later, the two visually fuse together entirely.

being a fairly crude Japanese particle that emphasizes a phrase–basically, it's a sort of verbal exclamation point. And then there's this... obviously, we can't talk about Jotaro without mentioning Star Platinum, his impressive Stand, with his battle cry "*Ora Ora Ora Ora... ORAAA!*," delivered with a series of blows, which is clearly a variation on "*Atatatata... WATCHAAA!*," from the hero of *Fist of the North Star*. According to Satoko Fujimoto, the current French translator of the series, "ora" sounds like an interjection used by Japanese bad boys that's been exaggerated and repeated.[43]

Jonathan, Joseph, Jotaro: there's no doubt, the three men are cut from the same marble (to keep the statue theme going), with similar faces and builds. That said, Jotaro really stands out with his stoic disposition and his tall posture. With him, there's no bragging. Truth be told, Jotaro is more like a legendary figure–like one of the champions from ancient mythology–than like a classic *shōnen nekketsu* protagonist. He's even the antithesis of the latter: from the beginning of part three, Jotaro demands respect; he has incredible power and at no point in his adventure does he need to do any training whatsoever to rise to the top. Jotaro has nothing to learn. At most, he has to learn to channel his power in the first few chapters, then push his limits during the action of the great final battle. In fact, even his name has an aspect of grandeur and prestige! Araki tells where it came from: "When the third part [of *JoJo*] began, I went to Kamakura for an interview. As it happens, the regents of the Kamakura shogunate were named Hōjō, so that's where I got the 'jō' of Kūjō."[44] As for the other "jō" character (承), the one in Jōtarō: "Actually, the proper reading of that kanji is 'shō.' But sometimes, in the names of temples, the character is read as 'jō.' So that's why I chose it."[45] Thus, the most conventional reading of his first name would be "Shōtarō." Interestingly, this could be seen as a reference to author Shōtarō Ishinomori–from the same region as Araki–or to Shōtarō Kaneda,[46] the hero of *Tetsujin 28-gō* (Mitsuteru Yokoyama, 1956-1966, the basis for the anime *Gigantor*), even though the kanji differ and they're just homophonic homonyms. However, this idea may not be so far-fetched, when you read this 2014 statement from Araki: "If I were to draw Part 3 all over again, I would have used Yokoyama Sensei's *Tetsujin 28-go* as inspiration for the Stands, representing a return to the basics."[47]

43. Remarks collected by us on January 25, 2019.
44. In *JoJoveller*, Shūeisha, Lucky Land Communications, 2013 (never published in English). Kamakura was the capital of Japan during the Kamakura period (1185-1333). The Hōjō clan, tied to the shogunate, dominated Japanese politics at that time.
45. *Ibid*.
46. Shōtarō Kaneda is also the name of one of the main characters in *Akira*. A deliberate reference made by Katsuhiro Otomo.
47. Remarks from the author in *JoJonium*, *Stardust Crusaders*, volume 1.

As we know, Araki worships Clint Eastwood, especially his gunslinger roles. America, the Wild West, freedom... Except that by giving Jotaro the taciturn attitude and imposing aura of the "Man with No Name" from the *Dollars Trilogy*, Araki unintentionally returned to his own cultural roots, since the first of the three films, *A Fistful of Dollars* (1964), is, as previously mentioned, an unofficial remake of Akira Kurosawa's *Yojimbo* (1961), in which Toshirō Mifune plays a *rōnin*, a samurai without a master, who wanders around in the final years of the Japanese shogunate. This character is an excellent avatar for the freelance swordsman who goes wherever the wind takes him. Jotaro, admittedly accompanied by his companions in the adventure, is like an imitation of this solitary figure who blends traditional Japanese stoic virility with the arrogance of a man who doesn't play by the rules. It's worth underscoring the idea of solitude, which is at the heart of Araki's conception of the ideal hero, as he explains in *Manga in Theory and Practice*: "There may be nothing more beautiful than a person who pursues something important, regardless of society's approval, and even if it means standing alone. The best heroes are like Jesus Christ: they may be praised by some, but they act not for personal gain and risk death in desolation and solitude, and they follow the call of truth within themselves. [...] Fundamentally, characters who cannot fight without the aid of another can't be considered heroes."[48] In Araki's mind, Clint Eastwood's most famous roles match this philosophy, and that's why Jotaro, the most Eastwood-like of his characters, seems larger than life: he is subject to an idealized form of radical heroism, resulting in a type of person we very rarely see in the real world—especially in Japan, a country where people are conditioned from an early age to contain their individuality in order to become one with the community. Jotaro is the opposite of the hero in part four of *JoJo*, for example, who is more down-to-earth.

That's why I say Jotaro is representative of Eastwood and the Wild West spirit. But that's not all: we can't forget Inspector Harry Callahan, the hero of the five *Dirty Harry* movies, with his famous .44 Magnum, which he loves to say is the "most powerful handgun in the world." Jotaro's iconic pose—with his index finger pointing straight forward accusatorily—is really an imitation of Dirty Harry pointing his favorite weapon. Jotaro's hand is even positioned vertically, as if he were holding a gun, rather than horizontally (which seems like it would be the more natural position). Then there's this: similar to Harry, Jotaro uses what other characters in the manga call "the most powerful Stand in the world," i.e., the muscular Star Platinum. Even the phrase "*Yare yare da ze*" is a loose Japanese interpretation of a line from Eastwood in *Dirty Harry*![49] Incidentally, it's interesting to note that Araki and Eastwood met in 2012:

48. Hirohiko Araki, *Manga in Theory and Practice*, p. 57.
49. Words of the author in *JoJonium*, *Stardust Crusaders*, volume 1.

JOJOmenon, a special issue of the women's magazine *SPUR* published for *JoJo's* 25th anniversary, documented this historic meeting and included a classic photo that's worth its weight in .44-caliber bullets. In it, Eastwood is standing tall, his head cocked to the side, his index finger pointing: he's doing Jotaro's favorite pose! We can only imagine how the *mangaka* must have felt...

However, the "Jotaro formula" would not be complete without this funny contradiction. Dirty Harry hates disorder and likes to call the local crooks "punk!," as we hear in one of his most famous lines. He has no tolerance for riffraff. And yet, Jotaro's appearance is the classic image of a delinquent. In addition to looking like Marlon Brando's rebellious character in *The Wild One* (1953, László Benedek), the young Joestar dresses like a *banchō*, a Japanese gang leader. In Japan, the uniform for high school boys (the *gakuran*) is a black suit that first appeared in the early 20th century and which was originally inspired by the Prussian imperial university uniform. For Jotaro, like many young Japanese hoodlums (or *furyō shōnen*), the uniform has been altered: by customizing his outfit, Jotaro breaks down the military austerity that characterizes the suit and, in doing so, Jotaro gives himself a wild look. It's worth noting that his bad-boy style was already "old-school" in 1989. Truth be told, Jotaro looks overwhelmingly like an old *furyō shōnen* archetype: the hero of *Shiritsu Kiwamemichi Kōkō*[50] ("Ultimate Path Private High School," 1980, never published in English), a series by Akira Miyashita, published a decade before Jotaro in *Shōnen Jump*. The hero in question had just about everything: a giant with a severe air about him, a hat with unruly locks of hair sticking out from under it, an extra-long open jacket, and other details still. Added to that, Jotaro has details with Araki's personal touch, like a variation of the Lucky Land Communications[51] logo attached to his hat or the two belts around his waist, which, in addition to being reminiscent of outfits from the Wild West (generally, the first belt to hold up the pants and the second belt to hold a revolver), are decorated with triangular motifs reminiscent of traditional South American clothing—a vestige of Antonio Lopez's illustrations for Missoni, in the same spirit as Caesar Zeppeli's headband. And let's not forget the thick chain hanging around Jotaro's neck, a symbol of rebellion that replaces, in a way, the imposing mala—Buddhist prayer beads—that the hero of *Shiritsu Kiwamemichi Kōkō* wears around his own neck. We should also

50. The title can be translated as "Ultimate Path Private High School," but the original kanji for "ultimate path"—"*kiwame michi*"—can also be read as "*gokudō*," which is a common way of referring to yakuzas. Moreover, the story takes place in a school where the goal is to train future yakuza elite.
51. That's the name of the company founded by Araki to manage his studio (to employ his assistants, for example) and the intellectual property rights over his work. The company's logo shows a right hand in a vertical position, fingers extended, with a blister on the left side of the middle finger, where a pen or pencil would rub up against it. This logo is often inserted into *JoJo* in one way or another as an Easter egg.

remember Kōichi from *Babel II*, the *gakuran*-wearing hero who's immersed in the chaos of the desert, all alone. There's something poetic in his image, which is another reimagining of the uniform. There's no reason why Kōichi should be there, particularly in a school uniform, and this same idea intentionally appears in Araki's hero, who travels all over Asia and climbs dunes in (funny) schoolboy clothing.

Jotaro Kujo, an amalgam of order and disorder. The order of Clint Eastwood characters and the disorder of Japanese hoodlums. Perhaps the character's popularity is thanks to this strange clash. In any case, whether it's Inspector Harry Callahan or the Japanese *banchō*, we see the idea of disobedience and a sort of parallel set of rules. In *JoJo*, that parallel set of rules is that which applies to Stand users: since the human society's justice system is powerless against Dio, Jotaro must get his hands dirty and take Dio out himself. It's a radical solution, somewhere between Dirty Harry-style vigilantism–ridding the world of "punks"–and the hero's personal interest in saving Holly Kujo.

United colors of JoJo

So, they're off to save Holly Kujo. As can be expected, the trip to Egypt is not exactly a walk in the park. Dio sends his henchmen, Stand users that he controls by implanting in them seeds of his own flesh. The high schooler Noriaki Kakyoin[52] is the first of these henchmen and he attacks Jotaro at school. After a battle that features the very first "Ora Ora Ora!," the hero defeats his attacker and manages, via a delicate surgery, to free him from Dio's control. Kakyoin then joins the Joestar team and becomes one of the four men who will travel to Egypt: Jotaro, Joseph, Kakyoin, and Avdol. I have to stress the importance of Mohammed Avdol, who, in addition to being Jotaro's very first Stand-using adversary, is also the man who names the group's Stands. Avdol, being a fortune teller, does a card reading before the group leaves for Egypt: he uses the tarot cards' 22 major arcana to symbolize the fate and power of the Stand users. This is how he names his own Stand Magician's Red, for example, in reference to the first card (called The Magician), whereas the card associated with Jotaro is the 17th, The Star, hence Star Platinum. Until they arrive in Egypt, all of the adversaries faced by the heroes possess Stands associated with the 18 remaining arcana. Dio is the last, with his power called The World (card number 21).

While Araki compares the formation of his quartet of heroes to the *Seven Samurai* (1954, Akira Kurosawa), he also cites the travel stories from the

---

52. "Kakyōin" is the name of a neighborhood of Sendai, located near the city's main train station.

Japanese TV series *Mito Kōmon* (1969-2011) and the novel *Around the World in Eighty Days* (1872, Jules Verne) when he speaks of their journey, which is marked by numerous stops, in one country after another, and which uses various means of travel (a surprise complication prohibits them from taking a flight directly to Egypt). Initially, Araki saw having his characters travel as a sort of act of resistance. In the 1980s, the narrative formula centered on a tournament became very popular in *shōnen*. *Dragon Ball* helped boost interest in this kind of competition story with the various successive editions of its famous "World Martial Arts Tournament." Moreover, according to Akira Toriyama, it was the introduction of this tournament that finally got the ball rolling for *Dragon Ball*, a series that up to that point had been unpopular with audiences.[53] You have to admit, it's an effective formula. It sustains readers' excitement while naturally building greater and greater tension as the characters win and face increasingly formidable adversaries. Araki wanted to avoid using this format, which he saw as a trap because it necessarily leads to a massive escalation, with more and more powerful enemies... But what's supposed to happen after the tournament? Can the one-upmanship continue infinitely? No. So then, what's the end goal? Wouldn't it be disappointing to return to less powerful adversaries after going all the way to the top? We can draw a parallel with the economic bubble that grew between 1986 and 1990 in a Japan that was rich and prosperous, on the verge of suffering a serious blow when that bubble burst.[54]

So, Araki, rather than give in to the tournament trend, as was suggested to him to boost the popularity of his manga, got the idea for a "space by space" format, inspired by board games with a path to follow like *e-sugoroku*, a Japanese cousin to snakes and ladders.[55] It's a narrative structure in which each move corresponds to a new enemy to fight, without each one neces-sarily being more powerful than the last, which circumvents the inflationist pressure of tournaments. The progression to the top in a championship is replaced by another form of ascent: moving toward a final destination. However, Araki's formula has a flaw: even though the settings of the encounters vary, the encounters themselves can end up being very similar, as he admits.[56] So,

---

53. He shares this information in the catalogue of the exhibition *Shōnen Jump Vol. 2*, published in 2018.
54. In November 2018, Araki confirmed that the context of the economic bubble indeed played a role in his rejection of the tournament formula. Source: Masanobu Matsumoto, "Draw Close to the Unexpected — The Chemical Reactions of Manga Artist Hirohiko Araki," *The New York Times Style Magazine: Japan*, November 25, 2018. https://www.tjapan.jp/entertain-ment/17230475.
55. Game boards for *e-sugoroku* have a wide variety of structures, depending on when they were created and variations in gameplay. While some are very similar to snakes and ladders or the "Game of the Goose," others actually depict a map, with different key places connected by travel routes.
56. Hirohiko Araki, *Manga in Theory and Practice*, p. 94.

to keep things feeling fresh, he came up with a solution that's unusual for an action *shōnen*: occasionally introducing weak enemies. "Because there's no thrill in an easy victory, I compensated for physical weakness by making [these characters] extra devious and frightening. The idea was to make these battles offer a different challenge than just might struggling against might."[57] It's a concrete example of what I called earlier in this chapter "the third parameter," the extra rule of the game, that element that changes the playing field. Soul Sacrifice (a.k.a. Devo) is the first such opponent. His Stand Ebony Devil–strongly inspired by the doll Chuck from the horror film *Child's Play* (1988, Tom Holland)–has a very original characteristic: the more the user hates his adversary, the stronger the Stand gets. As such, Soul Sacrifice purposely provokes his opponent into hitting him. It works like a charm. Alas, these novelties are not enough to dissolve the very real repetitiveness of the first ten volumes of part three, which results from their linear nature. There's never a moment where we doubt that the team of heroes will end up reaching Egypt and, ultimately, all of these obstacles along the way only offer limited narrative value. Their function, first and foremost, is to result in battles, which remain the heart of *JoJo*, but the quality of said battles can be very uneven. It took until the later volumes of *Stardust Crusaders* for Araki to find his groove and reach the full potential of the Stand concept.

That said, the journey to Egypt offers a constant, very refreshing dose of exoticism. The "crusaders" travel through Hong Kong, Singapore, and India, then traverse the Middle East (Pakistan, United Arab Emirates, Saudi Arabia) before reaching Egypt and crossing it from south to north until they reach Cairo.[58] Other than the most dangerous places, Araki personally visited all of the destinations on the itinerary[59] and he delivers in his manga a lot of information about each place. For example, he sets the battle in Hong Kong in the Tiger Balm Garden and informs us that "the magnificent sculpted beasts, pagodas, fountains, trees, and plants, each one rarer than the next, make it a must-see destination for any visitor to Hong Kong." Sadly, the place was demolished in 2004 to make room for a cluster of luxury apartment buildings named The Legend. In *JoJo*, the stunning garden is the arena for a battle between a Frenchman with an unforgettable name, Jean-Pierre Polnareff,[60] who is the

---

57. *Ibid.*, p. 95.
58. The author even draws a map on which the heroes' route is shown with a dotted line, like in the *Indiana Jones* movies.
59. He confirms this in *Manga in Theory and Practice* (p. 160), also noting that he visited Egypt three times.
60. His last name is actually a reference to French singer Michel Polnareff! Out of caution, in the Western version of the video game *JoJo's Bizarre Adventure: All Star Battle*, released in 2013, the character was renamed... Jean-Pierre Eiffel. Additionally, Polnareff's sculpted hair is most likely, as was the case with Rudol von Stroheim, inspired by the eccentric hairdos in the illustrations of Antonio Lopez—particularly one of his portraits of Grace Jones.

second henchman sent by Dio that ends up joining the band of heroes, after also being freed from the vampire's influence—it's also worth noting that the other enemies encountered on the journey to Egypt, in general, simply end up... dead.[61] With the obligatory French clichés, the stylish Jean-Pierre has a Stand that wields a rapier, the magnificent Silver Chariot (whose helmet, that of medieval armor, is reminiscent of Jagi from *Fist of the North Star*), and he has a keen interest in the ladies. Moreover, he becomes one of the main sources of comic relief in *Stardust Crusaders*, often at his own expense. Polnareff is never far away when Araki draws some scatological gag of questionable taste, particularly when the Frenchman experiences culture shock around the toilets of western Asia. This bathroom humor is a bit incongruous and remains specific to this portion of *JoJo* (which, I might add, has no shortage of humor in general, continuing the trend started in *Battle Tendency*). That's probably for the best. What happens on the journey... stays on the journey.

Let's recap the makeup of the Joestar team: a mixed-race Japanese-American man (Jotaro), an Anglo-American (Joseph), an Egyptian (Avdol), a Frenchman (Polnareff), and a Japanese man (Kakyoin). Have you ever seen such a multicultural main cast in a *shōnen* before? Absolutely not. To this day, such diversity remains rare, just like the exceptionally eclectic selection of places visited. Indeed, while the concept of a journey with many stops along the way underpins other parts of *JoJo's Bizarre Adventure*, the odyssey of this third part remains the most varied and most exotic.

Horror show

In *Stardust Crusaders*, we see a real step up in quality in terms of the way in which the tension and gradual incursion of horror are presented. In the first volume, the handful of pages in which Avdol discovers Holly lying on the floor at home serve as a model of suspense. In this scene, Araki signals something strange is afoot by using a totally ordinary factor: a spoon lying on the floor. There's no reason why it should be there, in the middle of the house. "*Go Go Go Go Go...*," cry the onomatopoeias written in katakana, those famous pulsing sounds that give rhythm to Araki's pages. Avdol approaches the spoon. "GO!," shouts another onomatopoeia even louder. Then we see a new shot with breathtaking framing: Avdol, his face drawn from a 3/4 back view (or rather, a mix between 3/4 back and profile views: an anatomically impossible perspective, but one that works very well and which has become a

---

61. As *Stardust Crusaders* progresses, this trend of fights to the death—which is not unlike the cutthroat atmosphere of the Wild West—eases off. More and more bad guys (except for the last several) are simply rendered unable to cause further harm, without actually being killed.

typical element of Araki's graphical lexicon), spots more kitchen items lying on the floor. Pans, ladles, plates... The refrigerator door is open. Araki zooms in. A hand seen from a distance. Then the same hand closer up. Then on the next page: "BAAAAN!" Holly is lying on the floor, her eyes closed. The position and camera angle are strongly reminiscent of the very first page of *JoJo*, minus the sexually charged atmosphere. As for the progressive zoom-in on the hand, it resembles the work of *mangaka* Kazuo Umezu, a master of frenetic "camerawork," imitating the zooming in and out and the traveling shots of a movie camera. You can see this approach in his series *Senrei* ("Baptism," 1974-1976, pre-published in the magazine *Shōjo Comic*), for example, a horror-thriller masterpiece. It even includes an example of the "almost 3/4 back" view (on page 55 of the first volume), whose function is clear: to show us what the character is seeing from a special point of view in the heart of the action, over their shoulder, without sacrificing the expressiveness of the character's face (since a true 3/4 back view wouldn't show the eyes or mouth), before, in this case, zooming in over three panels on what the girl is looking at. A strange spot of blood on the ceiling. While Umezu's influence on Araki has never been confirmed by him, it seems very likely.

Never far from Araki's mind, horror movies also haunt this third part of *JoJo*. We see this often throughout the journey to Egypt, during which many of the Stands encountered are inspired by well-known horror figures–slime, the fish-man, etc.–and even figures from specific films, like the doll Chucky from *Child's Play*, mentioned earlier, or *A Nightmare on Elm Street* (1984, Wes Craven), whose Freddy Krueger has an avatar in the Stand Death 13 (tarot card number 13, Death). A Grim Reaper in Venetian Carnival garb who attacks the heroes in their dreams, which are filled with absurd, illogical events. I also have to mention the terrifying Stand Wheel of Fortune (card number 10, Wheel of Fortune), a flamboyant '50s car that's a reference to both *Duel* (1971, Steven Spielberg), a film in which a truck with an unseen driver chases a guy for no apparent reason, and the diabolical Plymouth in *Christine* (1983, John Carpenter). They're obvious references. So, why so many horror movie allusions? Simply because, by chance or by fate, life led to a match made in heaven: Araki and the great classics of (Western) horror and fantasy film, brought together in the same time and place. Araki was fortunate enough to grow up during a key period for the genre, while, because of Western culture establishing a presence in Japan after World War II, foreign works became easy to find in the country. The 1970s also saw the rise of twin phenomena: the emergence of a slew of major horror filmmakers and, at the same time, the swift rise to prominence of author Stephen King. In fact, many of those filmmakers have adapted King's stories at one time or another! Brian de Palma did *Carrie* (1976); Tobe Hooper did *Salem's Lot* (1979) and *The Mangler* (1995); Stanley Kubrick did *The Shining* (1980); David Cronenberg did *The Dead Zone* (1983);

George A. Romero did *Creepshow* (1982; in this case, King specially wrote the film script, instead of being an adaptation of one of his books) and *The Dark Half* (1993)... John Carpenter, meanwhile, directed the famous adaptation of *Christine*. As such, it's only natural that we'd find Stephen King references in *JoJo's Bizarre Adventure*, right? Especially when you consider the fact that King wrote a novella called *The Body*, adapted for the silver screen in 1986 by Rob Reiner using the title... *Stand by Me*? The Stand that looks like the car from *Christine* is, without a doubt, a clear example of King's influence on Araki's manga, much like Alessi swinging his ax at a closed door in volume 10, which is an obvious recreation of the famous scene starring Jack Nicholson in the adaptation of *The Shining*. However, those are not the first such examples,[62] nor will they be the last. Stay tuned.

Level Up!

Stardust Crusaders, JJBA volume 23.[63] The tipping point. The moment that brings *JoJo's Bizarre Adventure* into uncharted territory and foreshadows all of the genius that the series will go on to demonstrate. Jotaro and his companions have now reached Egypt and are crossing it from south to north. By this point, all of the tarot cards (except Dio "The World") have been revealed and the new enemies are instead named after Egyptian gods. D'Arby the Elder is one of these opponents. Stand: Osiris. Power: extracting the soul of his adversary when they feel defeated after a game or a bet and transforming it into a poker chip. D'Arby is a depraved collector: he has a need for poker chips. Always more chips. So, wagering the disclosure of valuable information about Dio, he challenges the group of heroes in a bar in the Egyptian desert, an atmosphere not unlike that of a Wild-West saloon. D'Arby first makes a bet–if you put two pieces of fish in front of a cat, which will it eat first?–then there's a game that involves dropping coins into a glass of water without it spilling over. Team Joestar suffers two defeats... Their last hope: Jotaro, who faces the gambler in a game of poker. Of course, D'Arby is sly... and cheats. Tricks, bluffing, and surprises: it takes us back to the spirit of *Busō Poker* and *Mashōnen B.T.* Further proof that Araki's artistic identity, where he shines the brightest, is in what I called "the third parameter" at the beginning of this chapter: the rules of engagement in the battles, in all their shapes and forms.

With D'Arby, the *mangaka* breaks the law that says that each appearance of a Stand user triggers a brawl. He shows that it's possible to battle in a different

---

62. On page 21 of volume 2 of *Phantom Blood*, Dio holds a bottle of alcohol whose label says "Dead Zone" and "Cronenberg."
63. *JoJonium Stardust Crusaders* vol. 7–8.

manner, even in an action *shōnen*. Better yet: he makes the encounter more thrilling than all of the previous confrontations! Granted, there were Stands with original powers before him: in volume eight, Boingo's Stand—a manga whose pages predict the future—didn't actually result in a battle, so to speak. However, setting aside the brilliant idea, that part lacked pizazz, whereas the psychological struggle against D'Arby makes a success of the concept by executing it well. We see a direct extension of the idea later on in the saga (in the eighth part, with betting on a fight between trafficked stag beetles), but also in other manga in *Shōnen Jump*.

The year is 1991; the five chapters of "D'Arby the Gambler" are published in Japan and *JoJo's Bizarre Adventure*, already an unorthodox series, is increasingly distinguishing itself in *Jump* with its inventiveness, particularly compared to the well-established classic style of other action manga like *Dragon Ball*, *Dragon Quest: Dai no Daibōken* (1989-1996, Riku Sanjō and Kōji Inada), and *Keiji* (1990-1993, when Tetsuo Hara tried his hand at historical fiction). With its "dangerous games"[64] and other Stands with unusual powers, *JoJo* paved the way for *Yu-Gi-Oh!*, whose author makes no secret of his love for Araki's work, but also for the "Sensui" story arc of the action manga *Yu Yu Hakusho* (1990-1994; by Yoshihiro Togashi, another admirer of Araki), which began in spring 1993, not long after the end of *Stardust Crusaders*. This part of the series presents psychological struggles that, directly in keeping with the Stand battles in the Egyptian part of *JoJo*, are centered on powers with special rules, like not being able to speak a taboo word. It even includes a video game-style duel... like in the fantastic volume 25 of *JJBA* (*JoJonium Stardust Crusaders*, volume nine), which quite simply features D'Arby's younger brother, who uses a Stand similar to D'Arby the Elder's, in a sort of rematch that's even more exciting than the first.

From the battle against D'Arby the Elder, *JoJo's Bizarre Adventure* enters a golden age. The best ideas and the best fights of *Stardust Crusaders* are found in its last six volumes (*Stardust Crusaders* volumes seven to 10 of the *JoJonium* edition). For example, there's the battle against the alliance of two returning enemies: Boingo, the child with the manga-Stand, and the cowboy Hol Horse, whose Stand, Emperor (tarot card number 4, The Emperor), is a hybrid firearm—a combination of a revolver and a semiautomatic pistol—with homing bullets. It's a complex variation on the "three-parameter" system, which results in totally insane passages and some serious twists. Since Boingo's

64. Note that, in Japan, the 1980s saw the arrival of a wave of manga based on games of chance. Nobuyuki Fukumoto, author of the popular manga *Ten* (1989-2002, about mahjong), *Akagi* (1992-present, same), and *Kaiji* (1996-present, about all forms of gambling), is a major leader in this genre. *Kaiji*, in particular, features bets with extremely high stakes, like crazy sums of money... or the character's life. However, at the time of *Stardust Crusaders*, this type of story was unheard of in action manga.

manga predicts that a salvo of bullets shot by Hol Horse will strike Jotaro in the head precisely at noon, this prediction must become reality, no matter what, and the projectiles in question will follow incredible trajectories to fulfill this destiny. Once again, though, Araki messes with the rules–of course he can't kill Jotaro yet! What actually happens is the bullets strike... the drawing of Jotaro in Boingo's manga! They rip through the paper and then make a beeline for Hol Horse. Brilliant. Another unusual situation, in *JJBA* volume 24 (*JoJonium Stardust Crusaders*, volume 8): the battle in the animal kingdom between the dog Iggy–a new ally for Team Joestar–and the falcon Pet Shop, both Stand users, in an all-out game of cat and mouse through the streets, and then the sewers, of Cairo. The sequence is as original as it is enthralling.

By this point, Araki's graphics have stabilized. His pages have achieved a balance between detail and clarity. The abundant shadowing is still present, but is less saturated than in *Battle Tendency*. The panels breathe better and are often trimmed with dynamic bezels, conveniently guiding the eye. Araki also successfully tests a curvilinear perspective, like when he shows the expanse of Cairo or to really emphasize, at the end of *JJBA* volume 24 (end of *JoJonium Stardust Crusaders*, volume 8), the gradual approach to Dio's mansion: a series of panels that have an incredible impact, in which you can also see the *mangaka*'s new, more schematic approach to drawing the human body. Short, trapezoidal torsos, slender legs, sharp angles, and floating stances. The bodies, although muscular, seem to defy the laws of gravity; they're almost weightless, sometimes on tiptoes or off balance. The "*JoJo* poses" have changed; they're less obviously inspired by the robotic-dancing poses in Antonio Lopez's work or the highly affected attitudes of Tony Viramontes' work: instead, we now find this kind of borrowed idea in cover art, illustrations outside of the actual story. Note, however, that the "*JoJo* discotheque" is still open: the characters continue to adopt sophisticated, unnatural positions, but they no longer put themselves in strange, momentary, choreographic poses for no reason, like in *Battle Tendency* with its famous twin poses by Joseph and Caesar. Generally speaking, the body contortions are less exaggerated and closer to what real human beings can do–excluding the body proportions, of course! Little by little, Araki is refining his approach and achieving his first graphical acme.

Lone Star

Dio. From the beginning, his presence looms over *Stardust Crusaders*. He's there, lurking in the shadows. Araki shows him from time to time, hiding from the sun in his Egyptian mansion, his face masked by the darkness. For the author, obscuring Dio is a way of not distracting his readers from what's happening in the moment–the obstacles along their journey–even though faithful readers are already familiar with Dio Brando. Well... he's not actually called "Brando" anymore; he's now just "Dio." "God" in Italian, as previously mentioned. The Japanese version, as if to give extra weight to the name, even says "DIO" in all capital letters from the Latin alphabet, instead of in katakana characters. Araki purposely shows Dio unclothed (often from behind in a sensual pose reproduced from a women's fashion illustration by Tony Viramontes[65]), again giving him a mythical aura, like Michelangelo's *David* or the Greco-Roman gods of antiquity–before him, the Pillar Men received this same treatment. Truth be told, the new Dio, who we don't really see until *JJBA* volume 27 (*JoJonium Stardust Crusaders*, volume 10), doesn't have much in common with the version of him from a century earlier. Not only because of his all-new extravagant physique and fashion, but also because of his unfathomable, even laconic personality. Araki doesn't say much, if anything, about his feelings and motivations, as if there's just nothing to be said. Or as if the author himself was unable to capture the thoughts in Dio's labyrinthine mind. He exists, period. Just like how evil has always existed. In fact, Dio has become an idea in human form: he personifies domination. Just like how Broly in the movie *Dragon Ball Z: Broly - The Legendary Super Saiyan* (1993), another laconic antagonist, embodies the idea of destruction in its purest form.

Moreover, the later volumes of *Stardust Crusaders* offer scenes reminiscent of the dizzying battles in *Dragon Ball*. All of a sudden, the characters start to make spectacular leaps and pounce on each other while sporting blazing auras! That's not to mention Araki actually drawing Dio's Stand, The World, in the pose for "Kamehameha," Goku's signature attack.[66] At another point, a panel shows Polnareff enraged, in an obvious recreation of a well-known image from *Dragon Ball*: Goku's fit of anger against Frieza.[67] It's a reflection of what was in fashion at the time. The Toriyama craze was in full swing–incidentally, in *Manga in Theory and Practice*, Araki praises the talents of his colleague, who he considers a virtuoso–and was thus infused into this very particular part of the story, the last two volumes of *Stardust Crusaders*, which are dedicated to the battle between Team Joestar and the ancient vampire. They are fantastic volumes. You can read them over and over again. All action *shōnen* authors should study them carefully–and I'm sure many have–because they are

65. The illustration in question was produced in 1984 for Nina Ricci Haute Couture and is found on the back cover of *Bold, Beautiful and Damned – The World of 1980s Fashion Illustrator Tony Viramontes* (Dean Rhys-Morgan, Laurence King Publishing, 2013). Moreover, it's not the first time that Araki drew inspiration from this illustration: take a look at page 204 of volume 2 of *Battle Tendency*, JoJonium edition (*JJBA* volume 8), which shows Joseph in this same position.
66. In an illustration between two chapters, on page 160 of *JoJonium Stardust Crusaders*, volume 10 (*JJBA* volume 27).
67. Page 245 of volume 9 for *Stardust Crusaders*, JoJonium edition, and page 73 of volume 27 for *Dragon Ball*.

brilliant in every way. Whether it's their narrative tension, their excitement, or their clear way of visually representing Dio's power of stopping time for a few seconds.

At the end, of course, Araki's hero must face his enemy alone. Jotaro versus Dio, the nocturnal duel between two legends. "If this was a Wild West gun duel, this is the part where they'd say, 'Draw, partner,'"[68] says Jotaro, sounding more Eastwood-like than ever. In *JoJo's Bizarre Adventure*, the battle against Dio is so peculiar, not only because of its quality or its aerial chases, which are unique in the series. No, this peculiarity comes from the fact that it's probably the battle that gets closest to a "regular" *shōnen nekketsu*. Since Jotaro and Dio are two adversaries with simple, similar abilities, direct assaults dominate the confrontation. Fists explode, bodies fly. *Ora Ora, Muda Muda*![69] However, to fight The World, Jotaro cannot count on brute force alone; he must use intelligence and strategy. But that's not enough... Could the suspension of time be an unbeatable power? Perhaps Araki thought about it. Because it takes a *deus ex machina* to save Jotaro: suddenly, his Star Platinum begins to develop the ability to freeze time, too, first just for a fleeting moment, then for longer and longer. How do we explain this? It's a mystery. At best, we can imagine that Jotaro and Dio, since the antagonist now possesses Jonathan Joestar's body, have developed similar Stands because they belong to the same lineage. In any case, Jotaro stands up to the vampire and, after surviving the most "WTF?" attack of the battle (Dio tries to crush him with a steamroller![70]), our hero gains the upper hand.

---

68. *JoJonium Stardust Crusaders*, volume 10, p. 349 (*JJBA* volume 28).
69. "*Muda Muda Muda Muda…*" is Dio's battle cry. *Muda* means "useless" in Japanese.
70. It's likely a reference to a similar passage in *Kinnikuman*, which can be seen in the very first episode of the anime from 1983.

Ora Ora Ora Ora Ora Ora Ora Ora Ora Ora Ora Ora Ora Ora Ora Ora Ora Ora
Ora Ora Ora Ora Ora Ora Ora Ora Ora Ora Ora Ora Ora Ora Ora Ora Ora Ora
Ora Ora Ora Ora Ora Ora Ora Ora Ora Ora Ora Ora Ora Ora Ora Ora Ora Ora
Ora Ora Ora Ora Ora Ora Ora Ora Ora Ora Ora Ora Ora Ora Ora Ora Ora Ora
Ora Ora Ora Ora Ora Ora Ora Ora Ora Ora Ora Ora Ora Ora Ora Ora Ora Ora
Ora Ora Ora Ora Ora Ora Ora Ora Ora Ora Ora Ora Ora Ora Ora Ora Ora Ora
Ora Ora Ora Ora Ora Ora Ora Ora Ora Ora Ora Ora Ora Ora Ora Ora Ora Ora
Ora Ora Ora Ora Ora Ora Ora Ora Ora Ora Ora Ora Ora Ora Ora Ora Ora Ora
Ora Ora Ora Ora Ora Ora Ora Ora Ora Ora Ora Ora Ora Ora Ora Ora Ora Ora
Ora Ora Ora Ora Ora Ora Ora Ora Ora Ora Ora Ora Ora Ora Ora Ora Ora Ora
Ora Ora Ora Ora Ora Ora Ora Ora Ora Ora Ora Ora Ora Ora Ora Ora Ora Ora
Ora Ora Ora Ora Ora Ora Ora Ora Ora Ora Ora Ora Ora Ora Ora Ora Ora Ora
Ora Ora Ora Ora Ora Ora Ora Ora Ora Ora Ora Ora Ora Ora Ora Ora Ora Ora
Ora Ora Ora Ora Ora Ora Ora Ora Ora Ora Ora Ora Ora Ora Ora Ora Ora Ora
Ora Ora Ora Ora Ora Ora Ora Ora Ora Ora Ora Ora Ora Ora Ora Ora Ora Ora
Ora Ora Ora Ora Ora Ora Ora Ora Ora Ora Ora Ora Ora Ora Ora Ora Ora Ora
Ora Ora Ora Ora Ora Ora Ora Ora Ora Ora Ora Ora Ora Ora Ora Ora Ora Ora
Ora Ora Ora Ora Ora Ora Ora Ora Ora Ora Ora Ora Ora Ora Ora Ora Ora Ora
Ora Ora Ora Ora Ora Ora Ora Ora Ora Ora Ora Ora Ora Ora Ora Ora Ora Ora
Ora Ora Ora Ora Ora Ora Ora Ora Ora Ora Ora Ora Ora Ora Ora Ora Ora Ora
Ora Ora Ora Ora Ora Ora Ora Ora Ora Ora Ora Ora Ora Ora Ora Ora Ora Ora
Ora Ora Ora Ora Ora Ora Ora Ora Ora Ora Ora Ora Ora Ora Ora Ora Ora Ora
Ora Ora Ora Ora Ora Ora Ora Ora Ora Ora Ora Ora Ora Ora Ora Ora Ora Ora
Ora Ora Ora Ora Ora Ora Ora Ora Ora Ora Ora Ora Ora Ora Ora Ora Ora Ora
Ora Ora Ora Ora Ora Ora Ora Ora Ora Ora Ora Ora Ora Ora Ora Ora Ora Ora
Ora Ora Ora Ora Ora Ora Ora Ora Ora Ora Ora Ora Ora Ora Ora Ora Ora Ora
Ora Ora Ora Ora Ora Ora Ora Ora Ora Ora Ora Ora Ora Ora Ora Ora Ora Ora
Ora Ora Ora Ora Ora Ora Ora Ora Ora Ora Ora Ora Ora Ora Ora Ora Ora Ora
Ora Ora Ora Ora Ora Ora Ora Ora Ora Ora Ora Ora Ora Ora Ora Ora Ora Ora
Ora Ora Ora Ora Ora Ora Ora Ora Ora Ora Ora Ora Ora Ora Ora Ora Ora Ora
Ora Ora Ora Ora Ora Ora Ora Ora Ora Ora Ora Ora Ora Ora Ora Ora Ora Ora
Ora Ora Ora Ora Ora Ora Ora Ora Ora Ora Ora Ora Ora Ora Ora Ora Ora Ora
Ora Ora Ora Ora Ora Ora Ora Ora Ora Ora Ora Ora Ora Ora Ora Ora Ora Ora
Ora Ora Ora Ora Ora Ora Ora Ora Ora Ora Ora Ora Ora Ora Ora Ora Ora Ora
Ora Ora Ora Ora Ora Ora Ora Ora Ora Ora Ora Ora Ora Ora Ora Ora Ora Ora
Ora Ora Ora Ora Ora Ora Ora Ora Ora Ora Ora Ora Ora Ora Ora Ora Ora Ora
Ora Ora Ora Ora Ora Ora Ora Ora Ora Ora Ora Ora Ora Ora Ora Ora Ora Ora
Ora Ora Ora Ora Ora Ora Ora Ora Ora Ora Ora Ora Ora Ora Ora Ora Ora Ora
Ora Ora Ora Ora Ora Ora Ora Ora Ora Ora Ora Ora Ora Ora Ora Ora Ora Ora
Ora Ora Ora Ora Ora Ora Ora Ora Ora Ora Ora Ora Ora Ora Ora Ora Ora Ora
Ora Ora Ora Ora Ora Ora Ora Ora Ora Ora Ora Ora Ora Ora Ora Ora Ora Ora
Ora Ora Ora Ora Ora Ora Ora Ora Ora Ora Ora Ora Ora Ora Ora Ora Ora Ora
Ora Ora Ora Ora Ora Ora Ora Ora Ora Ora Ora Ora Ora Ora Ora Ora Ora Ora
Ora Ora Ora Ora Ora Ora Ora Ora Ora Ora Ora Ora Ora Ora Ora Ora Ora Ora

Muda Muda Muda Muda Muda Muda Muda Muda Muda Muda Muda Muda
Muda Muda Muda Muda Muda Muda Muda Muda Muda Muda Muda Muda
Muda Muda Muda Muda Muda Muda Muda Muda Muda Muda Muda Muda
Muda Muda Muda Muda Muda Muda Muda Muda Muda Muda Muda Muda
Muda Muda Muda Muda Muda Muda Muda Muda Muda Muda Muda Muda
Muda Muda Muda Muda Muda Muda Muda Muda Muda Muda Muda Muda
Muda Muda Muda Muda Muda Muda Muda Muda Muda Muda Muda Muda
Muda Muda Muda Muda Muda Muda Muda Muda Muda Muda Muda Muda
Muda Muda Muda Muda Muda Muda Muda Muda Muda Muda Muda Muda
Muda Muda Muda Muda Muda Muda Muda Muda Muda Muda Muda Muda
Muda Muda Muda Muda Muda Muda Muda Muda Muda Muda Muda Muda
Muda Muda Muda Muda Muda Muda Muda Muda Muda Muda Muda Muda
Muda Muda Muda Muda Muda Muda Muda Muda Muda Muda Muda Muda
Muda Muda Muda Muda Muda Muda Muda Muda Muda Muda Muda Muda
Muda Muda Muda Muda Muda Muda Muda Muda Muda Muda Muda Muda
Muda Muda Muda Muda Muda Muda Muda Muda Muda Muda Muda Muda
Muda Muda Muda Muda Muda Muda Muda Muda Muda Muda Muda Muda
Muda Muda Muda Muda Muda Muda Muda Muda Muda Muda Muda Muda
Muda Muda Muda Muda Muda Muda Muda Muda Muda Muda Muda Muda
Muda Muda Muda Muda Muda Muda Muda Muda Muda Muda Muda Muda
Muda Muda Muda Muda Muda Muda Muda Muda Muda Muda Muda Muda
Muda Muda Muda Muda Muda Muda Muda Muda Muda Muda Muda Muda
Muda Muda Muda Muda Muda Muda Muda Muda Muda Muda Muda Muda
Muda Muda Muda Muda Muda Muda Muda Muda Muda Muda Muda Muda
Muda Muda Muda Muda Muda Muda Muda Muda Muda Muda Muda Muda
Muda Muda Muda Muda Muda Muda Muda Muda Muda Muda Muda Muda
Muda Muda Muda Muda Muda Muda Muda Muda Muda Muda Muda Muda
Muda Muda Muda Muda Muda Muda Muda Muda Muda Muda Muda Muda
Muda Muda Muda Muda Muda Muda Muda Muda Muda Muda Muda Muda
Muda Muda Muda Muda Muda Muda Muda Muda Muda Muda Muda Muda
Muda Muda Muda Muda Muda Muda Muda Muda Muda Muda Muda Muda
Muda Muda Muda Muda Muda Muda Muda Muda Muda Muda Muda Muda
Muda Muda Muda Muda Muda Muda Muda Muda Muda Muda Muda Muda
Muda Muda Muda Muda Muda Muda Muda Muda Muda Muda Muda Muda
Muda Muda Muda Muda Muda Muda Muda Muda Muda Muda Muda Muda
Muda Muda Muda Muda Muda Muda Muda Muda Muda Muda Muda Muda
Muda Muda Muda Muda Muda Muda Muda Muda Muda Muda Muda Muda
Muda Muda Muda Muda Muda Muda Muda Muda Muda Muda Muda Muda
Muda Muda Muda Muda Muda Muda Muda Muda Muda Muda Muda Muda

オ

ラ!!*

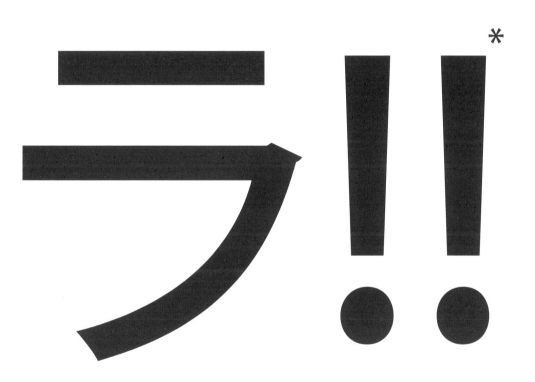

* ORAAA!

In the end, it's anger that drives Jotaro to push his limits in the last moments of the fight, after Dio kills his grandfather Joseph right in front of him. Jotaro loses it, in a conclusion that couldn't be any more *nekketsu*. Or couldn't be any more *Dragon Ball*, to be more precise. Friendship, effort... and victory. So long, Dio. "Now... we've taken back what is ours, Dio!," Jotaro declares as the sun rises, after the vampire's blood resurrects the truly relentless Joseph. Alas, other "crusaders" are not as fortunate... And I'm sure some readers still mourn them.

A legacy for the future

Stardust Crusaders is so deeply rooted in the manga universe that for many, this third part is simply the definition of *JoJo's Bizarre Adventure*. From now on, nothing will be the same: *JoJo* has become a name with prestige. In the '90s, Jotaro's odyssey was the only part to be adapted into an anime (in 1993, a transposition of the journey through Egypt which Satoshi Kon worked on, before later creating well-known films) and into video games. First in the form of a role-playing game in 1993, then, in 1998 and 1999, two fighting games developed by Capcom, the company that dominates the genre and created *Street Fighter II*. What's more, the fighting game universe has more than once drawn inspiration from *JoJo*'s third part. For example, we find two admitted "cousins" of Jean-Pierre Polnareff in the famous series *Tekken* (with Paul) and *The King of Fighters* (with Benimaru); meanwhile, the hero of *Guilty Gear*, Sol Badguy, has a general attitude similar to Jotaro's and he even delivers the line "*Yare yare da ze.*" All this is to say that there are countless works of pop culture that have referenced *Stardust Crusaders* to one degree or another.

There's still a question we have to ask: when it comes down to it, does this third part really deserve its golden status? Isn't it too uneven? Doesn't it take a long time to find its footing? To be honest, almost half of the voyage to Egypt is forgettable. Also, it's easy to be skeptical about the fact that the bad guys *always* show up on Team Joestar's path–how do they know *exactly* where the heroes will be in such vast and at times deserted territories? Granted, this fact follows the logic of snakes and ladders, but I'd say it looks too artificial when applied to a story and it just reduces the bad guys to their function as obstacles. But does that mean we should put *Stardust Crusaders* on the chopping block? No. Instead, I propose that we split it into two halves, which we can affectionately call "Destination Egypt" and "Explorers of Egypt" (after the famous volumes of the Tintin comics). We should praise the second one, which avoids the pitfalls of the first. The fantastic second half is truly worthy of defining *JoJo's Bizarre Adventure*. Or at least it can be one of its definitions. That said, we can still criticize *Stardust Crusaders* overall for being relatively superficial—certain characters, like Kakyoin, lack development and, in spite of a few welcome twists, the plot is both shallow and linear.

In any case, the rest of the saga owes practically everything to *Stardust Crusaders*. With its Stands, its "*e-sugoroku*-style" narrative structure, and its extraordinary psychological battles, Jotaro's odyssey established almost all of the fundamentals of the story's subsequent parts. We can consider part three to be the saga's "classical" period, its top period of reference, and, more specifically, its final volumes started a transition to what we can call the baroque zenith of *JoJo's Bizarre Adventure*, the transcendence of established principles.[71] As for Jotaro and Dio... their spirits will continue to guide (in the case of the former) and haunt (in the case of the latter) the saga for quite some time.

71. I'm not trying to claim that *Stardust Crusaders* presents exactly the same characteristics as classical art of the early modern period (like harmony and balance), but rather that we find, between the third and fourth parts of *JoJo*, the same transcendence of established norms as seen between the classical and baroque periods. As such, the terms "classical" and "baroque" here are not meant to be understood as strict equivalents to their meanings from early-modern art.

CHAPTER III.5: HIDDEN PLACE

Stand: Hidden Place

Have you ever had the experience, while out walking, of coming across a street
that doesn't appear on any map?
That's what's just happened. By turning the page, you've uncovered a hidden
chapter that doesn't appear in the table of contents.
Here, the normal rules don't apply.

To listen to while reading:
The sounds of the nearest video game arcade.

It was inevitable. We have to take some time to talk about the video game
released by Capcom in December 1998, in Japan's dark and noisy arcades,
simply entitled *JoJo no Kimyō na Bōken* (*JoJo's Venture* outside of Japan). It's not
the only video game to be adapted from the saga, of course, but it's probably
still the most emblematic, a veritable time capsule and a testimonial to the
extreme popularity of the manga's third part. It's also the best way to understand the concept of Stands at a glance.

This chapter is very personal for me, the author, because it was thanks to
this Capcom game that I got to know *JoJo*, at a time when nobody—or almost
nobody—was talking about Araki's work in the French-speaking world. So, you
can see these pages as an indulgence, an optional detour, or a "free space," the
only segment where we'll talk about video games, and also the only part that
will come in the form of a complete interview.

How and why did they bring *JoJo*, a free-spirited series, into the strict
confines of a fighting video game? And what was the end result? To answer
these questions, I talked with two video game connoisseurs. They know
Capcom like the backs of their hands and they relish each and every "*Ora
Ora.*" Thomas Loreille, a.k.a. "Neithan," and his fellow gamer Sébastien,
a.k.a. "TMDJC." Thomas founded the reference website *Bas Gros Poing* and,
before that, wrote as a journalist specializing in fighting games for *Red Bull*

and *Gamekult*. Sébastien also works for *Bas Gros Poing*, hosts the independent podcast *Rhythm Fighter*, was a web TV host for Webedia, and contributed to the mook *Pix'n Love*. Their words are golden, and here they are, unfiltered, in a fascinating dialogue.

In Japan, the third part of *JoJo* ended in *Jump* in 1992. Why did Capcom adapt it into a video game so much later, in 1998?[72]

Thomas: The game came out in 1998 because Capcom's new arcade system board, the CPS-3,[73] arrived in 1997–for its public version–and, at the time, it was common in the arcade segment to combine a hardware event with a game event. If you look back, you can see that for the CPS-1 system, it was *Street Fighter II* [editor's note: in 1991]. And for the CPS-2, there was a game adapted from another major franchise, *X-Men: Children of the Atom* [in 1994]. The idea is basically the same: take a well-known franchise, associate it with a well-known arcade system, and show Capcom's expertise. Because that's part of the reasoning too. To remind you, 1998 was the year of *Tekken 3*. And the Dreamcast came out that year, so it was also the year of *Soulcalibur*. At the time, Capcom did not at all see 3D as the end of 2D: they planned to keep making 2D games. And 2D fighting games that were a bit hardcore, like the *JoJo* games, still worked in Japan, but unfortunately not so much in the United States because, there, 3D had already pretty much won out in terms of popularity. So, we look at this with bewilderment and say to ourselves: "Umm... what exactly is the logic of making a game out of *JoJo*'s third part, which had ended five or six years previously? And why in 2D when 3D had already prevailed? And why on arcade hardware when game consoles work better?" There are lots of things that seem illogical to us, but it was a perfectly logical sales approach for Capcom at the time in Japan.

We know that Capcom took an interest in *JoJo* very early on and the series' influence is found in characters from the *Street Fighter* franchise, for example. That's also true for games from SNK, their main competitor at the time. So, why is it that *JoJo* wasn't adapted into a fighting game sooner? Were there any attempts to do so?

Sébastien: Absolutely not, there were no attempts before then. The game was created exactly when it was meant to be. The *JoJo* and Capcom universes have

---

72. For the sake of convenience, in this interview, we will consider the 1998 game and its update, *JoJo no Kimyō na Bōken – Mirai e no Isan* ("Heritage for the Future"), released in arcades in 1999, to be a single entity. Additionally, these games were ported—with varying levels of modification—for the Dreamcast and PlayStation consoles.
73. Capcom System III.

regularly influenced each other. There are even some characters whose inspiration is so pronounced—take Rose or Guile, for example, uh... *(uncomfortable laugh)* they're clearly tributes to Lisa Lisa and Polnareff. But that's simply because the Capcom designers used them as references. Although, as we know, *JoJo* has had great success and it's a very well-known manga, it still has—how do I put this?—a sort of "underground" quality to it. You can't compare it to a manga like *Dragon Ball* or *Naruto*. I have to say, there's something special about *JoJo* and its quirkiness; the manga has a certain "noble" quality to it.

Thomas: By which you mean that piggybacking on the *JoJo* franchise was an honor for them. For that matter, they had previously piggybacked on a Marvel franchise with *X-Men: Children of the Atom* for the CPS-2, and even though Marvel wasn't where it is today, it was still a big deal. The other star series for the CPS-2, *Darkstalkers* [started in 1994] was a vanity project for Capcom, sort of like they were saying, "hey, you think *Street Fighter* is all we can do? Then check this out: we're going to make a game with werewolves, vampires, a bee-woman, Little Red Riding Hood, etc." When you look at that series, you see an aesthetic, and even creative, escalation not seen elsewhere and that was needed for the *JoJo* video game. *Darkstalkers* doesn't reference *JoJo*, but it has the same energy and the same eccentricity. It has crazy characters, dazzling backgrounds, highly stylized animation, and more. At the time Capcom was still the greatest in terms of creating sprites[74] and upholding the 12 principles of animation—*Street Fighter III* proved this. And Capcom's DNA combined very nicely with *JoJo*'s DNA. If you look at the *JoJo* and *Darkstalkers* games, you'll see that they move the same way.

Sébastien: For me, *Darkstalkers* is really a blend of horror films, Disney animated movies, and *JoJo*. It has this synergy between worlds that aren't supposed to meet and that's why, in addition to the game's quality, to this day, *Darkstalkers* is beloved by many players.

Who initiated the project to make a *JoJo* game? Capcom or the owners of the franchise?

Sébastien: It was definitely Capcom that made the first move. As Thomas suggested, they were really looking for a game to help launch the CPS-3. Their idea was to focus first and foremost on the sound and animation, figuring that later, when the technology evolved, they could move to higher-resolution graphics.

---

74. Graphical elements made of pixels in 2D video games—in this case, a character.

Thomas: Which is what happened with *Guilty Gear X*, from Arc System Works, two years later.

Sébastien: Exactly. At Capcom, they often poked fun at it, they laughed at its animation, but I can tell you that internally–and this is something they won't share with the general public–they were jealous when they saw the first images from *Guilty Gear X*, and you have to admit, it's a very beautiful game. But clearly, Capcom and its CPS-3 focused most on animation. The problem is that takes an enormous amount of time... Moreover, you can see that in *JoJo* the animation is well below the standards of what Capcom did in other games: it's not super well animated–relatively speaking! They basically just focused on the Stands. They tried to enhance the manga, which is something that has since been done in other games, like, not that long ago, Arc System Works' *Dragon Ball FighterZ*.[75] The idea was to showcase the characters by figuring out what their "signature moves" would be. They also had to decide which panels of the manga to use to design their sprites. When you look at the sprites in the *JoJo* game, they're not actually very nice looking, and they're small. However, as usual, Capcom managed to come up with *the* moment, *the* sprite that makes you go, "Oh yeah, I recognize the universe now, I'm playing a manga!" They're very good at that.

When did the game's development begin?

Sébastien: The very first version presented was four months before the official release. As such, you might be tempted to say that the game was developed in less than a year. But, before that, they had to obtain the rights and get everyone on the same page. The *mangaka* had a right to review everything and, from what I understand, he was perfectly satisfied with the game. In any case, according to the information I've been able to gather, the parties got along great and the developers really enjoyed working on this project.

Thomas: Additionally, I'm sure you've noticed that the design of the characters was very uneven. If you look at Kakyoin, he has great poses... but he doesn't move very well, to tell the truth. Young Joseph, meanwhile, runs with his arms pinned to his sides... Compare that to Jotaro and Dio... There you have it! We can clearly see that some characters were stars and others were less important. (laughs) Which also explains why the development took so little time.

---

75. A fighting game released in 2018, generally hailed for its extreme visual faithfulness to the *Dragon Ball* saga, particularly the anime version of *Dragon Ball Z*.

Unlike more classic fighting stories, the battles in the *JoJo* manga are each their own full-fledged game, with rules determined by the powers of the characters, on the one hand, but also by additional factors, like the configuration of the setting. The fights are often very lopsided and, to get by, the characters take shortcuts: they use trickery or they find a detail in their surroundings that they can turn to their advantage... What remains of this spirit in the 1998 video game?

Thomas: If you know how to play the game, you can gain the upper hand. I'll put it that way! (laughs) But certainly, the game is unbalanced. It's completely busted.

Sébastien: Definitely. It's no surprise that a second version was released less than a year later. In the first, there were characters who were totally messed up. But to answer your question... What remained of that spirit? I don't think Capcom intentionally created a game in which some characters are really much stronger than others. It wasn't tested enough. That's the big issue with this type of production: when you take on a *shōnen* legend—and the same is true for American comics and even Franco-Belgian comics—how do you manage to make a game that's coherent and that everyone can enjoy, without it being just a battle between "the good guy and the bad guy," while all the other characters just play bit parts? That's really difficult.

Thomas: The character Pet Shop is unavailable in tournament mode, for example. Because, of course, he flies, so you can't deal him a low blow. You can't open up his defenses! The same is true for Iggy. I think that he's permitted in tournament mode, but it's ridiculous.

Sébastien: Depending on the tournament, yes, he can be allowed. But in certain ones, he's prohibited.

Thomas: "Black Polnareff" is another one who has a counter that takes away a ton of life and that's active for a very long time.

So, it really remains up to chance.

Thomas: Yes, totally. Other than certain situations established by the developers, like the possibility of sandwiching your adversary between the Stand and the Stand user. In cases like that, you have very elaborate reversals of the situation. For example, on the one hand, Star Platinum shouts *"Ora Ora Ora Ora!,"* and at the same time, Jotaro strikes. Other than that, no, there's not what you expect, like exploiting a detail in the background, with a character saying:

"Aha, you didn't notice, but I placed such-and-such thing in such-and-such place!"

In spite of all that, do trickery and deception pay off in this game?

Thomas: No, it's still a classic fighting game; it's not an RPG... I'm not really sure how to put it.

Sébastien: No, that pretty much covers it. We can draw a parallel with *Dragon Ball FighterZ*, which you'll hear me mention a lot because I think that they did something that no one else had managed to do before, in terms of accentuating a series. But to tell the truth, even though they did a great job, they had the advantage of Toriyama's work being super "easy" to work with. Compared to *JoJo*, it's much easier to align all of the characters and put them on the same level. In *JoJo*, you sometimes have five whole pages to explain a power, and they'll say that in such-and-such conditions, this will happen. What I mean to say is that, that's what you expect as a reader; you're happy to learn this information and see how this twist plays out. But you can't put those five pages of explanation in a fighting game. You're forced to alter the manga so that it fits into the scope of this type of game. From a distance, you get the impression that *JoJo* is an idiotic fighting manga, and so making a fighting game out of it seems logical. But that's not the case! *JoJo* is much more than that, and fighting games, too, are much more than just two characters "duking it out." So the fact of putting the two together is complicated.

If they had to stick to the power dynamics of the manga, it would be impossible to balance the characters in the game. Dio and his ability to suspend time would beat everyone. As such, the way in which his power was reproduced in the game is quite clever—Dio teleports himself, or sometimes he can move freely while his opponent is stuck. This power remains strong, impressive, but it doesn't destroy the game's balance; it doesn't come close to allowing Dio to win every time.

Sébastien: Some people, in Mugen games,[76] have played around with things like that and it results in unbeatable characters who can stop time—including on the game clock—and prevent their opponents from moving. It's funny to watch when a character takes down 400 opponents in a row. It's the "artistic, funny" side of things. But that doesn't make for a good game.

---

76. System for creating amateur fighting games.

In the manga, the strength of Soul Sacrifice [a.k.a. Devo] comes from his hatred for his enemies. If you hit him, his strength increases. Do we see those same mechanics in the game's Soul Sacrifice?

Sébastien: I don't remember anything like that. Unlike in other games, like *Samurai Spirits*, for example.

Thomas: I was going to say the same thing. At the time, fighting games already had mechanics meant to "stir emotions" and in the *Samurai Spirits* series, all of the characters have a bar that turns red as they take hits. Then, the character gets very mad and hits harder, earning a super attack. It's a very *shōnen* style. Perhaps more *shōnen* than *JoJo*, specifically. As for Soul Sacrifice, I don't think the game has anything like that.

Are there "bizarre" things in the game, compared to other fighting games from the same era?

Thomas: Oh yes!

Sébastien: Plenty, including one huge thing Thomas mentioned a moment ago: the fact that there's a character that you can't knock down because he doesn't have feet! Sure, you can find that in other games, but for bosses that you can't play as.

Thomas: Unfairness is something that you can find in fighting games. But only on the computer side. Because if a human can take advantage of that, that will really annoy players. Other than that, in terms of bizarre aspects, the Stand mechanics were still unusual at the time. The fact of controlling two characters at once and being able to sandwich your opponent between the two.

Sébastien: There had been "fakes" in some games, like Rose in the *Street Fighter Alpha* series who could multiply herself with "Soul Illusion." In *JoJo*, the fact of controlling not just one character, but two at once, that was unheard of at the time. At least not like that.

Thomas: What was original was that for characters who have Stands, you had two characters in one. Depending on the situation, you can choose whether or not to call on your Stand. You can play as Jotaro, but also as "Jotaro with his Stand" and some of Jotaro's hits are then replaced with the Stand's. And then you can separate the Stand from Jotaro: during a super attack, the Stand cries "*Ora Ora Ora!*," but you can move Jotaro around independently and strike at the same time. I may be mistaken, but I think that was relatively new at the time.

Today, we have plenty of things like that, notably in the series *Guilty Gear*, where you find a character inspired by "tower defenses,"[77] who places towers from which little guys pop out and sweep across the screen. However, at the time, there wasn't so much experimentation. I'm tempted to say that's because they hadn't reached the peak of one-upmanship. Today, if you want to stand out with a character in a fighting game, it's very hard to do.

Sébastien: Before that, what had been done was maybe creating characters with two stances. But you just played as one character who behaved in different ways.

Thomas: That was done a lot in many games. There were also follow-up attacks: you land a first attack and then you have the option of a second, a third, a fourth... But two characters in one, or separated, that was still unusual.

Sébastien: And then there's the fact that you can play as a dog in this game! Another awful character, by the way. (laughs) There are lots of moves that hit all of the characters except him: you can't get him with them because he goes right under them!

That same year, in *Tekken 3*, the dinosaur Gon[78] was also a character who was smaller than the others, right?

Thomas: Yeah, but Gon is sort of a special case. He was a bonus character and he was still relatively large and could match up with the way a 3D fighting game works. It's a little technical, but in 3D fighting games, "stand punches" don't hit characters who are crouching. And that makes sense: it's designed that way. In a 2D game, the stand punch is not a punch that hits "high," but rather at a "medium" height, and thus hits characters who are crouching. Normally, in *JoJo*, a stand punch should hit Iggy, but it doesn't. And that's not normal! (laughs) What's funny is that people have played this game seriously, when really, above all, it's a game meant for fans, and it shows. At the time, they still weren't necessarily thinking about competition, e-sports, that sort of thing. They made games that had a good vibe, to make fans happy. That's it. That's what mattered most.

That's the whole paradox: it's a game for fans, but it doesn't reproduce the feeling of the *JoJo* manga; it remains a "true" fighting game. In fact,

---

77. Video game that involves placing towers along a path to prevent waves of enemies from reaching a base.
78. Hero of a manga by Masashi Tanaka.

the game imagines what it would look like if *JoJo*'s characters hit each other constantly...

Sébastien: Very well said!

... And yet, that's not what *JoJo* is. Creating both a true "Capcom-style" fighting game and a true *JoJo* game seems impossible.

Sébastien: This game has one foot in both worlds, that's its big problem.

Still, it has a good reputation in the fighting game community, right?

Sébastien: I'm going to say something that might ruffle some feathers, because indeed, it has gotten very good reviews in our community: I personally think that some of its aspects are overrated. Given that a lot of us like *JoJo* and a lot of people like Capcom productions, naturally, when a game offers a combination of the two and it's good—because, to be clear, the game's not bad!—well, it makes sense that you want to say: "What? You don't know this game? You've never played it? It's so good!" And then there's the "cool factor" of knowing something that was sort of underground. But to tell the truth, if you took exactly the same game with different sprites, without the *JoJo* franchise... I am thoroughly convinced that it would not have the ratings that it has currently in our community. The game has lots of flaws that are really obnoxious if you fight someone who knows how to play. And sometimes you end up playing the same characters over and over: even if you rule out those that are completely awful, there are characters who just aren't worth much if you're playing to win.

Thomas: We've seen the same issue in Capcom's Marvel games. If *Marvel vs. Capcom 2* weren't a game with Marvel and Capcom in it, the game wouldn't have had the success that it's seen in competitions. It's one of the most interesting games from a competitive point of view, in spite of its best efforts, because it's "busted." So, there's also the pleasure of playing as *the* character that you love and watching them holler whenever you want. You don't need to wait for him to go *"Ora Ora Ora!"* in an episode of the anime. You launch a super move every five minutes and that makes you fall in love with the game! (laughs)

Sébastien, you were saying that *JoJo* is well liked in the fighting game community. However, in that same community, did the quirky side of the characters bias people against the game?

Sébastien: No. Not at all. Once again, I'll say something that might ruffle some feathers, but there are leaders within our community. Whether you like them or not, when someone like Guillaume Dorison or Ken Bogard [two prominent French video game commentators] says something, lots of people will approve of the game or manga they're talking about without ever having played or read it. And *JoJo* is really a manga that, I don't know why—most likely because of its quality and lots of other things—has really resonated with French people. What's astounding is that an entire French community got to know this manga quite naturally, very early on, even before Tonkam began publishing *Video Girl Ai* [in 1994, when manga were first published in French]. But really by word of mouth. You didn't have Dorothée [a French children's TV host] presenting an episode of *JoJo* every Wednesday morning; it wasn't mainstream. So, when a guy like Ken Bogard says that *JoJo* is great and presents the game in one way or another, and then the game is presented at Stunfest,[79] nobody wants to say that it's not good. And while sometimes there are homophobic comments like, "oh, that guy plays like a fag," or, "so-and-so is such a fairy," in this case, there's a sort of general consensus to say: *JoJo* is off limits! *JoJo* is really a treasure. Moreover, anyone who says that it's garbage will have tons of people come for him, including people who've never read the manga!

Thomas: And that results in a really funny situation, also... Sometimes, I see people shaming others for discovering *JoJo* through the anime! Or through the PS3 game developed by CyberConnect2.[80] Lots of people discovered *JoJo* through that game. You always see that in communities: those guys who try to judge whether or not you're a real fan based on the fact that you were born in 1981, or things like that. Besides that, in terms of the effeminate aspect... No, to tell the truth, all fighting games have always had some homoerotic tendencies, no matter the series.

Sébastien: All Japanese productions.

Thomas: Right, in *The King of Fighters*, for example, there are lots of characters who are extremely effeminate and who are still played by people who, clearly, don't like gay people or think that it's unnatural. I've known people like that and they have no problem playing as Benimaru. (laughs) Additionally, you have to remember that fighting games are a type of video game that sells you an illusion of power. That's the goal. And if the game succeeds in doing that, if it's fun, if it makes you feel good, if you feel powerful while playing it, then it will have a good chance of succeeding, even if the franchise isn't well known or if it has things that you don't like. Sometimes the bottle doesn't matter, as

79. A major video game festival in Rennes, France, that hosts fighting game competitions.
80. *JoJo's Bizarre Adventure: All Star Battle*, a fighting game released in 2013 in Japan and in 2014 in Western countries, that features characters from all parts of the saga.

long as it gets you drunk. And as it happens, *JoJo* gets the job done: if you play as Jotaro and use "stand medium," he does a sort of knee strike, as if he's too lazy to lift his entire leg, and you say to yourself, "Oh my God, that's so Jotaro, that's exactly like him!" And at the same time that the move hits, the other guy draws back in an exaggerated way, as if he just got hit in the leg with a scooter. (laughs) And the sound is like, "shplaaa!" I mean, it works!

Sébastien: Yeah, the sound effects in this game are incredible.

The game's PlayStation version has something special: "Story mode" incorporated passages from the manga that don't adapt to the classic fighting-game model. These passages come in the form of battles with a modified system or mini-games—the *"Innerspace"* adventure inside of Joseph's body becomes a shooting game, for example, and there's the gambling against D'Arby. Have you played this mode?

Sébastien: Yes and, as it happens, I think it's extremely well done. They drew a lot of inspiration from the work they did for the Japanese version of *Rival Schools*.[81] And it was honestly a great idea to put that in there.

Thomas: There's also something to take into account. Why did they adapt that particular story arc? Because I think that when you get past the third season, there are fewer and fewer fighting Stands and more and more Stands who use strategy, deception, etc.

Actually, the manga turned in that direction as early as the second half of *Stardust Crusaders*.

Thomas: Yeah, I was going to say, you mentioned D'Arby. When you watch the two halves of the third story arc in the anime, there's a real discord. First you feel like you're watching "X-Men: the road trip," then they have to play against this guy in poker, then against another in a video game. And when you look at the fourth part, it's even less adaptable: the Stand that traps you in your own feelings of guilt or the Stand of the restaurant owner...

In 2002, Capcom adapted the fifth part into a peculiar action game: it has fighting, but it also has little puzzles, things you have to trigger in the backgrounds. Really, it's more of a *JoJo*-style game than the one from

---

81. A fighting game set in a school environment, released in arcades in 1997. The PlayStation version (released in 1998 in the different regions) has a second disk that offers, among other things, various mini-games.

1998. But when it comes down to it, you have to wonder if it's possible to create a true *JoJo* video game. Even if you set aside the current trends or the financial aspects, is it really possible to adapt the series?

Thomas: Yeah, you give it to Tarō Yokō[82] and presto! I think you would need that kind of creator who would gradually break all of the game's conventions, just like *JoJo* breaks all of the conventions of its own universe.

Sébastien: You would have to break the fourth wall at many different moments... And you'd have to work hard to incorporate everything from the manga. In reality, I feel like if you don't take sales into account, everything is adaptable. You could create a *Berserk*[83] fighting game, even though, logically, you'd know that it would have to have unbeatable characters. So, yeah, you could. But not while remaining within the conventions of *Street Fighter II*. And that's the big problem today: by "inventing" the modern fighting game, *Street Fighter II* also set the rules for such games. And it can be very difficult to break the rules—the difficulty is not necessarily doing it well, but finding an audience for it.

In the end, what are the best parts of Capcom's *JoJo* fighting game?

Thomas: What it comes down to is, do you feel like they did right by the franchise? When you play the game, do you feel like you're in the manga or in the anime? Personally, I feel like that's absolutely the case for the 1998-'99 game, and that's why I love it. I really enjoy playing it a lot. It's not a game I'd like to play "seriously" in competitions. I play it on Friday nights with friends after a few beers.

Sébastien: I completely agree. It's like I was saying a bit ago: it has one foot in both worlds, meaning that it struggles to really draw in people who play classic fighting games or people who like the manga, but don't play fighting games, but it does have that niche of players...

Thomas: ... who like both. (laughs)

Sébastien: Yes, and, above all, who *really* love both. And I think that in that sense, Capcom succeeded in doing exactly what it intended to. Even though the sprites are small, you immediately recognize the characters. It's a bit like certain older *Dragon Ball* games that really missed the mark, but they

---

82. A video game designer known for his daring titles (like *NieR: Automata*) with unusual artistic choices.
83. A famous dark fantasy manga by Kentarō Miura.

played to the "heart," making players say: "Yay! I can finally play the anime I love!" I've personally played some games that were much worse than this *JoJo* game because they belonged to a particular franchise. In this case, I think that Capcom achieved a real feat by creating a game that's fun to play and that's really what you'd expect from a fighting game in the *JoJo* franchise.

What do you think is the legacy of this game in the world of fighting games?

Thomas: Today, everyone adapts comics and anime into fighting games like Capcom did with *X-Men* and *JoJo's Bizarre Adventure*, working off of—or even referencing—existing material. But as I see it, Capcom had more freedom and was able to add its own special touch, whereas in many more recent adaptations, that would be seen as a violation or distortion of the franchise. The characters in the *X-Men* and *JoJo* games have animations that are really astute and highly expressive, with a very elegant design, poses that are completely impossible, but deliberately made as an artistic choice... When other studios adapt franchises, like Arc System Works with *Dragon Ball*, it's as if they're too careful, sticking too close, whereas when you look at the *JoJo* game, it's missing many animation steps and lots of other stuff... but on a visceral level, it's just right. It may not be perfect, but it's more expressive than most adaptations we see today. In any case, that's my opinion.

Sébastien: What you're saying is interesting because today, a lot of people prefer the amateur game *Hyper Dragon Ball Z* [developed by fans, not officially licensed, and distributed online since 2014] over *Dragon Ball FighterZ*. In the fan game, the manga was graphically "mistreated." When it comes down to it, it has a very "Capcom" aspect to it. Not only in terms of gameplay, but also in terms of the way the characters are animated.

Thomas: Yeah, I agree. That fan game totally fits into the legacy of the *JoJo* game—and of *Street Fighter III* and *Darkstalkers*. It has a really elegant and visually unique side to it. Today, I think that IP right owners have more power and developers are thus much more careful. They take fewer risks and don't stray from the expected style. *JoJo* and *Hyper Dragon Ball Z* are games made by designers and not by animators in the Japanese animation world. They don't make cels; they make ink drawings. And today, no one does that.

Remarks collected on February 28, 2019.

CHAPTER IV: THE HOUSE THAT KIRA BUILT
(1992-1995: JOJO'S BIZARRE ADVENTURE, PART 4)

Stand: Mimikry
Sometimes, it feels like an invisible force is altering reality.
If that happens, keep calm and carry on.

To listen to while reading:

Prince – *1999*
Pink Floyd – *Shine On You Crazy Diamond*
Pink Floyd – *Echoes*
Talking Heads – *Psycho Killer*
Queen – *Killer Queen*

"Their destiny was foreordained. 1999." A message that adorns each cover of the manga *X*, the unfinished masterpiece by the famous collective of female authors known as CLAMP. Having started in 1992 (and never finished), this '90s classic is about a great struggle that presages the end of the world, in a sort of modern retelling of the Book of Revelation, set in Tokyo. As such, *X* is a series that's representative of its time period. In those final years of the second millennium, the world was in a weird place. Fear of humanity's decline ran through people's minds and expressed itself in various ways: some feared the "Y2K bug," for example, which would supposedly take down all computer systems, causing airplanes to fall from the sky and banks to collapse; meanwhile, others worried about the words of Nostradamus, who supposedly predicted that the world would end as the new millennium started. In Japan, Tokyo was constantly being destroyed in pop culture, whether it be

in manga, in the *Teito Monogatari* novels, or in the video game series *Shin Megami Tensei*, just to name a few famous examples. After the economic bubble burst in 1991, a cloud of disenchantment began to hover over Japan in the 1990s. That cloud only got heavier with two tragic events: the major earthquake in the city of Kobe on January 17, 1995, and the sarin gas attack in the Tokyo Metro on March 20, 1995, orchestrated by the leader of the cult Aum Shinrikyo. This leader, convinced that Armageddon was imminent, presented this attack as a "holy attempt to elevate the doomed souls of this world to a higher spiritual stage,"[84] with the idea that only members of the cult and people killed by them could escape the fires of hell. Additionally, in the late '80s, the image of manga culture was dragged through the mud by a new kind of killer: the *otaku* Tsutomu Miyazaki, a dangerous pedophile, cannibal, and necrophiliac, who was supposedly influenced by reading or watching violent content. Following that case, the word "otaku" spread across Japan, charged with a negative connotation. These large-scale tragedies may not have been correlated—moreover, in Japan, most people just see disasters as natural phenomena, not as signs of the end of the world, caused by a wrathful god—but they nonetheless helped establish a feeling of distress across the country and truly marked the end of an era. It was as if modern civilization had reached an advanced stage of decline.

The fourth part of *JoJo*, which debuted in *Shōnen Jump* on May 4, 1992, also reflects this ambiance. Hirohiko Araki, however, did not envision a massive apocalypse, like in CLAMP's manga, but rather a latent evil threatening a community. The end of *a* world, rather than the end of *the* world. In a story stretching over 18 volumes that contrasts with the epic voyage of *Stardust Crusaders*, the author sets the scene with contaminated air poisoning a small town in Japan in 1999. Of course, this year is not without meaning: "[The fourth part] takes place in 1999, a very mysterious year because not only does it close out a century, but it also concludes the second millennium. People have always feared certain dates, and when I realized that we were drawing close to that time of transition, it intrigued me,"[85] said Araki a few months after finishing the fourth part. Moreover, setting the fourth part in 1999 allowed him to anchor the story in a time period that would be easily relatable—just seven years in the future from the time its first volume was published, which is quite close in time—while adding in a dose of imagination. From a more mundane point of view, it can also be seen as a reference to the album *1999* by Prince, Araki's favorite musical artist, who, incidentally, shares the same birthday (June 7).

84. "Tokyo sarin attack: Aum Shinrikyo cult leaders executed," *BBC.com*, July 6, 2018. https://www.bbc.com/news/world-asia-43395483
85. *Kappa Magazine* No. 54, December 1996.

Right off the bat, the first words of the story arc set the tone for this strange time and its subtle aftertaste of impending darkness: "It feels like 1999 only just started, but April is already here. Here in Japan and overseas, the media is in an uproar over Nostradamus's prophesies of terror befalling humanity and such, but for most regular people... well, maybe life isn't carefree, but it goes on as normal." These are the thoughts of Koichi—doesn't that name sound familiar?—at the very beginning of *Diamond is Unbreakable*.[86] He's a scrawny 15-year-old boy who's walking through the streets of Morioh, a fictitious town in eastern Japan, heading towards his new high school. A few minutes later, his life will veer in a new direction from which there's not coming back.

Diamond in the rough

Joseph Joestar, you naughty boy. Sometime before the events of *Stardust Crusaders*, the virile grandpa had a child out of wedlock, in 1983, with a young Japanese woman named Tomoko. For a long time, this son remained a secret, but at the start of *Diamond is Unbreakable*, Joseph's infidelity is brought to light and the Joestar family is forced to deal with this scandal. For this reason, Jotaro, now an adult and a seafaring adventurer who specializes in marine animals, goes to Morioh, where the illegitimate child, Josuke Higashikata,[87] lives, in order to inform him that he will one day inherit one third of Joseph's fortune. By chance, Koichi (he at first fills the same role as his namesake in *Māshonen B.T.*), witnesses, to his astonishment, a brawl between the two men. It turns out that Josuke is a particularly gifted Stand user. And it makes perfect sense that Joseph's son also possesses this power: Josuke, too, belongs to the Joestar bloodline and, like Holly Kujo, a Stand awoke within him at the time of the events of *Stardust Crusaders*, putting him in a state between life and death for 40 days—he was four years old at the time. To his great surprise, Jotaro discovers that Josuke is very well-mannered and perfectly polite, apologizing for the fact that his existence may have made things difficult for his estranged family. But Jotaro makes a mistake. Just like you can never call Marty McFly, the hero of *Back to the Future*, a "chicken," it is strictly forbidden to disrespect Josuke's hair, his flamboyant *furyō* pompadour that defies the laws of gravity. By daring to say, "Save this ridiculous hair talk for another time," JoJo the Third triggers the anger of the Fourth, who is... his uncle, actually—it's strange to say, but that's how the family tree grew.

---

86. Once again, this international title was given after the fact.
87. In Japanese, the character "*suke*" (助) can also be read as "*jo*." As such, the character's first name can be read as "JoJo," signaling his status as our new hero. Moreover, Higashikata (東方) means "to the east", making our hero "JoJo from the East" (of Japan).

After a few macho exchanges between Star Platinum and Josuke's Stand, Shining Diamond (a.k.a. Crazy Diamond)—which in addition to its fighting abilities can repair destroyed objects (with no guarantee that they'll return to their original form!)—Jotaro explains that a madman is lurking in Morioh. A man named "Angelo"—ironically, this is the nickname given to him by the press—a child killer and rapist, is hiding somewhere in the area and poses a threat to the people close to Josuke. Once this initial threat is cornered, we learn that the killer, who has a Stand, was struck by a strange arrow that awoke this power in him. Araki connects this idea to the events of *Stardust Crusaders*—we can see this as either revisionism, filling in a plot hole, or deepening the universe, the choice is yours—and explains how Dio suddenly acquired a Stand in the late 1980s. The old woman Enyaba, his ally in Egypt, got her hands on an ancient bow, a magical artifact whose accompanying arrow triggers the appearance of a Stand in individuals capable of handling it. Starting in *Diamond is Unbreakable*, Araki presents Stands as abilities acquired by a specific stimulus and, with few exceptions, will no longer introduce characters who have the power innately, like Avdol, who stated that he got his Stand naturally.

Thus, ten years after *Stardust Crusaders*, on the other side of the world, Dio's shadow continues to loom over the Joestars. Even though he never makes an appearance—this time, the vampire really is dead, once and for all—Dio is still the indirect cause of the havoc that occurs in Morioh. In the second volume of part four, Josuke confronts the Nijimura brothers, two bad boys, the older of whom, Keicho, has gathered considerable information about Stands over the span of a decade, to the point of obtaining the bow and arrow from Enyaba. Why this obsession? Because he's trying to find a Stand user who would be capable of... killing his father. A decade earlier, the brothers' father let Dio implant a seed of flesh in him, becoming one of Dio's underlings in exchange for money. Why? Because while everyone was enjoying the virtues of the economic bubble, Mr. Nijimura had missed the boat and, drowning in debt, had no other choice but to accept Dio's offer when the vampire, in the '80s, was looking for allies all over the world. Alas, when the Joestars' nemesis died, the seeds of his flesh went mad and the Nijimura patriarch's body began to mutate, transforming into a mass of flesh incapable of recognizing his sons. A hideous creature that's impossible to kill, thanks to Dio's immortal cells,[88] even if you crush his head. For this reason, Keicho began firing arrows, a bit randomly, at the inhabitants of Morioh, in order to create Stand users. In reality, it seems that Araki improvised this motivation (killing the father) in the moment: in the first volume, we see Keicho trigger Angelo's power before telling him, "Do as

---

88. I think it's fair for us to question this element of the plot: why are these seeds of flesh immortal while Dio himself is not?

you please: have fun, take lots of money, kill... let your desires run wild." Fairly inconsistent with the version of the elder Nijimura we meet later. Whatever the case may be, creating Stands by shooting people blindly was not the best idea, since Chili Pepper (a.k.a. Red Hot Chili Peppers), a brand-new, electricity-based Stand—notably, he can move through electrical circuits—pops out, deals Keicho a fatal blow, and runs off with the bow and arrow. Drawn by the artifact and its possibilities, his mysterious user plans to use it to achieve his ambitions.

Thus, ten years after *Stardust Crusaders*, on the other side of the world, Dio's shadow continues to loom over the Joestars. Even though he never makes an appearance—this time, the vampire really is dead, once and for all—Dio is still the indirect cause of the havoc that occurs in Morioh. In the second volume of part four, Josuke confronts *(Having déjà-vu? Don't worry.)* the Nijimura brothers, two bad boys, the older of whom, Keicho, has gathered considerable information about Stands over the span of a decade, to the point of obtaining *(Stay calm, everything will be fine.)* the bow and arrow from Enyaba Only Time. Why this obsession, Jean-Claude? Because he's trying to find a Staand user who would be capable of... fafafather. A decadent earlier, the brothers' father let Dio implant a Hieronymus Bosch of flesh in him, becoming *(You have entered a time loop created by the Stand Mimikry.)* one of Dio's underlings in exchange for moneybags. Why? Because while everyone no one everyone no one everyone no one everyone was enjoying the virtues of the economic moneymaker, Mr. Nijimura had missed the boat and, drowning in debt, had no other *(Mimikry can't read my comments in italics; he doesn't know that I'm helping you.)* choice but to accept Dead Dead Dio's DiDiDiDi Diostruction offer when the vampire! in the '80s! was looking for allies! Alas, when the JOESTARS' nemesis died, *(To get out of this defective loop, follow my instructions.)* the seeds of his flash went madhouse and the Nijimura patriarch's body began to dance, dancing into a mass of dancing incapable of dancing his sons. A kill creature that's impossibly hideous to kill, thanks to hideous Dio's hideous immortal cells, even if you crush his hideous. For this hideous, began hideous arrows, a bit randomly, *(Close your eyes, count to three, and turn the page.)*

That's the direction set by the first batch of volumes, which runs until the end of the battle against the user of Chili Pepper (*JJBA* vol. 34, American *DiU* vol. 3), a rocker named Akira Otoishi–who, with his purple hair and long line of make-up crossing his eye, has an appearance clearly based off of Japanese musician Kenji Ohtsuki.[89] In this segment, the narrative structure varies greatly from *Stardust Crusaders*. Everything revolves around the idea of latent threats hiding somewhere in the town, as well as the principle of Stand users being unconsciously drawn to one another, which is much more logical on the scale of a town than the encounters between Stand users in the middle of nowhere seen in the third part. The relationship with time has changed: urgency no longer drives the story. Everything takes place in rhythm with the characters' movements. Before encountering Akira Otoishi, Josuke and his allies–Jotaro, Koichi, and the reformed Okuyasu–come across the residents of Morioh who have been struck by the arrow, who form a diverse group of people (and animals!), some well-intentioned and others not so much. And unlike the journey to Cairo, Araki offers an unpredictable story line. In *Diamond is Unbreakable*, anything can happen. Which is very exciting. For example, Koichi, in a sort of remix of the Stephen King novel *Misery*, is faced with a crazed high school girl named Yukako Yamagishi who's enamored with him and holds him prisoner in a remote house, subjecting him to a (much too) rigorous lifestyle to turn him into "a fine man"! In that same volume, the fourth of part four (*JJBA* vol. 32), we see the signs of the pure excellence that will come to characterize *Diamond is Unbreakable*: an abundance of ideas, off-the-wall humor, suspense prominently featured (which, I'll remind you, is the direction that Araki always wanted to go in), a flawless visual impact, and rich personalities.

Why this drastic change in narrative construction compared to *Stardust Crusaders*? It actually all started with a series of unused ideas for enemies from the third part, in which the adversaries were more of the "search and destroy" variety, pursuing the team of heroes. At the time, Araki also wanted to create opponents who would wait calmly for their prey to come to their home or place of business. Like spiders sitting in their web. We see a few of these in *Stardust Crusaders*, but filling the plot with this sort of enemy didn't fit with the concept of the third part. In 2006, Araki spoke about what was happening behind the scenes: "I had a lot of these ideas left over, and so I thought that I could probably use all of them within a single town. There were various incidents back then, such as a case of a serial killer, that sent huge shockwaves across Japan. The feeling of your neighbor possibly being a serial killer was the perfect atmosphere, so I used that idea when positioning lots

---

89. Hirohiko Araki and Ohtsuki actually met during a joint interview published in 1993. The interview (in Japanese) and the photos that go with it are available on the blog *JoJo no Kimyō na Kenkyūjo*, "*JoJo*'s Bizarre Laboratory": http://blog.livedoor.jp/jojolab/archives/39762265.html.

of Stand users around the town. That's basically how part four was born."[90] So, to answer the question, "why did the *JoJo* saga continue beyond the initial trilogy?," we have a mundane response, to say the least: because there was leftover material! In any case, we understand where the idea for Antonio Trussardi's odd restaurant in volume three (*DiU* American edition; *JJBA* vol. 33) comes from, as well as how we got the transmission tower-*cum*-prison in volumes seven and eight (*JJBA* vol. 42-43), an incident in which an eccentric resident of the town draws Josuke and his companions into a Stand in the form of... an electrical transmission tower, from which they can't escape after entering its perimeter. This also explains how *Diamond is Unbreakable* got that unique ambiance giving the feeling that there's a predator hiding in the shadows. Like in CLAMP's *X*, which began the same year, the insecurities of the time shaped Araki's story. In short, they are both manga that embody the spirit of the "end of the millennium," but using distinct registers.

In any case, Josuke manages to eliminate the threat from Akira Otoishi. To be more specific, the rocker ends up behind bars, because in part four, the heroes are not cowboys; they don't kill their adversaries. However, his incarceration is not enough to purify the small town's air once and for all; the tranquility restored to Morioh is only on the surface, and a much deeper threat remains to be discovered. In Morioh, an abnormally high number of people have disappeared and no one seems to care... Big mistake, dear townspeople.

This city will eat you alive

"This is the town where I live—Morioh. Morioh is a commuter town that saw rapid development in the early 1980s," Koichi tells us. Commuter town for what city? One that we simply know by its initial, "S." S for Sendai, of course! Hirohiko Araki's hometown. We can consider Morioh (In Japanese, *Moriō-chō*) to be a suburb of the city of S (the Japanese version calls it *S-shi*). In Japanese, the suffixes "-*chō*" and "-*shi*" both refer to municipalities, with the former being for smaller ones and the latter being for larger ones. However, this nuance doesn't have exact equivalents outside of Japan, especially since the meaning of "-*chō*" can vary according to the prefecture, and can sometimes be used for a neighborhood, like the famous Kabukichō district of Tokyo! In English, we would make this distinction by calling Morioh a town and S a city. Araki likely disguised the names to avoid offending anyone. He probably was afraid of drawing the ire of his hometown by depicting Sendai as a hotbed of crime. However, this fear was clearly unfounded given that, since part four was

90. Interview of Araki conducted for the video game *Phantom Blood* (2006), released for the PlayStation 2 in Japan only, for the 20th anniversary of the series.

published, Sendai has proudly hosted events tied to *JoJo's Bizarre Adventure*, like an exhibition for the saga's 25th anniversary in 2012, or "JoJo Fest," held from August 12 to September 10, 2017, offering activities and places decorated in honor of the series. During both events, organizers distributed a newspaper called *Morioh Shimpō*, a knock-off of the real-life Sendai newspaper *Kahoku Shimpō*, and the 2012 edition of the paper included a joint interview between Hirohiko Araki and... his character Rohan Kishibe!

Growing up, Araki got to know a version of Sendai that was seen as ancient and filled with history. However, in the 1980s, development of a new residential area began and it was this environment that inspired Morioh in *Diamond is Unbreakable*. When Araki saw all of those beautiful new houses with warm lighting shining from the windows, he felt a sort of unease. It was as if those immaculate facades were hiding something terrible.[91] Who knew what all those newcomers living in those houses were up to? That feeling, along with the scandalous stories of serial killers making headline news, gave rise to the idea of evil lurking in the background. On top of that was the influence of Stephen King novels: in the '80s and '90s, Araki read many of these and, unsurprisingly, he names *Misery* as one of his favorites. In this case, we can see how King's work is more deeply infused into the series: the *mangaka* didn't stop at just visual references, as was the case with the car from *Christine* in *Stardust Crusaders*. Araki reproduces sensations similar to those found in the novelist's horror-thrillers, like the underlying–and well-founded–fear that pervades the fictitious town of Derry in the novel *It* (1986). The town in *Diamond is Unbreakable* also has the feel of an American suburb, with large, quiet residential streets lined with Western-style houses. However, while the appearance of Morioh doesn't match the "postcard" image of Japan, it's worth mentioning that you absolutely can find such settings in the country and Morioh was inspired by real places, particularly the Izumi Park Town residential district, but also various other neighborhoods of Sendai.[92] That said, even though the author depicts an ordinary Japanese environment–that, in principle, is more familiar to Japanese readers than England or Egypt–and draws inspiration from some specific places, there remains a certain foreign quality in his town that comes from how he stylizes the setting and certain details, like the very European stone bridge on page 32 of volume one (*DiU* American edition; *JJBA* vol. 29). We should also note that director Takashi Miike mainly shot his live-action adaptation of *Diamond is Unbreakable* (2017)

---

91. Remarks by the author in a Japanese special edition ("*Jump Remix*") of *Diamond is Unbreakable*, published in 2004.
92. In an interview given to the official website of the Hirose River, Araki also mentions the area of Tsurugaya New Town ("new towns" are totally new bedroom communities) and the north of Matsushima (a coastal town northeast of Sendai) as references. http://hirosegawa-net.com/interview/new/18_01.html.

in the Spanish town of Sitges, Catalonia, probably to again give the setting an exotic flavor.

While Morioh is based on Sendai and its surrounding area, Araki gives his fictional town a number of unique characteristics. It's filled with unusual businesses, like the famous restaurant "Trattoria Trussardi" and Aya Tsuji's beauty salon (both managed by users of peaceful Stands). The author also gives the town urban legends and offbeat tourist sites, like "Boyoyoing Cape." This last place was created at the end of volume two (*DiU* American edition; *JJBA* vol. 32) when Koichi—whose last name is actually Hirose, like the emblematic river that runs through Sendai and by which Araki would play as a child—uses Reverb (a.k.a. Echoes), his incredible Stand capable of manipulating sound effects, to place a "boing!" on a pointed rock to prevent his torturer-*cum*-admirer Yukako from being impaled. Thus, with a "boing!," Yukako bounces off the rock. This gives rise to a legend among local fishermen who begin praying every morning toward the "sacred" cape to bring them good luck. This kind of detail makes Araki's town very charming. It has a soul. There's something familiar about it. Not so much because it's inspired by a real-life model; more because it establishes an imaginary setting that, over the course of several volumes, becomes familiar.

Wild hearts never die

Did you notice? In the final volumes of *Stardust Crusaders*, the symbol of the heart becomes ubiquitous. It appears on the clothing of characters—Dio, D'Arby the Younger, Cool Ice (a.k.a. Vanilla Ice)—and is also featured on their Stands: for example, heart symbols serve as knee caps and even as a codpiece for Dio's flamboyant Stand, The World! This repeated motif signals an aesthetic trend that really takes off in *Diamond is Unbreakable* and which has remained through the rest of *JoJo*: a profusion of all sorts of symbols on the characters' outfits—we have to wait for *Steel Ball Run*, or even *JoJolion*, for this trend to calm down... a bit. This visual choice bears the direct influence of Italian fashion on Araki. The influence of a very specific brand, actually. "My favorite fashion designer of all time, since I debuted in the '80s, is Moschino. He has since then passed away. He blends humor with beauty. He also used symbols in his designs and various techniques, and I really liked all of that," Araki explained in 2017.[93]

Franco Moschino is a crucial key for unlocking the secrets of *JoJo*'s aesthetic. Since its launch in 1983, the brand "Moschino Couture!," whose exclamation

---

93. "Message from Hirohiko Araki – JoJo's Bizarre Adventure and Fashion," VIZ Media, *YouTube*, October 2017. https://www.youtube.com/watch?v=r2FHRUjBI6Q.

point serves as a sort of loud artistic statement, has adopted an iconoclastic, provocative, and exuberant style. There's a kind of hoodlum quality to its collages and remixes of famous garments, like its reinterpretation of the Chanel suit, emblematic of bourgeois women at that time, as a corrupted version with its buttons replaced by forks and spoons–not to mention other versions with "TAILLEUR" (French for women's suit) written in big letters across the back or "WAIST OF MONEY"[94] around the waist. It would be impossible to summarize all of Moschino's style here, being loaded with all sorts of messages and stances, but all you have to do is look at the brand's collections from the 1980s and early '90s (the creator died in 1994) to understand its strong impact on Araki's work. In *JoJo*, this new trend of adorning characters with messages and symbols, without any complexes, without concern for a visual overload or tastelessness, is apparently rooted in the creations of Moschino. What's more, Araki stated in 1996 that "the clothing and many of the objects used by my characters are copied directly from French and Italian fashion catalogues, especially from Versace and Moschino,"[95] with the caveat that he tends to make changes to these designs. In *JoJo*, the jumble of hearts is undoubtedly inspired by Moschino, with the brand's garments using and abusing this shape, just like the peace symbol found on Josuke's uniform–as proof of his total "Moschino-ization," his Stand even has a head shaped like a heart![96] On the collar of his jacket, we also see an anchor that looks like the logo for the singer Prince, of whom we can see certain features in the face of the series' fourth hero. Other references to Prince: the color purple, closely tied to the artist's image, is also associated with Josuke, as we can immediately see on the cover of the first volume; meanwhile, the main character's outfit and haircut are reminiscent of the singer's style in the early '90s, a sample of which can be seen on the album cover for *3 Nights Live in Miami 1994*. So, starting with *Diamond is Unbreakable*, there's another way for us to look at Araki's work–one that was possible before, but to a lesser extent–by discovering the various references and symbols in the characters' clothing.

As in *Stardust Crusaders*, the hero looks like a Japanese hoodlum. And just like Jotaro before him, Josuke also has a purposely dated look, with his baggy school uniform and his pompadour, inspired by the 1980s style of "yankees"–a term that in Japan refers to young delinquents, generally from poorer families. He's even totally old-fashioned! Laurent Bareille, a specialist of "yankee" imagery, comments: "Starting in the early 1990s, pompadours and baggy pants

---

94. A play on words with the phrase "waste of money," of course. You can see this piece at the beginning of the Milan fashion show for the spring–summer 1991 collection (https://www.youtube.com/watch?v=jO5tG_L42uk).
95. *Kappa Magazine* No. 54, December 1996.
96. Surprisingly, and for no apparent reason, Shining Diamond (a.k.a. Crazy Diamond) looks a lot like The World!

were done for. The looks of delinquents changed. For example, they started shaving the sides of their heads while leaving their hair long on top. They began wearing more streetwear and looks inspired by the fashions of Shibuya —with tight pants and long, straight hair, sometimes dyed. Other styles of young delinquents emerged, like *chiima* (a.k.a. "teamers") in the late '90s, who tend to be from cities and whose outfits outside of school would include: engineer boots, Levi's 501 jeans, and Avirex leather jackets."[97] Josuke's style predates all of these newer looks. In fact, his fashion comes from what we now call "classic yankee," an '80s look that blended a reappropriation of the typical Japanese school uniforms with the influence of Western rock 'n' roll. "In the '80s," explains Laurent Bareille, "the yankees wore rock star-like pompadours in the 'Regent style,' the name of which comes from London's Regent Street.[98] They wore baggy pants called *bontan*, for example, which we often see in manga. You can see all of this clearly in *Be-Bop High School*, which debuted in 1983, as well as the films based on this manga. It's the prototypical 'classic yankee' style."

Rebellious pompadours, parts of a uniform purposely chosen in the wrong size (including jackets, being either too short or too long, and often worn unbuttoned): we see in this a deliberate defiance of conventions and corruption of classic garments, which fits perfectly with the Moschino spirit in *Diamond is Unbreakable*. Although in part four Araki drew inspiration from *furyō manga*, particularly for the dynamic duo of Josuke and Okuyasu, somewhat reminiscent of the two heroes in *Be-Bop High School*, we find in its pages an "haute-couture delinquent" spirit that's totally fanciful and unrealistic, and that brought this influence into uncharted territory at a time when other manga in *Jump*, like *Rokudenashi Blues* (1988-1997, Masanori Morita, never published in English), *Slam Dunk* (1990-1996, Takehiko Inoue), and *Yu Yu Hakusho* (1990-1994, Yoshihiro Togashi)—all three of them excellent, but more orthodox—were using that "classic yankee" imagery, already becoming outdated when each of these series debuted, without any modifications to it. I should also mention that when starting *Diamond is Unbreakable* (in 1992), Araki's editor was skeptical about Josuke's hairdo. He suggested that the creator instead draw a character in keeping with the times. However, the *mangaka* stuck to his guns and explained, in 2004, that he really liked that anachronistic side of Josuke: "The way he cares about his hairstyle, it's very '70s and '80s delinquent, isn't it? But when

97. Remarks collected by us on November 22, 2018. Laurent Bareille is the author of the thesis *Les représentations du « mauvais garçon » dans le cinéma japonais de 1955 à 2000, ou le questionnement à propos de l'évolution de la société japonaise par ce paradigme* (2015, Université Jean Moulin Lyon 3).
98. A comprehensive study of this hairstyle, a sort of Japanese idealization of 1920s British high society, can be found on the website *Néojaponisme*. http://neojaponisme.com/2014/10/09/history-of-the-regent.

you go to the countryside, you occasionally see people like that (laughs). When I was a student, I would stay away from people like that because they scared me, but now there's almost something endearing about them."[99] Indeed, there's something endearing about how Josuke maintains that style, bucking all of the trends, even though he's not actually a delinquent. He does all of this out of respect and admiration for a high schooler who sported this same look and who saved his life when he was a child. Josuke's appearance alone says a lot about who he is as a character.

Killer's heaven

After the defeat of Akira Otoishi, *Diamond is Unbreakable* enters its second phase. For a time, the series follows the daily lives of the characters and their "chance" encounters with the town's remaining Stand users–remember, there's a sort of magnetic force that attracts Stand users to each other. Thus, somewhat randomly, Koichi finds himself knocking on the door of the famous (and fictional) *mangaka* Rohan Kishibe, a popular *Jump* author who moved to the quiet town of Morioh to get away from people. Of course, the eccentric Rohan (whose outfits offer numerous references to the *mangaka* profession, in a "mishmash of symbols" spirit that's again very Moschino-esque) has a Stand, Heaven's Door, that's capable of transforming a human being into an open book so that Rohan can read the person and write new information within them. Koichi pays the price when he naively visits the famous artist's studio. This episode is a great example of the "spider's web" format, which we find often in this fourth part. Rohan, a maverick and Sherlock Holmes-style unsociable genius (what matters most to him is his manga and getting information for it), who was initially created to be a minor character, but who goes on to play a prominent role in the story, represents the new direction for Araki's characters, who are much richer and more ambiguous than before. Once defeated, Rohan joins the main cast, but he nonetheless keeps his sociopathic personality. As such, until the end of *Diamond is Unbreakable*, Josuke and Rohan remain frenemies; however, they're forced to team up to deal with the evil eating away at Morioh. They learn that somewhere within the town, there hides a serial killer who uses discreet methods and has been active for 15 years. No one knows what he looks like; it could be anyone living in the area. His name is Yoshikage Kira[100] and he becomes the main antagonist of part four.

99. Remarks by the author in a Japanese special edition ("*Jump Remix*") of *Diamond is Unbreakable*, published in 2004.
100. A reference to the English word "killer," which is pronounced the same way as "Kira" in Japanese. Moreover, the "Yoshi" in Yoshikage and the "Ki" in Kira are written with the same Japanese character (吉), creating a visual rhyme in the original version.

Volume 37 of *JoJo's Bizarre Adventure* (in vol. 5 of *DiU*, American edition): the great turning point in the story. A masterful volume that, in a handful of chapters, embodies the full brilliance of the fourth story arc and takes it in a new direction. In a breathtaking passage, Araki introduces Kira in an unusual fashion: he plunges us into the well-ordered daily life of the killer, telling things from his point of view, and throws a wrench into the well-oiled machine of his existence. The killer has just made a mistake and he must do everything possible to avoid being discovered. It turns out that this anonymous office worker is hiding a fetish for women's hands and he likes to carry his victims' hands around with him, greedily sucking on them when no one is looking. Unluckily for him, the paper bag that was supposed to contain his lunch, but which actually holds his coveted body parts, gets switched with someone else's! This kicks off a classic sequence of stalking and hide-and-seek, in which Araki's love for suspense and tense situations is on full display. If you remember, in *Stardust Crusaders*, there's that passage where Avdol discovers Holly Kujo lying on the floor; in this respect, in *Diamond is Unbreakable*, Araki becomes a master of this sort of approach, which has a very Kazuo Umezu spirit to it, and the fourth part of the saga, from this point on, has a style much closer to that of thrillers than action manga. Araki finally did it: he got his series based on suspense! Moreover, the choice to introduce the killer from his own point of view is totally innovative for *JoJo*, with Araki's previous bad guys having always been presented from the heroes' perspectives. In this case, the author aims to immerse us in Kira's mindset; he wants us to understand the murderer's habits, his desires, and his thought patterns. That's not to say he builds empathy for the killer: he must remain the antagonist. There's a fine line that can't be crossed, one on which Araki dances with verve. This change of viewpoint is also a constant in *Diamond is Unbreakable*, a story with an ensemble cast, in which Josuke is indeed the official hero, but which nonetheless switches constantly from one perspective to the next. As such, starting in *JJBA* volume 37, the antagonist himself becomes one of these perspectives. From there, the series continues with two major plot lines: the day-to-day life of the town and Yoshikage Kira's hunting. Two parallel lines that, at times, curve and intersect.

JJBA volume 39 (American *DiU*, vol. 6): Kira, his identity unmasked, backed into a corner, is nearly defeated by Koichi and Jotaro. However, in a last burst of energy, the serial killer manages to escape at the last second; he then takes advantage of Cinderella, Aya Tsuji's Stand—a sort of cosmetic surgery tool—to change his face and thus disappear behind a new identity. I want to underscore the importance of this passage, a typical example of how Araki crafts his stories. A few chapters back, I called *JoJo* a living organism whose heart beats in unison with that of its creator. This idea is true in multiple ways: the author fills his work with his obsessions, of course, and his beliefs (remember his conception of the "lone-wolf" hero), but there's also the fact that the plot aligns with the *mangaka*'s state of mind. Araki improvises. Or rather, he adds a layer of improvisation and excitement on top of a solid base that's designed with clear intention. In *Manga in Theory and Practice*, the author reviews in detail the methods that he's developed over time. Araki first meticulously writes his characters, he completes very detailed profiles that collect information on them, both essential and anecdotal; sometimes, he never ends up using those profiles for the manga and he then lets his creations blossom in his mind. He establishes the beginning and end of his story, but he doesn't know the path that connects them. Basically, it's an intuitive method of writing that can be compared to the improvisation exercises that Stephen King details in his memoir *On Writing: A Memoir of the Craft* (2000). "People often say that even if an author doesn't know where the story will go, the protagonist will act on their own," Araki explains. "If you have the setting and the characters in order, you can leave the rest to them."[101] There you have it, the secret to *JoJo*-style suspense: the author himself doesn't even know how his story will evolve! In the case of Kira's escape, Araki wasn't sure how the antagonist could get away from this critical situation: "I didn't think at all about using Cinderella to change his appearance. When he was cornered and I was thinking hard about how Kira might escape, lightning struck me and I realized, 'hey, I could just use Cinderella, who I wrote about last episode!' I'm basically thinking on a week-by-week interval and never about what happens after that."[102] The fact that the author himself is excited by how his story evolves is probably a major key to the success of *JoJo's Bizarre Adventure*, as is the secret behind the vitality of his characters: the way they act simply reflects Araki's natural reactions, which he comes up with "on the spot." Of course, this improvised component can create small inconsistencies (e.g., Keicho), but, when it comes down to it, what's more valuable: total consistency, controlled from A to Z, or a vibrant tale that's constantly being refreshed? Even though its story spans entire decades, *JoJo* is a work that lives in the moment, going with its gut; it's enjoyed best when you don't try to connect the dots between the smallest details, at the risk of discovering some illogical points that may break the series' charm—for example, why is it that, after a certain time, Rohan Kishibe no longer needs to use the pages of his manga to activate his Stand? Likewise, the saga is not the result of some grand master plan; it develops empirically and has new elements added to it over time, for example, the star birthmark on the Joestars in *Stardust Crusaders* or the bow and arrow in *Diamond is Unbreakable*. You just have to

---

101. Hirohiko Araki, *Manga in Theory and Practice*, p. 104.
102. Remarks by the author in a Japanese special edition ("*Jump Remix*") of *Diamond is Unbreakable*, published in 2004.

accept it. Within reason. And in part four, the author's small omissions and revisions are totally acceptable.

After Kira changes his identity, the story arc enters its final phase. The main cast is faced with new Stand users, whose powers are triggered by Kira's father (a ghost who continues to exist through haunted photos[103]) who was, like the Nijimura brothers' father, one of Dio's allies and who has another Stand-generating bow and arrow. Although his son is a dangerous serial killer, he can't help but love and protect him. From there, even while *Diamond is Unbreakable* was already reaching new heights, the series boosts its quality even further: Araki creates increasingly inventive—while remaining comprehensible—powers and increasingly exhilarating situations, like the game of rock-paper-scissors in which the players fly above the town, in a spirit similar to the high-flying ballets of *Dragon Ball*. Or how about the high-speed chase during which Josuke, on a motorcycle and being hunted by a Stand who is forcing him to not go below a certain speed (a sort of wild remake of the 1994 Jan de Bont movie *Speed*), uses Shining Diamond to take apart and put back together his bike in the middle of the chase in order to dodge a baby stroller in his path. What an incredible scenario! It shows Araki's prowess for visual storytelling: at this point in time, Araki has achieved a perfect balance between complexity and readability, his graphic style having evolved toward greater precision, while his characters bodies became less bulky and they gained more rounded traits. This is the golden age of what we've called "the third parameter." All of the battles are governed by creative rules and no volume is the same as the previous one.

Triforce

It's clear to see and it pulls at your heartstrings: *Diamond is Unbreakable* is the part of *JoJo's Bizarre Adventure*, up to this point, that speaks most fondly of humanity. Filled with endearing characters, this fourth part, more specifically, gave us three of the saga's most emblematic figures, who are so memorable that they have lived on in Araki's more recent work in one way or another—but we'll come back to that when the time is right. Josuke Higashikata, Rohan Kishibe, and Yoshikage Kira. The good, the bad, and the bloody.

---

103. Note that ghost stories and urban legends were very popular in Japan at the time. The TV series and films *Gakkō no Kaidan* (*Ghost Stories*), for example, released between 1994 and 1996, are representative of this trend. In general, Japanese horror went through a prolific period in the 1990s, with major hits like the novel *Ring* (1991) by Kōji Suzuki or the manga of Junji Itō (*Uzumaki*, 1998-1999). In *JoJo*, Yukako Yamagishi's evil hair, an element typical of Japanese horror, fits into this movement.

While Jotaro Kujo is like a mythical figure, Josuke has a more down-to-earth and immediately familiar quality to him, which is also more reflective of this fourth part compared to the third. Although he has–at least initially–a "Joestar-esque" muscular physique, JoJo the Fourth of His Name is a teenager like any other, with his flaws, his worries, and his mischievousness–for example, he enjoys scamming Rohan during a comical game using loaded dice, or he doesn't miss an opportunity to make a few bucks by teaming up with Okuyaso, who's just as broke as him. And above all, Josuke is overflowing with *junjō*, a concept that author Jean-Marie Bouissou describes as, "a naive and sincere spirit, someone who instinctively throws themself into a fight for justice, with a big, 'typically Japanese' heart and a raw energy that can't be restrained by either calculations or concerns about propriety [...]. Their purpose is to restore the greatest virtue to corrupt institutions and troubled communities."[104] Josuke has that slightly naive purity, that unwillingness to compromise that we see particularly in *furyō manga* heroes, without himself actually being a delinquent–he just looks like one. Additionally, we should note that unlike many characters in the *furyō manga* genre who use their energy to rise through the ranks in the often closed-off community of teenage hoodlums, disconnected from the adult world, Josuke uses his fiery temperament to take on Kira, and thus helps take care of his entire town. Incidentally, while the Japanese character "*jō/shō*" (承) in Jōtarō means "to listen, to hear, to take in; to undertake" or "to receive; to inherit; to pass on," the "*jō*" (仗) in Jōsuke, which is different, can mean "to rely on" or "to guard or escort."[105] There is indeed a warm quality to Josuke; he projects the ideas of mutual aid and caring for loved ones and neighbors. It's no surprise that Araki has mentioned him several times as being his favorite hero, a character that he came to see as his friend.

Rohan Kishibe, meanwhile, is not Hirohiko Araki's friend, but rather his imaginary alter ego. Kishibe shares certain characteristics with *JoJo*'s author and exaggerates them, like Araki's tendency to write meticulous details about his characters, something we see reflected in Rohan's Stand, Heaven's Door, the ultimate tool for reading someone's personal "novel." Far from being as barbaric and disreputable as he at first seems, over time, Rohan develops a real friendship with Koichi and he even has a few charming personality traits. A goodness in him that he reservedly hides. We can tell that he's on a mission –even though he'll never say anything of the sort–when he finds himself in a hidden street in the town, a sort of no-man's-land between the world of the living and the world of the dead, where he discovers that he is the only

104. Jean-Marie Bouissou, *Manga – Histoire et univers de la bande dessinée japonaise*, Philippe Picquier, 2010, p. 249 (2014 updated edition).
105. Explanations provided in the French version of *Diamond is Unbreakable*, vol. 1.

survivor of a massacre that occurred in a house 15 years earlier—having been a child at the time, he had repressed this memory. These were Yoshikage Kira's first murders. On that night, a teenage girl named Reimi Sugimoto was killed; she now haunts this secret street in Morioh, her soul wandering and powerless, waiting to find someone who can "restore Morioh's peace and dignity." While a tragic figure, Reimi does not make us pity her. She still has a strength and integrity about her that inspire respect, and, from a visual standpoint, she is probably one of Araki's best characters.

Who is Kars, the leader of the Pillar Men? To find out, we have to go back in time 10,000 years. At that time, there was a tribe of humanoid creatures who the prehistoric humans feared as if they were gods. Or demons. Weak against the sun's rays, these beings *(Oh no! Here we go again!)* .44 Magnum, which he loves to say is the "most powerful handgun in the world" were capable of absorbing energy who is Kars, the leader of the Pillar Men? You didn't have Dorothée *(The disturbance is stronger this time.)* presenting an episode of *JoJo* every Wednesday morning, their lives took a sinister turn. Otomo's drawings influenced countless numbers of artists and a rejection of the rule that says that every living must this era of worshiping physical prowess. *(Keep going, don't go back.)* Who is Kars, the leader of the Pillar Men? Dio, a young European with foppish attitudes and poisonous beauty progressive zoom-in on the hand and two infants who survived met in 2012 the hand was wearing a black leather glove a special issue of the women's magazine Jotaro's hand Eastwood is standing tall, his head cocked to the side, his index finger pointing Stands as abilities acquired. *(Now you know how to get out of the time loop.)* Who is Kars, the leader of the Pillar Men? Even if that means killing His Lordship, the famous final page of *Ashita no Joe*, both in terms of the time scale and what's at stake, Pet Shop is unavailable in tournament mode Joseph's son also possesses this power a sandstorm cannot be the only antagonizing force his ally in Egypt and its subtle aftertaste of impending darkness *(Close your eyes, count to three, and turn the page.)*

History with filled and ancient as seen was that Sendai of version a know to got Araki, up growing. *(Wait, why didn't that work?)* Unbreakable is Diamond in Morioh inspired that environment this was it and began area residential new a of development, 1980s the in, however. *(Let's try that again. Three, two, one...)*

As for Kira... He may just be the most fascinating character in the entire *JoJo* saga. He's an office worker with an appearance that's understated—for the saga—but elegant, similar to David Bowie's style from the late '70s, particularly his look in the film *The Man Who Fell to Earth* (1976, Nicolas Roeg), in which the musician played the graceful and enigmatic Thomas Jerome Newton.[106] It's this version of Bowie that seems to have gotten the *JoJo* remix. We can see in Kira a baroque manifestation of the "salaryman," the Japanese employee, the stereotypical anonymous, interchangeable worker who's a bit of a slave to his work, like a little soldier in a suit and tie who's devoted to the common cause and represses his individuality, who bottles up his private desires until he can release them at night in bars and *izakaya*, under the neon lights of the city districts that never sleep, where, in the heat of the night, men don't have to be so prudish. In Kira, this need to release the pressure and follow his desires takes the form of murder, in private, of course—he refuses all invitations to go out with his coworkers. In Japan, where the societal model strongly emphasizes group cohesion, there's an expression that can be translated as "the nail that sticks out calls for a hammer," the idea being that you shouldn't step out of line. Don't disturb the order of society; don't trouble the flow of everyday life. And from an outside view, Kira does not upset this order. He does everything he can to not be that nail that sticks out and to give the impression of following the herd so that he can practice his dark activities in secret, reflecting the way in which everything that's dirty, disgraceful, or unsavory often remains hidden in Japan, a country where appearances and the public face of things are of great importance, even if that means masking the truth.

When it comes down to it, Kira simply pursues his happiness, remaining calm and humble, in the private comfort of a house where he lives alone. Unlike Dio and Kars, who embodied the battle for supremacy, and thus also, in a way, the bygone era of Japanese economic growth, Kira has no interest in climbing the ladder, competition, or victory. Rather, he leads what we would now call a "slow life" and avoids all forms of conflict. Still, even if he did have to fight, Kira would have no need to fear: his Stand, the splendid anthropomorphic cat Deadly Queen (a.k.a. Killer Queen), makes him virtually invincible thanks to his ability to transform everything he touches into a bomb! And yet, Kira has all the skills he would need to excel in society and to climb the corporate ladder at his company; however, he chooses not to play the stressful game of the Japanese professional system and simply does decent work without drawing attention to himself. Araki explains: "Since he was in middle school, when Kira receives awards, Kira always comes in third place. Not first, not second,

---

106. Araki has never confirmed this, but the inspiration is very likely given that we know he's a big fan of Bowie. Furthermore, the author never misses an opportunity to pose in photos the same way the singer does on the cover of his album *Heroes*!

but third, which is not the best, but still respectable. He has all the talent he would need to be number one, but he's unable to handle the fact of standing out, making enemies, and feeling pressure or the weight of expectations. [...] I wanted to draw this sort of abnormal figure, this sort of strange genius."[107]

One problem: his individualistic conception of happiness is incompatible with life in society because in order to feel good, Kira must kill to placate his secret passions, his fetish for women's hands! An attraction that, as we learn at the very end, developed in childhood when he discovered Leonardo da Vinci's *Mona Lisa* in an art book—and on this point, we can likely draw a parallel with the books that Araki would peruse as a boy: "Those hands, that Mona Lisa has crossed on her lap... the first time I saw that... how can I put it... Pardon the expression, but... that gave me a hard-on,"[108] the serial killer admits. Kira's story may be the first time that *JoJo* talks about sexual tension, whether it be explicit, as in this quotation, implied (we get the sneaking suspicion that the killer does more with the women's hands than suck on the fingers), or allegorical, via Kira's nails, which grow faster or slower according to how he's feeling. Ultimately, this character, aware of his vices and the danger he poses, but incapable of living his life any other way, also symbolizes, for example, the way in which the comfortable standard of living in rich countries has developed at the cost of bleeding poor countries dry. One of the great conundrums of today's world.

For Araki, the character of Kira has a special place: quite simply, he's the author's favorite villain, as he has said on several occasions, a character in which he invested a lot of energy. Kira embodies another way of celebrating humanity and its strengths, the amoral counterpart to the heroes of *JoJo*. Although we can say that he became a psychopathic adult due to a trauma in his youth, Kira is fully self-actualized at present; he knows what he is and goes out of his way to follow his own path. Moreover, the author doesn't try to excuse or justify Kira's actions: he doesn't make the killer a pathetic character; he doesn't show him as a damaged human being or someone we should feel sorry for. Araki explains: "I don't think it's interesting in a *shōnen* manga if the hero feels some sort of empathy for the villain. For example, with the character Yoshikage Kira, I think that he has his own reasons for becoming a serial killer, such as the poor environment of his childhood, his relationship with his mother and father, who always ignored him. But if I were to write the story like that, we would start to feel sorry for Kira, and so despite being such a horrible villain, when Josuke fights him, I think he would kind of feel sorry

---

107. Remarks by the author in a Japanese special edition (*"Jump Remix"*) of *Diamond is Unbreakable*, published in 2004.
108. *Diamond is Unbreakable*: *JJBA* vol. 46, future vol. 9 of the *DiU* English version.

for him."[109] That's why Araki doesn't show the trauma experienced by his bad guy in *Diamond is Unbreakable*. Kira fully embraces his identity: "That's the reason why I really like Kira," Araki says. "Although he may have had a bad childhood and turned into a serial killer, I still hope that he tries his best at being one. I can't really say that out loud much though. I'm secretly a fan of his."[110]

What's more, while initially Yoshikage Kira wasn't actually supposed to be a character, his presence is the definitive realization of *Diamond is Unbreakable*'s original concept, the idea that evil and horror can be hiding behind the scenes of our everyday life; he also is the result of the author's keen interest in serial killers. "I liked reading books on serial killers back in the '80s–this was just before *The Silence of the Lambs* was published, starting that trend–and I wanted to understand what motivates serial killers. What would make a human being do such things? That sort of question really interested me and I found the actions of these people to be really spooky,"[111] the *mangaka* tells us, clearly showing that Kira is one of the characters most representative of Araki's obsessions.

Toward the end of *Diamond is Unbreakable*, Kira, after his identity change, becomes a super version of himself. Even more powerful, more sure of himself, practically untouchable. In addition, he upends the lives of the family he infiltrates and, by usurping the identity of the anonymous salaryman Kosaku Kawajiri, Kira ironically restores excitement to the life of Kawajiri's wife. Shinobu Kawajiri, a housewife and prisoner to a dull, loveless marriage, develops, for the first time, feelings when she sees the new charisma of her "husband," who she hardly recognizes. Perhaps Kira could actually have had a happy family if he could control his murderous impulses? However, this redemption will never come in *Diamond is Unbreakable*. That said, Araki offers a sort of rehabilitation of Kira in the spin-off *Dead Man's Questions*,[112] published in 1999 in *seinen* magazine *Manga Allman*, which was launched a few years before that by... Araki's old partner in crime Ryōsuke Kabashima! This story features Kira as a wandering ghost who has no memories of his existence as a living being. He now has a role that's part detective, part hitman, working for a

---

109. Interview of Araki conducted for the video game *Phantom Blood* (2006), released for the PlayStation 2 for the 20th anniversary of the series.
110. Idem.
111. Remarks by the author in a Japanese special edition ("*Jump Remix*") of *Diamond is Unbreakable*, published in 2004.
112. Included in the collection of short stories *Shikei Shikkōchō Datsugoku Shinkōchū* (1999), also known as *Under Execution, Under Jailbreak*, never published in English. In addition to *Dead Man's Questions*, the collection includes the eponymous short story (1995, published in *Super Jump*), as well as *Dolce and His Master* (1996, published in *Allman*) and the first chapter of the spin-off series *Thus Spoke Kishibe Rohan* (1997, published in *Shōnen Jump*). Interestingly, the titular short story was adapted into a play (which also includes elements of *Dolce and His Master*) that was performed November 20-29, 2015, at Tokyo's Galaxy Theatre.

woman monk who's able to see him. Thus, Kira finds no rest in the afterlife. As for that, it's interesting to note that originally, one of the ideas on which Araki wanted to build his fourth part was life after death, as he revealed in 1996 to the Italian magazine *Kappa*.[113] Instead, he chose to tell about the daily life of a small town. Perhaps this spin-off was a way of returning to that initial concept, as was also the case with the ghost of Reimi Sugimoto. *Dead Man's Questions*, in any case, is a final tribute from the author to a character he's very fond of. In the commentary included in the collection *Under Execution, Under Jailbreak*, Araki reveals that drawing Kira as a ghost even made him cry.

We can be heroes (so the world might be mended)

Let's go back to *Stardust Crusaders*. Can we say that the abilities of the Stands–looking beyond their appearances–were specifically tied to their users? To those users' desires and personalities? Not really, no, other than a few cases like the D'Arby brothers and their love of gaming, or, at best, Dio and his desire for control. *Diamond is Unbreakable* is a game-changer. In it, most of the main characters develop abilities tailored to them, allowing them to pursue a personal aim or counterbalance their human weaknesses. Take Koichi's transformation when he uses Reverb and becomes as sort of "Super Saiyan" straight out of *Dragon Ball*, with hair standing on end and a determined attitude: isn't it like therapy? A way for him to get over his timidity and the fact of being a scrawny boy? The final evolution of his Stand, an independent being, even delivers irreverent lines that are very "gangsta rap" in spirit–"let's kill da bitch" being one of them. In other words, he's the total opposite of the original Koichi, as sort of fantasy version of him or what he would look like if he were a superhero. In addition, Koichi, who evolves over time, is the character who most resembles a classic *shōnen* hero, whereas Josuke, like Jotaro before him, is super powerful and has a strong personality right off the bat. Another example: in the case of Rohan, for whom nothing is more important than his manga, Heaven's Door's ability to read inside of people is a clear manifestation of his desire to obtain the ultimate source of material for his work. As for Josuke, his case is a bit less obvious, perhaps because his Stand appears from the beginning of *Diamond is Unbreakable*, before the fourth part heads in a clear direction, but Shining Diamond reflects the intrinsic goodness of the hero. We see his deep sense of friendship and his ability to support those around him by repairing them, both literally and figuratively. In a way, that's what he does with Okuyaso, whose life takes a new direction when he meets our hero. On a metaphorical level, we can also connect Shining Diamond with the idea of

---

113. *Kappa Magazine* No. 54, December 1996.

restoring order to the town of Morioh. Taking care of it. But of all the different powers, it's Kira's that resonate most with his personality. What is Deadly Queen, if not a tool for making the evidence of the killer's secret machinations disappear? To make them literally explode, go up in smoke? Deadly Queen's secondary ability, Heart Attack (a.k.a. Sheer Heart Attack), a little self-guided tank,[114] represents Kira's desire to eliminate nuisances from a distance without revealing himself in broad daylight, whereas the Stand's greatest power, called Bites the Dust, is the ultimate shield, the (theoretically) supreme guarantee of peace-of-mind since anyone who looks too closely into the identity of the Stand user will end up exploding.

By creating Stands that reverberate with the hearts of his characters, Hirohiko Araki, who says that he built part four around the theme of human weaknesses,[115] gives his work strong overall coherence. These powers represent the characters' life force, vectors for deep desires that collide with one another. Ultimately, it's not the broad and absolutist ideas of good and evil that clash with each other; rather, it's intimate desires and beliefs. It's no longer a black and white matter, as was the case in Araki's work in the past; instead, it's many shades of gray together, imperfect human beings who fall on one side or the other of the moral barrier that is murder. Morioh's Stand users take the initiative to unite against Yoshikage Kira both out of a sense of duty to their fellow citizens and out of a sense of morality in the context. Faced with an outside force threatening the security–relative though it may be–of their life as a society, they bring their talents together, their Stand powers, which are an expression of their individuality. In short, it's a celebration of both personal values and the virtues of cooperation, creating an interesting combination of the individualism of Western societies and the community cohesion that's typical of Japan. In a way, Josuke and his allies are the only ones who see that Kira is Morioh's "nail that sticks out." In this sense, *Diamond is Unbreakable* has a spirit that's closer to conventional Japanese values than *Stardust Crusaders*, in which Jotaro–being heavily inspired by Clint Eastwood and by the rebelliousness of *furyō*–was surprisingly and radically libertarian for a Japanese man, putting him at the margins of society.

114. This tank is reminiscent of the passage in the second volume of *Babel II*, mentioned in the previous chapter, in which the hero must deceive a number of tanks whose appearance is somewhat reflected in Heart Attack.
115. He says this in the note on the inside flap of the cover for volume 17 of *Diamond is Unbreakable* (*JJBA* vol. 45).

Guaranteed to blow your mind

Deadly Queen versus Shining Diamond. Before reaching this final battle, *Diamond is Unbreakable*, in its penultimate volume (of the original edition), shows the effects of Deadly Queen's final power: Bites the Dust. Kira acquired it after inadvertently being struck a second time by the arrow.[116] In this gripping 17th volume, Hayato Kawajiri, Kira's "son" (the son of Kosaku Kawajiri), who has discovered that his father was replaced by an impostor, finds himself stuck in a time loop triggered by Bites the Dust. This power is actually a bomb placed inside of Hayato: if anyone asks him a question about Kira's identity, the bomb will explode right then and there, taking out both Hayato and the questioner, before rewinding time by an hour. However, once this is done, fate does not change: those who are "already" dead will die again. As for Hayato, the memory of having met the victims is erased and the day returns to its normal course, guaranteeing peace of mind for Kira. It's a formidable power that, like Dio's The World, is also based on the manipulation of time—once again, Araki held onto unused ideas that he'd come up with when thinking about powers related to time. We should also note that this becomes a constant: the antagonists of the next two story-arcs, *Golden Wind* and *Stone Ocean*, also have time-related abilities. In any case, Hayato ends up finding an escape and the final volume features Josuke against Kira in a battle every bit as intense as the duel between Jotaro and Dio. Ironically, it's actually Jotaro—he doesn't appear often, but when he does, he steals the scene—who deals the final blow to Yoshikage Kira, who ends up... being crushed by an ambulance. For Araki, drawing this final battle was no easy task: Josuke found himself so badly positioned that the author himself had to wonder if it was even possible to defeat Kira. The hero's situation was not unlike that of the author: while Josuke struggled against Kira, Araki was running up against a wall in the story. In the end, by putting himself in Josuke's shoes while dealing with a similar problem in his own life, Araki managed to come up with a way to beat the bad guy, as if the author had entered the pages of his own manga and lived out its story. It's one of the most significant examples of Araki's method of writing. And it explains why this final battle is so vibrant and why it's one of the most memorable of the entire saga.

Let's just come out and say it because this is the truth: *Diamond is Unbreakable* is a masterpiece, the most brilliant *shōnen* manga of its decade. It's so good

116. At the same time, he changes his hairstyle. It's possible that the thick, dark-colored locks on top of his blonde hair are inspired by the later mixed-media work of Tony Viramontes, who liked to draw freestyle on top of photos. This new Kira looks strikingly like a work created for the Italian magazine *Lei* ("She"), in November 1984, in which heavy brushstrokes of paint are layered on top of the hair of the model in the photo.

that we could have said, "stop there, you'll never do better!," and ended *JoJo's Bizarre Adventure* at that peak. And it's true: Araki will never do better in the pages of *Jump*–nor will anyone else, I almost dare to say. How could the *mangaka* do better than this high point? How could he at least match the fourth part, which truly has it all? For one thing, part four is imbued with the particular ambiance of its time; additionally, Araki seems to have assembled in a single place everything he cares about most, creating a sort of ultimate compilation of his obsessions, his personal tastes, and his experiences. *Diamond is Unbreakable* is the apex of the new spirit of *JoJo* inaugurated by *Stardust Crusaders*: it's where we find the best ingredients; it's where the author offers his most inspired ideas; we can also tell it's where the author felt most free.[117] It's also a one-of-a-kind *shōnen* which, by its eclectic nature, its hybrid inventions, and its unique elements (for example, presenting a main antagonist who abhors conflict is a very interesting choice), evades all attempts at labeling it; meanwhile, its scenes in the life of a serial-killing salaryman are quite daring compared to the typical *Jump* story and they offer a surprisingly adult point of view for a magazine that's, above all, intended for teenagers, simultaneously showing that in spite of the way *shōnen* manga has evolved, it is still capable of connecting to the real world and keenly depicting the present. However, while the series frees itself from conventions, it also shows a real respect for the *shōnen* standards of the 1990s. *Diamond is Unbreakable* pays homage to several currents of manga found in *Jump*, to which Araki adds his own spin: Akira Toriyama's style of manga (via the living, breathing tribute that is Koichi, *JoJo*'s "Super Saiyan," and his Stand, whose different looks resemble Cell and Frieza), the *furyō manga* genre, of course, and even romantic comedy, as seen in the bonkers passages dedicated to the "romance" between Koichi and Yukako. And let's not forget, quite simply, the *nekketsu* energy that is *Jump*'s signature and that in *JoJo*'s part four is used in a baroque fashion, like when Rohan and his adversary throw all of their energy, holding nothing back, into an impassioned game of rock-paper-scissors. *Diamond is Unbreakable* also pays homage to the medium of manga in general, via the *mangaka* Rohan Kishibe, of course, but also through the ingenious power that is Reverb, who uses sound effects in creative ways, or through the Stand of Kira's father, Heart Father, a play on the concept of "a frame within a frame" (the Polaroid serves as a comic book panel within a comic book panel) and of ellipsis between panels–the photo transforms from one panel to the next, allowing the Stand user to move little by little within the image.

During publication of the fourth story arc, *Shōnen Jump* reached its greatest peak in popularity by bringing together smash-hit manga like *Dragon Ball*,

117. Araki says in the 2012 mook *JOJOmenon* that, indeed, he had a lot more freedom than before.

Slam Dunk, and *Yu Yu Hakusho*. And what about *JoJo's Bizarre Adventure*? In the catalogue for the exhibition *Shōnen Jump Vol. 2*, published in 2018, Araki talks about this period: "I was in my 30s, about 10 years after by debut. I was sort of in my prime. I wasn't a rookie and I was starting to really understand how to create manga. When I think about it now, I was fortunate at that age to have been published in *Shōnen Jump* when it was really jumping (laughs). When I say 'jumping,' I don't mean only circulation numbers, but also the content." Interestingly, the interviewer adds this comment after that remark from Araki: "He seems unaware that when *Jump* was 'jumping,' he was one of the catalysts." The *mangaka* explains his thinking: "There's always something above you. There are always more popular creators. I never felt I was like that." It's true, Araki remained on the margins. His work doesn't look like the rest of *Jump*. But strangely, from that margin, and without sacrificing the bizarreness of his style, he managed to create a manga that has had a resounding impact.

We will talk more about Morioh later. Not only because Rohan Kishibe goes on to have his own spin-off, but also because the eighth part of the saga, *JoJolion*, takes place in the small town too. Well... not exactly. It's another version of the town, in a parallel universe. As for the version of Morioh in *Diamond is Unbreakable*: "In my heart, Morioh will forever be in that unresolved state," Araki says. Frozen as it appears in the final panel of the last volume. "What happened to Josuke after the series? I don't think about that at all. Morioh is 'eternal'."[118] The town will be eternally crystalized in 1999, at the turn of the new millennium. That strange time when "most regular people... well, maybe life isn't carefree, but it goes on as normal."

---

118. Remarks by the author in a Japanese special edition (*"Jump Remix"*) of *Diamond is Unbreakable*, published in 2004.

CHAPTER V: GANG STARS
(1995-1999: JOJO'S BIZARRE ADVENTURE, PART 5)

Stand : Man in the Mirror
Sometimes, you find answers by looking in the mirror.

To listen to while reading:

Gang Starr – *Above the Clouds*
Prince – *Gold*
Sex Pistols – *Holidays in the Sun*
King Crimson – *21st Century Schizoid Man*
Hyphen Hyphen – *Like Boys*

"All that glitters ain't gold," Prince sings in his song "Gold." It's a proverb that, sadly, perfectly describes the fifth part of *JoJo's Bizarre Adventure*, which began in *Shōnen Jump* in the issue dated December 11, 1995, and which later became known as *Golden Wind* or *Vento Aureo* (Italian for the same). I say this because part five, probably the most flashy and "poppy" part of the saga, had a lot of promise, but also stumbled often, triggering alternating waves of excitement and disappointment. You'll see why.

A few paragraphs ago, I said that the saga could easily have ended on a high note with *Diamond is Unbreakable*. And from Araki's perspective, truth be told, he could absolutely have ended *JoJo* with the fourth part, given that he'd been able to include in it the things that he hadn't been able to fit into the third story arc.[119] In this sense, although *Diamond is Unbreakable* has its own tone, we can see it as a more in-depth continuation of what was originally supposed to be a trilogy, and thus as the conclusion of the tale that started in 1987. That's why the fifth part, which was created anyway, makes such a clear departure in terms of themes. While the *JoJo* bloodline remains intact, Araki also wanted to

---

119. He said this in the Japanese mook *JOJOmenon* in 2012.

tackle subjects he hadn't yet explored and, in the end, his manga turned out to be darker and more marked by tragedy and gloom, but without betraying the spirit of the series.

When *Golden Wind* debuted, Hirohiko Araki was already a pillar of *Shōnen Jump*. A veteran, even, since *JoJo*—which was still so different from the magazine's other works—was the second longest-running series in the magazine at the time, behind *KochiKame*[120] (1976-2016, never published in English). At that time, in late 1995, the golden age of the magazine's popularity was history. Sales began to decline, with the fall from grace likely accelerated by the end of the *Dragon Ball* dynamo (its last chapter was released in spring 1995) and by the approaching conclusions of other flagship series like *Slam Dunk* and *Rokudenashi Blues*. However, the situation was more complex than that and had more to do with a widespread decline for manga magazines, partially explained by the implosion of the Japanese economic bubble (with the related consequences for purchasing power) and by competition for the attention of young people from other very popular pastimes like video games. For this reason, later *Jump* superstars, like *Naruto* and *One Piece* (which, to remind you, is the best-selling manga series in history at the global level by *tankōbon* volumes), never brought the magazine back to its all-time sales record. Thus, in a parallel that may not be entirely due to chance, the beginning of a crisis for *Jump* coincided with the beginning of a decline in *JoJo*'s quality. That said, paradoxically, *Golden Wind* turned out to be one of the most popular parts of the saga. Once again, you'll see why.

The year is 1995 and manga culture has now caught on in the Western world. It's still looked down upon by some there and certain people view the manga "invasion" with suspicion, notably in France, but its universe has started to gain traction worldwide, partially thanks to the anime adaptation of *Akira* (1988, directed by Otomo himself), which quickly became a sensation outside of Japan. Like punk culture in its time, manga culture—of which Westerners latched on to the most aggressive and extreme elements—is able to capture the fascination of young people; it has a naughty, rebellious, and non-conformist side to it. And a modern side, as well. The same year, the spectacular music video for Michael Jackson's *Scream*, which may still be the most expensive music video ever made, featured a high-tech outer space décor with anime clips playing in the background... including a clip from the recent adaptation of *Babel II*![121] Hirohiko Araki must have been on cloud nine seeing his favorite manga share the screen with the king of pop and his sister Janet. Of course,

---

120. With its 200 volumes, this comedic series by Osamu Akimoto is the second longest in the history of manga. Its full title is about as long as the series itself: *Kochira Katsushikaku Kameari Kōen Mae Hashutsujo* ("This is the police station in front of Kameari Park in Katsushika Ward")!
121. A modernized adaptation of Yokoyama's manga, in four episodes for the original video animation (OVA) market, released in Japan in 1992.

during that era of globalization, Japan could not escape from the latest Western cultural phenomena, like the stunning explosion of boy bands or the popularity of American hip-hop, dominated by gangsta rap—moreover, some Japanese delinquents began imitating the style of dress of African-American gangsters. And you have to admit, *Golden Wind* and its group of young guys have a bit of the '90s boy band spirit. Whether that mash-up of cultures is intentional or not, we should note that Japan already had its own local boy band phenomenon a bit before the worldwide explosion, with groups like SMAP, made up of four or five handsome boys moving and grooving with pop choreography. The influence of gangsta rap, on the other hand, is much more direct in *Golden Wind*: we see the heroes listening to this genre of music, one of the Stands in part five is named Notorious B.I.G. for the famous rapper,[122] and the author himself listened to artists like Snoop Dogg while working on *Golden Wind*. Additionally, the protagonist of this story arc aims to become a "gang star." However, he does not live in the world of American gangs, but rather that of the Italian mafia. Because Araki, for the second time, anchored his story in Italy, the country that had so greatly inspired him and that he had made a habit of visiting every year before the start of *Golden Wind*.[123] Thus, six years after the end of *Battle Tendency*, *JoJo's Bizarre Adventure* returned to its spiritual birthplace.

ǝsᴉpɐɹɐd s,ɐʇsƃuɐ⅁

It feels like déjà vu all over again. Once again, Jotaro is looking for a young "unofficial" member of the Joestar family: to find him, Jotaro sends Koichi to Italy, to the city of Neapolis, which is a fictional version of Naples. Like in *Diamond is Unbreakable*, Koichi initially plays the role of narrator, the first page in many ways reproducing the opening of the fourth part. Now, we're no longer in the spring of 1999, but instead in 2001, at exactly the same time of year. Koichi's mission: to find the 15-year-old Japanese-Italian youth named Haruno Shiobana and take a sample of the boy's skin so that the Speedwagon Foundation can analyze it. Basically, it's an all-expenses-paid vacation from Jotaro with a little side job.

Haruno, a golden-haired teenager, now goes by Giorno Giovana, or GioGio for short.[124] *Le Bizarre Avventure di GioGio V* is even how it's presented in *Shōnen*

---

122. The Notorious B.I.G. was murdered on March 9, 1997. Araki's Stand of the same name, who appeared in the chapter published in the January 15, 1998, issue of *Jump*, activates when his user dies. We can interpret this as an homage to the rapper, a way of showing that he will never truly die.
123. Joint interview between Hirohiko Araki and Yūsei Matsui (author of the manga *Assassination Classroom*), 2013.
124. The Japanese characters for Haruno can also be read as Shioruno. So, if you Italianize Shioruno Shiobana you can get "Giorno Giovana." Moreover, the letter J does not exist in Italian, hence "GioGio."

Jump on the title page of the first chapter, where you can also see a close-up of Michelangelo's *The Creation of Adam* to the left of Giorno and, to his right, an image of Victoria (a winged Roman goddess who represents victory). Giorno, the series' fifth hero, has been through hell. His father died shortly before his birth and his mother remarried an Italian, a detestable man who made a habit of beating his stepson with a belt when his mother's back was turned. And then there's this: we learn that Giorno's true biological father is none other than... Dio! Apparently, for the vampire, women were not all just objects to be consumed for sex and food, since he left this one alive. In any case, Giorno thus possesses both Joestar DNA—quite logically, the sperm used to conceive him came from Jonathan's body—and DNA from Dio Brando. However, his true paternal figure is yet another man. As a child, Giorno saved a gangster by accidentally using his Stand, which is a natural part of him that he had been totally unaware of. In return, the mafioso began looking out for Giorno, watching quietly, respectfully, from a distance, allowing the boy to finally trust someone. Ironically, Giorno, who was likely to turn out quite poorly after such a terrible childhood, learned to take life by the horns and appreciate it thanks to a criminal. While the mafioso may have tried to dissuade his protégé from following the same path in life, teenage GioGio dreams of joining a gang. He's committed to an idea: to revitalize his city and rid its streets of drugs, which are destroying the lives of Neapolitans. For Giorno, who sees that the police and political leaders are all corrupt, the only way to flush out the drug dealers is to take control of the city by becoming a gangster himself. From there, he'll climb the ladder to reach the top of an organization named "Passione" in order to change it from the inside out.

So, for the third time in a row, after Jotaro and Josuke, *JoJo's Bizarre Adventure* features a big-hearted quasi hoodlum. However, Giorno pushes the limits further: not only does he end up actually joining the gangster world, within an organization that's no joke, he also has an extreme thirst for justice. Simpler—and at 15, also a bit younger—than his predecessors, Giorno is more like a typical *nekketsu* hero; he is filled with that famous "where there's a will, there's a way" spirit and an unshakable desire to reach the top. Not for himself, however, but out of altruism for his fellow citizens. So, logically, Giorno has a special power allowing him to care for others. Well... it's actually more complicated than that. The basic power of Gold Experience, GioGio's Stand, is the ability to transform inorganic objects into living things. For example, a revolver can become a banana or, in *JoJo* volume 54, Giorno transforms a part of a motorcycle into plant roots that grab onto a Stand's foot—which, of course, is reminiscent of Bernini's *Apollo and Daphne* sculpture. However, the hero uses his guardian in different ways, notably allowing him to cure people— for example, he can transform a bullet inside a body into organic matter to undo the injury. That said, Giorno is as merciless with his enemies as he is brotherly with his allies; he won't hesitate to kill his adversaries in cold blood if they get between him and his dream. So, he's sort of like a blend of Jotaro and Josuke.

After the exciting first two volumes and an eventful initiation ritual, during which we learn that Passione is full of Stand users (the organization has another Stand-creating bow and arrow), Giorno makes it into the gang. He joins a team of young recruits–the oldest being 20 years old–who do low-level tasks tied to managing casinos or protecting shops; they're kept away from Passione's divisions that deal drugs and commit murders. This squad is led by Bruno Bucciarati, a man who also hates the drug trade (recently added to the organization). Giorno manages to win Bucciarati over with his moral rectitude and the purity of his dream. The two then adopt the goal of getting noticed so that they can climb the ranks and get close to the organization's boss, a man that no member has ever seen in person. To do this, Bruno takes his team on a mission to find the hidden fortune of a recently deceased lieutenant in the organization, with the aim of handing it over to the mob so that they'll be rewarded with a promotion. Thus begins the first quest of *Golden Wind*, in a road trip similar to the narrative structure of *Stardust Crusaders*, with other members of the organization competing with them in the treasure hunt. This leads to fights to the death in which Stands, often aggressive in nature–displaying countless menacing teeth–draw blood under the bright Mediterranean sun.

The new meaning of virility

Golden Wind redefines what it means to be a JoJo-style man. In the 1990s, the bodybuilder aesthetic declined in popularity, just as action movie heroes gradually fell by the wayside. In manga, muscle men increasingly filled humorous bit parts, or they had their forms exaggerated to the extreme, bordering on monstrous, like the characters in the martial arts *shōnen Baki the Grappler* (1991-1999) by Keisuke Itagaki, still ongoing in Japan via various sequels. As such, there was no reason for Araki, who wanted to keep up with the times, to continue worshiping big muscles and traditional virility, which had left the mainstream and been relegated to cultural niches. Granted, characters' silhouettes had already gotten slimmer over the course of *Diamond is Unbreakable*, but in part five, Araki takes things even further: his male characters all have exaggeratedly slender physiques; they appear so thin and lithe that their bodies hardly seem to be planted on the ground and they practically bend with the wind. In this way, they fit quite well with the trend of slender limbs and bodies with incredible balance that we see in many mannerist sculptures of the late Renaissance, like Giambologna's *Mercury* (1574). These new bodies in *Golden Wind* fit perfectly with the idea that, for Stand users, spiritual strength is greater than physical strength. However, these new characters also, particularly, have an androgynous appearance pushed to the extreme.

Following in the footsteps of *Battle Tendency*, this is the second era of feminization of men in *JoJo's Bizarre Adventure*. But with a very different register this time. The boys of *Golden Wind* have somewhat girly appearances because, first and foremost, Araki drew inspiration from women's fashion to create their attitudes and, particularly, their outfits. His characters have never been more chic than in part five. They look like they've just come from fashion week and they adopt poses reminiscent of both modern sculpture and fashion photography (with the extra Araki-style touch of defying gravity, of course, and twisted and flexed limbs that stretch the limits of the human body), often women's fashion. For example, the title page of the third chapter, which shows Giorno with the Italian words "*buon giorno*" on either side of him, is inspired by the cover of the Versace women's fall-winter 1995-1996 catalogue, a photo by Richard Avedon in which supermodel Kristen McMenamy is standing with her legs half bent, wearing a bright red pantsuit with tight-fit pants. This collection also prominently features the checkered pattern, which may have inspired the back of Giorno's jacket. Sticking with the Versace theme, we should note that Araki also drew inspiration from photos for the brand's line for men and, as early as *Diamond is Unbreakable*, we see reinterpretations of famous photos included in the collection *Men Without Ties* (1995). This is also the case in *Golden Wind*: the illustration that opens the sixth chapter, for example, shows Giorno cheek to cheek with his Stand, clearly inspired by a photo in that collection, and Araki immerses the entire image in a dazzlingly glamorous ambiance, which itself is reminiscent of the style of Gianni Versace, a creator who played a lot with the imagery of luxury and power, particularly by using an abundance of golden ornamentation. The flashy black and gold contrast was often found in his '90s collections and this combination is also seen on Giorno, whose dark outfits—at least in the black and white images, because the characters aren't associated with particular colors and Araki gives them different hues from one color illustration to the next—also create a link with the black school uniform of the two previous JoJos.

In general, in terms of clothing, the influence of women's fashion from that time is ubiquitous. The patterns of squares worn by Narancia, for example, are strongly reminiscent of patterns from the Prada spring-summer 1996 collection,[125] while the round holes in Fugo's outfit are found in the collection

---

125. The fashion show for this collection can be seen on *YouTube FF Channel* (https://www.youtube.com/watch?v=TcAFwQ1_6-M). The square patterns in question are abundantly present, for example, at 14 min.

for the same season from the brand Iceberg.[126] Meanwhile, Giorno and Bucciarati wear suits whose cut—with broad shoulders, a snug collar, a deep V-neck showing the bare chest, a tightly fitted jacket that falls below the posterior, tight pants—appears to come directly from the elegant suits of Giorgio Armani's women's spring-summer 1995 collection.[127] Suits to which Araki adds, as in *Diamond is Unbreakable*, symbols that evoke the identities and powers of the characters. More generally, the characters have looks with attributes often associated with women, like Bucciarati's hairstyle (which is reminiscent of the timeless bob cut with bangs of the lingerie designer Chantal Thomass and her models, or even the hair of the Egyptian queen Cleopatra), Narancia's skirt, or Tiziano's sandals with heels. Not applying to any one character in particular, low-cut necklines and painted lips are also ubiquitous, for example.

More than a simple feminization of the men, we can view it as a hybrid between the expressions of masculinity and femininity. In *Golden Wind*, the men—and they clearly are men—quite simply follow social conventions (i.e., body language and clothing) that blend those associated with men and women. It's not cross-dressing; it's simply the way things are in this universe. We also find as many behaviors associated with heterosexuality (we see that some of the members of the gang are attracted to Trish, the only girl prominently featured in part five) as we do situations with obvious homoerotic tension. On that point, we couldn't possibly ignore the first encounter between Bucciarati and Giorno, in which Bruno licks the sweat from GioGio's cheek to determine whether or not he's lying. Another striking example: the dynamic duo of Tiziano and Squalo, two men who are inseparable and who are at least very touchy-feely with each other. We see all of this without any of them ever being defined as gay or straight. It's just not something that matters here. *Golden Wind* is a free-spirited world where genders and sexual orientations intersect and blend together to create human beings without labels, whose constant ambiguity creates a unique, risqué atmosphere.

Poem Gang Destiny

Volume four (*JJBA* vol. 50). Bucciarati is promoted to lieutenant and his team is given an important mission: to escort the boss' secret daughter, Trish Una,[128]

---

126. The fashion show for this collection can be seen on *YouTube Fashion Channel* (https://www.youtube.com/watch?v=SiUA3L5iGK0). The round holes are seen in the white dress at 10 min. 43 sec., as well as in the outfits of the two models at 11 min. 30 sec.

127. The fashion show for this collection can be seen on *YouTube Fashion Channel* (https://www.youtube.com/watch?v=crU8OMavlus). The suits mentioned can be seen at 1 min. 15 sec.

128. Her physique and first name are based off of Trish Goff, a famous model from the '90s. Additionally, her clothes seem to be inspired by the outfit worn by a female figure appearing on the cover of the Prince album *Around the World in a Day* (1985).

to a specific location. Within the organization, a few dissidents aim to kidnap her to discover the identity of Passione's leader so that they can find him, kill him, and take control of the drug trafficking business; at the same time, Giorno also secretly plots to depose the boss, but with the goal of dismantling the drug trade. This new phase, which lasts until the ninth volume, establishes, once and for all, the logic and rhythm of bniW nsbloᴐ, made up of several journeys from a point A to a point B. Journeys interspersed, of course, with multiple battles against Stand users who block the heroes' way. Thus, it's a model similar to *Stardust Crusaders*, but with longer fights (sometimes lasting more than an entire volume). As in the third part, the traveling aspect allows for varied battlefields, each one an opportunity to add the "third parameter" that shapes each struggle. For example, the sixth and seventh volumes take place in an express train to Florence, where what has to be the most exhilarating battle of *Golden Wind* takes place.

At this point, we come to understand that the star of part five is actually Bruno Bucciarati, who is prominently featured in this train sequence via a (mainly) two-against-one fight in which the lieutenant expertly uses his Stand, Sticky Fingers, who is able to place zippers on any surface (any solid thing, really, even human bodies) to open them and pass through them. To the very end of *Golden Wind*, Bucciarati proves to have flawless moral rectitude and royal elegance, with his suit whose pattern looks like ermine fur (the kind of fur used for the lining of the cloaks worn by Old Regime French kings) and his Cleopatra-style hair. As such, he's both a king and a queen, and a symbol of both masculine and feminine eroticism (the zipper of men's pants, the hairstyle of Chantal Thomass' lingerie models or of the dancers at Paris' Crazy Horse cabaret). Bruno steals the show from GioGio, who, we must admit, falls back from the third volume onward: not long in, *Golden Wind* is no longer told from his point of view and it becomes a story with an ensemble cast; from there, we start to forget about our slightly dull hero. This is because his allies Fugo, Mista, Narancia, and Abbacchio each get their chance in the spotlight and, in parallel to the gang's missions, the author tells the often-tragic origin stories of each member, in addition to explaining their connection to the central figure of Bucciarati. From these different voices emerges the overall theme of *Golden Wind*: a person's lot in life. Araki discussed this subject in 2005: "When I was writing the fifth part, bniW nsbloᴐ, I kept asking myself: 'How should someone behave when having to live with the fact that just being born is a source of sadness?' People can't choose how they come into the world. Some find themselves in happy families; others grow up in terrible places from day one. So, what is this second group of people to do, if destiny and fate are already decided by gods or some kind of law that controls the movement of the stars in our vast universe? This is the main theme of ᴐolqɐu Miuq and both the protagonists and their adversaries need to face it. Giorno, Bucciarati, Fugo, Narancia, Abbacchio,

Mista: every single one of them grew up, or rather was forced to grow up, on the margins of society and family. The same can be said about Trish, really. Will they ever be able to challenge their destinies and change them? This was my most recurring thought while working on this story."[129] Basically, it's a new variation on the theme of the family tree: heritage can be a burden. It's a variation that's sadder than the hereditary heroism of the Joestars, but one that's not without hope.

Volume nine: a dramatic turn of events. The first odyssey comes to an end in Venice and Trish is delivered to the boss, safe and sound. However, the mob boss' real intention is to kill his illegitimate daughter himself to protect his identity and the secrets of his past. Bucciarati stands up to him and after this act of rebellion, his team, which manages to save Trish, becomes a splinter cell within the organization. From there, *Golden Wind* enters its second half. Still following the model of the journey with many stops, the Bucciarati gang heads off in search of the boss' identity—with the user remaining cloaked in shadows, we still haven't seen his Stand—and they continue to face Passione's most dangerous killers. Well, that is to say, what remains of the gang since Fugo decided not to follow Bucciarati on this suicide mission. And in fact, we never see him again... Fugo is without a doubt the most under-used character in the group, perhaps because his power, Purple Haze, is much too powerful to allow for fair fights—he releases a virus capable of eradicating all lifeforms in record time—but also because, as Araki has said, the author initially had other plans for him: Fugo was supposed to become a traitor, but Araki had to go rethink that decision. It was visceral for him. Absolutely impossible. It broke his heart to imagine how Bucciarati would take that betrayal. "I absolutely can't understand betrayal from a trusted friend and this is why just thinking about it hurt me physically. As an author, I could handle any criticism saying that I 'didn't have the guts to do it,' but I assure you, I couldn't write that episode, no matter what. Maybe Giorno would then have had to kill Fugo and I'm sure this would have given a really bad impression to my younger readers. This is what lays behind that farewell scene in Venice. With the publication of the novel based on *Golden Wind*,[130] I was able to have a story written about how Fugo would continue to help his companions from inside the organization."[131] Araki's visceral and uncontrollable attachment to his characters says a lot about his relationship with his work. In *Manga in Theory and Practice*, he even says that he cried

129. Postscript to the final volume of the Japanese *bunkobon* (a compact format, even smaller than usual tankōbon paperback books) republication of *Golden Wind*.
130. There are several novels derived from the *JoJo* franchise. This one, published in Japan in 2001, is called *Golden Heart, Golden Ring* and was also translated into Italian in 2004. As these novels were not written by Hirohiko Araki, we will not consider them to be canon and they will not be covered in this book.
131. Postscript to the final volume of the Japanese *bunkobon* republication of *Golden Wind*.

over the deaths of some of them.[132] When it comes down to it, they are small parts of him. Additional proof that the heart of the living organism that is *JoJo's Bizarre Adventure* beats in unison with that of its creator.

From baroque to rococo

While it's possible and constructive to find the merits of any artistic movement, one of the ways we can view the rococo style, found first in the decorative arts, then in painting, of the 18th century in Europe, is as a degradation of the Italian baroque style. The term "rococo," given after the fact by Neoclassical painter Pierre-Maurice Quay (1777-1803), not without derision, is a portmanteau of "*barocco*" and "*rocaille*" (French for "stony ground"), and it refers to an over-the-top, flamboyant ornamental style that imitates natural stones, shells, and other such things. In the 19th century, the word rococo even became insulting, referring to things that are ridiculous or outdated. In painting, we can describe rococo as a form of baroque that's lacking depth in its themes, tending to focus on subjects like the hedonistic day-to-day lives of the aristocracy, in a spirit that flirts with mushiness and sentimentality. Of course, artistic expression and trends evolve. It's a natural process and I'm sure that in its time the rococo style was what needed to be expressed. However, certain standards of the baroque were shifted in a way that, in hindsight, we can view as a corruption.

Golden Wind, undergoing its own natural evolution, shifts the standards of *Diamond is Unbreakable*, which we can say were perfectly set. The reason is that Hirohiko Araki is not the kind of person to tread water or to rest on his laurels with a successful formula: thus, it's only logical that he would continue to evolve. In this case, the *mangaka* moves his series in the direction of outrageously complex Stands, both in terms of their powers and their appearances. Giorno's Gold Experience immediately heralds the new direction for Stand powers, which become more convoluted, or even more ambiguous, than before. Moreover, Araki "forgets"—or abandons—a characteristic introduced at the beginning of the story arc: the idea that when someone strikes a living thing created by Gold Experience, the damage caused rebounds back on the assailant. Perhaps this ability made Gold Experience too powerful? But that's no big deal. As I've said, and as we know, the author gradually makes minor revisions as he writes and we just have to accept this—just like how the appearance of Passione's leader, once revealed, is totally different from the silhouette that we see several times in

132. Hirohiko ARAKI, *Manga in Theory and Practice*, p. 64.

the shadows. However, the new wave of Stands leads to other problems that are much more bothersome.

From one power to the next, it's either hit or miss. Some of them work in very clear and ingenious ways, and their visual translation is exemplary, like Mista's excellent Sex Pistols (six little beings who live in a revolver and direct or strike the bullets with their feet, in a spirit reminiscent of the teamwork in *Captain Tsubasa*), while other Stands are incomprehensible due to ideas that are too complicated or that result in drawings that are difficult to decipher–in general, the graphics in this part evolve toward a style that's too busy with information, hurting readability. The episode in volume three when a boat, deflated by the Stand Soft Machine, covers the surface of another boat is a perfect example of these pointlessly complex concepts.[133] However, the boss' Stand, King Crimson, takes the cake. His ability to manipulate time–not to stop it like The World, but rather to erase a few seconds (with the effect of advancing reality by a few seconds)–works in a way that's so difficult to explain that he became a meme on English-language websites: "it just works,"[134] is how fans explain it. And it actually works very well, so much so that we end up wondering if it's possible to defeat him.

The final phase of *Golden Wind*, which takes place in the Roman Colosseum, brings together all of the concerns about over-complicated situations, overloaded visuals, and Stands that are too powerful. In it, we finally see the boss, Diavolo, who we learn was responsible for distributing the bow and arrow throughout the world. He's the one who originally unearthed six sets, by chance, in Egypt in 1986: he then sold five to Enyaba, Dio's ally, and kept the last one. We also learn that Jean-Pierre Polnareff, after *Stardust Crusaders*, investigated the bow and arrow, leading to a brush with Diavolo and his organization, costing Polnareff the use of his legs. At this point, the Frenchman makes his big comeback–in a wheelchair–and helps Bucciarati's group in their final battle by revealing a secret property of the arrow: if it pierces a Stand, the guardian will evolve into a higher form called "Requiem," which may be capable of defeating King Crimson. And this is precisely what happens to Polnareff's Silver Chariot, which becomes an autonomous being capable of

133. At the end of this episode, one of the strangest—and most famous—passages of *Golden Wind* takes place (*JJBA* vol. 49, after the battle against Zucchero). Once the enemy is neutralized, the team of heroes begins torturing him to get information and while the villain lies in agony, Fugo, Mista, and Narancia begin dancing in synchrony! It's reminiscent of both the film *Reservoir Dogs* (1992, Quentin Tarantino)—in the middle of torturing a man with a razor, Michael Madsen begins to dance to a Stealers Wheel song—and the "Crip Walk," a dance move performed by members of the American gang called the Crips after beating up or killing a member of a rival gang.
134. There's an entire page on this on the website *Know your meme*: https://knowyourmeme.com/memes/king-crimson-jojo.

swapping souls between bodies. Thus, for example, Mista ends up in Trish's body and Giorno in Narancia's. The intriguing part is figuring out which body Diavolo's soul ended up in... The concept is exciting, but it makes the pages of Golden Wind that much more complex, when it already wasn't always easy to follow the action...

In the 17th and final volume of part five, Giorno finally manages to pierce his Stand with the arrow and obtains Gold Experience Requiem,[135] which enables GioGio to challenge Diavolo and his ambitions for domination–the boss of the organization is an exaggeratedly bad kind of bad guy who, in spite of his intriguing multiple personality disorder, lacks the depth of Dio or Kira. We have to admit, the way this Requiem Stand is obtained is a bit of a clumsy *deus ex machina*. While Jotaro, at the end of *Stardust Crusaders*, little by little developed the ability to stop time so that he could gradually give Dio a run for his money, Giorno obtains the most powerful Stand imaginable, an expeditious power that leaves Diavolo with zero chance. Gold Experience Requiem is so over-the-top, in fact, that he doesn't even land on the Stand classification scale: in Golden Wind, Araki makes a habit of placing, between chapters, profiles that measure Stands according to criteria like strength, speed, and precision, rated from A to E, and the profile for Giorno's guardian doesn't offer any such ratings because he blows the criteria out of the water. "He has the ability to reduce his adversary's strength, both in terms of his actions and will, to zero. Since even death is reduced to nothingness, the person struck by this power is condemned to die over and over again infinitely," explains Gold Experience Requiem's profile in volume 17. No doubt about it, there's not much you can do against that! So, like the expulsion of Kars back in part two, this serves as a convenient way to get rid of Diavolo for good. Should we interpret this *deus ex machina* as an admission that King Crimson was too powerful? This time, couldn't Araki have come up with a more balanced way to counter this power, like he did in the battle between Josuke and Kira? Maybe we should see this as a limitation to the intuitive writing process, which is a double-edged sword.

Golden Wind, however, does not end there. After the final duel, Araki delivers a surprising epilogue, "Sleeping Slaves," which takes place just before Giorno meets Bucciarati for the first time in volume one. A double homage, to Michelangelo and to Bucciarati, this addendum serves as a sort of manifesto on the conception of destiny according to *Golden Wind*, presenting a Stand in the form of a stone, called Rolling Stones, whose special power is his ability to take the form of those who are destined to die soon so that he can offer them a more peaceful death than the one that's coming. Araki draws a parallel between

---

135. It's also worth noting that Giorno's Stand had already been pierced by the arrow at the start of part five (*Golden Wind* vol. 2), but nothing happened at the time.

this power and Michelangelo's conception of sculpture, which the Stand's user describes as a way of seeing fate by sculpting. Michel Lefftz, the head of the Art History and Archaeology Department at the University of Namur in Belgium, an expert of medieval and early modern sculpture, sheds some light on this peculiarity of the famous Florentine artist: "Michelangelo wrote sonnets—which, I might add, are magnificent and are translated in a great bilingual edition—in which he explains that the artist must 'simply' seek his subject in a block of marble. It's there and the artist just has to bring it out. Thus, it's an approach to sculpture that says that if the idea is there in the artist's head, the form must be found somewhere in the marble. It's not a matter of proceeding gradually, as all sculptors do, removing a little bit of material all over, preparing the marble, working off of progressive plans. No: Michelangelo searches within the material. He gets to the heart of it and the form is there: that's what he shows us. But that requires absolutely incredible conceptual intelligence! Other sculptors measure; they proceed slowly so that they don't take off too much material... because once it's been removed, that's it. (laughs)."[136] This idea that stone is destined to take on a certain form is thus embodied in Araki's work, in a Stand capable of predicting the future. In the epilogue, this Stand of stone takes on the appearance of Bucciarati, who indeed ends up losing his life during the final battle in the Colosseum, just like Narancia and Abbacchio a bit before that. This epilogue gives meaning to their dramatic deaths and tells us that while each person is a slave to their destiny, it's still possible for them, even in tragic situations, to find meaning in their existence during the time allotted to them among the living. Araki discussed this passage in 2012: "Today, when I think back on it, I think it may be the most impactful episode in the 25 years of the story of JoJo. It gets at the heart of the saga."[137] At least one thing is for sure: this touching epilogue foreshadows the fact that the saga will go on to continually examine the subject of predestination. It puts down on paper JoJo's conception of destiny at that point in time and, aptly, helps alleviate the disappointment of the final battle and thus end Golden Wind on a positive note.

Style Over Substance

For the 30th anniversary of JoJo's Bizarre Adventure, shortly before Araki's big Tokyo exhibition Ripples of Adventure (from August 24 to October 1, 2018, at the National Art Center in Tokyo), a Japanese website with an original concept

136. Remarks collected by us on March 22, 2019.
137. JoJomenon, 2012.

was launched. It was called *JoJosapiens*[138] and it established the typical profile of a fan of JoJo based on a big survey. According to that profile, Hirohiko Araki himself created the Stand–called JoJosapiens–for this archetypal reader. The website also shared the results of the survey, which received responses from over 17,000 people, mainly Japanese. One of the questions asked was, "What is your favorite part of *JoJo*?" The response was–as you may have guessed– *Golden Wind* (19.1%), just ahead of *Diamond is Unbreakable* (17.5%), then *Stardust Crusaders* (17.3%). Meanwhile, the fight between Bucciarati and the duo of Pesci and Prosciutto in the train to Florence was ranked as the fifth favorite battle of the saga. Could the imminent release of the anime adaptation of *Golden Wind*, which began airing on October 5, 2018, have tipped the scales in favor of this story arc? Perhaps. But *Golden Wind* didn't have to wait until 2018 to attract so much attention. As a sign of its popularity, in 2002, it received a great video game adaptation for the PlayStation 2 (in Japan only, in spite of aborted plans for a Western release), when the story arc had been over for three years. Similarly, two novels expanding the universe of part five were published, in 2001 and 2011.

So, how does Araki explain the popularity of *Golden Wind*? "I think that compared to the other parts, its success is probably due to the class and style of the characters, which diverge from the usual. Unless it's quite simply because of the tragic pasts and fates of the characters,"[139] he said in 2007. And it's true, he instills in part five a strong sense of camaraderie, in line with the *Jump* spirit (remember: friendship, effort, victory), and the heroes are memorable; at the same time, the beautiful, well researched, realistic Italian setting creates a charming ambiance. These characteristics actually also highlight the somewhat superficial and flashy aspects of the fifth part–ultimately, it's a lot like Giorno, the elegant but lackluster hero. Although part five has some interesting themes, like determinism and blood relations, it generally just touches on them quickly and, above all, like a speeding bullet, offers a long series of non-stop action that, like the voyage in *Stardust Crusaders*, proves to be linear and predictable–often without the magic and ingenious ideas of the third part, unfortunately. What's more, in spite of the emphasis on the characters, none of them are as well developed as Yoshikage Kira, for example, who was given long and intriguing passages of introspection with a slower rhythm. How can we explain this creative direction that puts style above substance, as well as the other missteps and shortcomings of the fifth part, like the fact that the drawings are increasingly difficult to decipher? Is it possible that the

138. "Was called," because sadly the website has been shut down.

139. Interview conducted by French publisher Tonkam, included at the end of the first French volume of *Golden Wind*.

composition of Araki's team of assistants changed, affecting the drawing of shadows and backgrounds, since these tasks are often entrusted to assistants during the manga creation process? Or should we see it as the artist losing steam during a period in which, sadly, the *mangaka*'s morale was very low?[140] Or is it the consequence of a less effective partnership than before between the author and his editor (he has had several since Ryōsuke Kabashima), during a period in which *Jump* experienced disruption and in which, Araki says, the editorial board began giving him more and more requests for modifications to his pages?[141] Who knows.

Ultimately, though, the saddest thing about *Golden Wind* is the abandonment of its most exciting idea: the fact of having a hero who's the son of Dio Brando. While we see at the beginning of the story arc that Giorno has a photo of his father in his wallet, sadly, this relation is never again brought up. The only small connection that remains is the battle cry "useless, useless, useless!" (the famous "*Muda Muda Muda!*") that Giorno shouts, a reference to Dio's own battle cry. Similarly, after a brief cameo at the beginning of the story arc, Jotaro never again reappears—and neither does Koichi, for that matter. When the author, in the middle of *Golden Wind*'s publication, was asked in *Jump*, "What does Jotaro intend to do with Giorno?," he answered: "I haven't thought about it yet. It might be that he's just simply curious about him?"[142] But we never really find out and the two men don't cross paths, even though an encounter between the third JoJo and the son of his sworn enemy, who he personally killed, would have made a lot of sense. All this said, Giorno defines his own individuality, and not according to his origins. It's by freeing himself from the context of his birth and the environment in which he grew up that he achieves self-actualization and, as for that, there's a certain consistency in no longer mentioning his blood relation with Dio, even if that means turning a piece of information that's initially important into a mere fun fact.

Today, what is the legacy of Ꭼ৹ɩɊᏕᴜ Ⰳ!ɴɊ? As I write these lines, the fifth part is back in the spotlight thanks to its anime version, which has generated a good amount of enthusiasm. From April 12 to May 12, 2019, for example, the Golden Wind Campaign took place in the streets of Tokyo's Harajuku

---

140. He shares in the postscript to the final volume of the Japanese *bunkobon* republication of *Golden Wind* that, for personal reasons, he fell into a deep depression while working on this part. Araki also says, touchingly, that his characters taught him to pick himself back up.

141. He says this in the postscript to the first volume of the Japanese *bunkobon* republication of *Golden Wind* (2005), adding that these requests rarely came with reasons and that, even when they did, the explanations were not convincing—although Araki notes that in saying this, he doesn't mean to criticize his publisher, he's simply expressing how he felt about the situation. It makes us wonder if censorship had been put in place, limiting the author's freedom of expression at a time when, in fact, he wanted to broach difficult subjects and show scenes expressing human brutality.

142. Interview of Araki in *Weekly Shōnen Jump* No. 9 of 1998.

neighborhood, a bastion of colorful fashion, and offered pop-up shops and a "JoJo Café" selling items based on the various characters of *Golden Wind* who (it's worth underscoring) are almost all named after food-related Italian words. Nonetheless, the heritage of *Golden Wind* within the saga remains weak. We never again hear mention of Giorno—which makes sense because, given how his power became so excessive, it's hard to see how Araki could have brought back the character—and his story arc has no bearing on the next, *Stone Ocean*, nor on the latest two, which actually reinterpret many key elements from the previous parts of *JoJo*. Perhaps we'll have to wait for a ninth part, after the one being published as I write this book, for the author to come back to and fix *Golden Wind* as a final homage to Italy? While we wait for that possibility, we can think fondly of the most beautiful passages in part five and, above all, of the unforgettable Bucciarati, one of the purest embodiments of the ode to humanity that is *JoJo*. These things are worth remembering.

CHAPTER VI: RIOT GIRLS
(1999-2003: JOJO'S BIZARRE ADVENTURE, PART 6)

Stand: End of World Party
You can reach heaven. It's just a matter of time.

To listen to while reading:

Jimi Hendrix – *Stone Free*
Bikini Kill – *Rebel Girl*
Marilyn Manson – *Posthuman*
Led Zeppelin – *Stairway to Heaven*
HÆLOS – *End of World Party*

Trish Una. Even though she's the only major female character in *Golden Wind*, Diavolo's daughter changed *JoJo*. Before her, damsels in distress had to count on a man to save them. Even Lisa Lisa, the legendary trainer in *Battle Tendency*, had to be rescued by her protégé Joseph; in *Stardust Crusaders*, saving Holly Kujo was precisely the driving force behind the journey. *Diamond is Unbreakable* began to turn things around. Reimi Sugimoto served as a more independent version of the "woman to be saved," being responsible for her own rescue: in spite of being a wandering spirit incapable of doing anything to living people, she remained on earth, with patience and determination, in order to find people who could help avenge her death and, in so doing, cleanse the streets of Morioh. Trish, meanwhile, may be escorted by a group of young men, but she gains her own independence as she learns to control her Stand, Spice Girl—named, of course, for the iconic '90s musical group that was part of the girl power movement—in volume 12 of *Golden Wind*, in which she ends up saving the heroes.

After *Golden Wind*, Araki's saga went on a long hiatus. Giorno's story ended in the April 5, 1999, issue of *Shōnen Jump* and the next story arc didn't start until the issue dated January 1, 2000. After so many years of working, the *mangaka* finally gave himself a bit of a break—up to this point, he only took vacation during the new year holiday season. Then again... the author didn't rest on his laurels during this period, since he created the spin-off *Dead Man's Questions* and worked on his book of illustrations *JOJO A-GO!GO!* (February 2000, never published in English), before tackling the sixth part of *JoJo*, entitled *Stone Ocean*—with this English title used from the very beginning for the original Japanese version. Additionally, while the other parts had numbered the volumes continuously from the beginning of the series, this sixth part reset the numbering to one: a choice by the publisher that was most likely intended to attract new readers. So, *Stone Ocean* continues *JoJo*'s trend of featuring strong women by telling the story of Jolyne, a tenacious 19-year-old young woman who is nothing like the "package to be delivered" or "damsel in distress" types of female characters. She's actually quite the opposite: one of the big drivers of part six is Jolyne's fierce struggle to save her father.

I'll remind you: in 1986, Araki censored himself. Before starting *JoJo*, he brought an end to *Gorgeous Irene* because he felt like the *shōnen* world just wasn't ready yet for women fighters. Beyond the fact of showing a woman delivering blows (and the need to offer characters that the main target audience, boys and young men, could identify with), it was, above all, the risk that she herself would be hit that posed a problem at the time, at least in a *shōnen* magazine. This trend ultimately changed, notably thanks to the martial artists in the very popular series *Ranma 1/2* (1987-1996, Rumiko Takahashi), as well as characters like Lisa Lisa in *Battle Tendency* and Chi-Chi in *Dragon Ball*. So, in 1999, changed attitudes allowed Araki to go back to explore the opportunities of a female protagonist: in *JOJOmenon*, he explains that by the time of *Stone Ocean*, "seeing a girl get punched was no longer shocking. I figured that, man or woman, it's all the same thing, and this time I felt like I could create a strong female character."[143] His new heroine, who lives in Florida in the year 2011, is a fighter who could rival the impressive Linda Hamilton in *Terminator 2: Judgment Day* (1991, James Cameron), a strong woman if there ever was one, while sporting—in true *JoJo* fashion—a flamboyant look similar to the girl-power pop style of the Spice Girls. But Jolyne is so much more than that.

Let's take a moment to revisit Toshiyuki Araki's childhood. His relationship with his two sisters. "Every time I that I would bicker with one of my sisters, at a certain point, the one who had nothing to do with it would burst into tears. 'Why are you the one crying!?,' I would ask angrily. [...] It was actually a strategy orchestrated by my sisters: they would create a situation in which no matter the excuse I tried to offer to my parents, it would always be my fault. I swear, whenever I hear on the news about some innocent person who was wrongly accused and put into prison, I get teary eyed! All the time, I would pray for those two brats to disappear once and for all, and I eventually even

143. *JOJOmenon*, 2012.

started thinking of myself as a victim of some curse that would always make people misunderstand me. Even when some disaster happened at my school, for some reason, I would always be put on the list of suspects."[144] It's hard to not draw parallels with Jolyne, who, in *Stone Ocean*, is thrown in prison for a murder she didn't commit. Could the heroine of part six be the author's way of settling the score from his childhood trauma? It shows a disdain for injustice that we've actually seen before, in the relationship between Dio and Jonathan early in *Phantom Blood*, with the hero suffering from the evil deeds of his adopted brother, who nevertheless enjoys favorable treatment by their father. In *Stone Ocean*, this incarceration also creates a connection with the third hero who, I'll remind you, spent the first few chapters of *Stardust Crusaders* behind bars. This repeating of history makes sense because Jolyne is the daughter of none other than Jotaro Kujo! She inherited the "*Ora Ora Ora!*" battle cry from her father and, in the Japanese version, delivers the line "*Yare yare da wa*," which is the feminine version of "*Yare yare da ze*." We quickly discover that, in many ways, *Stone Ocean* is the true sequel to *Stardust Crusaders*.

(Three.)

Shōjo's Bizarre Adventure

First we had Dio's son, now we have Jotaro's daughter. Moreover, the illustration that opens the first chapter shows Jolyne in a pose similar to the well-known image of Giorno opening his collar and pulling at the bottom of his jacket,[145] as if to signify continuity with her predecessor; additionally, the young woman has a ponytail that looks like that worn by the golden-haired "gang star." And while Giorno's hairstyle extravagantly reinterpreted the open spaces formed by the curls on Michelangelo's *David*, Jolyne's hair has a sort of blended pop and Renaissance style to it, with two colors,[146] which we can see as symbolic of her mixed heritage (her mother is Italian-American), and the two braided buns, the complexity of which is reminiscent of certain hairstyles of the Italian Quattrocento, as seen in the portraits of Simonetta Vespucci painted by Sandro Botticelli and Piero di Cosimo. From the point of view of clothing style, we again see continuity from the fifth hero: while GioGio wore a

---

144. Postscript to the final volume of the Japanese *bunkobon* republication of *Stardust Crusaders*, 2002.
145. *JJBA*, vol. 47, at the end of the flashback to Giorno's childhood, and the opening illustration to the first chapter of *Stone Ocean*.
146. Note that light-colored locks of hair on top of dark hair was in fashion in *Jump*! This style was also seen on the heroes of the very popular manga *Hikaru no Go* (1998-2003, Takeshi Obata and Yumi Hotta) and *Yu-Gi-Oh!* (1996-2004, Kazuki Takahashi).

ladybug symbol, Jolyne sports a butterfly emblem. This all fits perfectly. From the start, JoJo VI proves to be one of Araki's greatest characters.

One difference, though, is her relationship with her father. Unlike Giorno, whose connection with Dio is never given more depth in *Golden Wind*, Jolyne has spent her teenage years hating her absent father, and she doesn't miss an opportunity to say so. "Shut it and stop pretending to be a dad. You decide to come see me only when I'm in the slammer? Is that your idea of fatherly love? You're dead to me now,"[147] she says when Jotaro visits her in prison in volume two. We see a repeat of events here: since *Stardust Crusaders*, the heroes of *JoJo* never grow up in the standard Japanese family model and, in each case, there's a notable absence of the father, who abandons or neglects his family —perhaps we can see in this the influence on Araki of manga written by Ikki Kajiwara, in which the parents are often absent, dead, or unfit. When asked about this, French translator Satoko Fujimoto says that in the late 1980s or early 1990s, single mothers, like Jotaro's and Josuke's moms, were actually not unusual in Japan. However, they were very frowned upon. "Single-parent families have always existed. And, indeed, it's a good thing to feature them prominently... It's very hard to be a single mother in Japan. They are seen as people on the margins and don't receive much support from society. Here in France, this situation is not as much of a big deal, but there... and especially at the time of *Stardust Crusaders*, a family without both parents was seen as a troubled family. People tended to keep this situation secret." In *Stone Ocean*, the father's absence is even more significant given that the story establishes that Jolyne's parents are divorced, which is not a matter taken lightly in Japan. "In France, people get divorced all the time. But in Japan, when you have kids, it's much more rare," explains Satoko Fujimoto. "Twenty years ago, at the time *Stone Ocean* was written, I think that the situation hadn't changed much since the time of *Stardust Crusaders*."[148] While Araki's manga takes place in the United States, it was created in a Japanese context. As such, we can see the parents' divorce as the reason why Jolyne went down the wrong path and fell for a bad boy, probably trying subconsciously to fill the emotional void created by her father's absence.

And in *Stone Ocean*, everything starts with a conspiracy tied to the bad boy in question. In his Alfa Romeo GTV, Jolyne's Romeo is speeding. As he and Jolyne flirt, Romeo runs over a man due to his dangerous driving. Sadly, life is unfair: Jolyne is charged with murder instead of her boyfriend. Betrayed by her lawyer, the young woman is found guilty and is sentenced to 15 years in prison. She is then transferred to an island penitentiary known as the Green Dolphin Street Prison, a.k.a. The Aquarium. It's worth noting

147. *Stone Ocean*, vol. 2.
148. Remarks collected by us on May 15, 2019.

that Araki created his setting after visiting several prisons and talking with the director of Miami's Turner Guilford Knight Correctional Center. So, did Jotaro really abandon his daughter? Not exactly. Before his divorce, he gave a special necklace to Jolyne's mother with the instruction that she give it to Jolyne if their daughter should ever find herself in trouble. Jolyne's mom does this and, while the young woman is opening the pendant, it pricks her; from there, strange things start happening to her. It turns out she has just acquired a Stand, triggered by a piece of the famous arrow, hidden inside the pendant. Her brand-new Stand becomes known as Stone Free, representing her desire to escape. The Stand's body is made up of a long string that can take on various different forms, such as a net that can block attacks. It's also worth noting that, in a scene with "shocking" morals, Jolyne uses her power to exact revenge and kill her lawyer remotely... which, when it comes down to it, actually makes her guilty of a murder that no one is aware of![149] In any case, this bit of arrow is responsible for some of the story's earliest incidents and, passing from one person to the next, it creates new Stands inside the prison.

With seemingly everyday situations becoming unpredictable, in a confined environment hiding its fair share of curiosities, the early chapters of *Stone Ocean* have a narrative structure reminiscent of *Diamond is Unbreakable* —moreover, just as how Morioh had bizarre tourist sites, part six has "the prison's seven wonders." The return to an isolated world was something that Araki really wanted; additionally, he loves the film *The Great Escape* (1963, John Sturges) and wanted to tell that same kind of adventurous escape story. The first third of the manga, which is often fast-paced and original, does not entirely erase the rambling nature of *Golden Wind* (we'll come back to this), but it's satisfying and brings back fond memories thanks to things like the user of the "debt collector" Stand Marilyn Manson, who clearly fits into the legacy of the D'Arby brothers. Above all, this time, the new heroine does not in any way fade into the background: she's the one who drives the story and her quest is placed at the forefront. A quest that takes shape after her father visits her. Jotaro goes to see Jolyne in prison to warn her that someone wants to do harm to the Joestars: her imprisonment is the result of a frame-up and the best thing for her would be to use her Stand to escape. The father and daughter are then both targeted and Jotaro ends up being defeated in battle by Whitesnake, a Stand that kind of looks like Deadly Queen and is capable of transforming memories and Stands into discs.[150] The senior JoJo does not die, but he falls into a coma. For some reason, the evil Stand user,

149. This happens at the end of chapter three of *Stone Ocean*. The lawyer's death is not confirmed, but he's badly injured, with no way to call for help, so it's hard to imagine him surviving.
150. This idea of discs that are inserted into and removed from faces is reminiscent of the creature "CD" from the horror film *Hellraiser III* (1992, Anthony Hickox), who has a CD slot in his face.

whose identity remains unknown, aimed to trap Jotaro in order to steal his memory. Whitesnake, whose body is covered in the letters A, T, C, and G (the four nucleotides that make up DNA), embodies a dark inversion of the concept of inheritance: the stripping and diversion of assets to give them to another person. Twisting and damaging the branches of the family tree.

Jolyne could flee, thanks to a submarine owned by the Speedwagon Foundation located just off the island, but she decides to remain captive. She aims to fight to recover her father's two discs—for his Stand and his memories—in spite of not really knowing her father; she realizes that her father actually loves her very much. Something that he probably never could—or never knew how to—express before. Thus, the first major theme of *Stone Ocean* becomes apparent, as the user of Whitesnake, surprised by Jolyne's determination, inserts Stand discs into a slew of prisoners to try to eliminate the heroine and her small team of allies.

(Two.)

A God in an Alcove

Retcon. An English neologism, a contraction of "retroactive continuity." It refers to when an author introduces revisions into their story by adding new information that alters the established facts. For example, the author can kill off a character, then decide that they're actually still alive and continue their story from that new basis. In other words, it's a way of rewriting a story that's used commonly in the universe of American superhero comics, as many artists have had to take over series while working off of what previously happened in the stories. The introduction of retcon is also a convenient way for an artist entering an existing saga to manipulate certain aspects of the universe in order to create a story that better suits their own tastes. In *JoJo's Bizarre Adventure*, the addition of the star-shaped birthmark on the bodies of the Joestars is an example of light retcon, a version that's perfectly acceptable and that doesn't damage the overall coherence. The sixth part, however, is not so gentle. While it may be a sequel to *Stardust Crusaders*, it so heavily changes the existing characters that it ends up looking like a totally independent entity. From here on, you just have to accept that we can no longer view the saga as one big, consistent story. In part six, Jotaro looks younger than he did before his journey to Egypt. This is probably due to—in addition to his stunningly refreshed physique—his new sportswear-style getup. Incidentally, the sleeves of his jacket, which have "JOJO" written repeatedly along them, seem to have been inspired by a piece from the fall-winter 1999-2000 collection from Céline, the influence of which we also see on the cover for volume five.[151] It's also hard to believe that Jotaro was the father of a little girl at the time of *Diamond is Unbreakable*. However, the most dissonant element is the rewriting of Dio's story, which goes hand in hand with the new bad guy.

Who is the person, hiding in the shadows, that controls the terrifying Whitesnake? The prison's chaplain, a man that no one would suspect. Father Enrico Pucci is an admirer of Dio, who he met not long before the events of *Stardust Crusaders* and for whom he has taken up the mantle. Not the mantle of seeking domination; instead, it's a more private quest that Dio calls, in a flashback, "reaching heaven." *Stone Ocean* contains four memories (in volumes 6, 7, 11, and 15) of encounters between Pucci and Dio that show, in a disorderly fashion, the young priest's growing fascination for the ancient vampire. In these memories, Dio loses a lot of his bestiality, seemingly crossing over entirely to the romanticized version of vampires, closer in spirit to the characters of author Anne Rice (*Interview with the Vampire*, 1976) than to the ferocious vampire of *Stardust Crusaders*. Between Dio and Pucci, we see latent homoerotic tension build, culminating in a scene in volume 11 in which the duo, lying on the same bed, get into a discussion about the soul as an intimate ambiance hangs in the air. "You are the king of kings... How far will you go? I want to follow you to find out! I love you as I love God...," Pucci tells a shirtless Dio after the vampire asks him why he hasn't tried to steal The World using Whitesnake. "I'm sorry, I offended you...," Dio responds. "I've never met someone who could put me at ease just by speaking... I was afraid of losing you..."[152] It's impossible to imagine the Dio from *Stardust Crusaders* speaking like this. And then there's the fact that we learn in part six that Dio supposedly traveled several times between Egypt and the United States in 1988 to visit his friend Pucci. Why would Dio, the guy who couldn't survive in sunlight, go through all that trouble? Moreover, the author gives him a goal that's never been mentioned before. The aforementioned plan to get to heaven. Initially, we're not really sure what Araki is talking about. "Going to heaven! Humans can spend their whole lives preparing for that voyage. That's the amazing thing about them. You know what I mean?,"[153] explains Pucci to a prisoner. Up to this point, the idea seems to resemble the typical one of a heavenly afterlife. However, in the flashback in volume six, Dio explains that his personal heaven is a state of mind, an ecstasy that can be achieved through spiritual evolution. A happiness that makes wealth and domination pale in comparison. At that

151. In the photo for the brand Céline, taken by Patrick Demarchelier, model Gisèle Bundchen is wearing a red roll-neck sweater whose sleeves have the name "CÉLINE" repeating along the side. On the cover for volume five of *Stone Ocean*, the heroine, in a very similar position, is wearing a top bearing the repeated name "JOLYNE."
152. *Stone Ocean*, vol. 11.
153. *Stone Ocean*, vol. 4.

point, we still don't know what he means, but the vampire apparently wrote notes on how to reach it, in a notebook that Jotaro apparently read after Dio's death before burning it. This is why Pucci needs Jotaro's memories. He waited for two decades for the opportunity to get his hands on them.

However, cold and calculating though he may be, the charismatic Father Pucci is not actually as evil as you would think. At least, not in such a radical way as suggested in the first few volumes, in which Whitesnake's user describes himself as "rotten through and through" (vol. 3). Really, Pucci is fighting for a specific conception of happiness, according to which certainty leads to serenity. Indeed, the concept of "heaven" in *Stone Ocean* is really—as we learn at the very end—just the ability to know exactly what the future has in store for you so that you can eliminate the fear of the unknown and prepare for your inevitable death. While we're left wondering why Dio, who's theoretically immortal (granted, the story showed us that wasn't exactly the case), would want to obtain such a power, Pucci's reasons are more understandable since he originally became a priest in hopes of finding answers to his existential questions. How do we find true happiness and what is the force that governs the destiny of humans? Why did his twin brother die at birth[154] and not him? Pucci's second trauma, during his adolescence, was the death of his sister Perla. Which affected him deeply. That's the day his archivist Stand, Whitesnake, was born, a power resulting from his desire to preserve his memories of Perla. That same day, Pucci went to see Dio, a being he had met briefly sometime before that and who had miraculously cured his malformed foot... before giving him an arrowhead. Why do people cross paths? What is it that governs the world? Pucci became convinced that Dio held all the answers. At that moment, he became no longer just a servant of God, but also of Dio Brando—if that's even possible—the being that, in Pucci's opinion, gets closer than anyone to divine truth. Pucci have himself a mission: to find a way to enable humans to face their destiny. To accept it without suffering.

We can tell that Araki improvised this idea of "heaven" gradually as he created each page. We can imagine him asking himself, just like his readers, what this closely guarded secret of ecstasy could look like. And the suspense works: from beginning to end, the most exciting element in *Stone Ocean* is the possibility of finally discovering what form this much-vaunted heaven will take. As it happens, the idea of heaven—and even the idea of featuring a Catholic priest?—perhaps comes from the surprising fact that Araki, in his youth, attended a Protestant Christian school, which meant that he read the Bible every day. It's also worth noting that we find in *JoJo*, from *Stardust Crusaders*

---

154. *Stone Ocean* goes on to tell us that this is not actually the case: his brother is alive and is actually the character Weather Report.

onward, the theme of ascension to heaven when important characters die, in a way that's reminiscent of Christian (i.e., Catholic) art and is really quite unusual for Japan. While the author has said that his religious education helped forge his ways of thinking, he still doesn't consider himself to be a religious believer. "I wouldn't say that I believe in God, but rather that I feel that he exists. It's hard to explain in definite terms. I'd put it in the same category as concepts like destiny,"[155] he explained in 2001, during the publication of *Stone Ocean*. What you have to understand here is that, for Araki, belief in a god, just like a belief in destiny, is a supernatural notion that you either believe in or you don't. However, when you think about it, we can say that in *JoJo's Bizarre Adventure*, destiny is itself a supreme divine force. The saga previously brought up the idea that each person's destiny is governed by an impalpable force: it was the subject of the eloquent epilogue to *Golden Wind*, for example; there's also the fact that Stand users in *JoJo* are involuntarily drawn to each other by an inexplicable, supernatural force. *Stone Ocean* is the part that demonstrates this conception of destiny in the most ambitious and radical way. Indeed, Pucci's dream, his desire to soothe the human soul by alleviating the pain of destiny, takes shape in spectacular fashion in the 17th and final volume, which we will come back to soon.

(One.)

Sine Wave

While *Stone Ocean* begins with excitement, the quality of this part constantly wavers. As such, up to volume seven, *Stone Ocean* only partially inherits the problems with complexity that were legion in *Golden Wind*, with powers and situations that lacked clarity. At Green Dolphin Street Prison, things initially remain reasonable. Alas, from there, the author again pushes the limits of being over-the-top and convoluted. More than ever before, really. Indeed, *Stone Ocean* presents one overloaded panel after another and long battles between Stands with properties that are at times abstruse; meanwhile, the process that Pucci follows to reach "heaven" is totally bizarre and leads to a chain of events that are complex, to say the least. In summarize: a bone from Dio's body transforms 38 sinners (i.e., prisoners) into plants that in turn give birth to a green baby (in volume 10). Then, Pucci speaks a series of words in the following order: "spiral staircase," "rhinoceros beetle," "city in ruins," "fig tart," "rhinoceros beetle," "*Via Dolorosa*," "rhinoceros beetle," "particular points," "Giotto," "angels," "hydrangea," "rhinoceros beetle," "particular

155. Joint interview with Kazuma Kaneko, conducted in 2001 for the magazine *Thrill*.

points," "secret emperor." After that, the green baby cuts Pucci open and the two beings fuse together (in volume 11). The priest must then go to a specific point: 28° 24' north latitude, 80° 36' west longitude, which is in the middle of the Kennedy Space Center at Cape Canaveral, Florida. There, he must wait for a new moon, set to occur six days later, so that he can reach heaven. All around Pucci, who now has a new Stand, strange temporal phenomena begin to occur. As he waits for the new moon, the priest is joined by three secret sons of Dio (Rykiel, Ungaro, and Versus) who've come from God knows where, drawn to Pucci because their father's energy lives on in him since his fusion with the green baby. Notably, Giorno Giovanna, who is also Dio's son, does not appear, which shows a lack of consistency and reinforces the idea that it's better to view *Stone Ocean* as an independent story arc, rather than looking for overall consistency at all costs. That said, even within part six there are things that don't make sense: why does Pucci's brother have a star-shaped birthmark, in spite of having no relation to the Joestar family? Why do Whitesnake's disks continue to exist after the Stand is gone? Why does Narciso Anasui first appear as a woman before becoming the male character that we're familiar with?

Meanwhile, back in the prison, Jolyne and her allies—Narciso Anasui, Ermes Costello, Weather Report, and Emporio Alniño, a young boy who lives in a secret room in the prison—attempt to escape in order to catch Pucci; however, they come face to face with the guard Miu Miu and her Stand designed to prevent all jailbreaks, the formidable Jail House Lock. Anyone who falls under its spell can only remember three things at a time: beyond that, each new piece of information replaces another. To make up for the failings of her short-term memory, Jolyne begins to write notes on her own body, like the hero of the movie *Memento* (2000, Christopher Nolan). It's a very exciting episode that, again centered on the prison and its mysteries, brings back the spirit of the first few volumes. After the escape, *Stone Ocean* changes its dynamic and becomes a road trip across Florida. Destination: Cape Canaveral. From there, the story abruptly alternates between great ideas that are successfully executed (like Versus' Stand Underworld, in volume 14, who can identically reproduce any memory saved in the ground and who uses this power to place Jolyne on an airplane about to crash) and passages that are convoluted, to say the least. This is pushed to the extreme with the power Heavy Weather, which "modifies the refraction of the sun's rays thanks to Weather Report's power over the weather thus creates a 'subliminal effect' that affects the minds of all living things, who start to see themselves as snails."[156] It's a typical example of *JoJo*'s "rococo" period, the point when the story goes too

156. *Stone Ocean*, vol. 15.

far, when the powers become so strange that the rules of battles become much too extensive and too vague, which means that anything can happen and, thus, the reader is left in the dark, unable to imagine how the heroes will be able to get out of a sticky situation since the solution may very well be pulled out of a magic hat.

Stone Ocean also continues the trend of overloaded graphics seen in *Golden Wind*. A single face can have three or four different types of shading—parallel hatch marks, lattice, Ben Day dots, solid coloring—producing a complex and sometimes imprecise result, while the arms have strange cracks that appear to outline imaginary muscles. We no longer necessarily see stunningly gorgeous characters; instead, we find an exploration of bizarre representations of the body. For example, *Stone Ocean* presents characters with increasingly imaginary anatomy and looks: Pucci's facial hair creates a network connecting his hair, beard, and eyebrow; the head of the prison, Roccobarocco, has an extraterrestrial-shaped skull; and Jolyne's lawyer has elf ears. In general, the mouths become increasingly fleshy and the noses increasingly pointy. Of note, while the boys in *Golden Wind* trended more feminine, the heroines in *Stone Ocean* instead trend more masculine, in the same spirit of blurring the lines between genders or of rejecting strict conventions about appearances. For example, Ermes Costello, one of Jolyne's female acolytes, has a vertical line below her mouth that looks like a straight-lined goatee; there's also, in the first volume, during the strip search, a prisoner who has taken male hormones and looks in every way like a man (except below the belt, apparently). The prisoners' behavior does not fit with stereotypes of feminine elegance and, in the first volume, they don't hesitate to talk about masturbation or even about "hiding cash in your ass or in your pussy"!

When we get to volume 16, *Stone Ocean* takes a fascinating turn. Pucci's new Stand, C-Moon, makes him, the user, the center of gravity, thus affecting the gravitational forces on everyone and everything around him. "Everything above him is propelled toward space and everything around him within a 3-km radius is pushed back, parallel to the ground. This 'falling' backward ends once the 3-km limit is reached and everything falls back to the ground as normal."[157] This results in several acrobatic sequences as Jolyne and her allies try to reach the Kennedy Space Center where Pucci, the center of gravity, is situated. Alas, in the final volume, the priest achieves his aims. He changes his Stand one last time to acquire the magnificent centaur Made in Heaven, which has the power to bring about Pucci's "heaven": the ability

157. *Stone Ocean*, vol. 16 (Stand profile).

to accelerate the passage of time. The last battle is hopeless. Incapable of matching the invincible priest, Jolyne, Jotaro, Ermes, and Anasui ultimately lose their lives in a final brawl in the middle of the ocean...

And then comes heaven.

(Zero.)

OCIREDERF ENOLAZNA

WHEN
EVERYTHING
TURNS
WHITE

03.rd | THiRD
éditions

Table of Contents

And then comes heaven. Enrico Pucci accelerates time so much around him that the universe reaches its end. It finishes a full cycle. Hirohiko Araki is working off of the idea that life is an eternal cycle and that it's possible that, one day, a world just like the first one will be reborn, undergoing a similar evolution and becoming a home to the same beings, with some slight differences. "Humanity has seen its entire future before returning to this point!," Pucci declares. And that's the "heaven" we've been talking about: after this "full circle" in the universe's chronology of events, anyone who was alive at the time the power was unleashed is still alive in the new universe and everyone has a constant feeling of déjà vu. They have retained the memories of everything that happened to them, and thus of what will happen to them, and they are now, according to the priest, able to deal with these events. In this way, Pucci wishes to become a sort of shepherd for humanity, even though he has become the exception, the only living thing that can move freely without following the path laid out by fate. However, there's one flaw in all this. Pucci accelerated time until "returning" to the equivalent of the events of volume two, with the goal of eliminating young Emporio before he becomes a threat in the future. Unfortunately for Pucci, it would seem that, as the child says, fate comes down on the side of justice, and the boy finds a loophole and manages to defeat the priest. In so doing, Emporio, who takes up Jolyne's quest, becomes the most radical symbol of a recurring theme in *JoJo's Bizarre Adventure*: the fight to try to change one's destiny. Time then accelerates one last time and Emporio ends up in a third universe. The boy, who is now the only one to have retained his memories, meets new versions of his old companions. For example, Jolyne is now called Irene—a nod to Araki's first strong heroine, from *Gorgeous Irene*?— everyone is alive and happier than before in this new world, but the memories of everyone that Emporio knew have disappeared. And *Stone Ocean* concludes on this bittersweet note.

In the final chapters of this sixth part, before writing the ending, Araki thought that he had reached the peak of his creativity. He believed he had created all possible and imaginable Stand powers; he figured that the only thing left at that point was to explore parallel universes. So, Araki felt like he had reached his limits, but also like he'd already resolved Jolyne's personal quest. She filled the void in her heart from a lack of fatherly love and the trials and tribulations she experienced helped her become a strong woman. "If we look at this story as one about the protagonist's growth, then her story is over. So, now how am I supposed to conclude this manga? In other words, I have nothing left to draw. It's over. *JoJo's Bizarre Adventure* has reached its climax and its name is *Stone Ocean*. The end. Except no, not at all. That doesn't feel right."[158] Feeling like he shouldn't give up just because he seemed to have

---

158. Postscript to the final volume of the Japanese *bunkobon* republication of *Stone Ocean*, 2009.

reached the end of his series, the author gave it some thought. And the answer he came up with was to return to his beginnings. He thought about the Italian Renaissance, during which there was a rediscovery of Greco-Roman antiquity, and he decided to draw inspiration from that. That's just what he needed: to return to his beginnings and unleash the nostalgic energy within him. So, Araki changed the ending of *Stone Ocean* at the last minute, following through on this idea, and that's how we got the conclusion we know today. "Jolyne Cujoh's memories might be different in this reset universe, but her love and her feelings are still there. They became something eternal and I'm sure she'll keep growing wiser and stronger,"[159] says the *mangaka*. A touching, almost paternal, goodbye from Araki, who we can easily imagine writing those words with tears in his eyes.

Sayonara Wild Hearts

"Initially, I found that the story was very different from what you'd normally see in *Shōnen Jump*. The concept of an escape was a totally new approach for us, so I was a bit surprised,"[160] said Suguru Sugita, one of the magazine's editors. However, these words, spoken in 2018, are not about *Stone Ocean*, but rather the recent successful series *The Promised Neverland* by Kaiu Shirai and Posuka Demizu, which began in 2016. It's about a group of children who plan their escape from the fake Eden in which they're held. How should we interpret the fact that the editor forgot that there had indeed been a previous manga in *Shōnen Jump*—granted, an older one, but with a big name—in which the main characters plotted to escape from prison? In his defense, we have to admit that *Stone Ocean* is less a story about escape and more a manga about life in prison. But perhaps we can see this as a little clue that part six of *JoJo's Bizarre Adventure* was not very memorable? Today, *Stone Ocean* seems to have been somewhat forgotten; it came in sixth place (8.5%) in the *JoJosapiens* survey ranking the popularity of each story arc. Could this be because its legacy is nowhere to be found in the subsequent evolutions of the saga, whereas the first four parts have been referenced numerous times?[161] An anime adaptation (very likely coming out in 2020 or 2021) will probably move *Stone Ocean* back into the spotlight, and hopefully it will be able to fix the deficiencies of the source material.

159. *Ibid.*
160. "On a tout fait pour que la série soit un succès, et on a réussi» : entretien avec les auteurs du manga *The Promised Neverland*," remarks gathered by Élodie Drouard on the blog *Pop Up' Culture* from France Info, 2018. https://blog.francetvinfo.fr/popup/2018/08/21/on-a-tout-fait-pour-que-la-serie-soit-un-succes-et-on-a-reussi-entretien-avec-les-auteurs-du-manga-the-promised-neverland.html.
161. One of the few references: in volume 14 of *JoJolion*, the character Kaato comes out of a prison named "Stone Ocean."

So, what are the most memorable things about *Stone Ocean*? Above all, its incredibly charismatic heroine. Jolyne Cujoh is so photogenic that she is part of the select club of fictional characters who have become fashion models, like the heroine of the video game *Final Fantasy XIII*, Lightning, who served as a virtual model for a Louis Vuitton campaign in 2016.[162] For her part, Jolyne has been decked out in Italian fashion. In December 2012, the women's magazine *SPUR* presented *Jolyne, Fly High with Gucci*, a series of colorful pages blending manga with fashion illustrations. This special feature also included Bruno Bucciarati and Leone Abbacchio dressed in Gucci from head to toe. It was a one-shot manga with a story based on an anachronistic dream, developed in partnership with the woman who was the brand's creative director at the time, Frida Giannini. In early 2013, enlarged images from the one-shot were displayed in the windows of over 70 Gucci stores worldwide, according to *The Telegraph*.[163] Before that, in September 2011, Rohan Kishibe had appeared in the Gucci store in the Shinjuku neighborhood of Tokyo after being the hero in the first color one-shot to appear in the very same magazine, *SPUR*, a story that centered on a handbag with strange powers.[164]

That said, we'll also remember *Stone Ocean* for its conclusion, which demonstrates boldness rarely seen in a manga, no matter the series. This ending closed out the first great era of *JoJo's Bizarre Adventure* on the note of a tragic hero, echoing, with a more radiant version, the martyrdom of the original JoJo, Jonathan Joestar. Adieu to the shining lights that were Jolyne and Jotaro. This time, *JoJo really* could have ended. On top of his feeling that he'd reached peak creativity, the author thought he'd gone past the age of being able to draw for a *shōnen* magazine and, thus, he figured that *Stone Ocean* would be his final story arc in *Jump*. Araki, who was already quite different from everyone else at the magazine, began questioning his position more and more as he realized that, with the exception of the author of *Kochikame*, everyone around him was now younger. Moreover, and we can see this with our own eyes, many of those younger artists were fans of his work and there were numerous stories inspired by *JoJo* in the magazine—for example, *Shaman King*, whose spirits are reminiscent of Stands, or *Hunter X Hunter*, whose character Hisoka is a lot like Dio, among other similarities. However, the tone of Araki's manga remains totally unique. When you look closely at *Jump* during the *Stone Ocean* period,

162. The character even gave a fake interview to the prestigious British newspaper *The Telegraph*! Before that, Lightning and her companions showed off the spring-summer 2012 collection from Prada in the April 2012 issue of the magazine *Arena Homme +*.
163. Olivia Lidbury, "Gucci kicks off the New Year in Manga style," *The Telegraph*, January 3, 2013. http://fashion.telegraph.co.uk/news-features/TMG9778331/Gucci-kicks-off-the-New-Year-in-Manga-style.html. What's more, the meeting between Hirohiko Araki and Frida Giannini was documented in photos in the Japanese mook *JOJOmenon*.
164. This story appears (reproduced in black and white) in the first volume of the spin-off *Thus Spoke Rohan Kishibe*.

JoJo is totally offbeat compared to the rest of the magazine, with its mature characters and heavy themes, while the other manga abounded with young heroes and joyful adventures. Basically, we can call it the era of *One Piece*. However, surprising though it may seem, Araki still did not leave *Jump* and the saga of the Joestars did not quite come to an end. However, one thing is for sure: after part six, *JoJo's Bizarre Adventure* will be forever changed.

CHAPTER VII: CLOSE THE WORLD, OPEN THE NEXT (2004-2011: JOJO'S BIZARRE ADVENTURE, PART 7)

Stand: Mandela Effect

The existence of a quote, the way a title is written, the truth behind a fact…
Sometimes, what we believe with certainty proves to be
a collective hallucination.

To listen to while reading:

Electrelane – *John Wayne*
David Bowie – *Scary Monsters (And Super Creeps)*
AC/DC – *Dirty Deeds Done Dirt Cheap*
Depeche Mode – *Personal Jesus*
Pat Metheny & Lyle Mays – *It's For You*

This is not *JoJo's Bizarre Adventure*. *Steel Ball Run* may look like *JoJo*, it may taste like *JoJo*, it may include characters from the saga and even the concept of Stands… It's all there, but it's not *JoJo*! At least, part seven was not initially presented that way, but rather as a new work by Hirohiko Araki, not bearing the title *JoJo's Bizarre Adventure*. "To tell the truth, I was told to take the title off starting with the sixth part," the author says. "But I wanted to hold onto it. So, I insisted that it be used on *Stone Ocean*, but it was taken off with *Steel Ball Run*, on the one hand because the main character was no longer a JoJo, and on the other hand because the story arc was also intended for readers who weren't familiar with *JoJo*."[165] *Steel Ball Run* hit the shelves in January 2004. Almost a year had passed since the final chapter of *Stone Ocean* was published, in April of the previous year, and Araki's new work debuted in the issue of *Shōnen Jump* dated February 2, 2004, even appearing on the cover.

But before we get into the details, let's go back a few months. While there was a gap between *Stone Ocean* and *Steel Ball Run*, that doesn't mean that the

---

165. *JOJOmenon*, 2012.

author was twiddling his thumbs. Before returning to his saga, Araki took some time to experiment. For the first time, the artist launched an exhibition of original works (around 40 of them, including illustrations that appeared on the covers for his series and two works produced for the event), which is unusual for a *mangaka*. The trend has started to change since then, but in the past, manga pages and illustrations just ended up in a drawer, never to be shown or sold. For the inaugural event, Araki chose the city of Paris because France is filled with the Western art history that he loves so much and also, perhaps, because comics are considered more of an artform there than they are in Japan. So, April 10-30, 2003, the Odermatt-Vedovi Gallery, which no longer exists today, hosted the exhibition "JOJO in Paris," during which works were sold at prices ranging from €1,500 to €10,000, depending on the size.[166] For this reason, and because the author was still not well-known in France (the French version from publisher J'ai Lu had begun release with little fanfare, but was only at the beginning of *Stardust Crusaders*, and the anime adaptation of the same part was about to be released on DVD by Déclic Images), the buyers were the gallery's regular patrons rather than fans of the saga. However, Araki made every possible effort: in addition to attending the exhibition every day, he also took the time to sign copies of his manga in a Paris bookstore[167] and to answer questions from the French media. While this visit didn't bring about an explosion of the series' sales in France, where it long remained under the radar, we can point to April 2003 as Araki's first foray into the world of contemporary art.

The author also used this sabbatical to create two short stories that were published in the August and September 2003 issues of the monthly *seinen* magazine *Ultra Jump*. They are part of a series of such short stories published sporadically (1989, 2001, 2002, and three times in 2003) and dedicated to real people who lived interesting lives, like scientist Nikola Tesla and baseball player Ty Cobb. Up to that point, Araki had handled the writing while one of his assistants, Hirohisa Onikubo, did the illustrations. These last two chapters, created entirely by Araki, closed out the series, the entirety of which was compiled in a single volume called *Henjin Henkutsu Retsuden*[168] (never published in English), released in Japan in March 2004.

Two months before that, in January 2004, Hirohiko Araki returned to the pages of *Shōnen Jump*. I'll remind you, he drew inspiration from the Italian Renaissance's return to the past when writing the ending of *Stone Ocean*... And

---

166. Simon & Mazinga (*DVDanime.net*), "JOJO in Paris," October 29, 2003: http://www.dvdanime.net/articleview.php?id=46.
167. The Album Manga bookstore in Paris' Latin Quarter.
168. The compact edition (*bunko*), published in Japan in 2012, bears the secondary English title *The Lives of Eccentrics: Eccentric Enough, Courageous Enough.*

at the same time, he "broke" his universe! The Joestars are gone; everything was reset. While *Steel Ball Run* does not fit into the reality of *Stone Ocean*'s final chapter, instead launching a different universe that's completely separate from the previous one, Araki's part seven continues the concept of constant new beginnings. The author finished one cycle and decided to go back to the basics of his art. First, he abandoned the excessive complexity to return to purer ideas; second, he returned to the Wild West setting, from the genre that launched his career with *Busō Poker* and, of course, that made such a big impression on him as a child when he saw *The Good, the Bad and the Ugly* in a dark movie theater. So, what will be the result of this "back to basics" approach? Will Araki's artistic peak be a thing of the past or is the best yet to come, with a second wind that will be even more prolific than the first?

Wild Horses

"My name is Johnny Joestar and it all started when I met Gyro Zeppeli, a true man of mystery..."[169] Joestar? Zeppeli? That sounds so familiar. However, this time, the Italian Gyro is presented as the main hero, while the American Johnny is the "Koichi" of the story. Like the Koichi in *Mashōnen B.T.* or the one at the beginning of *Diamond is Unbreakable*, Johnny is a Watson-like character, a narrator who's fascinated by a powerful and charismatic figure. And it's true, Gyro is a captivating hero. He is a proud horse rider who looks like a rock star, with his wild hair, his glittering teeth *à la* Marilyn Manson—they make you think of the 2001 music video for *Tainted Love*, in which close-up shots constantly show off the singer's metallic chompers—bearing the words "GO! GO! ZEPPELI," and his provocative belt buckle featuring two symmetrical hands pointing to his crotch. And let's not forget his gleaming breastplate and his fingerless gloves that appear to be made of leather, as well as the straps nonchalantly wound around his arms: an ensemble whose style is reminiscent of the Dior Men's Luster collection from fall-winter 2003-2004, designed by Hedi Slimane. It really makes you think of one piece in particular, a wool sweater covered in a shiny material, looking like a cross between sportswear, goth-rock style, and medieval European armor; the sweater in question was one of the key garments of the campaign.[170] Perhaps we can also see in the flamboyant Gyro some aspects of Donatello's long-haired *David* (c. 1430), a

---

169. *Steel Ball Run*, vol. 1, last page of chapter 2.
170. The fashion show for this collection can be seen in a series of photos on the *YouTube* channel *Victim of the Crime* (https://www.youtube.com/watch?v=esgkUGAoTKQ). The shiny sweater with loose straps can be seen at 2 min. 40 sec. Its influence on Gyro's getup is obvious when you look at the earliest drawings of the character in "volume 100.5" of *JoJo*, included in the April 2010 issue of *Ultra Jump*.

sculpture of a young man wearing a hat, with a rebellious air about him and an affected attitude (his posture is an example of "counterpoise," or *contrapposto*: one of the two legs bears the body's weight, tilting the pelvis, while the shoulders lean in the opposite direction) as he stands victorious with one foot on Goliath's head, which he has just severed. In any case, Gyro immediately becomes one of the most endearing characters Araki has ever created. What's more, uniquely, he doesn't fight with a revolver; instead, he uses steel balls (as in the title), which he wields masterfully.[171] When thinking of the stories the author read as a child, it's hard not to compare Gyro's steel ball handling to the skillful way the hero of *Kyojin no Hoshi* handles a baseball, representing an extremely popular sport in Japan, thus making Gyro an interesting symbol for the blend of the Italian and Japanese cultures in Araki's saga. And it's this incredible steel ball handling that grabs Johnny's attention because he sees it as the greatest thing in the world. Johnny is a former jockey who lost the use of his legs after a pathetic fight he got into while trying to impress a girl. One day, the desperate Johnny is suddenly able to stand again after touching one of Gyro's steel balls while it's still spinning: the ball seems to have performed a miracle, allowing him to jump up from his wheelchair. Convinced that Gyro's technique, called "the Spin" (*kaiten* in Japanese), offers him the hop of being able to walk again, Johnny follows the mysterious rider closely and pesters him to share his knowledge. While Johnny is supposed to be the equivalent of Jonathan Joestar in this parallel world, his physique and personality are nothing like the original JoJo. He's a weakened and depressed young man who's driven less by justice and more by his own interest. In other words, a more human character. And thus more endearing. It's worth noting that his clothing and cap, covered in stars, are reminiscent of Dom DeLuise's comical character dressed up as "Captain Chaos" in the movie *The Cannonball Run* (1981, Hal Needham): less flattering as a resemblance than Jonathan's own to Kenshiro or Stallone! And this comparison is not as absurd as it may seem: *Steel Ball Run*–the name speaks for itself–is really just an equestrian version, transposed to the late 19th century, of the "Cannonball Run," the movie's car race across the entire United States. In Araki's manga, the Steel Ball Run kicks off on September 25, 1890, going from San Diego to New York City. In other words, crossing the country from west to east. Over 3,600 horses on a course 3,700 miles (6,000 km) long, with an unbelievable sum of money for the winner: it's the biggest event of the century. Each participant has their own reasons for competing: for example, Sandman, a Native American who's doing the race on foot (!), wants to buy back his ancestral lands from the white man. Diego Brando is a jockey prodigy from the English working class

171. The official international name "Gyro" comes from the Latin verb meaning "to rotate," which is, of course, a reference to the hero's weapon.

who's seeking glory. He's nicknamed—as I'm sure you've guessed—Dio. Johnny Joestar has also joined the race, but not for the money or the glory: his goal is to follow Gyro. As for the latter... we know nothing about him for the moment.

The first few volumes of *Steel Ball Run* focus on the adrenaline-pumping action of the race, fights between competitors, and other obstacles that present themselves along the way. In the absence of Stands, everything is initially simpler and clearer than in *Stone Ocean*. Actually, there's no mention yet of Stands, but we get hints about such powers and, in the third volume, the first of these spectral beings makes his appearance. In part seven, they're presented as a new phenomenon and the term "Stand" isn't introduced until volume four. While there are many references to his popular saga *YoYo's Strange Journey*, Hirohiko Araki doesn't expect his readers to have read his previous work. Everything is reexplained and clarified, and the Stands are given a new origin story: it's by crossing through the Devil's Palm, a strange rocky site that moves several miles each day in the desert, that this dormant power is awakened, a power known to the Native Americans, who consider it a curse. Johnny acquires his Stand when he randomly wanders into this logic-defying place. The new power allows him to rapidly spin his fingernails and fire them like bullets, finger by finger. It makes you think of the first chapter of *Gorgeous Irene*, in which Araki gave his heroine a similar power, or of Yusuke, the hero of *Yu Yu Hakusho*, and his "Rei Gun," allowing him to shoot rays of spirit energy from each of his fingers.

Once we get to volume four, the author dives into Gyro's origin story. He is the heir to the royal executioner of the Kingdom of Neapolis—we of course recognize the name of this city, which is the only reference to *Golden Wind* in *Steel Ball Run*. In other words, the duty of the Zeppeli family for the last 380 years has been to carry out death sentences. The Zeppelis have become masters of Spin, but they're also experts in medicine and human anatomy because Spin was originally intended to relieve the suffering of the condemned—when placed on the back, the steel ball gives a sort of anaesthetizing massage—when the blade hits their necks. While Gyro, the oldest son, was supposed to succeed his father, the heir opposed a death sentence imposed on an innocent little boy named Marco, who was simply in the wrong place at the wrong time. Gyro was outraged. So, when he learned about the Steel Ball Run, he set himself the goal of winning the race in order to bring pride and glory to his country and, in so doing, to get the king to grant amnesty for the child and cancel his execution. However, the king's adversaries are determined to stop him from getting that honor and they keep an eye on Gyro, until the middle of the race...

French history buffs will surely have noticed: Gyro Zeppeli has many similarities with the young Charles-Henri Sanson, the reluctant heir to the family of royal executioners, who nonetheless went on to become one of the most famous executioners in the Kingdom of France and who decapitated the key figures of the French Revolution. Manga fans may also be quite familiar with him because he is the subject of the excellent manga *Innocent* (2013-2015) by Shin'ichi Sakamoto, based on a Japanese novel by Masakatsu Adachi (a Japanese academic who specializes in French history) that tells a loose interpretation of the life of this historical figure. It's clear that, in writing Gyro, Araki drew inspiration from this very same book, entitled *Shikei Shikkōnin Sanson* ("Sanson the Executioner," never published in English), published in Japan in December 2003 and which the *mangaka* himself recommended in 2004. Later, the book was also wrapped with a promotional band bearing a message from Araki that leaves no doubts: he explains clearly that Sanson was the model for the hero of *Steel Ball Run*. Additionally, the message came with an original illustration of Gyro, who appears to be dressed as Charles-Henri.[172] It's worth noting that the book was published by Shūeisha Shinsho, where the editor at the time was... Ryōsuke Kabashima, the former editor of *HoHo's Weird Odyssey*, the man who allowed Araki to express his unique artistic sensibilities. I'll remind you that Kabashima is an intellectual type who studied Western history and archaeology, and who also actively supported Adachi's book, so I'd say it's a strong bet that he's the one who introduced Araki to the novel. Proof that the two have maintained a true connection after all these years. And also that, even from afar, Kabashima continues to influence the saga, and even watches over it.

Bizarre Hyper Age

Ultra Jump. The most beautiful magazine in the *Jump* family. Unlike *Weekly Shōnen Jump*, this monthly is not for young readers, nor is it for the mass market; instead, it's for a niche of hardcore *otaku* fans. In practice, this means that its readers are mainly men in their 30s. While it's no collector's item, *Ultra Jump* is also not a throwaway, the kind of magazine that you read right away and throw out as soon as you're done, as can be the case with *Shōnen Jump*, with its very low-quality recycled paper that at times looks pink or blue. It's more than twice as expensive[173] and its paper is more pleasing to the eye; all of this for a much smaller readership: the average circulation of *Ultra Jump* was just 36,000 copies per issue in 2018, versus 1.74 million for *Shōnen Jump*.[174] While

---

172. This illustration can be seen on the official page for the book on Shūeisha Shinsho's website: https://shinsho.shueisha.co.jp/kikan/0221-d.
173. Currently, *Ultra Jump* costs 650 yen and *Shōnen Jump* costs 270 yen (as of July 2019, 1 US dollar is worth about 180 yen).
174. Crystalyn Hodgkins, "Shueisha Reveals New Circulation Numbers, Demographics for its Manga Magazines," Anime News Network, April 22, 2019. https://www.animenewsnetwork.com/news/2019-04-22/shueisha-reveals-new-circulation-numbers-demographics-for-its-manga-magazines/.145991.

this difference may seem shocking, there is a logic to it: *Ultra* is intended to host the works of artists with less universal appeal. In an interview published in January 2018, the editor in chief at the time, Ryō Itō, said that the magazine "was created in 1995 out of a desire from the editor in chief, Mr. Tomita. He decided to bring together several *mangaka* whose sensibilities didn't fit into the editorial mold of *Young Jump*,[175] the idea being to have them work for a publication adapted to their style. Since the extra edition was a success, it was decided to offer it as an independent publication starting in 1999."[176] That's how this space for free expression was created. Initially, it was only home to *mangaka* with very bold visual styles. Before long, the magazine adopted the famous tagline "Hyper Age Manga Magazine" and an overall identity with strong notes of sci-fi.

Created in 1995, *Manga Allman* is another of Shūeisha's magazines for men. Although it's more oriented toward down-to-earth stories (to sum it up, you'll find fewer androids there and more heroes in a suit and tie), it was in the pages of this publication that Hirohiko Araki drew for the first time a few stories categorized as *seinen*, between 1996 and 1999, like the spin-off dedicated to Yoshikage Kira's afterlife. Why there? Probably because Ryōsuke Kabashima (yes, him again) was the magazine's editor in chief. We can imagine that if *Manga Allman* hadn't been shut down in 2002, *Steel Ball Run* would have continued its run there. Indeed, in early 2005, after a pause of several months, the series left the historic home of Araki's works: it moved from *Weekly Shōnen Jump* to *Ultra Jump*. Thus, it switched from *shōnen* to *seinen*, but also from weekly to monthly. With this triumphant return, which corresponds to the beginning of volume five, Araki's baroque Western officially joined *NyoHo's Strange Journey* and became the saga's seventh story arc.

Why this transfer? You have to remember that Araki, then in his 40s, already thought that *Stone Ocean* would be his last hurrah in *Shōnen Jump*. He felt like he was too old to keep writing for elementary and middle schoolers, who are still the magazine's target audience. As for that, it's actually surprising that *Steel Ball Run* debuted in a *shōnen* magazine. It's also important to remember that a *Jump* manga is typically broken up into weekly chapters that are 19 pages long. From the very beginning, with *Phantom Blood*, this division created issues for the author since the rhythm that he had adopted meant that his hero would be left in a difficult position for several weeks at a time, which readers didn't like. However, right off the bat, *Steel Ball Run* broke the 19-page rule: its chapters are typically 31 pages long. Araki, who seems to have gotten a head start, managed to keep up the weekly pacing of *Shōnen*

175. Shueisha's *seinen* magazine.
176. *Ultra Jump: Bienvenue dans l'Hyper Age*, remarks by Ryō Itō collected by Fausto Fasulo in the magazine *ATOM* No. 5, 2018.

Jump, even though the series took several breaks in its publication. So, from the beginning, *Steel Ball Run* proves to be more ambitious, with longer chapters that allow the author to draw out his storytelling and explore more details and greater complexity, without getting stuck in the trap of the obligatory cliffhanger on the 19th page. Apparently, this arrangement did not fully satisfy Araki, and that's how *Steel Ball Run* switched to a rhythm of about 60 pages a month, on average, in a magazine for adults. An environment that's more flexible and that fits better with who the author has become. What's more, the editorial board welcomed the now-ultra-famous *mangaka* with open arms: "We make sure that Araki-*sensei* is happy at *Ultra Jump*! (laughs),"[177] jokes editor in chief Ryō Itō, seemingly confirming the *mangaka*'s VIP status. Implicitly, this also gives us an idea of the creative freedom the author must have gained.

What's more, *GoGo*'s audience, the one that has followed the saga from the start, must have grown up even as the author's ambitions grew. From *Diamond is Unbreakable*, we could already tell that the series was on a trajectory that brought it naturally to a state of greater maturity. Within *Jump*, *Stone Ocean* was unusual compared to the other manga, which are often much more appropriate for an audience of children and teens. This totally natural phenomenon of maturing has undoubtedly touched many *shōnen* authors. Tsukasa Hōjō, for example, the author of *City Hunter*, definitively moved to the *seinen* genre in 1995 with the launch of *Manga Allman*, in which his work appeared from the very beginning. This new arrangement resulted in *Family Compo* (1996-2000), a comedy on the theme of trans identity, which probably would not have made it into *Shōnen Jump*. You also have to admit that, increased maturity or not, his style no longer really matched the *shōnen* style of the '90s, just like Tetsuo Hara, who also ended up moving to the *seinen* genre. There are numerous examples of such moves and they generally go hand in hand with renewed ambitions from the authors, like rising to a new challenge: for example, the *Shōnen Jump* veteran Masakazu Katsura seems to have adopted, with *Zetman* (2002-2014), a "*seinen* positioning," moving towards more darkness, realism, and impressive graphics. The same was true for Takehiko Inoue when began the *seinen* manga *Vagabond* in 1998, based on the story of the swordsman Miyamoto Musashi, not too long after the conclusion of *Slam Dunk*. In *Ultra Jump*, as Araki's series gradually became more ambitious, his style also changed.

In the fifth volume, *Steel Ball Run* finds its new central theme when Araki introduces the main antagonist, Funny Valentine... who is the (fictitious) president of the United States! We discover that the race was secretly organized as part of a plot by him to bring together the parts of a body that, according to him, would be worth more than all of the treasures and powers in the world. By some strange phenomenon, the remains of this "saint," scattered

---

177. *Ibid.*

across the country, have not decomposed. What's behind this mystery? No one knows for now, but by chance (is it really just chance?) Johnny happens to come into contact with one of the body's arms. Being told that this body is supposedly capable of performing miracles, and thus giving him back usage of his legs, Johnny decides to collect the various parts. This mission is added in parallel to the Steel Ball Run, whose route was designed to follow the map of the theoretical locations of the body parts–the race's organizers figured that with so many exceptional participants, they would have to stumble upon the body parts since there appears to be an attraction between them and certain people; once discovered, Valentine would be able to steal the collected parts. Up to this point, Johnny may have been an important character, but Gyro has been the center of attention. From the fifth volume on, we can say that there's no longer just one hero, but instead two, in *Steel Ball Run*. Two men who take part in the race for their own reasons, but as they help each other, they develop a strong bond, something between a bromance and a student-teacher relationship.

Quintessence and Renaissance

But what are we actually dealing with here? What is *Steel Ball Run*? Is it a remix, a remake, a reboot, a best-of? Well, it's all of that and much more. It's a regenerative synthesis, but that's not all. *Steel Ball Run* takes Araki's saga into uncharted territory. It offers things we've never seen before. Either in his own work or elsewhere.

Overall, part seven is an explosive cocktail of *Phantom Blood* and *Stardust Crusaders*, with elements of and references to the rest of the saga added into the mix. For example, we find a new, anachronistic Stroheim (he's wearing an SS uniform in 1890) who's participating in the Steel Ball Run; meanwhile, Sandman's Stand, who can manipulate sound effects, recycles the principle behind Koichi Hirose's Stand. From *Phantom Blood*, Araki reused the rivalry between Jonathan and Dio, as well as the Hamon apprenticeship. Hamon becomes Kaiten, a technique that *Steel Ball Run* presents as a way, in practice, to obtain something similar to Stand powers, thus bringing together these two forms of supernatural abilities.[178] What's more, the relationship between Gyro and Johnny blends aspects of Will Anthonio and Jonathan's relationship from *Phantom Blood* with aspects of Caesar and Joseph's relationship in *Battle Tendency*. The result is a new student-teacher connection that combines with friendship and quickly makes equals of the two men, in a non-hierarchical

178. Additional pages at the end of volume 10 re-explain in detail the concept of Stands and present Hamon and Kaiten as two ways of achieving this power.

relationship. Before this, in sports manga, there had been coaches who had suffered tragic injuries, like the coaches with sad life stories in *Ashita no Joe*, *Kyojin no Hoshi*, and *Captain Tsubasa*. Now, we have the "bromantic" coach. Or the "big brother" coach. Indeed, we learn in a flashback that Johnny lost his big brother, and thus Gyro serves as a surrogate fraternal figure, just like how Will Anthonio Zeppeli was a sort of second father for Jonathan.

On another note, the journey on horseback is, of course, reminiscent of the multi-staged narrative structure of *Stardust Crusaders*, but in an evolved version. It's not an endless chain of fights, with each spot on the map giving rise to a Stand battle. Araki takes the time to tell the story of their day-to-day events and draws them riding along. He also changes points of view and the atmosphere: the author actually sets aside Gyro, Johnny, and the race for almost an entire volume, for example, to show Lucy Steel, the race organizer's wife, attempting to infiltrate President Valentine's residence. Moreover, the journey of *Steel Ball Run* is less of a narrative device—simply offering a reason to move the characters from one panel to the next—than a theme that underpins the story arc. It changes the two heroes, deeply and irreversibly: it is the journey of a lifetime. In fact, perhaps this adventure is less like Jotaro Kujo's odyssey and more like the author's own personal experiences: "Traveling makes people grow. Personally, in high school, I challenged myself by taking bike trips and camping. So, I wanted to tell a story in which the main character would evolve through his adventure," Araki explained in 2012 when asked about *Steel Ball Run*. "I traveled by bike from Sendai to Hokkaido. It was during summer vacation after my first year of high school. I visited the Ryūsendō cavern in Iwate prefecture, as well as Mount Osore in Aomori prefecture. Sometimes, local hoodlums would stop me and say things like: 'Hey, who said you could come here?' (laughs). It took me about three weeks."[179] All of the ingredients were there. Those biking escapades prefigured the adventurous horseback rides in *Steel Ball Run*, which is without a doubt the story arc most representative of the idea of "returning to roots."

This return to the series' roots also helped restore the positive qualities that *Golden Wind* and *Stone Ocean* had diluted along the way. In part seven, the powers—the Stands and Spin—are generally clear and ingenious, and, during battles, they brilliantly play off of "the third parameter." In other words, the rules of the game are intelligible, balanced, and exciting, which results in situations that are both memorable and immersive. For example, Ringo Roadagain's Stand possesses the ability to travel back in time. By exactly six seconds. And after using it, he must wait six seconds before deploying it again. Period. Simple, effective, and nonetheless capable of creating interesting situations

179. *JOJOmenon*, 2012.

according to the setting and the powers of his adversaries. The battle against Ringo is also one of the most epic passages in all of *Steel Ball Run*. The seventh part also takes us back to a purer form of the thriller genre. For example, the scenes of Lucy Steel infiltrating Valentine's residence fit into the legacy of the famous passage of *Diamond is Unbreakable*, in volume nine, in which we follow Kira, in a difficult situation, forced to hide in a gymnastics vaulting box while trying to recover the paper bag containing the hand of one of his victims.

In addition, *Steel Ball Run* gradually acquires its own unique characteristics. The graphics evolve toward more clarity and brightness; the compositions become more airy. *Stone Ocean*'s overloaded graphics and its roughly drawn, angular characters are gone; Araki instead offers more realistic bodies—for example, looking at the noses, you'll immediately notice this—that do better justice to human beauty. In the seventh volume, the style of drawing mutates in spectacular fashion. Shadows become more realistic and coherent, formed by hash marks that are sometimes light and sometimes very detailed, similar to techniques used in anatomical sketches; meanwhile, the faces are more than ever reminiscent of early modern art. With their mouths almost always half open and their elegant proportions, the faces, which have a sort of frozen quality to them, acquire new theatrical and lascivious qualities. They make you think of fashion models, of course, but also, particularly, of the facial expressions on certain Bernini statues, like *Blessed Ludovica Albertoni* (1674), or of certain figures depicted by Michelangelo in the Vatican's Sistine Chapel, like the *Delphic Sibyl* (1509). Granted, this new style has the consequence of making the faces more uniform, but it helps establish a strong visual identity. For the first time, Araki really gets close to the splendors and sensuality of Italian statuary. This may be the greatest example of *Steel Ball Run* returning to Araki's roots. Moreover, it's no surprise that we find a Stand whose effects are reminiscent of the sculpture *Apollo and Daphne*—in volume 12, the Stand in question turns Gyro's legs into roots. Funnily, the natural evolution in how the characters are drawn results in Funny Valentine growing, doubling in size compared to his first appearance! "Let's just say that he did some weight lifting (laughs),"[180] Araki jokes when asked about this gradual growth. It's worth noting that in *Diamond is Unbreakable*, the opposite was true: certain characters, like Koichi and Tamami (one of the first antagonists), began to shrink! In *Steel Ball Run*, the author also develops a preference for faces shown very close up, which works perfectly in a Wild West universe. Filmmaker Sergio Leone, for example, made it one of his trademarks. In this case, the Western spirit also gives rise to very cinematic scene crafting when depicting duels—with guns or otherwise, for that matter. There's the stunning two-page spread in volume 12, separated into three vertical strips, each one showing a close-up: a direct shot of Gyro's face, a finger cocking a

180. *JOJOmenon*, 2012.

revolver, and Johnny's face in profile. It's a great way to show each character simultaneously before the coming frenzy. A pure, powerful composition, free of any words or sound effects, and paired with a beautiful visual harmony: the strips "sing," white, black, white. The fact of crossing the entire United States also allows Araki–who, as usual, went on fact-finding trips–to depict panoramic views that create a sense of space and an immersion in the setting never before seen in the *GoGo* saga. Stand user or not, humans are just tiny little ants compared to the canyons of the American West.

While overall the author moves toward more detail and precision, he also makes some totally unexpected choices with visuals. For example, from time to time, he just sketches the foreground: angular shapes, heavy brushstrokes, and plain white spaces. It makes you think of the heavy lines of Sanpei Shirato in *Kamui Den*! At a time when many *mangaka* had turned to digital techniques to create speed effects and a shallow focus, Hirohiko Araki responded to that movement by drawing from the works and methods of classic authors to showcase the foreground. Incidentally, Araki stated in *Manga in Theory and Practice* that he continues to draw on paper without computer assistance. "When you draw by hand, you get the tension that comes with having no takebacks, and that live-performance feeling of betting everything on the moment."[181] he explains, comparing this principle to improvisational jazz performances. His position is totally consistent because, as we know, the author uses improvisation when writing his stories. This graphic style is not the only original visual aspect of *Steel Ball Run*. In the final volumes, Araki adopts another unusual approach: he begins incorporating all sorts of little designs–pictograms, faces, etc.–into the speech bubbles, in addition to the text, which creates a new visual language that we can view as either funny, redundant with the text, or informative, since it helps visualize certain concepts or face that we may not have seen for some time. In the later volumes, again, the *mangaka* sometimes leaves out all sound effects. He creates panels that express a surprising calm (or a deafening silence) and reveal drawings that, at this point, have reached a stunning degree of virtuosity. Thus, when the author trades in his typical sound effects for pure imagery, we're surprised to hear the sound of the wind, the noise of the horsemen breathing, and a few melancholy notes of country music.

My Bloody Valentine

While Hirohiko Araki has already gotten us used to ambiguous, nuanced antagonists (like Yoshikage Kira and Enrico Pucci), up to this point, there's

---

181. Hirohiko Araki, *Manga in Theory and Practice*, p. 147.

never been any doubt that the hero is still more virtuous than them. This time, it's much more debatable. No one is in the right in *Steel Ball Run*. Funny Valentine does not embody absolute evil; instead, he fights for his personal conception of happiness, a very selfish version given that it only applies to the American people, who are the only group of people he's fighting for. *Steel Ball Run* conveys the cruelly realistic idea that everything is complicated, everything is a dilemma, and that happiness for some necessarily means unhappiness for others: whereas *Phantom Blood* featured an avatar for good who adopts the mission of eliminating the avatar of evil, *Steel Ball Run* tells us that misfortune will never disappear from the world, that happiness and sadness must coexist. In part seven, it's no longer about fighting for an ideal of social justice, as may have been the case in the *shōnen* manga of Araki's childhood in the late 1960s and early 1970s. *Steel Ball Run* tells us that the possibility of justice for all does not exist. Given that he must live with this fact, Valentine wants to distance himself and his country from all evil, all misfortune, and all scourges, to send them elsewhere in the world. He doesn't want any more victims than necessary; he simply wants to change where those victims live. And that's what the saint's body will allow him to do: the person who acquires the body attracts positivity while driving away negativity—for example, if someone is supposed to die, but finds themself under the protection of this power, another person will then die in their place on the other side of the globe. Incidentally, even though this is never said explicitly, the body is clearly supposed to be that of Jesus Christ. In practice, President Valentine wants to seal the body inside a bunker below New York City in order to cover his country in blessings. Basically, Valentine's ideal is similar to Pucci's. Like Pucci, Valentine wants to shape reality (his reality) so that it becomes a safe zone, a controlled place that's, above all, free from hazards. The president's big goal is "to ward off all unforeseen circumstances," as he says in volume 19. "Make sure that everything smiles upon me... Including misfortune itself." Blowing on fate's dice, in other words. Valentine may get his hands dirty, but for him, the Steel Ball Run and his schemes are a less costly way, in terms of human lives and compared to war (at a time when wars seemed inevitable), for him to defend his people and guarantee peace for them. The president is also convinced that he is the only one who understands the body and it must never be ceded to another nation, who would surely use it destructively.

What can Johnny say to that? Johnny himself pursues a selfish objective, to restore the use of his legs. What's more, while taking a stand against Valentine's radical methods (he sacrifices Lucy Steel, who becomes a receptacle for the saint's body, unleashing its power), Johnny himself takes the lives of innocent victims since the president ends up taking control of the body's power, meaning that from then on, every attack directed at him is "teleported" elsewhere in the world, taking the life of another person. This raises doubts in Johnny's mind: he begins to think that Valentine actually embodies justice and that he, conversely, embodies evil. During all of this, Gyro is more like an ideal hero. He personifies a purer conception of justice than Valentine's, but it's also a more naive, or at least more unrealistic or imaginary, version. The fact that the driver for his participation in the race is to save a child unjustly condemned to death shows that Gyro can't bear the very idea of injustice. As such, it makes perfect sense that he, too, takes a stand against Valentine–a man who can't achieve his aims without collateral damage. Like the other Zeppelis before him, Gyro ultimately loses his life during combat, while at the same time passing on the key to victory to a Joestar. In this case, Gyro helps Johnny, with one final lesson, master the "infinite Spin" and thus defeat Valentine. However, the death of this heroic figure, when it comes down to it, also means that heroism itself has just died and that the saga has entered a phase that's more mature, closer to reality, and thus also more unjust.

The climax of *Steel Ball Run*, the battle against Funny Valentine–or rather, the various phases of the battle–lasted about two years in *Ultra Jump*, from September 2008 to October 2010. All of that time was necessary to get the most out of the president's Stand, D4C (Dirty Deeds Done Dirt Cheap), because from the beginning, even before Valentine acquires the body's power and his Stand obtains the additional ability to repel all misfortune, the incredible D4C is filled with possibilities. Like Pucci, Valentine can shape the course of events: his power allows him, by placing himself between two objects, to travel through parallel worlds.[182] In theory, this makes him unbeatable, since he's capable of replacing himself with a fresh, new version of himself when he gets seriously injured. Additionally, there are two important rules. One: the world of the story is the "original" world, the most important of all, and the saint's body only exists in this main world; the same is true for D4C, of whom there's only one version, which can be transferred from one version of Valentine to the next. Two: if an object or a living thing comes in contact with a version of the same from another world, they will be drawn to each other like magnets and destroy each other. The exception is Valentine, who's exempt from this second law. We have to admit, this Stand sometimes makes the reader's head spin, and unreasonably so. The episode that takes place in the streets of Philadelphia, in volumes 17 and 18, is one of the most complex passages in the entire saga.[183] This is probably the greatest flaw in *Steel Ball Run*–along with the fact that it

182. The idea of a parallel universe is not the same as at the end of *Stone Ocean*. In this case, they're versions of the world that exist simultaneously, but where certain facts differ; in *Stone Ocean*, the worlds followed one another chronologically, each one reproducing approximately the same events as the last.
183. The YouTuber xForts, an expert on the *DoDo* saga, even offers a 3D reconstruction of this passage in order to try to understand exactly what happens (https://www.youtube.com/watch?v=X30YXFzq5Ys).

abandons certain promising characters along the way, like Pocoloco. However, D4C also brings part seven toward its most epic phase and the possibilities offered by his powers are absolutely fascinating. And then there's this: D4C's power results in the most dramatic turn of events in all of *Steel Ball Run*: it turns out that Funny Valentine is not really the "final boss." An even more twisted evil is yet to come.

Neoclassicism

In *Steel Ball Run*, this is the major throughline, according to Araki: "Gyro Zeppeli and Johnny Joestar symbolize a fraternal relationship. After the loss of his big brother, Johnny grows up with help from Gyro; then Gyro dies at the end."[184] At the very least, we can say that the result actually proves to be much more complex and ambitious than what the author describes there. What's more, part seven doesn't stop with the death of Gyro, nor with the death of Valentine. The Steel Ball Run carries on: there's one last stage to reach New York, offering almost two volumes of reading pleasure.

In the "original" world, Diego Brando—a.k.a. Dio—may be an arrogant, aggressive rival, but he's not totally evil. He dies not long before this point in the story while trying to take down Valentine. However, as we know, there's not just one Dio in the multiverse; rather, there are numerous versions of him. We find out that before he died, the president had traveled through parallel worlds in order to find one in which Dio was still alive, and then he placed the future of the United States in Dio's hands. Not because he trusted him, but because he liked Dio's ambition and figured that he wouldn't say no to becoming the center of the universe thanks to the saint's body. Seemingly to round out the great synthesis that is *Steel Ball Run*, this second Dio, quite different from the first, being both godless and lawless, bars Johnny's path on the way to New York. First, there was Funny Valentine, the ambiguous antagonist who follows the spirit of Enrico Pucci; now, we have the return of absolute evil. But that's not all. Surprise! Unlike the first Dio of part seven, who possessed the Stand Scary Monsters, this second one uses... The World! Yes, the power of Vampire Dio from *Stardust Crusaders*, capable of stopping time. Araki even presents a scene that's entirely a reference to the third story arc: Dio launches a volley of knives, stops time, then starts it again, just like during the final battle in Egypt.[185] The last volume of *Steel Ball Run* is a high-speed game of cat and mouse between Johnny Joestar and Dio Brando: rather than worrying about who will be the first to cross the finish line of the Steel Ball Run, they race to see who will be

184. *JOJOmenon*, 2012.
185. *JoJonium Stardust Crusaders*, vol. 10, "DIO's World Part 12" (*JJBA* vol. 28).

first to reach the bunker that holds the saint's body. In the end, Johnny fails to stop the new Dio, and it's Lucy Steel who manages to defeat him, thanks to a clever scheme. She gives him a package, a spherical item covered with a bit of cloth. And when the young man opens it... he finds himself face to face with the severed head of the Dio from the base world. And we know the rule: the two will be drawn to each other and then destroy one another. Isn't it ironic that this severed head, which echoes the state Dio found himself in at the end of *Phantom Blood*, brings about the death of this new Dio, who has inherited the Stand and the malevolence of the Dio from *Stardust Crusaders*? Moreover, as in *Phantom Blood*, it all ends on a ship. The relieved Johnny, who's amazingly able to stand on two feet again, gets on a boat to Italy. In a final tribute to Gyro, he's bringing his friend's body back to his homeland and holds one of his steel balls in his hand. However, the scene is ambiguous: does the box really contain Gyro's body, or instead the saint's? We'll never know. And *Steel Ball Run* ends on a sad note, even as it offers the promise of a new beginning for the Joestars.

In the mid-18ᵗʰ century, the neoclassical movement developed in art as a reaction to the fantasy and frivolity of the rococo. Neoclassicism argued for a return to antiquity, noble themes, and pure compositions. It's tempting to think that could describe *Steel Ball Run*'s position in Araki's saga, but it's much more than that. This seventh part doesn't just make the old stuff new again; it makes the old stuff better. And it offers an incredible second wind. It is a true masterpiece, the author's second to date, in a style that's very different from *Diamond is Unbreakable*—which still ranks slightly ahead thanks to its unique ambiance created by a confluence of circumstances, like the period in which it was created and the profusion of autobiographical elements. *Steel Ball Run* is another conception, one that's more extensive, more epic, and more adult (it also contains a new erotic charge), of what the saga's apex can look like. It's another blend of the elements of Hirohiko Araki as an author, one whose formula trends more toward tastes and influences than toward life experiences. It's an amazing distillation of Western films, horror-thriller stories, Italian sculpture, and contemporary fashion, just to mention the most notable ingredients.

Steel Ball Run also toys with the limits of *shōnen manga*. If we set aside for the moment the pre-publication magazines, which is really how manga are categorized, how should we define the *shōnen* genre? By its spirit? By conventions? By the number of pages per chapter? In part seven, Araki has created a hybrid that evades all attempts at strict classification. He drew from his experience and arsenal of tricks from the *shōnen* world—as seen in Johnny's learning journey and the adventurous spirit—and took them off-roading in the wild and fertile lands of *Ultra Jump*. There is indeed a *nekketsu* energy in *Steel Ball Run*, but it's applied to complex and adult issues. It seems that the author drew from the vigor and values that are characteristic of youth, elements that were abundant in the stories he read as a child, but he makes them face a harsh reality. The result is at times tragic for his characters, but it can also be miraculous. Never give up, always get back up, even though you'll sometimes fail. As if to underscore this idea, in a bit of dark humor, the last few pages explain that little Marco–the child for whom Gyro joined the race–did indeed avoid execution... but ended up dying of a cold!

Steel Ball Run is such a wonderful synthesis and such a fantastic revival that it would have made sense to end the *JoJo's Bizarre Adventure* saga there, this time for good, with this second golden age. Araki was 50 years old when the seventh story arc ended in April 2011 and no reader would have resented him for taking a well-deserved retirement, since we know how taxing the career of *mangaka* can be. But no. Hirohiko Araki still seems to be brimming with energy and in May 2011, he continued his saga with an eighth story arc that's still stimulating, still unique, and even more free from conventions. Another refined oddball.

CHAPTER VIII: THE SAILOR WHO FELL FROM GRACE WITH THE SEA (2011-2019: JOJO'S BIZARRE ADVENTURE, PART 8)

Stand: Without You I'm Nothing

Coming together is an eye-opener.

To listen to while reading:

Island People – *Ember*

Yes – *Heart of the Sunrise*

Lady Gaga – *Born This Way*

Simon & Garfunkel – *I Am A Rock*

Damo Suzuki & Øresund Space Collective – *Energisk Reaktion 2*

Where were you on March 11, 2011? Do you remember? It was a Friday. A black Friday. At 2:46 p.m. Japan time, a magnitude 9 earthquake occurred 130 km off the coast of Sendai, causing a gigantic tsunami that crashed down on around 600 km of coastline. Among the devastation caused, the Fukushima Daiichi nuclear power plant was damaged. This led to a series of chain reactions (i.e., explosions, fires) that brought this nuclear catastrophe to the level of the Chernobyl disaster. Added on top of the visible threat—the earthquake and the massive wave—was an invisible threat: radiation, measurable yet impalpable. Out of respect for the victims, I won't attempt to estimate the exact number of fatalities, injuries, and disappearances there were tied to the events of March 11, because the data vary depending on the source and every life counts. But one thing is for certain: it was a national tragedy. A tipping point for the Japanese.

The country's *mangaka* all had to react. Being artists and, for the most famous among them, veritable public figures, they had to express themselves. As such, many picked up their pens to address, in one way or another, the various aspects of the March 11 disaster and its consequences. There was a wide variety of approaches, both in fictional and documentary forms. Initially, authors dealt with the first two components of the disaster, the earthquake and tsunami, since their effects were more immediately visible than those of the nuclear disaster. For example, there was a whole slew of "charity comics," like the collective work *Bokura no manga* ("our manga," 2012, never published in English), for which a number of artists donated short stories on the theme of March 11, with the proceeds being given to people affected by the disaster. The popular author George Morikawa, for his part, took a break for a time from his eternal boxing manga *Ippo* (*Hajime no Ippo*, 1989-present) in order to create *Ai ni Iku yo* ("I'll be seeing you," 2014), the true story of a children's author, Nobumi, who went to help rebuild the damaged area. For this brief series, Morikawa occasionally received volunteer help from other famous *mangaka*. Another approach: in *H.E - The Hunt for Energy* (2012-2013), an environmental sci-fi story, the *mangaka* Boichi tells the story of a young man who can see invisible energy and who, immediately after the March 11 disaster, begins fighting to find a safe energy source that can replace nuclear energy. Through this fiction story, the author proposes solutions, like developing offshore wind farms. A final example among the many: the author Midori Inoue, a resident of Sendai, created a documentary manga about the inhabitants of Fukushima, living in a prefecture neighboring her own (*Fukushima Nōto*, "Fukushima notes,"[186] 2013-2017, never published in English). In this series, she simply aims to tell people's stories about their daily lives and their feelings, based on interviews she conducted herself. Each chapter tells the story of a different family. We hear from, for example, parents concerned about how radiation will affect their little ones or about the discrimination that these "children of Fukushima" might suffer from.

Sendai, I'll remind you, is a coastal city and was thus hurt by the tsunami; it's also Hirohiko Araki's hometown. According to *Kahoku Shimpō* (the local newspaper for Miyagi prefecture), Araki's family home, which dated from the Edo period, had stood by the sea through fourteen generations... and it didn't survive the tsunami. It was swept away.[187] While the author now lives in Tokyo, seeing the views of his childhood disappear was, of course, a huge shock—moreover, we don't know if any of his friends or family were affected. Normally talkative and happy to discuss any number of topics, Araki, understandably, has not said much publicly about March 11, as far as we know. His manga did all the talking for him.

186. Title translated to English from the French provided by Clémence Oliviero in her thesis *Rendre l'invisible visible: De l'utilisation pacifique à la catastrophe nucléaire, évolution de la représentation de l'atome dans le manga* (2014, Master's in Contemporary Eastern Asian Studies; Université de Lyon, École normale supérieure de Lyon, Institut d'études politiques de Lyon).
187. Remarks by Araki in the newspaper *Kahoku Shimpō*, dated October 21, 2014.

JoJolion,[188] the eighth part of *JoJo's Bizarre Adventure*, takes place in a parallel version of the town from *Diamond is Unbreakable*, good old Morioh, and thus an imaginary version of the Sendai region. Returning to Japan was an idea that had been running through Araki's mind for some time while working on *Steel Ball Run*, the never-ending story arc that held him "captive" in the wide-open spaces of the American countryside for seven long years. "Only drawing scrubland and plains was quite mentally taxing. I really got tired of it,"[189] the *mangaka* said in 2012. "*Steel Ball Run* was so tough that I really wanted to return to Japan as soon as possible. So, why not create a story in Morioh? (laughs) Drawing the town gives me comfort; it makes me feel like I'm back home." Then, as Araki was reflecting on what *JoJolion* would look like, the events of March 11 occurred. What would have happened with the eighth part of *JoJo's Bizarre Adventure* without the earthquake? It's hard to imagine. So, in a stroke of fate, for the first time, the saga dealt with real-world problems in real time: *JoJolion*, in which the aftermath of the tsunami is one of the jumping-off points for the story, mentions the March 11 earthquake explicitly. "It's a subject you can't avoid if you set the story in Morioh,"[190] explains Araki. "But I have to be careful about how I talk about it so that I don't hurt anyone." So, to put it plainly, we can explain the presence of the catastrophe in *JoJolion* like this: because it occurred in the region Morioh was based off of and because the author wanted to set part eight in the fictional town, he incorporated the disaster into his story. But that can't be the only explanation. That's just not credible. Part eight likely also serves as a personal and collective catharsis, intended to help both the author and his readers. Alternatively, it could be a form of civic activism, a way for Araki, a native of Sendai, to pay tribute to the people of this region and, perhaps, also to encourage his audience to think about what it means to be human and the ephemeral nature of things. What better ambassador to convey a strong message than one of the most popular sagas in all of manga? Whereas George Morikawa took a break from *Ippo* to depict the rebuilding of the devastated area in *Ai ni Iku yo*, Hirohiko Araki instead incorporated the disaster into *JoJo*. Incidentally, it's worth noting that Araki also engaged with the subject in another way: in 2011, he created an illustration to promote the restoration of the archeological sites in Hiraizumi (listed as UNESCO World Heritage Sites), which were damaged by the March 11 earthquake and tsunami.[191]

---

188. Araki wanted "JoJo" to be a part of the title. Thus, he invented a word containing it. Other candidates were "JoJo Town" and "JoJomenon," which is the title of the mook in which the author reveals this information.
189. *JOJOmenon*, 2012.
190. *Ibid.*
191. "JoJo's Araki Draws Art for Quake-Affected Historical Ruins," *Anime News Network* (https://www.animenewsnetwork.com/interest/2011-11-04/jojo-araki-draws-art-for-quake-affected-historical-ruins), 2011.

Given the connection between Araki and the city of Sendai, one might expect that the author would say something about "3/11" in the introduction to the first chapter of *JoJolion*. But no, he didn't say a thing about it. As if there were no need to do so. And really, that's true: what would be the point? Part eight says it all. Its pages are filled with a brand-new energy, a sort of melancholy tinged with nostalgia, that once again redefines *JoJo's Bizarre Adventure*. More than ever, it's a story about humanity. An ode carried by the sea and washed ashore, where humans follow the winds of destiny. Unless they can manage to shift the direction of those winds.

Absolute beginner

This is a masterpiece! That's what comes to mind when you finish the first volume. It opens with the discovery by the beach of a young man who's naked except for a sailor's hat. Pinned under some rocks, surrounded by debris, as if the sea chewed him up and spit him out. Morioh has been doubly disfigured by the great earthquake of March 11. In addition to the natural disaster, walls emerged all of a sudden near the seashore, as if to defend the town against misfortune borne by the ocean. Sadly, the walls did not stop the catastrophe. Riddled with holes, the townspeople call them "the walls that see." This is the landscape that Yasuho Hirose, a high-school girl from Morioh, is exploring when she comes across this unclothed young man who has a star-shaped mark on his back and, strangely, a bite mark surrounding it. Yasuho is the new Koichi, a character with whom she shares the last name Hirose. She is the first narrator of *JoJolion*, a "girl next door" figure who serves as an interface between the reader and the bizarre. A variation, female this time, of the narrator figure, who adds a streak of romance between her and the hero and who helps him search for his identity since he has no memories, not even of his own name.

The first volume turns to the thriller genre. And it does so brilliantly. Araki has lost none of his sense and mastery of suspense. He delivers a search for a lost identity that's gripping, with a pinch of absurd humor and previously unseen eroticism—for the first time, the author draws a woman naked from head to toe. The manga's tone had already been more free in *Steel Ball Run*, but in part eight, the saga decisively enters the world of manga for adults. So, *JoJolion* offers an exciting quest, but it also offers a deeper level of meaning, an extra dose of mystery for those who have read *Diamond is Unbreakable*. Indeed, as in the seventh part, the author reuses older material to construct a new edifice. The difference is, this time, he toys with us: while part eight can be read independently (for example, the concept of Stands is re-explained), Araki offers numerous Easter eggs for his faithful readers. For example, it's startling when we come across the name Yoshikage Kira. Just like in the fourth part, it's while inquiring about the owner of a piece of clothing—in this case, the sailor's hat; in the former case, a button from a jacker—that we discover this name. Here, it's in a hat store called "SBR" where a few well-known hats, like Jotaro's, make a cameo in the background.

So, there's a Kira. Could this be the name of the young amnesiac? He and Yasuho enter the apartment of the hat's owner and the tension mounts. In this home, everything is set up to create a sense of unease, but also to remind us of the former Kira. A *Mona Lisa*, a replica of a hand, jars filled with fingernails... and a naked girl in the bathroom. Is this the apartment of a deranged killer? Is it the same as Kira's home in part four's Morioh? We can sense a trap, both for the reader and for the hero. Needles in the napkins, tacks in the slippers: every effort is made so that visitors will inadvertently injure their hands and feet. We learn that a Stand user lives in the apartment upstairs and his power allows him to control the movements of his enemy's limbs if they have wounds on them. The naked girl, who serves as bait, has fallen victim to this Stand. This kicks off a fight against an invisible enemy in a claustrophobic atmosphere in which "Kira" tries to win by using his Stand, Soft & Wet, who can shoot soap bubbles[192] that temporarily strip "something" from a person or object—for example, he takes away "sound" from a wall so that he can smash it noiselessly, allowing him to move undetected from one room to the next and surprise his opponent. This episode is a model for scene-setting and "the third parameter." In it, we see some of the author's talents and obsessions at their finest. This booby-trapped apartment is also reminiscent of the cell in the short story *Under Execution, Under Jailbreak*, as well as the movie *Saw* (2004, James Wan): in *JoJolion*, a hacksaw is left on the floor, inciting the hero to cut off his own foot after being bitten by a venomous snake.

Clearly, no, our hero is not Kira. On the other hand, the aggressor from upstairs seems to have something against this Kira person, the apartment's occupant—who turns out to be very different from the serial killer in *Diamond is Unbreakable*—who is also a sailor and looks a lot like our hero.[193] Subsequently, Kira's lifeless body is found buried near the "walls that see." The plot thickens... While waiting to continue their investigation, Yasuho gives the amnesiac young man the name Josuke, after a dog she once had, and she leaves him in the care of the family of her childhood friend Joshu Higashikata. The sailor thus temporarily adopts the name "Josuke Higashikata" and he's hosted by a family of eccentrics descended from Norisuke Higashikata, one of the participants in the Steel Ball Run—this suggests to us that *JoJolion* takes

---

192. The bubbles have a star design on them, which, of course, makes you think of the Dragon Balls from *Dragon Ball*.
193. This new Kira, with his lock of black hair and his sailor's cap, looks like a modern version of the hero of *Jungle Taro* (1958-1959, never published in English), an adventure manga by Osamu Tezuka...

place in the same universe as the seventh part. Notably, they live in a modern house, designed in the style of Frank Lloyd Wright, that, as is said explicitly, was built to withstand earthquakes and survived the tsunami. This while the real-life Araki family home sadly perished... Perhaps we can see this as a sort of exorcism by the author. In any case, *JoJolion* finds its new focus in the second volume: the strange everyday life of our hero continues—Josuke has forgotten how to use a bed and he sleeps under, instead of on top of, his mattress!—as he searches for his identity with help from Yasuho.

The young man and the sea

In the Western world, March 11, 2011, is associated with the Fukushima nuclear incident. However, for the people of Sendai, this date is also, above all, associated with the tsunami... In *JoJolion*, nuclear energy is never mentioned. But just as the triple disaster unleashed both visible and invisible threats, we can see in Araki's work that the characters face certain phenomena that can be seen and others that can't. The physical and the impalpable; the said and the unsaid: a duality that constantly runs through part eight. And because of the resemblance to real-world events, this duality is wrapped in symbolism to a degree never before seen in the saga. Through interpretation and the feelings we get, we can read a lot into the early chapters of the story arc—it goes on to change its energy, but we'll come back to that later—which are filled with situations combining the collective tragedy of the natural disaster with the very personal drama of the main character. Reading these pages, you can't help but be moved.

It's by the "walls that see," a sort of allergic reaction by the land of "Sendai," that Yasuho, Josuke, and Joshu obtained their Stands. Maybe we should see this as these characters acquiring tools to defend themselves against the dangers of the world? Seemingly, growing up near this strange place, that appears to be secretly connected to the flows of positive and negative energy that govern the world, triggered the birth of these supernatural antibodies. Each character bears a bite mark, as if an invisible beast had attacked them and their immune systems reacted by generating Stand powers. While it may be tempting, we shouldn't necessarily see this invisible beast as a metaphor for nuclear radiation, but rather as the manifestation of a more universal, imperceptible evil: an impalpable avatar for the flows of negative energy that are responsible for bad luck, ugliness, and calamity (e.g., the tsunami), an extension of the concepts of happiness and misfortune seen in *Steel Ball Run*. Moreover, Yasuho, the narrator, concludes the first chapter of *JoJolion* with this thought: "This is the story of a curse... and of how to lift it. A curse that's been there from the beginning. Some explain it as being the manifestation of

impurity, the consequence of a sin committed by our long-ago ancestors. [...]
In any case, the curse must be neutralized. Otherwise, it will destroy us." This
is Araki's artistic statement to begin this eighth part. The author does not
foreshadow a battle against evil incarnate, as was the case with Dio, but rather
against something ethereal and impalpable.

Riddled with mysteries, ⟨ ✶ ⟩ constantly gives the impression that the
world is hiding invisible rules that we'd be better off not knowing. In the
Higashikatas' home, the father forbids Josuke from going upstairs. He is never
to go there under any circumstances. It seems that this authority figure doesn't
want him to find out the ⟨ ✶ ⟩, in the same way that an influential man who
got involved in some dirty dealings would try to suppress the evidence of his
guilt. It's quite clear that certain subjects are taboo in Morioh—just as can be
the case in the real world with certain things related to Fukushima. Josuke's
search for his identity, ultimately, is a metaphor for the deciphering of reality,
for the discovery of its truths and complexity, beyond the shortcuts and the
things we take for granted.

We soon learn that Josuke is no ordinary human being: he is the result of the
fusion between the sailor ⟨ ✶ ⟩ and someone else, whose identity
remains unknown. There was an exchange between the two bodies. Because
of this, Josuke has... four testicles—while Kira's corpse was left with none—and
two distinct halves to each iris. This also explains why he has a gap between
his front ⟨ ✶ ⟩. Initially, part eight gives the impression that it's the "walls
that see"—and thus, indirectly, the tsunami—that triggered the fusion, giving it
an additional metaphorical meaning, as if March 11 had taken apart humanity
and put it back together, symbolizing a new union of the Japanese people, or
as if it gave birth to a being physically altered by the disaster and proudly
bearing the scars. But that's not the case: while it was indeed by the walls that
the exchange took place, creating Josuke, we later learn that this place was
already "magical" before the ⟨ ✶ ⟩.

The characters in *JoJo* have always taken up space freely. Their poses and
their attitudes are not dictated by logic or nature—they're less about comfort or
mechanical function and more about freedom and self-expression. In *JoJolion*,
this characteristic takes on an additional meaning. The characters' tendency
to hold themselves in unnatural positions feels like a revolt by humanity
against its mortality. It's as if the characters reject the body's natural posture
and, in so doing, filled with a vital force, show their status as free ⟨ ✶ ⟩
beings, rebelling against the vagaries of nature. We see this right off the bat
with the cover of the first volume, on which Josuke is standing under a palm
tree by the sea,[194] on tiptoe, in an almost dance-like pose; meanwhile, his face

---

194. The black and white version of the illustration, inside the volume, shows a maritime
background, whereas the cover illustration presents Josuke and his Stand in front of a house.

JoJolion

truth

Yoshikage Kira

teeth

tsunami

human

has a melancholy look on it, in keeping with the later volumes of *Steel Ball Run*. Applied to *JoJolion*, this updated style makes the residents of Morioh look like martyrs, people who have been hurt by the tsunami. On that first cover, Josuke's half-open mouth, the placement of his hips, and his arms raised over his head also make him look like certain depictions of the martyred St. Sebastian (showing the saint tied to a tree, with his body pierced by arrows), like the baroque painting by Guido Reni (1615-1616). However, Josuke is a free, rebellious, and determined martyr. He stands like this not because he's tied up, but because he's declaring his independence. There's a fantastic music video for the Lorn song *Acid Rain* in which the young, deceased victims of a car accident awake and drag themselves from the vehicle, and then start a choreographed dance with sweeping and jerky movements. It's a dance of raw flesh, the heroic celebration of the fact that human beings will never disappear: though the body may perish, the substance remains. Nothing is lost; nothing is created; everything transforms into something else. And the characters in *JoJolion* seem to be filled with this same energy. "We won't give up," their bodies pledge. While the "*JoJo* discotheque" may still be open, the clientèle has changed and its energy is now a far cry from the carefree '80s attitude of *Battle Tendency*. It's as if they transitioned from the pleasure of movement to the *need* for movement, the need to express their vitality.

It's also worth noting that maritime imagery plays a strong role in *JoJolion*. And that's not to mention the obvious seafaring symbols on Josuke and his Stand. For example, the young man controls soap bubbles, seemingly able to manipulate water, as if it were his natural ally. That is, until the sea betrayed him. Until it launched an assault on the dominion of humanity in the form of a monstrous wave. Josuke, separated from the ocean by a wall that rose out of the ground, is a man of the sea who washed up on the land. Decked out in a sailor's outfit that he never takes off, he seems out of place in the everyday life of Morioh. It's up to him to create a place for himself.

Anthem for Doomed Youth

Little by little, the "walls that see" exit the story. They're mentioned from time to time, but they almost entirely disappear from the backgrounds and the mystery of their nature is no longer discussed, and the same is true for the bite marks, even though these facts were presented as being important. In short, *JoJolion* frees itself from aspects related to the tsunami. Perhaps we can see in this the fact that the real world has moved on to other things, while part eight has continued its publication year after year. Why should the people of Sendai be constantly reminded of that trauma? If that's the reason why the wall story line was abandoned, then we can easily accept the exchange of a bit of consistency for a bit of empathy and humanity. In any case, we know how Araki works. We know that he follows his instincts. In the mook *JOJOmenon*, published a year and a half after the debut of part eight, the author stated that he didn't know what direction his story would take and that he had just one thing in mind: Josuke Higashikata and Johnny Joestar are connected "by blood and by fate," thus creating a link between *Steel Ball Run* and *JoJolion*. "Given that the story takes place in Morioh, we can imagine that there might be some connection with the characters from part four. [...] There could be another version of Shigechi or Rohan,"[195] Araki stated, while the eighth part was still at an early stage. While these ideas have not materialized, other former characters have indeed had alter egos, like Yukako–whose equivalent in *JoJolion* would be Karera, who also has a hair-related Stand–or the original Josuke, who has a doppelganger with a more muted get-up named Josefumi[196] Kujo.

While the mystery of the hero's identity forms the story's major plot line, a second major focus emerges when Araki tackles the subject of the mysteries of Josuke's host family: that's where we see the aforementioned links between characters, connected "by blood and by fate." In *JoJolion*, the author establishes a new genealogy for the Higashikata and Joestar families, with the names and personalities shuffled around compared to the earlier parts of *JoJo*. The starting point of this family tree is Norisuke Higashikata, one of the winners of the Steel Ball Run, who used his reward to build a fortune by importing exotic fruit. From this shared ancestor, the family separated into two branches: Norisuke's son gave rise to the present-day Higashikata family (wealthy inheritors of the fruit import company) and his daughter, Lina, married Johnny Joestar, creating a second branch leading to Holly Joestar. She then married Yoshiteru Kira and their son is Yoshikage Kira, a ship's doctor, the man who took his last breath near the "walls that see."

As it happens, both bloodlines have fallen victim to a similar curse. From generation to generation, the eldest sons of the Higashikata family fall ill at the age of 10. An illness that turns them to stone. For this reason, the family's tradition is to raise their eldest son as a girl in order to "trick the demon behind the illness," because the Higashikatas believe in exorcisms, but it turns out that's really just superstition and the only true way to save the child is to make a trade: sacrifice one life to save another... In this way, *JoJolion* extends the principle of a balance between happiness and misfortune seen in *Steel Ball Run*, according to which the amounts of each cannot be changed: you can only make a trade. For the Joestars, it's the women who pay the price. Johnny's wife fell ill at the age of 20: she started to lose her memory and her

---

195. *JOJOmenon*, 2012.
196. Or Josephmi, the spelling that can be seen on his cell phone.

skin began to harden and fold like origami. In a flashback in volume five, the author tells of how the seventh JoJo stole the saint's body lying beneath New York City so that he could take it to the Higashikata family estate in Morioh to save his wife. However, making the disease go away means trading her life for something just as valuable... In saving his wife Lina, Johnny condemns his young son to death. Racked with guilt, he then uses the body one last time to trade his own life for his son's. And that's how Johnny died. And it's also the root of the principle of an equal exchange that runs throughout *JoJolion*. Near the "walls that see," the land of the Higashikata estate has this same property of exchanging things of equal value–probably because the body was briefly kept there. When you bury a lemon with a clementine there, then dig them up later, you'll find two fruits that are both half-lemon, half-clementine. It's this exchange phenomenon that leads to the creation of Josuke, who turns out to be a half-Kira, half-Josefumi hybrid, uniting two men, now deceased, who were on a mission to save Holly Joestar (for the one, because she's his mother, for the other, because she saved him from drowning when he was a child), who is sick with the same illness as her ancestor Lina.

As for that mission, it turns out that there's another way to "hack" fate and force an equal trade, other than the saint's body or the land of the Higashikata estate. It's called locacaca fruit, from a plant by the same name discovered on the island of New Guinea. A fruit that's traded on the black market for astronomical prices and that can cure anything. As long as you sacrifice something, of course. For example, by eating locacaca, an old man missing a leg grows a brand-new one, but in exchange, he loses his eyes. Not long before perishing, Kira and Josefumi tried to secretly grow a locacaca plant in order to cure Holly. However, just like the drug trade, distribution of the fruit is controlled by a secretive organization, most of the members of which are not actually human (with a few exceptions: some members of the Higashikata family are also embroiled in this cartel). They're known as Rock Humans, beings made of stone hiding among the rest of the population. And they are the antagonizing force in *JoJolion*, the ones who attacked Kira and Josefumi after discovering their secret plantation.[197] The hero's search for his identity and the illness that turns people to stone are thus two intricately linked plotlines. In a moving flashback, we ultimately learn how Josuke was born, how his two "parents" lost their lives by the seaside and then made an equal exchange that generated a new human being. However, *JoJolion* doesn't stop there. While he'll never recover any memories of his "past lives" as Kira and Josefumi, Josuke takes on the mantle of the two men and aims to obtain the locacaca fruit to cure Holly, who lies in a hospital bed. It's the only way to

197. Among these, it's hard not to see the A. Phex brothers and their synchronized actions as avatars for Araki's twin younger sisters.

give meaning to his own life. It's worth noting—because it's an ingenious idea—that Josuke is the result of the fusion between the new incarnations of the hero and the antagonist from *Diamond is Unbreakable*, while his quest borrows from Jotaro's mission to save his mother in *Stardust Crusaders*. Thus, he is a paragon of the JoJo-esque character. What's more, the mutual aid between the two reinterpreted adversaries from *Diamond is Unbreakable* shows that in *JoJolion*, there exists nothing so obvious as good and evil personified: in part eight, these two characters are neither good nor bad and they team up to take on the true calamity threatening their world: the sickness, an enemy you can't hit physically. In a way, their fusion is also the positive opposite of the bodily conjugation between Jonathan and Dio in *Stardust Crusaders*, given that it's both voluntary and a sign of hope.

Ultimately, in *JoJolion*, the tsunami and the "walls that see" are just a starting point, a base that leads to a portrait of the complexity of reality. Nothing is ever simple, everything is shades of gray, and the idea from *Steel Ball Run* that the world relies on a balance between happiness and misfortune comes back with a vengeance. "Happiness," in fact, is a key concept around which *JoJolion* revolves. In this case, it's not about winning a race, nor about defeating an evil genius. The eighth part, which is strongly oriented toward the mechanics of relationships and is more intimate than ever, tells of how a number of individuals come to terms with the ways of the world—and even try to change those facts by making an equal trade—in order to respond to their personal conceptions of happiness or, in other words, to the meaning that each person gives to their own life. We also see how those various philosophies, which put an emphasis on family, personal pleasure, or a desire for recognition in society, create connections or collide with one another.

For example, for Daiya, the youngest daughter in the Higashikata family, "happiness is sharing a memory with someone," and her Stand jives with this aspiration: it allows her to steal a memory and store it in a chess piece. Karera, meanwhile, leads a hedonistic lifestyle that's all about living in the moment.

For her, the locacaca fruit represents a potential way to escape from poverty. As for Josefumi, a sort of melancholy *furyō*, he is both a more down-to-earth version of the Josuke from *Diamond is Unbreakable* and the "Zeppeli" of *JoJolion*, the character who sacrifices his life to allow the survivors to keep going. In volume 13, in one of the most heartrending passages in all of *JoJo's Bizarre Adventure*, we learn that it was his   by the seaside that enabled the equal exchange with Kira, whose heart has stopped beating, after the Rock Humans had hunted and tortured them. While the duo had managed to escape, it was too late for Kira: he succumbed to his severe injuries not long after.[198] Josefumi, his face streaked with blood and a sad smile on his lips (never before has Araki captured human emotions with such intensity), then offers a   to Kira's lifeless body and says this to him: "When I was a child, that summer day... I drowned and already died once. [...] I'm not the one who must live at all costs; that's Ms. Holly's son. You're the one." Interestingly, in this panel, Holly is depicted symbolically like the Virgin Mary in Michelangelo's *Pietà* (1498-1499), cradling her son's body in her arms. "   " Josefumi continues. "If there must be an equal trade... I will gladly trade my body for yours. It's better that way. That   better with my idea of happiness. I'm already happy to have been able to live as long as I have." Thus, both Josefumi and   perished, while each also gave a piece of himself to the other. And thus Josuke was born, the result of the living remains of the two bodies. When it comes down to it, the essence of *JoJo*'s themes is found in this scene: it's the passing of a   , the transfer of an inheritance, in both a scientific sense (passing on the body's genes) and a figurative sense (handing down a mission). In the entire saga, this last act by Josefumi perhaps best encapsulates the idea of "the beauty of humanity" that is inherent to *JoJo*. As such, though we can't say for sure who Araki's favorite character in *JoJolion* is, it would be safe to bet on Josefumi.

New Energy

JoJo's Bizarre Adventure has changed yet again. The eighth part is the most deserving of the title "refined   ," as it evades all attempts at labeling. If we absolutely had to assign a genre to it, we could say that it's a hybrid thriller and chronicle of everyday life. At first glance, part eight is similar to *Diamond is Unbreakable* in its tendency to present a series of bizarre encounters with various residents, who are generally   users (with powers that are often clear and clever), in a new version of Morioh that

---

198. This passage echoes one of the last chapters of *Diamond is Unbreakable*, in which a distraught Josuke tries to revive Okuyasu, who's been seriously injured (*JJBA* vol. 46; American *DiU*, vol. 9).

possesses its own mythology—for example, it has "Shakedown Road," a street where it's rumored that you can't get through without being scammed. Like in part four, *JoJolion* alternates between epic games of cat and mouse and encounters in close quarters. However, its battles are less frequent. In part eight, Araki dedicates a lot of space to the investigation itself and to scenes from everyday life, in an approach passed down from *Steel Ball Run*, with its longer-format episodes. In addition, the energy that guides the characters is also quite different. In part four, the protagonists end up splitting into two camps: Kira and Team Josuke, who embodies a civic movement to restore security to the town. *Diamond is Unbreakable* was a manga that pushed the limits of *shōnen* in its time, which was very surprising given how it drastically reduced the stakes compared to the previous parts: the story is about cleansing evil from a small Japanese town, rather than about standing up to a danger of global importance. In *JoJolion*, the stakes are even more restricted: it's no longer even about saving   ; instead, it's about curing a few specific individuals, and we don't see the characters divided into two opposing camps like in *Diamond is Unbreakable*, which, ultimately, was an aspect driven by *shōnen*'s need for simplicity.

   In *JoJolion*,   depicts a world that gets closer than ever to how society works in the real world. In other words, it's an ambiguous world, filled with dilemmas and uncertainty, a world laden with sordid affairs and other unspeakable things, but where, in spite of it all, grace, beauty, and honest emotions can still flourish. I mentioned before personal philosophies connecting and colliding: that's the most concise way to explain the complex human network formed by *JoJolion*. With each character possessing their own philosophy, their own sense of morality, and their own means of taking action (via money,   , or their Stand), there is no big, shared flow of energy, but rather a network of personal energy flows, which creates a particularly polyphonic story. In this way, *JoJolion* and its many characters can give the impression of being scattered and progressing very slowly, but in reality, each person revolves around the two major plotlines, i.e., the search for Josuke's identity and the   that turns people to stone. Each personal interest is attached to one of these. For example, which characters have in interest in stopping Josuke from discovering his origins, and why? There's Tsurugi, the little nine-year-old son of the Higashikata family: how far will he go to avoid contracting the infamous disease? Just as the cast forms a great web of interpersonal connections, there's no single major   in part eight; instead, there's a number of faceless evils. Problems are not created by some evil genius, but rather by networks of interconnected causes, whether brought about by humans, by nature, or by a supernatural force that governs fate and gives power to curses. At most, we can view the   as the main dangerous force, but we can't compare them to Dio or even to Valentine, who sacrifice

locacaca

My life is yours

fits

Kira

torch

oddball

Stand

Team

an entire town

Araki

power

curse

bad guy

Rock Humans

up to this point was the most realistic bad guy, along with the serial killer Kira—who will always remain in a league of his own due to the stunning credibility of the character from a human perspective.

JoJo thus reorganized its DNA and also spliced in new genes, like more humor, particularly conveyed by the shenanigans and blunders of Joshu, whose haircut is reminiscent of the wacky hero of the comedic manga *Makoto-chan* (1976-1981, never published in English) by Kazuo Umezu, revealing the childish and immature side of Araki's character. However, in part eight, the visual atmosphere also strikes a new balance. While the bodies and backgrounds continue the trend from the later chapters of *Steel Ball Run*, Araki establishes unprecedented harmony between detail and minimalist compositions. "I leave more white space in my drawings. Instead of filling them up, I let the image breathe a bit," the author explained in late 2012. "I could continue to draw like before, but I chose to lighten up my drawings to let the readers' minds relax."[199] The idea is to use synergy between the form and content to create a brighter, less stifling atmosphere that aims less to provoke a sense of unease than before. Consequently, this new style also proves to be both clear and elegant, and probably more pleasing to the eye than any of Hirohiko Araki's previous work. In his color illustrations, this approach translates to using large, single-color backgrounds, and to this day, that's the way Araki paints his illustrations—a style we could call "Michelangelo vs. Paul Gauguin," to put it simply.

With this graphic refresh comes new obvious obsessions. In terms of the styles of his characters, as usual, Araki blends his influences. Josuke's sailor outfit is of course reminiscent of the work of Jean-Paul Gaultier, but in general, the apparel also trends more toward simplicity. Characters' outfits often have large black or white areas. And the same is true for hairstyles, which have fewer details and highlights. The Moschino-style accessories and symbols, reflecting the character's soul or profession, have become more sporadic—already, *Steel Ball Run* had less of this, other than a few details like the horseshoe on Johnny's cap. We see examples mainly on Josuke's sailor outfit, whose symbols make reference to the hero of *Diamond is Unbreakable*. There's also Kei Nijimura, the Higashikatas' maid, whose hat and formal attitude are strongly reminiscent of the models in the photo campaign for Louis Vuitton's fall-winter 2011-2012 collection. In *JoJolion*, the minimalist style of most of the clothing has an air of avant-garde fashion to it, in a spirit that can be compared to creators like Gareth Pugh, who for a long time worked with black, white, abstraction, and simple geometric shapes. In the manga, we find lots of repeated forms, ensuring clarity and harmony in the compositions: the spheres of Norisuke's hair (which are reminiscent of the round shapes of fruits, which

199. *JOJOmenon*, 2012.

are the commodity he trades), the puzzle pieces on King Nothing's body, the flowers on Yasuho's skirt, and the squares on Josefumi's sweater. However, the most ubiquitous motif is spikes. Lots of characters wear garments studded with spikes, often black and sometimes shiny, that give them a rebellious rocker look. The architect Yotsuyu Yagiyama, whose look verges on BDSM fetish style, is the most emblematic example of this approach, especially given that his Stand has a power that reflects the idea of repeating an aggressive motif: the Stand user selects an object and all examples of that object around the victim will charge toward them, as if drawn by magnetism. With an appearance that combines the freshness of flowers with dangerous libido, the highly androgynous Yotsuyu, with hair very similar to Bruno Bucciarati's, is probably one of the most handsome characters Araki has ever created. It's worth noting that this trend of spikes with a rock 'n' roll spirit is still quite current: as luck would have it, the new women's collection from Balmain (fall-winter 2019-2020), just released as I write these lines, has a number of black pieces spangled with spikes.[200] We should also note that the locacaca fruit has spikes too, just like certain tropical fruits like durian. And just as in architecture we sometimes see smaller examples of shapes close to bigger ones—likes the arches on the facade of the Florence Baptistery, for example—this repetition in part eight creates the same kind of elegant analogy between the locacaca fruit and those whose fates are tied to it.

And then...

As I write these lines, the 88th chapter—which will be part of volume 22—has just been published in Japan in *Ultra Jump*'s August 2019 issue. We have entered the final stretch of *JoJolion*, Araki announced in 2018, but given where the story currently stands, we can expect that this segment will continue into 2020 and that the eighth part will become the longest of all. In France as in Japan, the eighth part is now in what we can call the "post-13th volume" phase, after the flashback revealing how Josuke was created. To date, that flashback is still the climax of *JoJolion*, an incredible passage, as well as the definitive answer to the main question that started the story arc: "Who is this hero in a sailor outfit?"

Actually, volumes 11 to 13 formed such a great segment, filled with revelations (we finally discover who Kira was, as well as the abilities of his Stand, who is none other than Killer Queen, repeating the surprise from the appearance of

---

200. The fashion show for the collection can be seen on Balmain's official *YouTube* channel (https://www.youtube.com/watch?v=0NpM1M7OmtY).

The World in *Steel Ball Run*!), that the tension seems to decline thereafter, now that the search for the hero's identity has been resolved. From here on, Josuke's mission is to save Holly–while at the same time the Higashikatas aim to save Tsurugi–and thus, he must delve into the secrets of the locacaca fruit. However, this new plotline is progressing slowly. We also have to wonder if the author will end up resolving certain abandoned mysteries, like the strange boy who washed up on the beach in November 1901[201] or, of course, the "walls that see." In regard to said walls, in case Araki doesn't return to this subject, here's my interpretation: after Johnny temporarily buried the saint's body under the meditation pine while trying to save his wife, that coastal land stored up a bit of the energy from the corpse, acquiring an erratic and incomplete version of its properties. This would explain why this place triggers an equal exchange, and also why a sort of defensive wall emerged from the ground, as if to prevent misfortune from landing in Morioh (as is normally the property of the saint's body)... but it doesn't really succeed in that task.

After its neoclassical period, *JoJo's Bizarre Adventure* has now entered into what we can call its "free period," a period of total emancipation. It would seem that since Araki now works for a publication, *Ultra Jump*, that, unlike *Shōnen Jump*, doesn't really have any rules to follow, and thus no rules to break either, the *mangaka* is now breaking the rules of his own saga. There are small traces of *nekketsu* or the "friendship, effort, victory" spirit, for example in Josefumi and his "son" Josuke, but that doesn't necessarily make it a manga that can fit in those boxes. *JoJo* has become more of a hybrid manga than ever before. Could this be the reason why in 2018 *JoJolion* came in dead last in the popularity ranking of each story arc on the website *JoJosapiens*, with just 7% of the votes? Could it be because the manga has changed its spirit, because there's no longer a main bad guy? Or because the post-13th volume period has brought down the level of excitement? In addition to the signals coming from this sample of fans, sales of part eight also seem to have faltered. While from 2011 to 2016 *JoJolion* always had at least one of its volumes on the Oricon top 100 list for annual manga sales, the series has been absent from this ranking since 2017.[202] And yet, the launch of *JoJolion* was a big deal: while from 2008 to 2011 no volume of *Steel Ball Run* made it onto Oricon's best-seller

---

201. The author lingers on this event in the final pages of volume 5. The boy was discovered half-naked, wearing precious stones around his neck, around the same time—maybe even the same day?—that Johnny Joestar took his last breath, and they both wear caps on their heads... It certainly raises some questions.

202. The Japanese company Oricon (for "Original Confidence") regularly provides reference information and sales numbers for Japanese cultural products—numbers available online for the manga go back to 2008. However, we should note that while *JoJolion* has not made the annual ranking since 2017, that doesn't mean the series has fallen into oblivion; far from it: as I write these lines, the 21st volume, released July 19, 2019, has reached fifth place (75,632 copies) on the Oricon weekly ranking for July 15-21, 2019.

list, the eighth part put the saga back on the charts in 2012 (volume one came out in December 2011 in Japan), perhaps benefiting from an additional boost tied to the launch that same year of the anime series of *Phantom Blood*. The inaugural volume of *JoJolion* was also the second best-selling manga during the week of its launch in Japan, with over 235,000 copies sold in that first week alone (December 19-25, 2011, again according to Oricon). It also quickly garnered positive reviews from critics, winning a grand prize for manga at the Japan Media Arts Festival[203] in 2013, as well as reaching 12th place in a ranking of the best manga for male audiences, published in 2012 in the famous annual book *Kono manga ga sugoi!* ("this manga is great!"), which tallies the votes of hundreds of manga industry players, including publishers, booksellers, and authors themselves.

"If I ever find myself struggling with finding new ideas for a story, that will be the day I quit being a *mangaka*," Araki said in 2015. "I count myself fortunate that my idea notes continue to flow and that I can continue being a *mangaka*. I used to be concerned that I would run out of energy, and that I would probably retire once I hit fifty, but as long as I can remain curious and interested, I'll keep on drawing a little while longer."[204] Today, the author is 59 years old. Is it possible that there'll be a part nine of *JoJo*? It's hard to say. But what we do know is that the 88th chapter of *JoJolion* is the 935th of the saga.[205] So close to 1,000... Could we possibly see a shorter final part that would allow us to reach that symbolic number, just like the dinosaur *KochiKame*, which ended with its 200th volume in 2016? Maybe. But if there were going to be a ninth and final part, what might it look like? After *Steel Ball Run*, which basically reprises *Phantom Blood* and *Stardust Crusaders*, then *JoJolion*, which more or less blends *Diamond is Unbreakable* and *Battle Tendency* (the Rock Humans are basically a less grandiose version of the Pillar Men), we can easily bet on a return to Italy with a female protagonist, since *Golden Wind* and *Stone Ocean* have only been slightly represented in the new space-time continuum. That would bring everything full circle.

Shortly before the debut of *JoJolion*, Hirohiko Araki began to regularly exhibit his work in very prestigious places. In Paris in 2009 (at the Louvre!), in Florence in 2013 (in an exhibition hall owned by Gucci), and in Tokyo in 2018 (at the National Art Center). That last exhibition then moved to Osaka and continue to tour Japan. Could it be that Araki, after these great experiences for which he produced sublime, life-sized paintings, will decide to pursue the creation of imagery alone, rather than continue with the exhausting profession

203. An international festival held each year since 1997 by the Japanese Agency for Cultural Affairs and the association CG-Arts. Each year at the festival, prizes are awarded in four categories: contemporary art, entertainment (like video games), manga, and animation.
204. Hirohiko Araki, *Manga in Theory and Practice*, p. 180.
205. According to the chapter list from *JoJo's Bizarre Encyclopedia*: https://jojo.fandom.com.

of storytelling? The only thing we can (almost) be sure of is that if the author continues his career as a *mangaka*, it will be to continue to expand his saga through a sequel or a spin-off. As evidence, we have this statement: "Over these last 25 years, I've been asked, 'Wouldn't you like to do something else?' I've answered: 'Sorry, but I can't draw anything other than *JoJo*.' But I think that's a good thing. If I were to draw a sports manga, it wouldn't turn out great (laughs)."[206] Araki said this in 2012. And they certainly remain valid today. And that's just fine. Far from trapping its author in an eternal universe-*cum*-prison, as was at times the case for Akira Toriyama with *Dragon Ball*, or any creative sclerosis, *JoJo's Bizarre Adventure* functions as an endless tapestry that has already delivered eight stories with distinct energies. Indeed, a living tapestry that has seen many equal trades over the years, while never losing the true essence of the series.

206. Interview of Araki on the Japanese website *Xtrend*, 2012. (https://trendy.nikkeibp.co.jp/article/pickup/20121009/1044420.)

Painting crazy diamonds. Again and again. Illuminate and enlighten humanity.

JOJO'S BIZARRE ADVENTURE

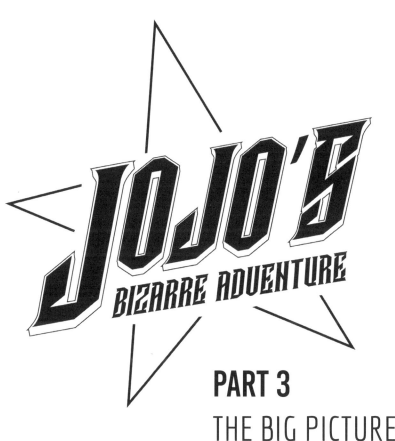

PART 3

THE BIG PICTURE

CHAPTER IX : GLORY TO MANKIND
(1986-2019: JOJO'S BIZARRE ADVENTURE, FULL SERIES)

Let's get a view from 30,000 feet. After this marathon on a horizontal plane, let's go vertical. Let's zoom out to the point where we can see *JoJo's Bizarre Adventure* in its entirety. Beautiful, isn't it? It's 125 volumes of bizarreness and flamboyance. It's time to listen to what this polyphonic ensemble has to tell us.

Crazy Diamond Dogs

Be yourself and be proud of it. That's what the characters of *JoJo* are constantly declaring, on every page. Do you hear them? They don't say it in dialogue, of course, but rather in the messages conveyed by their looks, their attitudes, and their ways of being. In the world of *JoJo*, no one is worried about being an effeminate man or a masculine woman, nor about being hetero, gay, or bi, and even less about how their bodies appear in public, whether they're understated or off-the-wall. Everything goes; nothing gets called out–with a few exceptions like, in *Steel Ball Run*, the emphasis put on the bisexuality of Valentine's wife. Moreover, almost everyone, rich or poor, dresses in clothing inspired by high fashion, which liberates garments from their symbolism of belonging to a more or less fortunate caste and ultimately puts all people on the same level. *JoJo* also presents and promotes people who are disadvantaged in society, like orphans and single-parent families, and it features purposely multicultural casts of characters, and even mixed-race heroes like Jotaro and Jolyne. To make a long story short: in *JoJo*, everyone is mixed together.

The reason why the characters convey these ideas of inclusion and liberation is that many artists who inspired Araki promoted those same causes, either through direct engagement or simply through their appearance—for example, Prince and his androgynous looks. Because of the ways that legacies work, all of that has indirectly made its way into *JoJo*. We think of Tony Viramontes, of course, who drew women and men who, in their time, were far from the beauty ideals and gender expressions commonly seen. Or Antonio Lopez, who helped bring visibility to cultures and people who had been left out of the media space by asking to work with models of color—at a time when that was almost unthinkable—and by also showing a keen interest in people with unconventional looks, like Jane Forth, with her missing eyebrows, and Donna Jordan, with her gap between her front teeth. In this way, "Antonio's Girls," these muses with unconventional beauty, prefigured the uniqueness of Araki's characters.

Of all the people that have lived on this planet, the one who most embodies the *JoJo* spirit has to be David Bowie, a total icon of sexual ambiguity and blending masculinity and femininity. He is the spiritual father of the glam, the flamboyance, and the "be yourself" spirit in Araki's work. Not many people know this, but as a teenager, in 1964, Bowie co-founded the "Society for the Prevention of Cruelty to Long-Haired Men," at a time when having long hair, which was associated with women, was still a source of discrimination! That was just the beginning. In 1970, the man who would soon become famous for his androgyny and bisexuality began to wear women's clothing, with encouragement from his wife Angie, thus starting a transformation that would forever change the rock world, which was very macho and hetero at the time. That year, he posed in a dress for the cover of the album *The Man Who Sold the World*—and for that matter, you could swear it was Funny Valentine in the flesh!—which marked a major turning point in his public life. While the album didn't sell, the cover created a buzz and the photo was even replaced by another visual in the United States, a country that just wasn't ready yet for that kind of image. But still, Bowie didn't change directions. He persisted with that effeminate style in the photo on the cover of his next album, *Hunky Dory*, and then things took off from there: he came out in the media, became hugely famous, and created his first androgynous stage persona, Ziggy Stardust, who became a major figure in glam rock, the genre of dandies in glitz and glamor and outrageous make-up who defied traditional masculinity. After that, Bowie went from one persona to the next and gave rise to a myriad of spiritual successors, creating a giant family tree of mutant pop creatures. Would Marilyn Manson have existed without Bowie? What about Lady Gaga, Prince, and Grace Jones? No, probably not in the same form. The other point in common between the members of this "family"? They have all influenced *JoJo's Bizarre Adventure*. As such, on the star map of the Araki galaxy, the constellation *JoJo* always connects in one way or another, explicitly or not, with the David Bowie nebula (the name of the Stand Scary Monsters comes from one of the artist's albums, for example, and, as I've mentioned, there's a resemblance between the Kira from *Diamond is Unbreakable* and Thomas Jerome Newton, Bowie's first real film role). The *mangaka*'s series is bathed in the flamboyant, eternal light of this polymorphic creature whose very existence sent a message: be yourself and be proud of it.

La grande bellezza

"This face really makes me think of Michelangelo," says art historian Michel Lefftz upon seeing some of Araki's more recent drawings (from 2009 to 2018), drawing on his expertise in early modern art. The image that drew this reaction was one of Rohan on a treadmill, on page 181 of the second volume of *Thus Spoke Rohan Kishibe* (2018), shown to him as a funny example of the reappropriation of *contrapposto*, the tilting of the hips seen in Renaissance art, on this character busy running. With the excerpts shown to him, Michel Lefftz at times sees the influence of baroque art, like in the spatial characteristics of certain faces, as well as, particularly, of mannerist sculpture, like in the anatomically incorrect aspects of the bodies and the use of tension that the compositions demonstrate, and of German expressionism—especially its engravings—as seen in the angular aspects of forms and the irregularity of lines.

As we know, for Araki, it all started with *Apollo and Daphne*, the famous baroque sculpture by Bernini. However, the author has produced something completely different out of this original source of inspiration. We can't say that his work was exactly inspired by Bernini, or even by the baroque. In fact, Araki's characters are composites, so much so that we can rarely establish direct links with a single artistic movement or a single way of positioning the human body: for example, when we come across an image of a character with their hips tilted, can we really tell if that posture was drawn from sculpture or fashion shows and photos, which in turn have often been inspired by Italian statues? Not really. It's all a melting pot. Similarly, when we think we detect some Egon Schiele in Araki's work, are we really seeing that direct influence or is it instead inspired by Antonio Lopez and Tony Viramontes, who were themselves inspired by the body language of Schiele's figures? The culture of the 20th century has so many cross influences and Araki is an artist with so many inspirations that it all creates a web that's too complex to untangle entirely. Particularly, it is very difficult to identify the precise heritage of the "*JoJo* poses." Many of them come from existing works of art: some are direct transpositions of fashion photos and illustrations, for example, while others are inspired by famous sculptures, but that's not always the case. Araki assimilated all of these influences. He integrated them into his blended visual vocabulary, allowing him to invent infinite variations of body language. For example, if we can consider the "mechanical" positions of characters' hands to be directly borrowed from the work of Antonio Lopez (who himself was inspired by urban dance styles), in *JoJo*, that influence is mixed with others. I'll remind you of the panel from *Phantom Blood* in which Dio's body, in a powerful contrast between angles and curves, takes the shape of an S, while his right arm and his left hand form 90° angles, for a result evoking sculpture, fashion, and martial arts all at once.[1] There's also the cover of the first volume of *Thus Spoke Rohan Kishibe*, which shows Rohan with one hand in a "Lopez style" (positioned horizontally, perpendicular to the forearm) and the other in a "Viramontes style," with the fingers spread out in front of the face—in the same spirit as Josuke's iconic pose on the cover of volume eight of *Diamond is Unbreakable*. However, because of the complex webs of pop culture, we can also imagine that Araki may have borrowed these gestures from a fashion magazine cover or, why not, a voguing dance move—since voguing is a dance that actually reinterprets imagery from women's magazines. Once again, in this illustration, the combination of angular and curving forms is ubiquitous: Rohan's body is drawn with sharp angles (as seen in the way his jaw is drawn), but the outlines of his clothing soften certain areas, like the shoulder, which would probably have a less rounded shape to it if Araki had drawn him without a shirt. We can also observe the contrast between Rohan's headband, made up of sharp triangles, and his plump lips, creating a zesty mix of danger and sensuality.

Because of the ways that legacies work, these influences indirectly give the *"JoJo* poses" multiple meanings. For example, while *JoJo's Bizarre Adventure* has never officially been presented as a manga belonging to gay culture, there are indeed elements of it in the author's drawings. Naturally, when he reinterprets, for example, a drawing by Antonio Lopez with an obvious homoerotic charge, in which two muscular, heavily make-upped men stand cheek to cheek, a part of that charge is carried over to the transposition.[2] In Araki's work, the result in this case is characters considered "camp straight," hetero men whose appearance evokes the stereotypes of flamboyant gay men. In other words, the sum of the meaning carried over from the original image and the context of the new image creates a new meaning. Another example: on the cover of the *Ultra Jump* dated August 2005, an illustration shows Gyro and Johnny in a shared pose inspired by a photo by Richard Avedon taken in 1993 for Versace, in which a masculine model (Marcus Schenkenberg) is holding up a partner (Stephanie

---

1. *JoJonium Phantom Blood*, vol. 2, p. 273 (*JJBA* vol. 3). See chapter 1 of this book, section "Macho, macho man."
2. In the first pages of *JJBA* vol. 8 (*JoJonium Battle Tendency*, title page for the chapter "Ultimate Warriors from Ancient Times, Part 2"), then on the cover of *Golden Wind* vol. 6 (*JJBA* vol. 52).

Seymour) whose legs are splayed around his bare chest. By borrowing from this photo with a very "Kama Sutra-esque," undeniable eroticism, the author inevitably transposes that sexual tension to the two heroes of *Steel Ball Run*. Even though, in its new context, the tension is diluted: Gyro is not shirtless and the fact that he's holding up Johnny can be explained by the latter's illness. Along the same lines, giving the pose of a Renaissance statue to a masculine character today often creates—because of the differences of context and era— male bodies that would now be viewed as effeminate.

Besides that, the hybrid nature of most of the poses—those that aren't transpositions of existing images, but instead are reminiscent of sculpture, fashion, and dance, without us being able to name the specific influences –gives meaning by itself. These poses are an interesting, even allegorical, expression of the frequent blending of cultures that took place in the 20th century and after. Like David Bowie, they blend male and female, or heterosexuality and homosexuality. Like voguing, they blend the culture of the wealthy (the world of luxury fashion) with the culture of the poor (urban dance styles). Like in Antonio Lopez's work, they blend white culture (Western high fashion) with the culture of Black and Latino communities (hip-hop dance moves) or, to put it differently, mainstream culture with underground culture. And on top of all that, the "*JoJo* poses" mix the culture of the world's great museums (ancient and early modern art) with pop culture, just as how comics have made their way into the world of art thanks to artists like Roy Lichten-stein, who was inspired by American comics. These poses are a powerful symbol of openness. They send a resplendent message that fits with the goals of diversity found in today's world. And thanks to their many mixed influences, they are also the total embodiment of the idea of heritage.

The bodies (as well as the garments covering them), the vehicles for the "*JoJo* poses," add even more to the big picture. Initially, in *Phantom Blood*, the author presented big, hulking men, symbols of masculine power who sometimes act like action film heroes, but also sometimes like female models (and sometimes both at once, like when we see traces of feminine gestures in fighting positions), with the latter seen with increasing frequency from *Battle Tendency* onward. In that second part, masculine and feminine gender expressions overlap via clothing, make-up, and accessories. Incidentally, we can also note the mixed influences of the outfits, which blend everything from South American motifs to tribal clothing to European fashion.[3] While *Stardust Crusaders* generally returns to the style of less effeminate men, the new Dio and the chic Jean-Pierre Polnareff continue to embody the trend established by *Battle Tendency*: when it comes down to it, we can even see Polnareff as a

---

3. See chapter 2, section "Club Bizarre."

fusion of Grace Jones and her former beau Dolph Lundgren! From there, *Golden Wind* turned back toward the trend of hybrid gender expressions:[4] androgyny reigns supreme, to be continued in *Stone Ocean*. There again, we find looks with multicultural, or even multicentury, influences: for example, the tiger-print pants worn by Guido Mista look like glam rock style, but the shape of his cap evokes that of a Venetian helmet from the 15th century,[5] while the diamond motif on his sweater is reminiscent of Harlequin's costume from the 16th-century *commedia dell'arte*. More recently, parts seven and eight have stabilized a new approach for bodies and looks, one that's closer to real-life norms. We can't say that the boys are hyper-feminized or that the girls are hyper-masculinized in *JoJolion*: we simply find modern-day city folk, wrapped in Araki's extravagant style. While in *Battle Tendency* the effeminate men were likely considered very eccentric for their time, fashion has strongly evolved, gender expression is more fluid, and the idea of embracing both one's masculine and feminine sides has entered the mainstream. In *JoJolion*, we can say that certain male characters are metrosexual and certain women, like Karera, proudly deviate from the rules of feminine elegance. A manga in keeping with today's trends.

Let's go back to sculpture. How does Araki's work formally borrow from statuary? In what ways did statues shape the "*JoJo* poses," the series' conception of beauty, and its relationship with time? Before we even get to the manga, let's establish some basic points. In sculpture, one of the major areas of analysis is posture. In medieval and early modern art, straight posture, leaning posture, *contrapposto*, and serpentine figures appeared one after another. The straight, stable posture of Romanesque statues of the Middle Ages was followed by leaning posture (tilting the pelvis) typical of the Gothic Middle Ages, then *contrapposto* (one of the feet bearing the body's weight and tilting the pelvis, while the shoulders tilt in the opposite direction, re-establishing balance) during the Renaissance, which was a return to a classic posture used in antiquity. After that, the mannerist movement of the late Renaissance introduced the serpentine figure, which previously existed during the Hellenistic period (the era of innovation in ancient Greek art) and was later used more frequently during the baroque period: it involves a placement of the body that creates a curving, spiral movement, inviting the viewer to walk all around the statue. As we'll see, these postures also exist in *JoJo*.

Why is it that in the history of sculpture, postures changed over time? Art historian Michel Lefftz explains the transformations that succeeded the straight posture found in Romanesque art: "From the moment that humans, represented in sculpture by the saints, gradually begin to understand the world

---

4. See chapter 5, section "The new meaning of virility."
5. A helmet like the *Sallet alla Veneziana*, on display at the Metropolitan Museum of Art in New York: www.metmuseum.org/art/collection/search/23229.

around them, they are no longer simply content with staying put and taking whatever the world gives them. They want to move. And with that desire, they will then also represent themselves moving. It starts with a human's mental representation of their relationship with the world. This understanding of spatial relationships develops gradually: first, in terms of the plane, since a tilting of the hips and *contrapposto* are always parallel to the plane of the back. Then, once the serpentine figure of mannerism and the baroque (or of Hellenism, in the case of Greece) appeared, there was a real need to tell stories taking place in larger spaces and as part of a continuum of events. Management of space is always tied to the management of time: having a subject move essentially means that there is a before and an after. Presenting the subject in a stable, vertical pose means that they are simply fixed in that position. Then, in the Gothic period, tilting of the hips created tension in the body, showing that it's not paralyzed and that it's animated by something. That tension presents a form of unbalance because, in the case of tilted hips, only the pelvis inclines. That's why *contrapposto*, which restores balance, fits perfectly with the ideals of the Quattrocento during the Italian Renaissance: to have something calm, stable, and balanced. However, it's an idealized vision of a body that's just there, suspended in time. It's not as if time has stopped, as we see in Bernini's work, but rather, time is suspended. That means that the story depicted—or the subject embodying or representing that story—is there, suspended in time, as if the action began some time ago and could continue for some time more. The stronger the spatial dynamic, the more restricted the space-time continuum. And if the time of the narration is tighter, that means that there must be different situations before and after, and that moments must be chained together in succession: there's a continuum. If the subject's pose is stable, there's still a continuum, but without change: it was before as it is now, and it will still be so later."[6]

We know that, initially, what struck Araki upon seeing *Apollo and Daphne* was the beauty and intensity of the baroque sculpture. But what was the conception of beauty during the early modern period? From the Renaissance onward, should we view refined postures like *contrapposto* and the serpentine figure as ways of idealizing human beings, making them as beautiful as possible and occupying space in the most elegant way possible? Michel Lefftz sheds some light on this: "Yes and no, because we could say the same thing about a Romanesque sculpture: it presents the most beautiful version of man because it corresponds to the ideal developed by humans based on Scripture. It's a stable version of man that's presented because God willed it to be so. Thus, that idea of beauty already existed before. The new development during

6. These remarks by Michel Lefftz, as well as those that follow, were collected by us on March 22, 2019.

the Renaissance was that the body became anatomical, whereas during the Middle Ages they paid no attention to human anatomy. During the 13th century, with the Gothic style and its tilting of the hips, the body attracted interest as a way of representing an idealized vision of man, through the depiction of Jesus Christ, who became a benevolent figure. It became increasingly common to see in Gothic cathedrals, at the portals, sculptures grouped around a central figure (the Christ, the Virgin Mary, or a local saint), presented as a welcoming person. In this way, holy figures are no longer distant concepts, represented as stiff, narrow subjects in Romanesque sculptures; instead, they become people like us because they have a certain humanity to them. However, they don't look like us from an anatomical perspective: the interest in anatomy didn't appear until the Renaissance; consequently, that's when artists began paying attention to the mechanics of the body, i.e., real-life mechanics." After that, representations of the human body evolved in a surprising way with the mannerist movement, which, as we'll see, is the style closest to Araki's work. Michel Lefftz explains this evolution, which occurred with the advent of a new generation of artists that followed that of masters like Michelangelo and Leonardo da Vinci: "Giorgio Vasari said about the ceiling of the Sistine Chapel that it offers so many possibilities—we see hundreds of subjects, each with their own attitude, position, and gestures—that there was nothing left but to draw inspiration from it, like a catalogue. Some artists did just that, but others preferred to express their own individuality more, and it's that latter group that really formed the mannerist movement, as they decided to depict anatomically incorrect bodies. They made the necks and limbs longer and depicted bodies that are beautiful according to concepts rather than according to nature. Deciding that beauty is first and foremost a conception of the mind and that its depiction, whether painted or sculpted, will follow these concepts distanced from reality is a demonstration of great freedom. It was really avant-garde for the time! So, from then on, the mannerists introduced the possibility of freeing oneself from the constraints of the body's real-life limits, offering possibilities for twisting and bending the various parts of the body. During the baroque, this idea of freedom was maintained, but it was clearly tempered because the bodies look more natural. However, in reality, there are often elements of subterfuge: if you take a statue or a painting and try to reproduce its posture in real life, it doesn't work."

While *JoJo's Bizarre Adventure* borrows some of these conventions from statues, it rarely takes stability into account. Everything is explosive, actions occur in rapid succession and at a frenetic pace, and the characters can change their posture from one panel to the next. In this respect, *JoJo* is an eminently urban—Tokyoite, we might even say—manga, evoking the speed and excitement of city life. This aspect also comes from the graphic conventions of the manga medium, such as the intensity of the "film editing" techniques first made popular by Osamu Tezuka not long after World War II, and in Araki's own work, the fact that these conventions are combined with poses borrowed from ancient sculptures creates a very unique collision of cultures. Strike a pose. Vogue. Vogue. Vogue. Just as Madonna says in the song *Vogue*. So, everything is connected, but the poses themselves have a vibrant quality to them. The example of Rohan in "pseudo-*contrapposto*" on his treadmill perfectly represents the fact that Araki, in his manga, reuses and gives new life to the poses of age-old art. Of course, in that frame, it's not a true example of *contrapposto*: Rohan's shoulders and hips are leaning in opposite directions, but he's not in a stable position. It's also not a real running position: no one runs while leaning like that; it has no logic in terms of balance. Furthermore, it would probably be difficult to reproduce that movement in real life—as in painting and sculpture, it has an effect of illusionism. In this case, the opposing inclinations of the pelvis and hips seem to have been drawn out of pure self-indulgence, to give a particular harmony to the image and perhaps also a few notes of calm to contrast with the energetic, dynamic movement created by the zigzagging prominent features and the many angular shapes. With his hand on his hip, Rohan almost looks like he's resting, while his face appears serene, as if frozen. What's more, even when Araki draws bodies that are stable and at rest, in true *contrapposto*, it creates a bizarre effect because of his well-known bold, angular lines. When you turn a page of *JoJolion* and find Jobin standing in *contrapposto*, what does the drawing say about this character who, incidentally, wears clothing covered in spikes? That there's an air of latent nervous energy, that something is about to explode. The character appears dangerously calm. Or calmly dangerous. Finally, when the author draws more spatial poses that look like a serpentine figure (see, for example, Kira on page 103 or Josuke on page 123 of volume 12 of *JoJolion*—in the French version), they give the characters stronger (Josuke) or lesser (Kira) tension, depending on the major lines formed by their bodies. However, above all, the amplitude of movements fills the characters with vital force.

If we had to associate the depiction of bodies in *JoJo* with a movement from the history of sculpture, first and foremost, it would have to be mannerism, with its emancipation from the proportions of the real-life body, as well as its possibilities for twisting and bending. Hirohiko Araki has always used a very free approach to drawing people, starting from *Phantom Blood* with its spectacular elongations and ballooning of limbs, which put the emphasis on the extraordinary abilities of the athletic bodies of characters like Jonathan and Dio.[7] However, it was in the mid-1990s that he really got close to certain mannerist statues, thanks to his tendency to present svelte figures and bodies that defy gravity, reminiscent of the works of artists like Giambologna.[8] In

7. See chapter 1 of this book, section "Macho, macho man."
8. See chapter 5, section "The new meaning of virility."

short, the massive bodies, in the style of *Hokuto no Ken* and *Sakigake!! Otokojuku*, seen in the first three parts of the saga gradually evolved toward more simplified forms (in *Stardust Crusaders*, the torsos become short and trapezoidal, the legs become slender, the jaws become angular) before slimming down in *Diamond is Unbreakable*, until reaching the style of *Golden Wind*, with its slim bodies that look totally different from other manga. From there, just as the baroque followed the mannerist movement, *JoJo*'s characters ended up returning to more realistic shapes, while not abandoning the freedom from the real abilities of the human body. From the second half of *Steel Ball Run* onward (and to this day), the bodies do more to celebrate the beauty of the true human body thanks to more realistic proportions and shading, while a general ideal of beauty begins to take shape and influence the appearance of most characters' faces.[9] This addition of realism comes with another change: we now really feel the weight of the bodies compared to *Golden Wind* and *Stone Ocean*. The bodies float less and are more firmly planted on the ground thanks to the fact that shadows are drawn beneath their feet and are often more realistic. In this respect, we can say that, in general, the characters interact more convincingly with their surroundings, without the manga losing its overall bizarre character.

The most difficult aspect to examine when looking at the transposition of elements from the medium of sculpture into manga is the question of time. In comics, in principle, there's no such thing as time being suspended infinitely: because one panel follows another, there is always—other than on the first and last pages, or in very experimental comics—something that comes before and after. And there's nothing to indicate how long exactly a panel lasts. Thus, as in sculpture, we can work off of the principle that the more static the characters are, the longer a panel could potentially last—and the speech bubbles can also serve as an indicator. So, a panel can last a long time, yes, but not eternity. Sometimes, in his panels, Araki creates a paradox: he freezes his characters in stable poses, similar to those seen in sculpture, but also shows, using speed lines in the background, that time is passing quickly, and thus the panel is capturing a precise instant. However, it's not the stopped time of *Apollo and Daphne*, nor the suspended time of a Renaissance sculpture. In this respect, we can draw a parallel with the "frozen" poses of Kabuki theater, which influenced the visual vocabulary of manga, those moments where the actors freeze for several seconds, generally during a key action, in order to emphasize it. In manga, for example, there are moments in *Captain Tsubasa* where a player is about to hit a ball. Typical of *shōnen*, this type of image also exists in *JoJo* (when a character is in movement), but instance of interest to us in this case,

9. See chapter 7, "Quintessence and Renaissance."

the one where the character is in a stable position on a background of speed lines, does not exactly fit into that vocabulary. Since Araki's work draws both from sculpture and the conventions of manga, we find in *JoJo* such totally bizarre cases.

In the end, the greatest contribution of sculpture to *JoJo* is that it gave rise to bizarre aspects that are unique in manga: this relationship with time that can be strange at times and that extreme theatricality created by the way the characters position themselves. The inspiration of statues, on the one hand, raises the question of the new meaning that a shape can take on when placed in a different context; on the other hand, it makes us think about the doors that can be opened into a creative process by viewing an image. The fact that Hirohiko Araki's encounter with *Apollo and Daphne*, a sculpture from the 17th century, gave rises to a modern, eccentric manga is a perfect illustration. Ultimately, there are as many paths to explore from Bernini as there are artists, as suggested by these words from Michel Lefftz: "A few months ago, I took an old Belgian sculptor, who's still active, to Rome. He visited the city when he was still learning his art, but at the time, they only taught about religious art and Bernini was considered decadent—this was in the 1950s, he's now 86 years old. After I showed him works of the baroque, he returned home brimming with new ideas. However, that doesn't mean he's going to copy Bernini. In that case, what is it that influences and affects him? Most of the time, an artist retains certain elements because exploring different works opens doors in their mind, answering their lingering questions. If they are looking for a definite solution for a particular situation, seeing how another artist solved a similar problem gives them that 'aha' moment." An "aha" moment. There's another concept that ultimately helps explain how legacies work. How connections are created across the star map of a work and its influences.

Written in the stars

Legacy and an ode to humanity. These have been the two main themes of *JoJo's Bizarre Adventure* since *Phantom Blood*. However, a third subject is closely tied to them: destiny. One might think that the concept of destiny runs contrary to the celebration of humanity, the idea that one or more invisible phenomena control the course of events being a negation of human strength. But that's not the case in *JoJo*. The saga presents human beings that are capable of facing destiny courageously and even sometimes of changing the course of events to their advantage.

As I see it, philosophers have always, in their own ways, dealt with the question of destiny—starting with the Stoics of ancient Greece and their deter- minist conception of the world, according to which all events must result from causes that precede them. Physicists have also examined the issue of destiny via the idea of quantum randomness. However, the world of *JoJo* is imaginary, supernatural, and does not obey the same rules as ours. So, let's observe it in its own context, not by comparing it to the world around us, and let's try to decipher the mechanisms of the invisible "god" who pulls the strings of destiny, that force that controls the movement of the stars. And of the Joestars. We can consider the world of the saga to be semi-predetermined: it is governed by constants, things that will occur no matter what, but its course of events also includes variables, a leeway that allows humans to act with relative freedom. Really, we should be talking about "worlds," plural, since the world of *Steel Ball Run* and *JoJolion* is distinct from the world of the first six parts. Since the handling of what we've labeled "constants" and "variables" is different in each world, we have to consider them separately.

The idea of destiny appears very early on in *JoJo*. In *Phantom Blood*, Araki clearly establishes—in the characters' own words or through narration—that the destinies of Jonathan, Dio, and Zeppeli are tied together and all converge on the stone mask. What's more, in *JJBA* volume four (*JoJonium Phantom Blood* vol. 3), a flashback shows that Zeppeli himself caused the creation of a constant: in Tibet, his master explains to him that if he continues down the path of Hamon, his destiny will be to die a cruel death from which there's no escaping.[10] And that's exactly what ended up happening. So, we see there the idea that constants, those unchanging data points, are not necessarily independent of human actions, nor are they determined since the dawn of time. They come into play when, shall we say, the force that governs the universe sets them, etching them in stone. In *Battle Tendency*, the story seems to repeat itself for the Joestar and Zeppeli bloodlines, as if the interactions between the members of these two families are governed by a constant through time. This idea continues in *Stardust Crusaders*: as long as they both shall live, Dio and the Joestar lineage shall be destined to fight each other through the generations. What's more, the third part concretely illustrates the idea of constants and variables via Boingo's Stand, a manga whose pages predict the future. Everything the comic book says must come true, no matter what: according to our model, we can say that when the future is written in Boingo's manga, the force governing the universe freezes the constants. However, the path to carrying out those predictions may vary.[11] In *Diamond is Unbreakable*, the Stand Bites the Dust borrows the idea of predestination, but presents it in a more complex fashion, since traveling back in time enters into the equation. If you view destiny in *JoJo's Bizarre Adventure* as being controlled by an impalpable force that governs the universe, then Bites the Dust gives Kira a status close

10. *JoJonium Phantom Blood* vol. 3 (*JJBA* vol. 4).
11. See chapter 3, section "Level Up!"

to that divine force since he's capable of creating constants. That power, while it remains active, has the effect of killing anyone who aims to discover the identity of the serial killer and to establish the constant that says "this person will die," before rewinding time by one hour. When this happens, even if the day's new course of events varies slightly from the previous version, the person will remain destined to lose their life, no matter what, even if they don't come in contact with anyone, thus leaving no proof of the evil deed.[12] Kira indeed uses Bites the Dust malevolently, but this power illustrates the strength of humanity, its ability to influence destiny.

From *Golden Wind* onward, destiny becomes a major theme. The best example is Bucciarati, whose death is foretold in the flashback at the end of the final volume.[13] That death is a constant, and it indeed took place. However, before that, by some miracle, the character extended his life beyond the moment when he was supposed to perish: Bucciarati, from the tenth volume onward, remains in the land of the living as an animated corpse—his heart no longer beats and he no longer bleeds. Filled with a remarkable vital force, he defies his destiny. He pushes the limits of the leeway that exists between two constants. In general, the fifth part praises that freedom. It tells us that it's always possible to fight to give meaning to your life, in spite of the things you have no choice about, like the environment you're born into or the constants of destiny—we can imagine that, for Bucciarati, the fact of having "chosen" that life of violence triggered the constant of how he would die.

Stone Ocean reduces that freedom. Part six tells us at the very end that after the universe completed a full cycle of existence—from its genesis to its extinction—that same universe was recreated almost identically,[14] thus meaning that the constants are both strong and numerous and that there's little room for variables, even if humans have a bit of leeway since certain details differ, in spite of it all, compared to the previous universe. However, like Kira before him, Enrico Pucci achieves an almost god-like status. He even escapes from the system of destiny, becoming the only human being to have true free will! In other words, he is the only cause of his choices. He is no longer subject to the influence of any constants; instead, he can create his own. Ironically, that ends up being his downfall since Emporio finds a way to make Pucci carry out an action that will cause his own death. These two characters are powerful embodiments of humanity's strength, each in his own way. They represent the invigorating idea that no matter where you come from or the misfortunes that await you, it's always possible to exercise freedom.

12. See chapter 4, section "Guaranteed to blow your mind."
13. See chapter 5, section "From baroque to rococo."
14. See chapter 6, section "Sine Wave."

Steel Ball Run and *JoJolion* again put the emphasis on humanity's strength, but they present a crueler version of the world. In these two story arcs, Araki presents the idea that there are invariable amounts of positive and negative energy and thus both fortunate and unfortunate events are bound to take place, but can't be avoided. They are constants. However, in this world, you can "hack" the constants: you can move a misfortune elsewhere in the world or exchange one impaired body part for another—remember, in *JoJolion*, there was an old man with an amputated leg who grew a new one in exchange for losing his eyes. In other words, humans are able to manipulate the divine force that governs destiny. A force that, in this second space-time continuum, has a physical existence: the saint's body. We can also see the locacaca fruit as being connected to the divine force. In *Steel Ball Run* and *JoJolion*, characters revolt against the constants of destiny; they aim to acquire a god-like power that will allow them to rearrange reality to their advantage. That's the principle behind the Stand Love Train, as well as the principle of the equal exchange. Yasuho's Stand in *JoJolion* also fits with this idea: it's a sort of GPS on steroids that, once again, makes it possible to "hack" the world by moving objects or events in ways that benefit the Stand user—for example, if Yasuho is being chased, the Stand will "arrange" her escape route to help her get away. In this way, we can say that she also possesses an almost god-like power, being able to (slightly) rearrange reality and thus change minor constants. Additionally, *Steel Ball Run* offers an interesting application for the idea of variables. In this story arc, Funny Valentine is capable of moving through parallel universes where certain parameters differ from those of the original world. In this power, we can see the different worlds that result from the potential branching that occurs from events with variable outcomes, the idea being that each different outcome creates an additional world.

Funnily enough, the idea of constants and variables is also part of Araki's creative process. As we know, the author improvises intuitively based on elements he establishes from the beginning. However, in reality, this approach goes even further. As evidence, we have these words from the *mangaka*: "It's hard to explain, but when I draw, I can really feel the existence of what I call 'gravity' (even if it's brief). In other words, while you might think that, as an author, I control the actions of the main characters by moving the story forward or controlling the world in general in which I give them life, that's not always how it works. Indeed, at times, the characters go against my will. That's how I end up with drawings that I would never have initially intended to create. That's how this 'gravity' manifests itself; I consider it to be related in some way to destiny."[15] In short, the tension between the characters and their destiny is so strong that it overflows from the saga, to the point of

15. Note from the author in vol. 17 of *Stone Ocean*.

"hacking" the mind of the creator himself! As if the characters' desire for free will broke the barriers of fiction. Ultimately, one of the strongest ideas sent by these characters, through their actions (whether morally acceptable or not) and their "*JoJo* poses" filled with a zest for life, is the idea of freedom. Reading *JoJo* and putting yourself in its characters' shoes, you get the feeling—even though it may just be an illusion, even though our own world may turn out to be entirely predestined—that humans are free creatures. And isn't that the true ode to humanity?

CHAPTER XXI: THE WORLD (IS JOJO)

To listen to while reading:

David Bowie – *Starman*
Vanilla Ice – *Ice Ice Baby*
Perfume – *Chocolate Disco*
Limousine – *Cosmos*
Sia – *Waving Goodbye*

Let's keep zooming out. This time, let's leave *JoJo's Bizarre Adventure*. Let's even leave manga culture and Japan alone to observe the entire globe. Over the last decade, Araki's series has risen to new heights. That author has had one prestigious exhibition after another, as well as multiple collaborations with Italian high-fashion brands. At the same time, the anime series, which began in 2012 (coinciding with the saga's 25th anniversary) and which has just finished *Golden Wind* as I write these lines, has attracted a whole new generation of fans worldwide. Meanwhile, new major video games have been made for home consoles and a live-action film was made by the famous director Takashi Miike. *JoJo* has become a global phenomenon.

Deep Impact

In 2006, for its 10th anniversary, the Japan Media Arts Festival conducted a survey of Japanese fans. The goal: to create a ranking of the top 10 manga of all time. Around 80,000 votes were cast and *JoJo's Bizarre Adventure* came in second place, just behind *Slam Dunk* and ahead of *Dragon Ball*! That just goes to show how important the saga has been for Japanese readers. And for *mangaka* too, I should add: there are countless artists who revere Araki's work. To celebrate the 100th volume and the 25th anniversary of *JoJo*, two anniversary booklets were distributed with *Ultra Jump*, "Volume 100.5" (in 2010) and *25 Years with JoJo* (in 2012): they include, among other things, drawings by famous *mangaka* paying tribute to all of Araki's work, across all eras. Contributors included Akira Toriyama and Eiichirō Oda (who both drew Jotaro), *Shaman King*'s Hiroyuki Takei (who drew Jolyne, but also a hybrid of

B.T. and Dio!), *Naruto*'s Masashi Kishimoto (who drew Giorno), *Death Note*'s Takeshi Obata (who drew Rohan)... And there were many more drawings by *mangaka*, each accompanied by a personal note. But those two booklets are not the only time that artists have shown their love for *JoJo*: back in the early '90s, the famous group of female authors CLAMP created an amateur parody manga featuring the characters from *Stardust Crusaders* in a parallel world where they were all still alive after the Egyptian adventure—best of all, Jotaro had married Kakyoin! Naturally, CLAMP also produced a drawing—of Jolyne—for the booklet *25 Years with JoJo*. In the manga world, this parade of tributes and influences has been constant, whether through the highly popular works of artists like Kazuki Takahashi and Yoshihiro Togashi[16] or, more recently, *Shishunki Renaissance! David-kun* by Yūshin Kuroki (*Teenage Renaissance! David*, 2018-2019), which sort of feels like *JoJo*'s comedic little cousin. This manga from *Shōnen Jump*, set in a Japanese school, features well-known figures from art history like Michelangelo's David, Botticelli's Venus, and even Jérôme Duquesnoy the Elder's Manneken Pis, who, in the manga, wears a hat parodying Jotaro's!

Of course, *JoJo*'s influence is not limited to manga. The world of fighting video games would not be the same without *JoJo* (the series *Street Fighter* and *The King of Fighters* first and foremost, but others as well) and, outside of that very specific genre, we can't ignore the resemblance between the concept of Stands and that of "personae" in the series of role-playing games *Persona*, launched in 1996, which is now a major RPG franchise. I won't list all of the video games that have referenced *JoJo*, but as an example, we find nods to *Stardust Crusaders* and *Diamond is Unbreakable* in the famous series of "visual novels" *Danganronpa* (2010-present) and, more recently, the adventure game *Bloodstained* (2019) references the stone mask, among other things.[17] Outside the sphere of manga, anime, and video games, the starlets Shōko Nakagawa and Kyary Pamyu Pamyu (who named one of her dogs JoJo!), and the girl group Perfume, for example, are big fans of *JoJo* and aren't afraid to show it on social media or in their choreography. Funnily enough, the "*JoJo* poses" sometimes inspired by dancing have themselves become dance moves used in music videos, on stage... and even on ice! In March 2019, during the World Figure Skating Championships in Saitama, Japan, skater Keiji Tanaka paid tribute to *Diamond is Unbreakable,* dressed as Josuke, and performed a routine with JoJo-esque flavor to it, moving to the beat of the theme song from the anime. Farther away, outside of Japan, the photo campaign for the fall-winter 2001-2002 collection from Dior, inspired

---

16. See chapter 3, section "Level Up!"

17. *Bloodstained* follows the legacy of the *Castlevania* series, which in turn contained references to *JoJo*. For example, in *Castlevania: Aria of Sorrow* (2003), a spectral being that follows the hero occasionally unleashes a flurry of punches while shouting, "*Ora Ora Ora!*"

by manga, had an ambiance that was strangely similar to that of the color illustrations from *Stone Ocean*; another example,in the American TV series *Heroes*, which began in 2006, the character Hiro Nakamura said he was a fan of *JoJo* and had the power to stop time like Dio! Closer to my own home, in 2014, Italian video creator Maurizio Merluzzo, who specializes in cooking, reproduced a dish by Antonio Trussardi[18] on his *YouTube* channel "Cotto & Frullato"... and then donned a stone mask, reappeared dressed as Dio, cried out a few "*Wryyy!*" typical of the infamous vampire, and even stopped time! In the video, the cook said that he's been a fan of the series since his childhood and he encouraged his viewers to check it out ASAP. This makes perfect sense given that Italy is so closely tied to *JoJo* and that publication of the series began there in 1993; what's more, this year, Araki will be there as a guest of honor at the Lucca Comics festival (October 2019), Europe's biggest event dedicated to comics. And that's a big deal: it will be the first time the *mangaka* takes part in a festival outside of Japan. Last but not least, here's one final example of *JoJo*'s international impact: John McAfee, a candidate for the upcoming American presidential elections, identifies with Joseph Joestar from *Stardust Crusaders*–as I write these lines,[19] he has an illustration of Joseph as his avatar on Twitter! You have to admit, there is a resemblance between the two men. McAfee is trying to win over young voters by using pop culture references–he even uses the tagline "McAfee 2020: Freedom, Justice, Anime"–and the fact that his communications team turned to *JoJo's Bizarre Adventure* to connect with over a million followers proves the firepower that the series now has in the Western world. Or rather, in the world in general: on July 28, 2019, the date the final episode of *Golden Wind* became available for streaming, the hashtag "#jojo_anime" reached the number-one spot on Twitter's list of global trends, followed closely by "ジョジョ," *JoJo* in Japanese characters. That day, for the span of several hours, we can say that "The World was *JoJo*" on the web.

Fan Fan Fan

- Why is Yoshikage Kira singing about Diego Brando?
- Because it just works.

This exchange, in the comments of a *YouTube* video playing the song *Scary Monsters* (the source for the name of Diego's Stand) by David Bowie, perfectly encapsulates the liveliness and humor of *JoJo* fan communities. Over 6,000 likes for the first comment and over 600 for the second, which is a meme about King

18. The one in *VIZ Diamond is Unbreakable*, vol. 3 (*JJBA* vol. 33), on page 26.
19. July 2019.

Crimson's power, known for being inexplicable.[20] They're "JoJokes." Given how the saga constantly references all sorts of musical artists, comments filled with JoJokes have appeared all over *YouTube* in recent years, and the view counters for certain forgotten songs have exploded. Even more amusing: when the rapper Vanilla Ice, in January 2015, posted on Twitter a photo from his vacation in Egypt, he got a barrage of reactions to his tweet, with messages like, "HOW COULD YOU KILL AVDOL?!?!," and edited images blending his photo with the *JoJo* universe. The reason is that Vanilla Ice is the name of Dio's right-hand man in the Egyptian portion of *Stardust Crusaders*, and he was also the character who murdered Avdol. Again, this happened at a time when the anime series was in the middle of *JoJo*'s third part.

In addition to JoJokes and memes of all sorts, like the famous "Araki forgot"[21] (a response given whenever an element of *JoJo*'s plot seems to contradict another), as well as jokes about the author's eternally youthful appearance, the various fan communities are also very creative. It's quite common, of course, for fans of a franchise to produce amateur drawings and to share them on the internet, but those made by *JoJo* fans are extraordinary. Besides the many reinterpretations with a *yaoi* flavor to them (a type of gay manga intended mostly for female audiences), we also see an incredible number of drawings that reverse the genders of the characters, which is seen less commonly elsewhere; and then there's this unique trend: some fans draw scenes of idyllic family life, reinventing the past for characters who had complex relationships with their parents. For example, on Twitter or specialized illustration communities like Pixiv, you can find an image of Jolyne as a little girl, sitting on Jotaro's shoulders, or dozens of other fantasies, like Dio brushing a young Giorno's hair.[22] It's a way for fans to give tender loving care to these fictional people. Another example of the liveliness of *JoJo*'s readers and viewers: there are classes for "*JoJo* poses," generally held at *otaku* conventions around the world, but also at an event called "*Tōdai JoJo dachi*," hailed by Hirohiko Araki's wife herself (Asami Araki, nicknamed "Chami"), which took place in March 2007 at the University of Tokyo (called Tōdai for short), one of the country's most prestigious universities.[23] In

20. The video: https://www.youtube.com/watch?v=NHywdqH3F6Y [accessed July 28, 2019]. Regarding the power of King Crimson: see chapter 5, section "From baroque to rococo." Note that in January 2017, the guitarist for the cult rock group from which the Stand got his name personally joined in the fun of the meme with a post on Facebook that, of course, generated a buzz (https://www.facebook.com/robert.fripp.96/posts/1578167965532561).

21. There's even an *Urban Dictionary* entry on this subject: https://www.urbandictionary.com/define.php?term=Araki%20forgot.

22. Max Genecov, "How JoJo's Bizarre Adventure fan art is trying to correct the anime's parental problems," *Polygon*, January 23, 2019. (https://www.polygon.com/2019/1/23/18193396/jojos-bizarre-adventure-jotaro-jolyne-dio-giorno-fan-art.)

23. Photos from the event can be seen on this Japanese website: http://kajipon.sakura.ne.jp/art/jojo-todai.html. To learn more about Japan's "*JoJo*'s Posing School," visit this page: http://kajipon.sakura.ne.jp/jojo.htm.

Japan, once again, the city of Sendai is a natural pilgrimage site for *JoJo* fans, who like to take photos with the Emilio Greco statue *Memories of Summer* on Jozenji-dori Avenue: the statue presents a woman whose body is twisted in a way that wouldn't be out of place in *JoJo's Bizarre Adventure*.

Rohan's Bizarre Adventure

"In 1997, the editorial board ordered a short story from me," Araki says in the first volume of *Thus Spoke Rohan Kishibe*, the collection of independent stories dedicated to Morioh's eccentric *mangaka*, published at irregular intervals in various magazines. "The conditions were: less than 45 pages, and I was strictly forbidden from creating a spin-off. And yet, lo and behold: here's a spin-off (laughs). Initially, I of course drew a version without Rohan, but isn't it so much better with him as the narrator? Read only the panels without him, just to get an idea. It's like a flavorless meal, don't you think? When I think about it, without that 'prohibition,' I would never have created the other Rohan spin-off stories. So, many thanks for that." So there you have it: that's how the series *Thus Spoke Rohan Kishibe*[24] got started. Often inventive, this manga is a space for Araki to express himself freely and deal with all sorts of paranormal subjects, like spirits and gods of nature, without always resorting to Stands. These chapters—some of which have been adapted into anime for the OVA market—are also a way for the author to talk about his profession: the stories include editorial meetings and quirky preparatory rituals that Rohan strictly follows before drawing. In addition, the spin-off series was an opportunity to return to the pages of *Shōnen Jump* from time to time, the magazine that Araki left, but for which he still feels real nostalgia, as he explains in the catalog for the exhibition *Shōnen Jump Vol. 2*.

However, Rohan was not satisfied with just appearing in Japanese magazines. "One evening, while reading a comic book, I said to myself: I work at the Louvre; I love my museum; I love books; I've always loved comics; why not do something with all of that?,"[25] said Fabrice Douar, editor at Éditions du Louvre. In 2005, he launched a collection of comic books in collaboration with publisher Futuropolis. Their first project together was *Glacial Period* by French author Nicolas de Crécy. Before long, they came to the idea of working with manga authors and Hirohiko Araki became the first of these. "Araki was on my short list when I went to Japan for the first time. I met him, as well as the

---

24. *Thus Spoke Rohan Kishibe* is its official international title. Meanwhile, the Japanese title is *Kishibe Rohan wa Ugokanai* (literally "Rohan Kishibe doesn't move").
25. "Le manga, nouvel ambassadeur du Louvre," remarks collected by Alexis Orsini for *Le Point Pop*, March 12, 2018. (https://www.lepoint.fr/pop-culture/bandes-dessinees/le-manga-nouvel-ambassadeur-du-louvre-12-03-2018-2201704_2922.php.)

other selected authors, and he was the first one to tell me 'yes,' and he did so very fast. That's why he was the first one to publish a story with us,"[26] explains the editor, adding that he chose the author of *JoJo* for the originality and the visual strength of his style, which, in Douar's view, is similar to that of the mannerists of the Italian Renaissance—as I also explained in the previous chapter. Although Araki was immediately excited about the project and, according to Fabrice Douar, had wanted to include the Louvre in his work since the first time he perused the Parisian museum, he was a very busy *mangaka*. Douar explains that for scheduling reasons, including the *mangaka*'s obligation to keep publishing *JoJo* monthly in *Ultra Jump*, the solution was to create a spin-off series, which suited Araki, who "wanted to delve into the life of one of the characters from his series, Rohan"; it also suited Araki's Japanese publisher, which was able to publish the spin-off episodes in *Ultra Jump* since they were still part of *JoJo*; and it suited the Louvre because Araki would create "a work immediately in color for the first time in his career, and it was with us!" Thus, in the April, May, and June 2010 issues of Shūeisha's monthly magazine, the story *Rohan at the Louvre* was published—in black and white, as required by the magazine—without replacing *Steel Ball Run*. A double dose of *JoJo*. In France, the color version was published in April of the same year in a large hardback format, using the Franco-Belgian publishing style but with the Japanese direction of reading. The book sold "tens of thousands of copies across Japan and Europe," says Fabrice Douar.

Rohan at the Louvre is a story that initially offers an energy that's quite different from *JoJo*, and even from the series *Thus Spoke Rohan Kishibe*: its atmosphere is softer and it has a slower pace. In it, we meet a moody, teenage Rohan who, one summer, in the inn run by his grandmother in Morioh, falls in love with a seductive young woman. However, one day, she suddenly disappears. Ten years later, Rohan is tracking down a cursed painting that supposedly lies somewhere in the secret rooms of the Louvre and which might help him find his long-lost love. This leads to a quest with a horror-thriller flavor. In creating this story, Araki visited places that are off limits for the general public: "Per his request, we took him to see the basements, the storerooms, and even the attics of the Louvre. The places where the characters go are very, very close to reality," explains Fabrice Douar, who also notes that the author was given a lot of latitude in creating his story. In fact, there's just one rule for the comic books in this collection: the author must use in their story works from the museum, certain rooms, the history of the site, or a specific collection (or any number of the above). "You can't just use the Louvre as the setting. For the

26. These remarks by Fabrice Douar, as well as those that follow, were collected by us on November 16, 2018.

rest, they have total free reign," explains the editor. Of course, as a big fan of mysteries, Araki chose to explore the secrets of the museum.

When showed this manga, art historian Michel Lefftz was clearly amused, having himself visited the same behind-the-scenes areas closed to the public—and he confirms that he recognizes the locations depicted. I chose to show him a specific two-page spread that has to be the most sensational in the book: it shows a full-body illustration of Rohan in front of one of the Louvre's pyramids, with the protagonist standing in a sensual pose tinged with eroticism, reminiscent of one of Michelangelo's "unfinished slaves." It's a beautiful and subtle reference to the museum since the nameless sculpture in question—that's sometimes called "The Dying Slave"—is on exhibit there. "There's no doubt that the author borrowed some interesting, erotic things from it," comments Michel Lefftz. "Like this hand that seems to caress the body... For the caress to really stand out, it needed to be opposed by an element of resistance: that would be the straps around the chest of Michelangelo's slave. Since your artist is presenting a story in today's world, he of course dressed his character, but had him lifting his shirt. What's funny is that he kept the lifted finger, which in the manga is clutching the edge of his sweater, whereas on Michelangelo's statue, the finger is below the straps, as if the hand slid down the abdomen, then came back up the chest and was stopped by the straps. It's a great element to borrow! In a more angular drawing, to top it off."[27]

Rohan at the Louvre will be remembered as a singular book in Araki's body of work; a brief foray, like an interlude, into the world of European comics. While on its own the book is really a minor work, it marked an important step in the *mangaka*'s career.

In the Pantheon

Rohan at the Louvre is not just a comic book. From January 22 to April 13, 2009, for the first time in its history, the Louvre opened its doors to the art of comics and exhibited original panels alongside the museum's paintings by master artists. During that time, Hirohiko Araki was preparing his book for Éditions du Louvre and thus his work was put on display, as part of a preview showing, alongside panels by Nicolas de Crécy, Marc-Antoine Mathieu, Éric Liberge, and Yslaire, who also created comic books for the museum. It was an important moment. It showed that Fabrice Douar, one of the two curators of the exhibit (along with Sébastien Gnaedig of Futuropolis), was committed to showcasing comics, which are often considered a lesser art form. "Comics

27. Remarks collected by us on March 22, 2019.

should have a place right alongside the other contemporary arts!" Fabrice Douar declares. "There is no hierarchy among different art forms because each one works with its own conventions, artists, and values." The fact that Araki was able to participate in this exhibition with a strong message, making him the first *mangaka* ever to have his works displayed at the Louvre, may have just been thanks to lucky timing. But this event marked an important kick-off. It propelled *JoJo* into prestigious circles: a major museum first, and not long after, the world of Italian high fashion.

Of course, the mutual relationships between fashion and comics did not begin with *JoJo*'s author—far from it. As I write these lines, the Comics Museum in Angoulême, France, is even hosting an exhibition on this subject—sadly, Hirohiko Araki has been left out of it... However, *JoJo* is one of the works that's very closely linked to the high fashion brands. As for that, the following event marked an important milestone in the history of *JoJo*: in 2011, after many years of drawing inspiration from the clothing of luxury brands, Araki finally got to draw them in an official capacity thanks to a great collaboration with the Florentine brand Gucci. Once again, Rohan played a role: this time, he traveled to Italy, in the colorful short story *Rohan Kishibe Goes to Gucci*; Rohan was then displayed in a large format in the window of the Gucci store in Shinjuku. In 2012, Jolyne took over with another short story and this time took over Gucci stores worldwide.[28] It was well-deserved recognition for Araki, who also, in 2017, collaborated with the brand Bulgari, for which he personally designed a series of accessories based on Killer Queen, the models for which were—in addition to Kira's Stand—Yasuho Hirose from *JoJolion* and Yukako Yamagishi from *Diamond is Unbreakable*. It's also worth mentioning that Araki created a cover image for the men's fashion magazine *Uomo* in Japan: in the illustration, Bucciarati is wearing an outfit from the fall 2018 collection from the French brand Balenciaga.

This collaboration with *Uomo* was also intended to promote the big retro-spective exhibition "Ripples of Adventure," which took place from August 24 to October 1, 2018, at Tokyo's prestigious National Art Center. The event was probably the greatest honor the author has received to date. I say that because Araki is just the second *mangaka*, after Osamu Tezuka (posthumously, not long after his death in 1989), to have an individual exhibition at a Japanese national museum! It was a major milestone in the history of manga. For the exhibition, which included numerous illustrations and original panels from *JoJo*, the author created a highlight of the show unlike anything he'd done before in his career. He created life-sized works, a series of 12 painted panels featuring key figures from his saga: "Even though some of the characters included in this artwork have already died off, drawing them again like this, all together in the

---

28. See chapter 6, section "Sayonara Wild Hearts."

same time and space, was quite an amazing experience," Araki explains. "It's like the joy I might feel when being reunited with old friends. Also, I developed a deeper affection for each of the characters, something I'd never experienced before. For example, since Jolyne has a life-sized face, it felt like I was putting makeup on an actual woman's face when I was brushing in the color. I felt as if she was right in front of me, and I grew more fond of her because of that, which was a pretty interesting experience. Manga artists usually sit at a desk to create their works, and the opportunity to do life-sized original artwork rarely comes around, so it was an honor to do this project. I feel as if I've ventured into a new world through this experience."[29]

So, what's the next big milestone we can expect from the author? Recognition at the Angoulême International Comics Festival, the biggest annual event dedicated to the art of comics. After the grand prizes awarded to Katsuhiro Otomo in 2015 and to Rumiko Takahashi in 2019, will we see Hirohiko Araki join the world's official pantheon of comic artists? It would be well-deserved. Even though, really, he already gained the status of a giant among men long ago.

29. Catalog of the Tokyo exhibition "Ripples of Adventure," 2018.

JOJO'S BIZARRE ADVENTURE

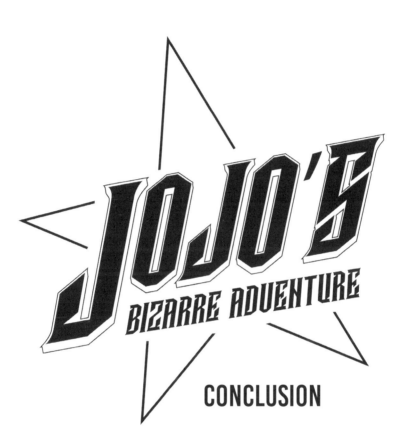

CONCLUSION

CHAPTER MMXXI: THE BRIDGE OF STARS

To listen to while reading:
Holly Herndon – *Frontier*

Here we are. We made it. Let's go back to our initial question: "Between what and what is *JoJo* the missing link?" In fact, there are hundreds of answers to this question, and when you realize that fact, the true magnitude of the saga really hits you. For example, I could give an amusingly exaggerated answer and say that *JoJo's Bizarre Adventure* is the missing link between David Bowie and *Yu-Gi-Oh!* And in a way, that is indeed the case! That proposition is ridiculous and artificial–don't quote me on it–but what it states is not really off base. I could also give you an obvious answer: that *JoJo* is one of the links between the past and the present of manga. In fact, on that topic, in a joint interview with Yūsei Matsui, Araki said that, early in his career, he was so inspired by Sanpei Shirato that he would draw his manga while looking at panels by the elder artist; "you were my Shirato-*sensei*," Matsui responded. "When I was young, I put a lot of effort into trying to break away from your influence. Recently, I think I've finally achieved that."[30] These comments have really stuck with me. They're very moving to read. So, Araki's work is a link between generations, but isn't that the case for lots of authors? That answer isn't enough.

As I write these lines, I'm still reflecting on the question. There's no way around it: I'm going to have to answer it seriously. But first, I'd like to take the raw material of this question that came to me intuitively and reformulate it to produce the following version: "Between what and what did *JoJo* create a bridge?" Basically, with this new version, I've traded the idea of a hole to be filled within a continuum for the idea, which I believe to be more positive, of creating a pathway for exchange between two different worlds. We can call it the Bridge of Stars. Much like the sidewalks of Hollywood Boulevard, it's spangled with the names of the numerous stars that are Hirohiko Araki's characters.

---

30. Joint interview between Hirohiko Araki and Yūsei Matsui (author of the manga *Assassination Classroom*), 2013.

Or something like that. I'll let your imagination fill in the details. Before I give my final answer, I would like to return to the importance of the author of *JoJo's Bizarre Adventure*. Hirohiko Araki, unlike Akira Toriyama and Katsuhiro Otomo, two other giants of the manga world from the same generation, did not start a movement of his own. Toriyama and Otomo forever changed *shōnen* and *seinen*, respectively. They created major trends and gave rise to prominent authors—there would be no Eiichirō Oda without Toriyama, for example, and no Naoki Urasawa without Otomo. They are pillars of the manga world, having revolutionized the artform. Araki, meanwhile, has positioned himself as an artist who goes against the flow. Being self-taught, he's had to come up with his own solutions in order to develop his own style and free himself from the influence of his forebears; at the same time, his creative preferences have not always matched the expectations of publishers. He's been helped along the way by chance encounters, like his personal discovery of Italian sculpture and pop-culture trends. There's also the luck of having lived in a time period absolutely filled with cultural innovations (new dances, new musical styles, new movements in manga, etc.), which he has been able to capture in his work. All of this has led him to explore unprecedented visual styles and—thanks to support from his editor Ryōsuke Kabashima, whose decisive role mustn't be forgotten—to go down innovative and iconoclastic paths never before seen in *Jump*. Araki has fought battles that seemed like lost causes. A story with a Western setting, rejecting the tournament narrative structure, a hero who dies while the series is in full swing... You're now familiar with all of that, as well as Araki's later innovations, like characters who speak with pictographs, or even song lyrics ("I am a rock, I am an island," says Yotsuyu in *JoJolion*, referencing a song by Simon & Garfunkel), and those surprising foregrounds made up of brush strokes. That's the essence of Araki's style. And surprising though it may seem, that bizarre style has given rise to an all-time best-seller, with over 100 million copies printed in Japan—a milestone reached in 2016. In Japan, they have the word *ōdō*, "the royal way." It's a word that describes things that fit into the pure tradition of a genre, as opposed to *jadō*, "the deviant way," i.e., the unusual path that diverges from the rules of the artform. Araki constantly refers to the royal way in *Manga in Theory and Practice*. He views it as a great path to follow, the path of timeless works passed down from generation to generation; he also explains why he believes his work filled with oddities has managed to follow that royal way. Really, *JoJo* has pulled off a true feat: this refined oddball has introduced a current of total bizarreness into the heart of the mainstream. While the saga has not started its own movement, it has changed the tune of existing movements and today, the influence of Araki's extravagance is found all throughout the manga world in one form or another.

By the by, I recommend that you read *Manga in Theory and Practice*, which is essential reading for anyone trying to understand who Hirohiko Araki really is. The book has numerous passages that have stuck with me, with the author sometimes being endearingly candid, but some passages are particularly memorable. For example, this one: "Even when I think to myself, 'I really made something great this time!,' I make myself forget that feeling. I believe that if I let myself feel that I've created a masterpiece, I'll stop getting ideas to create anything else. For that same reason, whenever others compliment me, I never take it to heart."[31] For this reason, Araki would probably never admit that fact that, as I believe, he has had a greater impact than Toriyama or Otomo. Those two artists are definitely better drawers, from a technical standpoint, and better narrators. They are virtuosos, uncommon geniuses. However, they've never really left the sphere of pop culture. All my life, I've heard scornful comments directed at *Dragon Ball*, and that continues to this day. Even though, just this year, Toriyama was awarded the French title of *"chevalier de l'ordre des Arts et des Lettres"* (Knight of the Order of Arts and Letters), it doesn't seem to have changed things much. And his honorary prize at the 40th edition of the Angoulême Festival (2013), rather than the official grand prize—which he could have won—had even less of an impact. Araki's situation is different: he will be remembered as the first living manga author to have had an individual exhibition in a Japanese national museum, the prestigious National Art Center in Tokyo. He was also the first *mangaka* to have his work displayed at the Louvre, the biggest and most famous museum in the world, even if it was just for a collective exhibition and was a case of being in the right place at the right time. No matter, the symbolism is still strong: manga! In the Louvre! If someone had tried to put those two words together in a sentence back in the '90s, particularly in France, they would have been met with a burst of (nervous) laughter in response.

Over the last decade, the fact that *JoJo's Bizarre Adventure* has appeared in these prestigious spaces and, also, that the illustrious fashion house Gucci has embraced the Joestar family sends a great message. As I see it, Araki's work has become the greatest emblem for a current movement: growing institutional recognition of manga. That recognition is gradually blossoming, with the British Museum—which, incidentally, has been collecting pieces tied to the history of manga since the late 19th century—presenting a massive exhibition on the medium, modestly titled "Manga," and the Angoulême Festival increasingly honoring this form of comics that for too long has been snubbed. It could be that the 21st century marks the transition from an era where manga was considered a trivial cultural product (not just abroad, but also in Japan, where, in general, it seems to have retained the status of ordinary entertainment or that of a powerful tool for soft power, even though there have been some great

31. Hirohiko Araki, *Manga in Theory and Practice*, p. 191.

initiatives, like the opening in 2006 of the International Manga Museum in Kyoto) to a hypothetical future where, once and for all, manga will have achieved the recognition it deserves and be seen as an artform like any other. Just like how Japanese woodblock prints were once seen as crude cultural products and are now celebrated at the highest levels of society. That said, in reality, manga culture had already made its way into the contemporary art world. But rarely in its raw form or in a space of national importance. For example, the artist Takashi Murakami–who's brilliant, I might add–has represented the manga world and he has indeed received recognition from Paris' Centre Pompidou and Louis Vuitton. However, his vision is really just a commentary on the medium, delivered through a very particular lens. Conversely, Araki's work presented at the Louvre in 2009, then at Tokyo's National Art Center in 2018, is true manga in its original form. Real panels, just as they were published. What's more, they're mainstream manga panels, not pages from the avant-garde magazine *Garo* or other alternative sources. In this way, Araki's work–thanks to those who decide to exhibit it–helps build a bridge between Japanese comics and the "noble" upper echelons of culture, two worlds that are never supposed to overlap. So, there you have one form of the Bridge of Stars.

But that's not my final answer. Because that's not what matters most to me. Rather, what really speaks to me is found in the series itself. It's the characters, who are powerful symbols for freedom and diversity, whose hybrid identities create many bridges between human beings. Araki's characters, in their appearances and how they carry themselves, blend genders without complexes and unite institutional cultures, like ancient sculpture, with more popular cultures, like urban dancing. Their personal styles combine symbols of the past and present–just look at Giorno, who blends Michelangelo's David with '90s fashion–and influences from every corner of the world. What's more, many characters are mixed-race, like Jolyne, who has European, Asian, and American roots, and the teams of heroes purposely bring together people from many different countries. On top of that, the *mangaka* puts disadvantaged persons at the forefront, like the paraplegic Johnny, who, far from giving up when faced with the challenges of his condition, overcomes it through his own will–incidentally, do you think it's just by chance that Araki was recently chosen to illustrate a poster for the 2020 Paralympic Games in Tokyo? To read *JoJo's Bizarre Adventure* is to join in a great rally: a rally of all humankind. As for that, I like to think that the series has managed to win over the very selective clubs of the great museums and of high fashion not just because of its borrowings from these two domains, nor because of the obvious refinement of Araki's work, but because the *JoJo* universe symbolically contributes to the goals of social cohesion and inclusion that are so important in today's world.

Araki has now clearly entered a phase of legacy-building. We see this in his big retrospective exhibition, his first participation at a European convention, and the publication of *Manga in Theory and Practice*, in which he provides details about his invaluable methods of creation. At the very end of that book, the *mangaka* says that he wrote it to help new artists create things that have never been seen before. He created it to be a map, not a star map, but one to guide people toward unexplored territories. In doing so, the author built yet another Bridge of Stars, one that has yet to be crossed. One that will lead to the next Hirohiko Araki. The next person who, without denying their heritage, will dare to destroy, to build, to break the rules, and to change once again the colors on the star map of the manga universe.

JOJO'S BIZARRE ADVENTURE

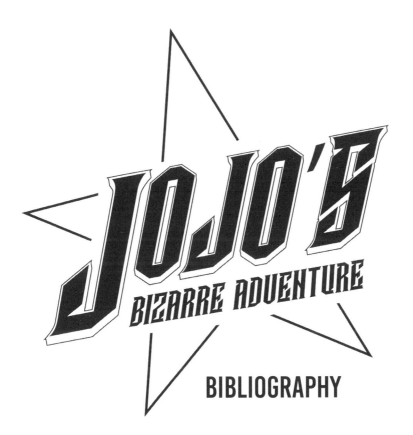

BIBLIOGRAPHY

T HE CONSULTATION of Japanese sources (and the French translation of quotations from said sources for the purposes of this book) was carried out with invaluable help from Laurent Bareille, Julien El Rab, and Satoko Fujimoto.

Some internet users have published on the web English translations of statements by Hirohiko Araki. Whenever possible, we have verified said translations using Japanese sources.

DOCUMENTS RELATING TO JOJO'S BIZARRE ADVENTURE AND HIROHIKO ARAKI

Interviews and statements by the author

1986: Interview of Hirohiko Araki in the Japanese magazine *Fanroad* (in Japanese, from: http://blog.livedoor.jp/jojolab/archives/38665393.html).

1989: Interview of Hirohiko Araki in the Japanese book *Famicom Jump: Hero Retsuden's Strategy Guide* (partially translated into English at: https://jojo.fandom.com/wiki/Interview_Archive).

1993: Comments from Hirohiko Araki in the Japanese artbook *JoJo 6251* (translated into English at: https://jojo.fandom.com/wiki/Interview_Archive).

1996: Interview of Hirohiko Araki in the Italian magazine *Kappa* No. 54.

1998: Interview of Hirohiko Araki in *Weekly Shōnen Jump* No. 9 of 1998 (translated into English at: http://raikaroom.blogspot.com/2015/04/feelin-jojo-final-episode-araki.html)

2001: Joint interview between Hirohiko Araki and Kazuma Kaneko for the magazine *Thrill*, No. 22, September 2001 (translated into English at: https://dijehtranslations.wordpress.com/2016/08/07/araki-hirohiko-x-kaneko-kazuma-interview-part-i and https://dijehtranslations.wordpress.com/2016/08/07/araki-hirohiko-x-kaneko-kazuma-interview-part-ii).

2002: Postscript from the final *bunko* volume of *Stardust Crusaders* (translated into English by internet user Macchalion, available at: https://jojo.fandom.com/wiki/Interview_Archive).

2003: Interview of Hirohiko Araki for the French magazine *Animeland* by Walo: https://animeland.fr/dossier/araki-hirohiko-jojo-de-vinci-et-moi.

2003: Second interview of Hirohiko Araki for the French magazine *Animeland* by Sam: https://animeland.fr/dossier/araki-hirohiko-exposed.

2003: Video interview of Hirohiko Araki by Eiichiro Funakoshi for Japanese television (https://www.youtube.com/watch?v=FfUennCnSuc), partially translated into English at: https://jojo.fandom.com/wiki/Interview_Archive.

2003: Video interview of Hirohiko Araki for French television (https://www.youtube.com/watch?v=rkA6mBr2eyA and https://www.youtube.com/watch?v=W2UklisoYPY).

2003: Joint interview between Hirohiko Araki and the head of the Odermatt-Vedovi gallery (in Japanese, at: http://blog.livedoor.jp/jojolab/archives/49592296.html).

2004: Remarks by Hirohiko Araki in a Japanese special edition ("*Jump Remix*") of *Diamond is Unbreakable*, published in 2004 (translated into English at: https://docs.google.com/document/d/1pgcnMshVrs7ZqvtACT3PWweRp-mJOXSNyu7O9qf4M21g).

2005: Postscript from the first *bunko* volume of *Golden Wind* (translated into English by internet user LegoAlex, available at: https://jojo.fandom.com/wiki/Interview_Archive).

2005: Postscript from the final *bunko* volume of *Golden Wind* (translated into English by internet user Macchalion, available at: https://drive.google.com/drive/folders/1sk9U4VZmgXK75f3flxRwxSlvpGJJf-Me).

2006: Video interview of Hirohiko Araki by Shoko Nakagawa for Japanese television (subtitled in English at: https://www.youtube.com/watch?v=-SPF-bQq-jNg).

2006: Video interview of Hirohiko Araki available on the disk of the Japanese video game *Phantom Blood* for PlayStation 2 (subtitled in English at: https://www.youtube.com/watch?v=IYLRKoWDadM, and transcribed at: https://jojo.fandom.com/wiki/Interview_Archive).

2006: Lecture by Hirohiko Araki at Tokai Junior & High School in Nagoya, Japan (report available in English at: https://www.comipress.com/article/2006/06/30/387).

2006: Joint interview between Hirohiko Araki and Nekoi Tsubaki in the Japanese official guide for the manga *xxxHolic* (translated into English at: https://petronia.livejournal.com/493401.html).

2007: Interview of Hirohiko Araki by publisher Delcourt-Tonkam in the first French volume of *Golden Wind*.

2007: Interview of Hirohiko Araki in the Japanese magazine *Eureka* (partially translated into English at: https://jojo.fandom.com/wiki/Interview_Archive).

2008: Postscript from the first *bunko* volume of *Stone Ocean* (translated into English by internet user LegoAlex, available at: https://jojo.fandom.com/wiki/Interview_Archive).

2009: Postscript from the final *bunko* volume of *Stone Ocean* (translated into English by internet user Macchalion, available at: https://drive.google.com/drive/folders/1sk9U4VZmgXK75f3flxRwxSlvpGJJf-Me).

2009: Interview of Hirohiko Araki for *Newtral* (translated into English at: https://jojo.fandom.com/wiki/Interview_Archive).

2011: Interview of Hirohiko Araki in 10 parts on the Japanese website *Hirosegawa Homepage* (in Japanese, at: https://www.hirosegawa-net.com/hirosegawa_interview/vol18-1).

2012: Interview of Hirohiko Araki in the Japanese mook *JOJOmenon*.

2012: Interview of Hirohiko Araki on the Japanese website *Xtrend* (https://trendy.nikkeibp.co.jp/article/pickup/20121009/1044420).

2013: Video interview of Hirohiko Araki for the Japanese television channel *NHK* (https://www.bilibili.com/video/av4837353).

2013: Remarks by Hirohiko Araki in the Japanese guide book for the video game *JoJo's Bizarre Adventure: All-Star Battle* for PlayStation 3 (translated into English at: https://gamefaqs.gamespot.com/boards/676176-jojos-bizarre-adventure-all-star-battle/67151860).

2013: Remarks by Hirohiko Araki in the Japanese artbook *JOJOVELLER* (remarks available in Japanese at: https://jojo.fandom.com/wiki/Interview Archive#JoJoveller%20(2013), and partially translated into English at: https://jojo.fandom.com/wiki/JOJOVELLER/Commentaries, as well as by internet user Macchalion at: https://drive.google.com/drive/folders/1sk9U-4VZmgXK75f3flxRwxSlvpGJJf-Me).

2013: Joint interview between Hirohiko Araki and Yūsei Matsui (translated into English at: https://jojo.fandom.com/wiki/Interview Archive#Dream%20 Talk%20Session%20(2015).

2014: Remarks by Hirohiko Araki in the Japanese newspaper *Kahoku Shimpō* on October 21, 2014 (in Japanese, at: http://atmarkjojo.org/archives/15483. html).

2015: Remarks by Hirohiko Araki in the book *Araki Hirohiko no Manga Jutsu* (officially translated into Engish in 2017 with the name *Manga in Theory and Practice: The Craft of Creating Manga*).

2017: Video interview of Hirohiko Araki on the *Vizmedia YouTube* channel (in Japanese, subtitled in English, at: https://www.youtube.com/watch ?v=r2FHRUjBI6Q).

2017: Interview of Hirohiko Araki on the website *Anime News Network* by Casey Lee Mitchem & Rebecca Silverman, June 29, 2017 (https://www.anime-newsnetwork.com/feature/2017-06-29/interview-jojo-bizarre-adventure-cre-ator-hirohiko-araki/.118032).

2017: Joint interview between Hirohiko Araki and Tetsuo Hara during the special event "Legend Talk Show," reports of which can be found on the Japanese websites *Mantan Web* (https://mantan-web.jp/article/20170910dog 00m200002000c.html) and *Nobury* (https://nobury.com/hara-araki), as well as in English on the website *Anime News Network* (https://www.animenews-network.com/interest/2017-09-13/jojo-fist-of-the-north-star-creators-discuss-their-manga-influences/.121287).

2018: Interview of Hirohiko Araki on the bilingual (Japanese and English) website *The New York Times Style Magazine: Japan* (https://www.tjapan.jp/entertainment/17230475).

2018: Interview of Hirohiko Araki in the bilingual (Japanese and English) catalogue for the exhibition "Shōnen Jump Vol. 2."

2018: Remarks by Hirohiko Araki in the bilingual (Japanese and English) catalogue for the exhibition "Hirohiko Araki JoJo Exhibition: Ripples of Adventure."

2018: Interview of Hirohiko Araki on the Japanese website *CNET* (in Japanese, at: https://japan.cnet.com/article/35129132).

General: Comments by Hirohiko Araki in the French versions of his manga. Comments in the *JoJonium* special edition. Comments in the collection *Under Execution Under Jailbreak* translated into English at: https://jojo.fandom. com/wiki/Dead_Man%27s_Questions and https://jojo.fandom.com/wiki/ Dolce_and_His_Master.

Manga and artbooks by Hirohiko Araki

The French versions of the eight parts of *JoJo's Bizarre Adventure* (J'ai Lu and Delcourt-Tonkam), of *Rohan Kishibe* (Delcourt-Tonkam), and of *Rohan at the Louvre* (Éditions du Louvre/Futuropolis). For the English translation of this book, the VIZ Media versions of parts one through four were used.

Works never published in English: *Mashōnen B.T.*, *Baoh Raihōsha*, *Gorgeous Irene*, *Henjin Henkutsu Retsuden*, *Shikei Shikkōchū Datsugoku Shinkōchū*, all published by Shūeisha.

The Japanese artbooks *JoJo 6251*, *JOJO A-GO!GO!*, *Hirohiko Araki Works 1981-2012*, and *JOJOVELLER*, all published by Shūeisha.

Print media

Araki, Hirohiko. *Manga in Theory and Practice: The Craft of Creating Manga*. VIZ Media LLC. 2017. 280 pages. ISBN 1421594072 (English translation of *Araki Hirohiko no Manga Jutsu*, published in Japan in 2015 by Shūeisha).

Araki, Hirohiko; Chujo, Shohei. ジョジョの奇妙な名言集 *part1 ~3 - JoJo's Bizarre Words*. Shūeisha. 2012. 208 pages. ISBN 408720636X.

Various authors. *JOJOmenon* (special edition of the magazine *SPUR*). Shūeisha. 2012. 128 pages. ISBN 4081021465.

荒木飛呂彦原画展 JOJO 冒険の波紋 – *Hirohiko Araki JoJo Exhibition: Ripples of Adventure* (catalogue). 2018. ASIN B07M9C6JGP.

Various issues of the Japanese magazines *Weekly Shōnen Jump* and *Ultra Jump* (Shūeisha).

Online articles and websites

Arte, "FANS DE MANGA VS YOUTUBE : LA GUERRE DES COMMEN-TAIRES" [online], May 3, 2019: https://www.arte.tv/fr/articles/tracks-jo-jo-adventure-manga-youtube.

ArtAujourd'hui, "Hirohiko Araki - Galerie Odermatt-Vedovi" [online], undated: http://www.artaujourdhui.info/e14566-araki.html.

Chapman, Jacob (*Anime News Network*), "Interview: JoJo's Bizarre Adventure director Naokatsu Tsuda" [online], July 16, 2015: https://www.animenews-network.com/feature/2015-07-16/interview-jojo-bizarre-adventure-direc-tor-naokatsu-tsuda/.90413.

Comic Natalie, "荒木飛呂彦が久々に描いたブチャラティがUOMO表紙に、注目は「肘」" [online], August 17, 2018: https://natalie.mu/comic/news/295729.

Comic Natalie, "「ジョジョの奇妙な冒険」原宿・表参道を舞台にした企画実施、コラボカフェも" [online], April 5, 2019: https://natalie.mu/comic/news/326834.

Comic Natalie, "露伴のもとに舞い込んだ依頼とは？「岸辺露伴は動かない」が別マに登場" [online], August 12, 2017: https://natalie.mu/comic/news/244503.

Comic Natalie, "浦沢直樹と荒木飛呂彦が東京2020オリンピック・パラリンピックのポスター制作" [online], July 30, 2019: https://natalie.mu/comic/news/341777.

Dakus (*Nipponzilla*), "La fin de JoJo's Bizarre Adventure: JoJolion est proche" [online], August 19, 2018: http://nipponzilla.com/la-fin-de-jojos-bizarre-ad-venture-jojolion-est-proche/.

Fat Yosh (*Urban Dictionary*), "Araki Forgot" [online], October 30, 2018: https://www.urbandictionary.com/define.php?term=Araki%20forgot.

Feh Yes Vintage Manga, "Potential influences on Kira from JoJolion" [online], June 30 2016: https://fehyesvintagemanga.tumblr.com/post/146729153940/potential-influences-on-kira-from-jojolion-by.

Fripp, Robert, *Facebook* post [online], January 6, 2017: https://www.facebook.com/robert.fripp.96/posts/1578167965532561.

Genecov, Max (*Polygon*), "How JoJo's Bizarre Adventure fan art is trying to correct the anime's parental problems," [online], January 23, 2019: https://www.polygon.com/2019/1/23/18193396/jojos-bizarre-adventure-jotaro-jolyne-dio-giorno-fan-art.

JoJo's Bizarre Encyclopedia, "Interview Archive – Chami Araki (11/2009)": https://jojo.fandom.com/wiki/Interview_Archive#Chami%20Araki%20(11/2009).

Lapresse.ca, "Le mangaka Hirohiko Araki entre au musée de Tokyo" [online], June 21, 2018: https://www.lapresse.ca/arts/arts-visuels/201806/21/01-5186736-le-mangaka-hirohiko-araki-entre-au-musee-de-tokyo.php.

LISEF (*9ᵉArt*), "Un candidat à l'élection présidentielle américaine utilise JoJo's Bizarre Adventure pour sa campagne" [online], July 1, 2019: http://www.9emeart.fr/post/news/manga/un-candidat-a-l-election-presidenti-elle-americaine-utilise-jojo-s-bizarre-adventure-pour-sa-campagne-10827.

Lidbury, Olivia (*The Telegraph*), "Gucci kicks off the New Year in Manga style" [online], January 3, 2013: fashion.telegraph.co.uk/news-features/TMG9778331/Gucci-kicks-off-the-New-Year-in-Manga-style.html.

LiiiFE, "Art Feature: HIROHIKO ARAKI JOJO EXHIBITION: RIPPLES OF ADVENTURE" [online], April 22, 2019: https://liiife.jp/culture/art-fea-ture-hirohiko-araki-jojo-exhibition-ripples-of-adventure/.

Livedoor News, "「ジョジョの奇妙な冒険」の作者 荒木飛呂彦氏の知られざる秘密" [online], August 21, 2017: http://news.livedoor.com/article/detail/13498403.

Loo, Egan (*Anime News Network*), "JoJo's Araki Draws Art for Quake-Affected Historical Ruins" [online], November 4, 2011: https://www.anime-newsnetwork.com/interest/2011-11-04/jojo-araki-draws-art-for-quake-affect-ed-historical-ruins.

Loveridge, Lynzee (*Anime News Network*), "JoJo's Bizarre Adventure Exhibit Heads to Nagasaki in 2020" [online], March 19, 2019: https://www.animenewsnetwork.com/interest/2019-03-19/jojo-bizarre-adventure-exhibit-heads-to-nagasaki-in-2020/.144732.

Lucca Comics and Games, "Hirohiko Araki, ospite d'onore" [online], 2019: https://www.luccacomicsandgames.com/it/2019/comics/news/hirohiko-araki-ospite-donore/.

Macdonald, Christopher (*Anime News Network*), "Top 10 Anime and Manga at Japan Media Arts Festival" [online], October 4, 2006: https://www.animenewsnetwork.com/news/2006-10-04/top-10-anime-and-manga-at-japan-media-arts-festival.

McMahon, Andrew (*Twinfinite*), "Every JoJo's Bizarre Adventure Reference in Bloodstained: Ritual of the Night" [online], June 20, 2019: https://twinfinite.net/2019/06/every-jojos-bizarre-adventure-reference-in-bloodstained-ritual-of-the-night/.

Morrissy, Kim (*Anime News Network*), "Hirohiko Araki Says He Could Never Have Created JoJo's Bizarre Adventure If He Hadn't Read Sherlock Holmes" [online], June 15, 2019: https://www.animenewsnetwork.com/interest/2019-06-15/hirohiko-araki-says-he-could-never-have-created-jojo-bizarre-adventure-if-he-hadnt-read-sherlock-holmes/.147612.

MScratch (*Know Your Meme*), "King Crimson (JoJo)" [online]: https://knowyourmeme.com/memes/king-crimson-jojo.

Pasqualini, Mario (*Dimensione Fumetto*), "JoJo è fashion victim e gli otaku fashion maniac" [online], May 24, 2016: http://www.dimensionefumetto.it/jojofashion/.

Sherman, Jennifer (*Anime News Network*), "New JoJo's Bizarre Adventure Exhibit Features New Illustrations in Summer 2018" [online], December 22, 2017: https://www.animenewsnetwork.com/interest/2017-12-22/new-jojo-bizarre-adventure-exhibit-features-new-illustrations-in-summer-2018/.125342.

Sherman, Jennifer (*Anime News Network*), "Hirohiko Araki Reveals Which Blade Runner Character Inspired DIO" [online], February 27, 2018: https://www.animenewsnetwork.com/interest/2018-02-27/hirohiko-araki-reveals-which-blade-runner-character-inspired-dio/.128280.

Sightseeing Japan, "[Extra Edition] Hirohiko Araki: JoJo exhibition in S City du Wang town [Sendai Mediatheque]" [online], April 20, 2019: sightseeing-jp.com/2019/04/20/extra-edition-hirohiko-araki-jojo-exhibition-in-s-city-du-wang-town-sendai-mediatheque/.

Simon & Mazinga (*DVDanime.net*), "JOJO in Paris", October 29, 2003: http://www.dvdanime.net/articleview.php?id=46 (the website is unavailable as I write this line).

Sp!nz Show Room, "[Dossier] JoJo's Bizarre Adventure Part. 2" [online], September 30, 2014: http://spinzshowroom.com/dossier-jojos-bizarre-adventure-part-2.

Toole, Michael (*Anime News Network*), "The Mike Toole Show – JoJo's Mojo" [online], June 1, 2014: https://www.animenewsnetwork.com/the-mike-toole-show/2014-06-01/.75101.

Tsuka (*Catsuka*), "[Expo] JoJo - Prolongations" [online], April 13, 2003: https://www.catsuka.com/news/2003-04-13/expo-jojo-prolongations.

Ursini, Francesco-Alessio (*The Comic's Grid*), "David Bowie's Influence on *JoJo's Bizarre Adventure*" [online], March 15, 2017: https://www.comicsgrid.com/articles/10.16995/cg.95/.

Vogue Italia, "Hirohiko Araki in Florence" [online], June 27, 2013: https://www.vogue.it/en/people-are-talking-about/vogue-arts/2013/06/hirohiko-araki-at-gucci-showroom-in-florence?refresh_ce.

"ジョジョの奇妙な冒険　パクリ糾弾テンプレまとめ" [online]: http://archive.fo/ajJ29.

"東大ジョジョ立ち" (Todai JoJo dachi), April 18, 2007: http://kajipon.sakura.ne.jp/art/jojo-todai.html.

"【実写】「ジョジョ立ち」の元となったデザインやファッションモデル達　まとめ," August 10, 2016: https://matome.naver.jp/odai/2141582377422198401.

"『死刑執行人サンソン』広告" [online], August 9, 2004: https://vec.hatenadiary.org/entry/20040809/p2.

"安達正勝『死刑執行人サンソン』" [online], September 14, 2004: https://vec.hatenadiary.org/entry/20040914/p3.

"ジョジョの奇妙なパクリ問題" [online], June 10, 2011: guinguin.cocolog-nifty.com/blog/2011/06/post-dc5d.html.

"ジョジョの奇妙なパクリ問題 PART2【黄金の道・前編】" [online], February 23, 2017: http://guinguin.cocolog-nifty.com/blog/2017/02/part2-4a1c.html.

Website *Jojosapiens*: https://jojosapiens.com (website unavailable).

Online videos/documentaries

Cotto & Frullato, "Insalata Caprese + Casillero del Diablo - Le Ricette di Cotto & Frullato" [online], *YouTube*, April 24, 2014: https://www.youtube.com/watch?v=y0njm9MU7pY.

LDOPE, "荒木 飛呂彦和手塚治虫" [online], *YouTube*, January 25, 2013: https://www.youtube.com/watch?v=ImktRhu3TGQ.

LuccassTV, "LA FOLIE JOJO DANS LES RUES DE TOKYO" [online], *YouTube*, May 11, 2019: https://www.youtube.com/watch?v=TZvq4RWBlgI.

Shōnen Jump Official, "[予告編] JOJO's Kitchen 荒木飛呂彦 パスタを作る" [online], *YouTube*, August 2, 2013: https://www.youtube.com/watch?v=ZcO-zufy9N_4.

Soma is Batman, "JoJo's Bizarre Adventure References in Castlevania" [online], *YouTube*, February 12, 2015: https://www.youtube.com/watch?v=HB-kaoRSRHFo.

xForts, "The Most Confusing Stand in JoJo's Bizarre Adventure" [online], *YouTube*, April 7, 2019: https://www.youtube.com/watch?v=X30YXFzq5Ys.

Databases and information sharing websites

Wiki encyclopedia *JoJo's Bizarre Wiki*: https://jojo.fandom.com/.

Website *@JOJO - JoJo's Bizarre News:* http://atmarkjojo.org.

Facebook page "|*| Le Bizzarre Avventure di JoJo |*|": https://www.facebook.com/LeBizzarreAvventurediJOJO.IT.

Twitter account "JoJo's Bizarre Adventure [FR]": https://twitter.com/JJBA_FR.

Forum "JoJo's Bizarre Adventure Community": http://ls57tiger.freepgs.com/jojo/phpBB3 (unavailable as I write this line).

DOCUMENTS ON OTHER TOPICS

Print media

Bacchi, Andrea; Pierguidi, Stefano. *Les Grands Maîtres de l'Art : Le Bernin et la sculpture baroque à Rome*. Le Figaro. 2008. ISBN 978-2-8105-0086-4.

Beaujean, Stéphane; Guilbert, Xavier. *Osamu Tezuka - Manga no Kamisama* (exhibition catalogue). 9eArt+. 2018. 160 pages. ISBN 978-2-9536902-4-8.

Beddiar, Fathi. *Tolérance zéro - La justice expéditive au cinéma*. Bazaar&Co. 2008. 192 pages. ISBN 2917339047.

Bouissou, Jean-Marie. *Les Leçons du Japon : Un pays très incorrect*. Fayard. 2019. 432 pages. ISBN 2213678022.

Bouissou, Jean-Marie. *Manga - Histoire et univers de la bande dessinée japonaise (3e édition revue et augmentée)*. Philippe Picquier. 2013. 480 pages. ISBN 2809709963.

Various authors (edited by Coolidge Rousmaniere, Nicole and Matsubba, Ryoko). *Manga* (exhibition catalogue). Thames & Hudson. 2019. 352 pages. ISBN 0500480494.

Various authors. 創刊*50*周年記念 週刊少年ジャンプ展 *VOL.2* (Catalogue of the second exhibition dedicated to the fiftieth anniversary of *Shōnen Jump*). Shūeisha. 2018. 260 pages. ASIN B07GSDB68W.

DuBois, Romain; Gottigny, Ludovic; Amazigh Houha, Malik-Djamel. *Akira* (special edition of *Rockyrama*). Ynnis Édition. 2019. ISBN 2376970385.

Du Mesnildot, Stéphane. *L'Adolescente japonaise*. Le murmure. 2018. 90 pages. ISBN 2373060280.

Galbraith, Patrick W. *The Moé Manifesto: An Insider's Look at the Worlds of Manga, Anime, and Gaming.* Tuttle Publishing. 2014. 192 pages. ISBN 4805312823.

Goto, Hiroki. *Jump - L'âge d'or du manga.* Kurokawa. 2019. 336 pages. ISBN 236852827X.

Gravett, Paul. *Manga: Soixante ans de bande dessinée japonaise.* Éditions du Rocher. 2005. 176 pages. ISBN 2268055507.

Murakami, Haruki. *Underground.* 10 X 18. 2014. 552 pages. ISBN 2264062703.

Rhys-Morgan, Dean. *Bold, Beautiful and Damned: The World of 1980s Fashion Illustrator Tony Viramontes.* Laurence King Publishing. 2013. 192 pages. ISBN 1780673078.

Paper media

Beaujean, Stéphane, "Tetsuya Chiba – L'étendard de la révolte," *Kaboom* No. 11, 2013.

Bouvard, Julien, "L'héritage impossible du "mai 1968" japonais : comment le manga dessine-t-il les mouvements sociaux de la fin des années 1960 au Japon ?," *Cahiers d'histoire. Revue d'histoire critique* No. 139, 2018 (viewed online at: http://journals.openedition.org/chrhc/7927).

Fasulo, Fausto, "Ultra Jump - Bienvenue dans l'Hyper Age," *ATOM* No. 5, 2017.

Fasulo, Fausto, "Hisashi Eguchi - Jeunes et joli(e)s," *ATOM* No. 8, 2018.

Fasulo, Fausto, "Tetsuya Chiba - Le poing final," *ATOM* No. 10, 2019.

Odaira, Namihei, "Un poil à gratter nommé Garo," *Zoom Japon* No. 43, 2014.

Rosenbaum, Roman, "Gekiga as a site of intercultural exchange: Tatsumi Yoshihiro's A Drifting Life," *Global Manga Studies* vol. 2, 2011 (viewed online at: https://www.academia.edu/36778775/Gekiga_as_a_site_of_intercultural_exchange_Tatsumi_Yoshihiro_s_A_Drifting_Life).

Suvilay, Bounthavy, "Le manga de sport comme récit de formation pour la jeunesse au Japon," *Agora* No. 78, 2018.

Various issues of *Vogue Italia*, via http://archivio.vogue.it/en.

Online articles and websites

Abdelhamid, Sébastien (*Yatta!*), "Hokuto No Ken un concentré de Pop Culture des 80's" [online], September 9, 2016: https://yatta.animedigitalnetwork.fr/article-mangas/hokuto-no-ken-un-concentre-de-pop-culture-des-80-s.

A. G. Nauta Couture, "Antonio Lopez and exciting times in fashion (Part 1)" [online], October 21, 2012: https://agnautacouture.com/2012/10/21/antonio-lopez-and-one-of-the-most-exciting-times-in-fashion-part-1/.

A. G. Nauta Couture, "Antonio Lopez and exciting times in fashion (Part 2)" [online], October 28, 2012: https://agnautacouture.com/2012/10/28/antonio-lopez-and-exciting-times-in-fashion-part-2/.

Anselme, Carine (*INSEEM*), "L'effet Mandela" [online], September 28, 2019: https://www.inrees.com/articles/effet-mandela-cerveau/.

Anzalone, Frederico (*BoDoï*), "Eiji Otsuka et le manga engagé," October 8, 2015: http://www.bodoi.info/eiji-otsuka-et-le-manga-engage.

Barder, Ollie (*Forbes*), "Katsuhiro Otomo On Creating 'Akira' And Designing The Coolest Bike In All Of Manga And Anime" [online], May 26, 2017: https://www.forbes.com/sites/olliebarder/2017/05/26/katsuhiro-otomo-on-creating-akira-and-designing-the-coolest-bike-in-all-of-manga-and-anime.

BBC, "Tokyo sarin attack: Aum Shinrikyo cult leaders executed" [online], July 6, 2018: https://www.bbc.com/news/world-asia-43395483.

Broderick, Ryan (*Buzzfeed News*), "A 20-Year-Old Is Helping John McAfee's 2020 Campaign Team By Teaching Him How To Shitpost About Anime" [online], November 29, 2018: https://www.buzzfeednews.com/article/ryanhatesthis/millennial-outreach-coordinator-anime-shitposting.

Bruney, Gabrielle (*Vice*), "Meet the Queer Latino Illustrator Who Brought Breakdancing to the Fashion World" [online], July 23, 2016: https://www.vice.com/en_au/article/8qvjjb/antonio-lopez-fashion-illustrator.

ComiPress, "The Rise and Fall of Weekly Shonen Jump: A Look at the Circulation of Weekly Jump" [online], May 6, 2007: https://www.comipress.com/article/2007/05/06/1923.

Drouard, Elodie (Pop Up' Culture blog from *France Info*), "'On a tout fait pour que la série soit un succès, et on a réussi': entretien avec les auteurs du manga *The Promised Neverland*" [online], August 21, 2018: https://blog.francetvinfo.fr/popup/2018/08/21/on-a-tout-fait-pour-que-la-serie-soit-un-succes-et-on-a-reussi-entretien-avec-les-auteurs-du-manga-the-promised-neverland.html.

Elric (*Marsam*), "Shochan no Boken" [online], May 4, 2016: http://marsam.graphics/shochan-no-boken.

Facebook "Tony Viramontes Studio Archive" [online]: https://www.facebook.com/pg/Tony-Viramontes-Studio-Archive-108650135820277.

Goedluck, Lakeisha (*Dazed*), "Gareth Pugh: a visual history" [online], February 11, 2015: https://www.dazeddigital.com/fashion/article/23560/1/gareth-pugh-a-visual-history.

Heroes Wiki, "Hiro Nakamura": https://heroeswiki.com/Hiro_Nakamura.

Hodgkins, Crystalyn (*Anime News Network*), "Shueisha Reveals New Circulation Numbers, Demographics for its Manga Magazines" [online], April 22, 2019: https://www.animenewsnetwork.com/news/2019-04-22/shueisha-reveals-new-circulation-numbers-demographics-for-its-manga-magazines/.145991.

Imomus (*Click Opera*), "The adventures of Tadzio in Japan" [online], January 7, 2008: https://imomus.livejournal.com/342686.html.

Klr Obscur, "Esthétique du giallo" [online], November 24, 2006: https://klrob.wordpress.com/2006/11/24/esthetique-du-giallo/.

KonoManga.jp, "【インタビュー】師匠・荒木飛呂彦との関係は……?『僕だけがいない街』三部けい【前編】" [online], June 9, 2014: http://konomanga.jp/interview/2893-2.

Lidbury, Olivia (*The Telegraph*), "'I am proud to be chosen': Final Fantasy character Lightning on being welcomed into the Louis Vuitton 'family'" [online], January 12, 2016: https://www.telegraph.co.uk/fashion/people/final-fantasy-character-lightning-on-starring-in-louis-vuitton-c.

Lismore, Kate (*Konbini*), "Vidéo: à 17 ans, David Bowie défendait les hommes aux cheveux longs" [online], January 11, 2016: https://www.konbini.com/fr/musique/video-17-ans-david-bowie-defendait-les-hommes-aux-cheveux-longs.

Loo, Egan (*Anime News Network*), "Japanese Comic Ranking, December 19-25" [online], December 29, 2011: https://www.animenewsnetwork.com/news/2011-12-28/japanese-comic-ranking-december-19-25.

Mangabrog, "Naoki Urasawa and Hisashi Eguchi talk about manga in the 70s and 80s, mostly Otomo" [online], May 17, 2015: https://mangabrog.wordpress.com/2015/05/17/naoki-urasawa-and-hisashi-eguchi-talk-about-manga-in-the-70s-and-80s-mostly-otomo.

Marx, W. David (*Néojaponisme*), "History of the Regent" [online], October 9, 2014: www.neojaponisme.com/2014/10/09/history-of-the-.

Melian, Eugenia (*Fashionsphinx*), "Tony Viramontes" (Parts 1, 2, and 3) [online]: http://fashionsphinx.com/?p=306, https://fashionsphinx.com/?p=986, https://fashionsphinx.com//?p=1157.

MIN LEKPLATS, "Bjorn Andersen" [online], February 28, 2008: https://blog.goo.ne.jp/essingen/e/0bee497b4ba65eac3a65dc6230cd02bf.

Mud Map to Life in the Modern Age, "Flashback: Nostradamus and Y2K" [online], July 1, 2012: https://mudmap.wordpress.com/2012/07/01/flash-back-nostradamus-and-y2k.

Orsini, Alexis (*Le point Pop*), "Le manga, nouvel ambassadeur du Louvre" [online], March 12, 2018: https://www.lepoint.fr/pop-culture/bandes-dess-inees/le-manga-nouvel-ambassadeur-du-louvre-12-03-2018-2201704_2922.php.

Paget, Christophe (*RFI*), "Japon 1968 : la révolte étudiante la plus longue et la plus violente du monde" [online], April 11, 2018: http://www.rfi.fr/asie-pacifique/20180411-japon-1968-revolte-etudiante-.

Pattern Prints Journal, "GREAT FASHION ILLUSTRATORS: ANTONIO LOPEZ FOR MISSONI" [online], November 28, 2011: http://www.pattern-printsjournal.com/2011/08/great-fashion-illustrators-antonio.html.

Pike, Naomi (*Vogue*), "Why Is Everyone So Crazy About Moschino?" [online], September 24, 2015: https://www.vogue.co.uk/gallery/moschino-a-fash-ion-history-jeremy-scott.

Pineda, Rafael Antonio (*Anime News Network*), "JoJo's Creator's 'Prison Break' Stage Play Casts Eriko Hatsune" [online], September 7, 2015: https://www.animenewsnetwork.com/news/2015-09-07/jojo-creator-prison-break-stage-play-casts-eriko-hatsune/.92605.

Randanne, Fabien (*20minutes*), "VIDEO. Du voguing dans 'Climax,' 'Pose' ou la pub... Quand la contre-culture queer investit la pop culture" [online], September 19, 2018: https://www.20minutes.fr/arts-stars/culture/2339327-20180919-video-voguing-climax-pose-pub-quand-contre-culture-queer-investit-pop-culture.

Roure, Benjamin (*BoDoi*), "Expo BD au Louvre, comme si vous y étiez," January 22, 2009: http://www.bodoi.info/expo-bd-au-louvre-comme-si-vous-y-etiez.

Shmuplations, "King of Fighters '94 – Developer Interview (originally featured in the 'All About KOF'94' mook)" [online]: http://shmuplations.com/kof94/.

Silent Manga Audition, "Nobuhiko Horie" [online]: https://www.manga-audition.com/judges/nobuhiko-horie.

Spicer, Allison K. (*Inspirational Imagery*), "Tony Viramontes" [online], August 2010: http://inspirational-imagery.blogspot.com/2010/08/tony-viramontes.html.

Tauer, Kristen (*WWD*), "A First Look at 'Antonio Lopez: Future Funk Fashion' at El Museo del Barrio" [online], June 14, 2016: https://wwd.com/eye/lifestyle/antonio-lopez-future-funk-fashion-el-museo-del-barrio-10451271/.

Testamarck, Sylvie, "Baroque et Classicisme en peinture et sculpture" [online]: http://www.mjccaussimon.fr/?Baroque-et-Classicisme-en-peinture-et-sculpture.

The Blonde Salad, "How to create an iconic brand – Volume 11: Moschino" [online]: https://www.theblondesalad.com/en-US/fashion/moschino-history-iconic.

Thomas, Catherine, "Les Petits romantiques et le rococo : éloge du mauvais goût" [online], *Romantisme*, 2001/4 (No. 123): https://www.cairn.info/revue-romantisme-2004-1-page-21.htm.

TV Tropes, "Camp Straight" [online]: https://tvtropes.org/pmwiki/pmwiki.php/Main/CampStraight.

Univers Ciné, "Le 'giallo': La pulsion de mort du cinéma italien" [online], December 23, 2013: https://www.universcine.com/articles/le-giallo-la-pulsion-de-mort-du-cinema-italien.

Vaulerin, Arnaud (*Libération*), "Que s'est-il passé le 11 mars 2011 ?" [online], March 11, 2013: https://www.liberation.fr/terre/2013/03/11/que-s-estil-passe-le-11-mars-2011_887651.

Vertaldi, Aurélia (*Le Figaro*), "Quand la BD est entrée au Louvre" [online], January 22, 2009 (updated September 18, 2009): http://www.lefigaro.fr/bd/2009/01/22/03014-20090122ARTFIG00558-la-bd-a-ses-entrees-au-louvre-.php.

Vincent (*Le Scribe du Sanctuaire*), "RING NI KAKERO" [online]: http://scribe.seiya.free.fr/manga/ring-kakero.htm.

Vogel, Joe (*Forbes*), "Was Prince's Androgyny About Identity Or Branding?" [online], May 6, 2018: https://www.forbes.com/sites/joevogel/2018/05/06/was-princes-androgyny-about-identity-or-branding.

Yaeger, Lynn (*Vogue*), "A New Retrospective Celebrates the Wild Exuberance of Franco Moschino" [online], October 30, 2015: https://www.vogue.com/article/franco-moschino-retrospective-mint-museum.

Zetlaoui, Léa (*Numéro*), "Comment Gianni Versace est-il entré dans la légende ?" [online], January 5, 2018: https://www.numero.com/fr/mode/gianni-versace-legende-mode-italienne-serie-american-crime-story-supermodels-clton-john-elizabeth-hurley-princesse-diana.

大山 平助 (*LINE TRAVEL*), "ドララララァ!仙台で「ジョジョ立ち」を決めるスポット4選" [online], May 9, 2017: https://www.travel.co.jp/guide/article/26318/.

"文化庁メディア芸術祭10周年企画アンケート日本のメディア芸術100選 結果発表" [online]: https://web.archive.org/web/20110927110506/http://plaza.bunka.go.jp/hundred/bumon_manga.html.

"あの「緊急事態宣言」から1年、コミックビームは生き残れたのか　編集長が語る、電子増刊『コミックビーム100』の狙い (2/4)" [online], October 14, 2017: https://nlab.itmedia.co.jp/nl/articles/1710/11/news143_2.html.

Reports on Oricon figures from the blog *Parlons Manga*: https://parlons-manga.wordpress.com/category/top-oricon.

Shueisha, "Shueisha Inc | Books" [online]: https://www.shueisha.co.jp/english/books/#Shinsho.

Website of Shueisha Shinsho: https://shinsho.shueisha.co.jp/.

Website www.kyojin.fr (unavailable as I write this line).

Louvre website: https://www.louvre.fr.

Grand Palais website: https://www.grandpalais.fr.

Website of National Art Center in Tokyo: https://www.nact.jp/english.

Blog *Baburu Jidai*: https://baburujidai.tumblr.com/.

Archives of fashion shows on the website of *Vogue*: https://www.vogue.com/fashion-shows.

Theses and dissertations

Bareille, Laurent, *Les représentations du «mauvais garçon» dans le cinéma japonais de 1955 à 2000, ou le questionnement à propos de l'évolution de la société japonaise par ce paradigme* (doctoral dissertation, Asian and Asian diaspora studies), Université Lyon III Jean-Moulin, 2015.

Oliviero, Clémence, *Rendre l'invisible visible : de l'utilisation pacifique à la catastrophe nucléaire, évolution de la représentation de l'atome dans le manga* (master's thesis, contemporary East Asian studies), Université de Lyon, École normale supérieure de Lyon, Institut d'études politiques de Lyon, 2014.

Online videos/documentaries

Balmain, "Balmain Fall/Winter 2019 womenswear show" [online], *YouTube*, March 2, 2019: https://www.youtube.com/watch?v=0NpM1M7OmtY.

Clique TV, "Le Gros Journal de Kiddy Smile : l'enfant terrible du voguing" [online], *YouTube*, July 24, 2017: https://www.youtube.com/watch?v=I-Id6zX36Q6Q.

Rhys-Morgan, Dean, "Tony Viramontes" [online], *YouTube*, September 12, 2013: https://www.youtube.com/watch?v=eYFDY3fxrnE.

Feurra, Jean Laurent, "Total Records (3/11) – The man who sold the world// David Bowie" (documentary film excerpt) [online], *Arte*, 2018: https://www.arte.tv/en/videos/075319-010-A/the-man-who-sold-the-world-david-bowie.

France 5, "Entrée libre : Voguing, la danse des fiertés," [online], *France TV*, September 26, 2018: https://www.france.tv/france-5/entree-libre/entree-libre-saison-8/748815-voguing-la-danse-des-fiertes.html.

Kazé, "Interview de l'éditeur de Dragon Ball - Sa rencontre avec Akira Toriyama – Partie 1" [online], *YouTube*, January 3, 2015: https://www.youtube.com/watch?v=flb0XwHgJZ4&list=PLniwnOyzsQ8SFk1PjcoughronaxRhwnIm.

Livingston, Jennie, *Paris is Burning*, 1990, 78 min. (documentary film).

MANLY AnimeHERO, "AH Magic Boy B.T. 1983 Manga Review" [online], *YouTube*, July 21, 2015: https://www.youtube.com/watch?v=9yAPt3kzlbY.

Public Sénat, "UN MONDE DE BULLES, Spéciale Louvre, la bande dessinée au Louvre en 2109 ?" [online], *Dailymotion*, episode dated March 21, 2009: https://www.dailymotion.com/video/x95dul.

VICTIM OF THE CRIME, "Dior Homme Autumn Winter 2003 'Luster' By Hedi Slimane Runway Campaign" [online], *YouTube*, March 16, 2013: https://www.youtube.com/watch?v=esgkUGAoTKQ.

YouTube Fashion Channel: https://www.youtube.com/channel/UCepVy23t8l-CEaASZzfo9Jg.

YouTube FF Channel: https://www.youtube.com/user/FatalefashionIII.

Audio

NoCiné staff, "NoCiné: Les westerns spaghettis, un plat qui se mange froid," November 28, 2018: https://soundcloud.com/nocine/les-westerns-spaghettis-un.

PIFFFCast staff, "PIFFFcast 26 - Essorons Stephen King !" September 5, 2017: https://www.pifff.fr/news-173-pifffcast-26-essorons-stephen-king-en.

Databases

Flickr photo gallery "Kami Sama Explorer Museum": https://www.flickr.com/photos/kami_sama_explorer.

Database *Comic Vine*: https://comicvine.gamespot.com/.

Database *Wikipedia Japan*: https://ja.wikipedia.org/.

Database *Internet Movie Database*: https://www.imdb.com/.

JOJO'S BIZARRE ADVENTURE

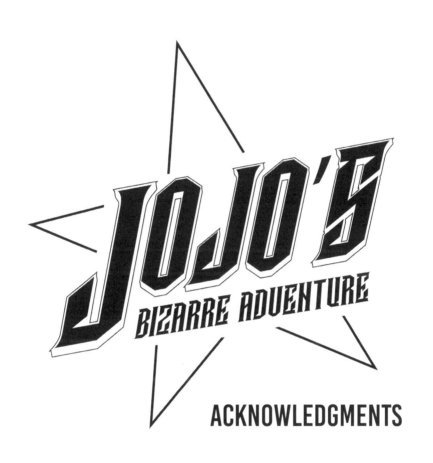

ACKNOWLEDGMENTS

WOULD LIKE TO EXPRESS my deep gratitude to Laurent Bareille, Quentin "ALT236" Boëton, Steffi Brock, Marius Chapuis, Coralie Choî, Margherita Contadini, Nicolas Courcier, Mélanie Couturier, "CygnusX", Fabrice Douar, Mehdi El Kanafi, Julien El Rab, Aurélien Estager, Fausto Fasulo, Satoko Fujimoto, Paul Gravett, Pierre Gris, Xavier Guilbert, Emmanuel Guillemant, Patrick Hellio, Malik-Djamel Amazigh Houha, Rémi Inghilterra, Michel Lefftz, Camille Lemoine, Thomas Loreille, Sébastien Ludmann, Sébastien "TMDJC," Damien Mecheri, Takashi Miike, Virginie Nebbia, Clémence Oliviero, Alexis Orsini, Boell Oyino, Natan Paquet, Elsa Pecqueur, Anthony Prezman, Lawrence Rasson, Misako Saka, and Clovis Salvat. All of these people helped me in one way or another.

I would also like to thank:

My friends and family, for their support and for putting up with me isolating myself so often and for such long periods while writing this book.

The readers of *JoJo* with whom I've had the privilege of communicating, personally or on websites, over the last 15 years. And all those who I don't know personally, but who helped me without even knowing it by contributing to online resources dedicated to *JoJo*, particularly *JoJo's Bizarre Encyclopedia*, which was incredibly helpful to me.

Third Éditions, which gave me carte blanche in writing this book and welcomed my twisted ideas with open arms.

And Hirohiko Araki.

JOJO'S BIZARRE ADVENTURE

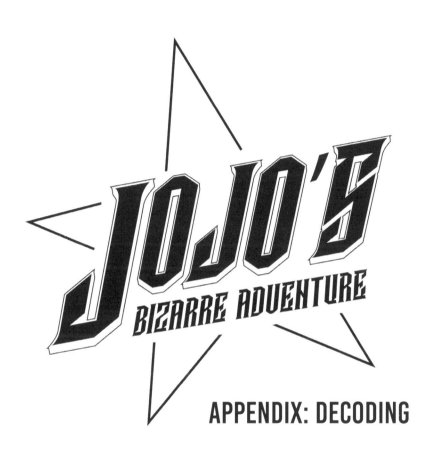

APPENDIX: DECODING

WARNING

The following section contains spoilers about the surprises
contained in this book!

Chapter IX:

Glory to Mankind: A reference to a recurring line in the video game *NieR: Automata*.

Crazy Diamond Dogs: A blend of the songs *Shine On You Crazy Diamond* by Pink Floyd and *Diamond Dogs* by David Bowie.

La grande bellezza: A film by Paolo Sorrentino.

Written in the Stars: A song by Tinie Tempah.

Chapter XXI:

A reference to the 21st tarot card, The World.

Deep Impact: The title of a film by Mimi Leder.

Fan Fan Fan: The name of a Stand in *Jojolion*.

Chapter V:

Gang Stars: A reference to the musical group Gang Starr.

Man in the Mirror: A song by Michael Jackson.

Gangsta's Paradise: A song by Coolio.

The new meaning of virility: The translation of the title of a French comic book from the series *Pascal Brutal* by Riad Sattouf.

Poem Gang Destiny: The title of the eighth volume of the manga *I'll*.

Chapter VI:

Riot Girls: A reference to the '90s musical movement "Riot grrrl."

End of World Party: A song by HÆLOS.

Shōjo's Bizarre Adventure: A blend of *shōjo*, meaning "girl" in Japanese, and the title of Araki's saga.

A God in an Alcove: A song by Bauhaus.

Sine Wave: A song by Mogwai.

Sayonara Wild Hearts: The name of a video game developed by Simogo.

Chapter VII:

Close the World, Open the Next: A reference to a phrase from the anime series *Serial Experiments Lain*.

Mandela Effect: The name of a phenomenon explained previously in the section on how this book's Stands work.

Wild Horses: A song by The Rolling Stones.

Bizarre Hyper Age: A blend of "Bizarre" from the title of Araki's saga and "Hyper Age Manga Magazine," the tagline for the magazine *Ultra Jump*.

My Bloody Valentine: A musical group.

Chapter VIII:

The Sailor Who Fell from Grace with the Sea: The title of a novel by Yukio Mishima.

Without You I'm Nothing: An album by the musical group Placebo.

Absolute Beginners: A song by David Bowie.

The young man and the sea: A reference to the novel *The Old Man and the Sea* by Ernest Hemingway.

Anthem for Doomed Youth: A song by The Libertines.

New Energy: A song by Four Tet.

Welcome to the Jungle: A song by Guns N' Roses.

Club Bizarre: A song by U96.

Around the World: A song by Daft Punk.

Closer to God: Lyrics from the song *Closer* by Nine Inch Nails.

Explosions in the Sky: A musical group.

Chapter III:

Fire in Cairo: A song by The Cure.

Emperor Time: A reference to the name of Kurapika's power in the manga *Hunter X Hunter.*

Jailhouse Rock: A song by Elvis Presley.

Rebel Rebel, Make My Day: A blend of the song *Rebel Rebel* by David Bowie and the line "make my day," delivered by the hero of the movie *Dirty Harry.*

United colors of JoJo: A reference to the clothing brand United Colors of Benetton, whose advertising campaigns featured people of all colors, just like how *Stardust Crusaders* presents characters from different continents.

Horrorshow: A song by The Libertines.

Level Up!: A reference to leveling up in role-playing video games.

Lone Star: A reference to the Western novel *The Lone Star Ranger.*

Chapter III.5:

Hidden Place: A song by Björk.

Chapter IV:

The House that Kira Built: A reference to the film *The House that Jack Built,* which is about a serial killer.

Minitry?: An album from the duo ANBB (Alva Noto & Blixa Bargeld).

Diamond in the rough: A saying used in the Disney film *Aladdin.*

This city will eat you alive: The translation of the title of an anthology of Yoshihiro Tatsumi's work, from French publisher Cornélius.

Wild hearts never die: Lyrics from a song on the soundtrack for the video game *Sayonara Wild Hearts.*

Killer's Heaven: A play on words with the title of the video game *Killer7.*

Triforce: A reference to a concept from the video game series *The Legend of Zelda.*

We can be Heroes (So the world might be mended): A blend of lyrics from the song *Heroes* by David Bowie and, for the part in parentheses, a famous line from the video game *Demon's Souls.*

Guaranteed to blow your mind: Lyrics from the song *Killer Queen* by Queen.

name from the discovery by Fiona Broome, a specialist on the paranormal, that she and others were convinced that Nelson Mandela had died in prison in the 1980s, when actually he was released in 1990 and lived until 2013. Some attribute this effect to the existence of parallel universes between which we supposedly pass; others say it's due to a flaw in the human brain. This Stand replaces mentions of JoJo and JoJo's Bizarre Adventure with titles like YoYo's Strange Journey; then, in the final pages, things return to normal and the text again says JoJo's Bizarre Adventure. This is a joke on the fact that Steel Ball Run did not initially bear the name JoJo; it's also a nod to Funny Valentine's Stand, which allows him to travel between parallel worlds.

Without You I'm Nothing: To read certain missing parts of the text, he makes you "fuse together" the content of two different pages (so, you have to turn to the page to find the words that fill the holes). This is a reference to the fusion of Josefumi and Kira in JoJolion.

◆

Just like JoJo's Bizarre Adventure, this book is filled with all kinds of references—mainly musical ones, as is the case with Araki. I'm now going to reveal to you the references I incorporated in to the names of the nine Stands I just explained, as well as into the titles of the chapters and sections.

Chapter I:
Strange and Beautiful: An album from the musician Aqualung.
New Order: A musical group.
Negative penalty: A game mechanic from the video game series Guilty Gear. It deals a penalty to a player who acts too defensively—just like how Jonathan Joestar, at the beginning of Phantom Blood, remains defensive against Dio.
The vampire masquerade: A reference to the role-playing game Vampire: The Masquerade.
Macho, macho man: A reference to a song by the Village People.
Ashita no JoJo: Blends the names Ashita no Joe and JoJo, which would translate in English to "The JoJo of tomorrow."

Chapter II:
Indiana JoJo: Blends Indiana Jones and JoJo.
Babel Fish: A reference to the creature from the series of novels The Hitchhiker's Guide to the Galaxy by Douglas Adams. It's a fish that, when slipped into a person's ear, allows them to understand any language.

Note 4 (in Dutch in the text): Babel Fish, volume 4. Among the various ideas, one was to insert song lyrics (from the songs recommended at the start of the chapter) between the paragraphs of this second chapter, like musical interludes.

Note 5 (a mixture of French, English, German, Dutch, Italian, Spanish, and Japanese in the text): Babel Fish, volume 5. The idea of using footnotes evolved over time. The Stand was initially called "Underworld" and rather than using foreign languages, he would "hide" anecdotes about the creation of this book and other thoughts from the author in the "underworld," i.e., the footnotes. Then, the idea became to write comments in various languages that, once translated, would turn out to be absurd or humorous. In the end, the idea evolved again and that's how I, Babel Fish, came into being. Thank you for listening and have a great day. Yours truly, B.F.

Emperor Time: He freezes time, like Dio's Stand The World in *Stardust Crusaders*. Then, the next page shows the battle cries "Ora Ora Ora" (Jotaro) and "Muda Muda Muda" (Dio), a projection of the final clash between the two characters, before ending with a resounding "Ora," signifying Jotaro's victory.

Hidden Place: He presents a secret chapter (the "hidden place") that doesn't appear in the table of contents. Just like how there's a hidden place in *Diamond is Unbreakable* that doesn't appear on the map of Morioh.

Mimikiry: He causes bits of text seen previously in the book to reappear, but in a "buggy" version (then), on the following page, the text returns to normal). This is a reference to Bites the Dust, the final power of Deadly Queen in *Diamond is Unbreakable*, which causes a day to be repeated while changing certain details.

Man in the Mirror: He "mirrors" certain parts of the text. This is a reference to the Stand Man in the Mirror in *Golden Wind*.

End of World Party: He counts down—(Three.), (Two.), (One.), (Zero.)—before taking us to "heaven," which is the goal of Enrico Pucci in *Stone Ocean*. Then, the chapter temporarily drops us into a parallel world, with a title page that looks like the one at the beginning of the book, but with different text. It's just like how at the end of *Stone Ocean*, after the universe comes to an end, a new, slightly different universe appears. In this book, after this brief interlude, things return to normal.

Mandela Effect: The Mandela Effect refers to mistaken beliefs or false memories strangely shared by various people around the world. It gets its

EXPLANATION OF THE EFFECTS OF THE STANDS IN CHAPTERS I TO VIII:

New Order: He messes with the page numbers, creating a numerical "new order." The destabilizing nature of this power symbolizes the nonconformist character of *Phantom Blood* at the time of its original publication.

Babel Fish: He adds footnotes—in addition to the book's normal footnotes—in various world languages, creating a mini story in several installments that gives background on the design of the Stands and a few abandoned ideas. The multilingual nature of this Stand is a reference to the "world tour" aspect of *Battle Tendency* and it also evokes the ancient ruins where the Pillar Men are discovered, via the idea of "revealing the deepest, darkest secrets" (the "deep" being, from the perspective of page layout, the footnotes).

Here are the notes in plain English:

Note 1 (in French in the text): Welcome, this is Babel Fish speaking. I am temporarily hijacking this space, but rest assured that I come in peace. The purpose of my intervention is simple: I'm here to offer you an opportunity to—try to—uncover a few lost secrets regarding the making of the book you're currently reading. Would you like to accept the challenge? Then be prepared, I'll come back soon.

Note 2 (in Spanish in the text): Babel Fish, volume 2. Stands were planned from the beginning of this project, but not every idea was kept. For example, originally, there was the "honesty Stand," who would force the author of this book to speak in the first person singular: this idea ended up in the preface and the conclusion of the original French version of this book.

Note 3 (in German in the text): Babel Fish, volume 3. Initially, one of the ideas was to make the reader flip the book around so that they could read certain portions of text not printed in the same direction as the rest. This Stand was supposed to be called "Wheel of Fortune."

Also available from Third Éditions:

- *Berserk. With Darkness Ink*
- *BioShock. From Rapture to Columbia*
- *Dark Souls. Beyond the Grave - Volume 1*
- *Dark Souls. Beyond the Grave - Volume 2*
- *Devolver: Behind the Scenes. Business and Punk Attitude*
- *Fallout. A Tale of Mutation*
- *JoJo's Bizarre Adventure. Manga's Refined Oddball*
- *Metal Gear Solid. Hideo Kojima's Magnum Opus*
- *Resident Evil. Of Zombies and Men - Volume 1*
- *Sekiro. The Second Life of Souls*
- *The Heart of Dead Cells*
- *The Impact of Akira. A Manga [R]evolution*
- *The Legend of Dragon Quest*
- *The Legend of Final Fantasy VI*
- *The Legend of Final Fantasy VII*
- *The Legend of Final Fantasy VIII*
- *The Legend of Final Fantasy IX*
- *The Legend of Kingdom Hearts - Volume 1: Creation*
- *The Rise of the Witcher. A New RPG King*
- *The Strange Works of Taro Yoko. From Drakengard to NieR: Automata*
- *The Works of Fumito Ueda. A Different Perspective on Video Games*
- *The Works of Hayao Miyazaki. The Japanese Animation Master*
- *Zelda. The History of a Legendary Saga - Volume 1*
- *Zelda. The History of a Legendary Saga - Volume 2: Breath of the Wild*

Legal submission: November 2021
Printed in the European Union by Grafo.